AF544917

## Cover Images

1 **Puerto Rico** City wall of Old San Juan
2 **Texas** Young girl at Cinco de Mayo Festival
3 **Florida** Florida Panther
4 **Florida** Lifeguard hut, Miami

Back cover: **Texas** Girl in Mexican dance costume, El Paso

HOLT SPANISH 1A

**Nancy Humbach**

**Sylvia Madrigal Velasco**

**Ana Beatriz Chiquito**

**Stuart Smith**

**John McMinn**

**HOLT, RINEHART AND WINSTON**

A Harcourt Education Company

Orlando • Austin • New York • San Diego • London



Acknowledgments appear on pages FL16 and R52, which are extensions of the copyright page.

Printed in the United States of America



ISBN 0-03-042668-5

4 5 6 7 8 9 048 10 09

# La Florida antes

From 1513, when Spanish explorers first set foot on the shores of what is now Florida, Hispanics have played an important role in shaping the state's history. In this section, you will learn about some of the influences of Hispanics on Florida's history and culture.

▲ 1 **The Lake Jackson Mound** Temple mounds, such as this one at Lake Jackson, were built by the native peoples of Florida and may still be found throughout the state. Long before Spaniards arrived in the 1500s, Florida was home to the Timucua, Apalachee, Ais, Tekesta, and Calusa peoples, among others. Relations between the native population and early Spanish explorers were hostile. Partly for this reason, the first permanent Spanish settlement was not established until 1565, more than 50 years after Florida was claimed by Spain.

◀ **Juan Ponce de León** The Spanish explorer Juan Ponce de León arrived in Florida in April of 1513 and claimed it for the Spanish crown. He named this land after "Pascua florida," the Easter celebration that coincided with his arrival. De León is thought to have landed near what is now St. Augustine. He then explored the Atlantic coast, the Keys, and the Gulf coast. He returned to Florida in 1521 intending to settle there, but was injured in battle and died before any permanent colonies were established.

◀ **Hernando de Soto** In 1539, Hernando de Soto landed near modern-day Bradenton with 550 men, 200 horses, and several priests, intending to establish a Spanish colony in Florida. He and his men were sidetracked when native inhabitants told them of riches to be found in a land called Ocale. Their search took them through central Florida and into what is now the southeastern United States. Journals and maps from de Soto's expedition provide a wealth of information about the customs and languages of the native peoples.

▲ 2 **Misión San Luis**
The Spanish settlers educated the native inhabitants of Florida in European customs, lifestyle, and religion through Franciscan missions. At one point there were dozens of them along the Atlantic coast and in northern Florida.

▲ 3 **Castillo de San Marcos, St. Augustine** Fifty-five years before the Pilgrims landed on Plymouth Rock, Pedro Menéndez de Avilés founded San Agustín, known today as St. Augustine, the first permanent European settlement in what is now the United States. Menéndez brought with him people of many professions as well as horses, cattle, sheep, goats, and sugarcane. St. Augustine became a strategically important port for the Spanish as they tried to protect their ships loaded with treasure from pirate attacks.

## ¿Qué tanto sabes?

1. How did Florida get its name?
2. What strategic significance did St. Augustine have for the Spanish?
3. What Native American peoples lived in your area? Are there any temple or burial mounds near where you live?

# La Florida ahora

Today, nearly 500 years after Juan Ponce de León first sighted the Florida coast, Hispanics are one of the most influential groups in the state. Virtually every aspect of life in Florida—from businesses to foods to the languages you hear and the people you meet—reflects the influence of the diverse Hispanic population.

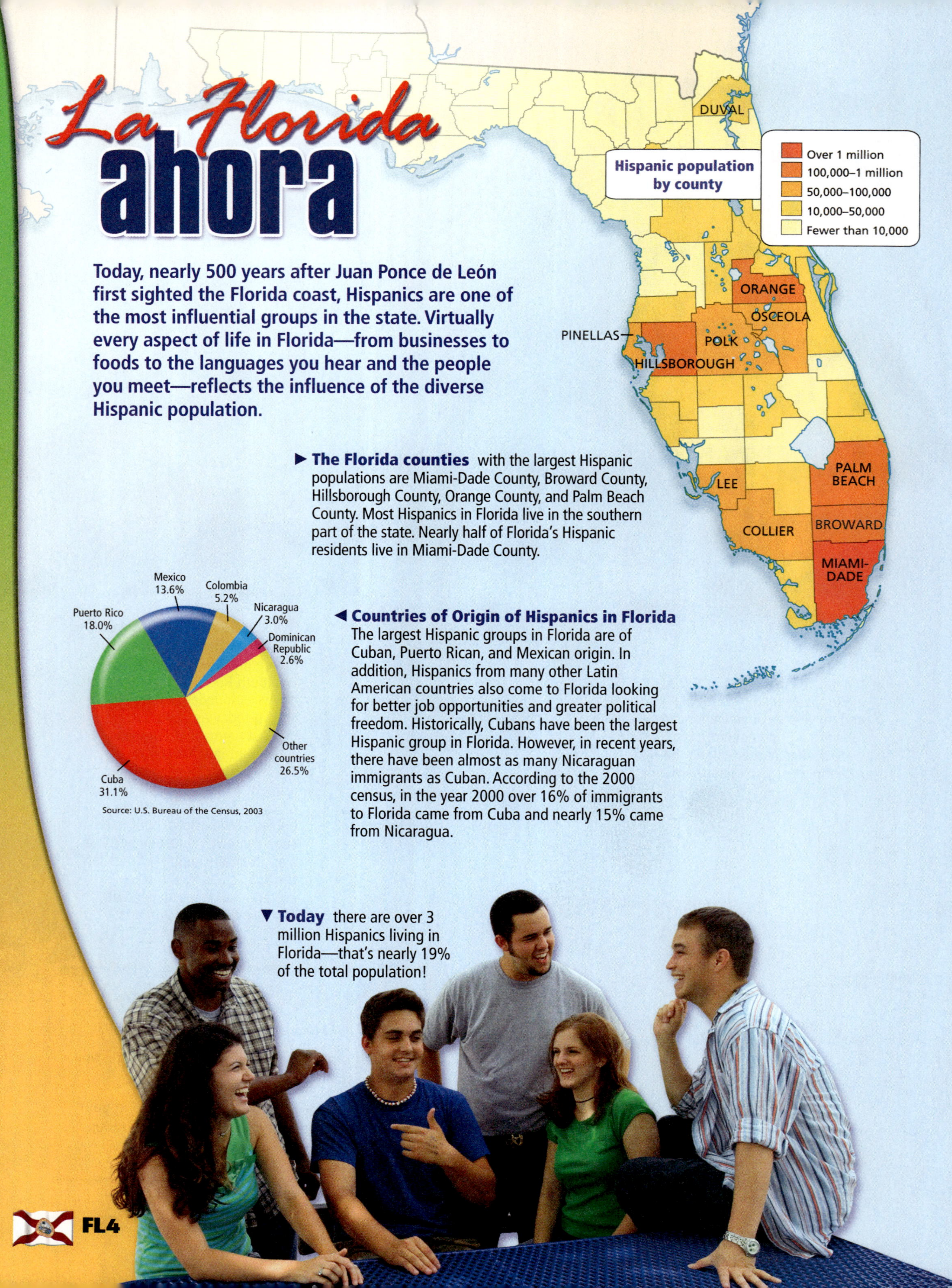


► **The Florida counties** with the largest Hispanic populations are Miami-Dade County, Broward County, Hillsborough County, Orange County, and Palm Beach County. Most Hispanics in Florida live in the southern part of the state. Nearly half of Florida's Hispanic residents live in Miami-Dade County.

◄ **Countries of Origin of Hispanics in Florida** The largest Hispanic groups in Florida are of Cuban, Puerto Rican, and Mexican origin. In addition, Hispanics from many other Latin American countries also come to Florida looking for better job opportunities and greater political freedom. Historically, Cubans have been the largest Hispanic group in Florida. However, in recent years, there have been almost as many Nicaraguan immigrants as Cuban. According to the 2000 census, in the year 2000 over 16% of immigrants to Florida came from Cuba and nearly 15% came from Nicaragua.

▼ **Today** there are over 3 million Hispanics living in Florida—that's nearly 19% of the total population!

▲ **Miami** Of all the metropolitan areas in the United States, Miami-Dade County has the highest percentage of Hispanic-owned businesses. The success of the Hispanic community here has greatly strengthened Miami's business ties with Latin America. The city is a hub for Latin American banking.

▼ **Doing business in Spanish** The large Hispanic population and many tourists from Latin America lead many businesses in Florida to hire people who speak both Spanish and English fluently. Many companies offer their employees basic Spanish classes. Seventy-seven percent of language students in Florida study Spanish.

▲ **Café cubano, Miami** In some neighborhoods in Miami you're more likely to find signs in Spanish than in English! Nearly 18% of Floridians speak Spanish at home. In some families, the older generations do not speak English very well, and it is not uncommon to see children who have grown up speaking English interpreting for their Spanish-speaking elders.

## ¿Qué tanto sabes?

1. **What is the second largest Hispanic population group in Florida? The third largest?**
2. **Why might a Florida employer prefer to hire someone who speaks both Spanish and English?**
3. **Do you know many people who speak Spanish? Why are you studying Spanish?**

# Hispanos *que triunfan*

◀ **Rep. Ileana Ros-Lehtinen** is the first Hispanic woman to be elected to the United States Congress. She has represented South Florida since 1989. Congresswoman Ros-Lehtinen came to Florida from Cuba when she was a child, and she grew up and went to college in Miami. In 1982, Ros-Lehtinen was elected to the Florida House of Representatives. She later became a state senator, and in 1989 was elected to the United States Congress. She is very involved in international and human rights issues, improving education, and protecting the environment.

▲ **Frank Caldeiro, astronaut** Born in Buenos Aires, Argentina, as a young child Fernando "Frank" Caldeiro did not suspect that someday he would become an astronaut. His family moved to the United States, and he went to high school in New York. He then went on to study aerospace technology and mechanical engineering in college. In 1985, he began testing planes for the U.S. Air Force, and was transferred to the Kennedy Space Center. In 1996, Caldeiro was chosen by NASA to become an astronaut. Since then, he has worked with the International Space Station and tested computer programs used on the space shuttle.

▲ **Ferdie Pacheco, painter and "fight doctor"** Born in Tampa to Spanish parents, Ferdie Pacheco is a painter who has had many different careers. Although he loved drawing and painting as a child, Pacheco was also interested in medicine, and decided to become a doctor. Pacheco opened a clinic in Miami and provided free medical services to newly arrived immigrants. He also volunteered as a doctor for boxers at a local gym, where he began working with Muhammad Ali. He stayed with Ali for 17 years, and worked to improve safety for boxers. After retiring as a fight doctor, Pacheco worked as a boxing commentator on television. He also began to devote more time to his painting. His works are lively and colorful, often depicting the Ybor City section of Tampa where he grew up.

▲ **Florida State Spanish Conference** Every year, students of Spanish from all over the state meet at the Florida State Spanish Conference. At this conference students use what they have learned about the Spanish language and the cultures of Spanish-speaking countries to compete for various awards.

Participants compete in categories based on their experience with Spanish. The primary categories for the competition are Impromptu Speeches, Declamations, and Dramatic Presentations. Prizes are awarded to school groups, but students also participate individually in costume, entertainment, and scholarship competitions.

▲ **A promotional poster for the Florida State Spanish Conference**

► **Fernando Bujones, dancer and choreographer** Miami native Fernando Bujones started dancing when he was eight years old. It was not long before he caught the eye of influential dance instructors and was awarded a scholarship to the School of American Ballet in New York. In 1974, at the age of nineteen, he gained international recognition when he became the first male American dancer to win the Gold medal at the Seventh International Ballet Competition in Bulgaria. Bujones continued his career as a dancer, choreographer, and artistic director with many of the finest ballet companies in the world. In 2000, Bujones returned to Florida as the Artistic Director of the Orlando Ballet, where he worked until his death in 2005.

# La cultura hispana de la Florida

▲ **Fiesta of Five Flags, Pensacola** The Fiesta of Five Flags celebrates the founding of Pensacola by the Spanish explorer Don Tristán de Luna. Its name refers to the five flags that have flown over Pensacola since it was founded: Spanish, French, British, Confederate, and American. Held every year in June, the Fiesta includes treasure hunts, reenactments, parades, and parties.

**With such a large number of Hispanics in Florida, the influence of Hispanic culture is not surprising—in everything from the food people eat, the music they listen to, the things they do for fun, and the way they do business.**

## Los festivales

**Festivals are one way for people to get together to celebrate their cultural heritage. Every year there are many festivals to celebrate the heritage and contributions of Florida's Hispanics.**

▲ **The ¡Viva Broward! celebration, Fort Lauderdale** Every fall, Fort Lauderdale comes alive to celebrate Hispanic Heritage Month with parades, concerts, art shows, craft fairs, and other cultural events.

▲ **Carnaval Miami** People come from all over to experience Carnaval Miami every March. On Calle Ocho, in Little Havana, thousands of people fill the street to celebrate the diversity of Miami's Hispanic cultures. At the "Festival de la Ocho," you can see and take part in parades, cooking contests, a jazz festival, and even a domino competition.

► **The Puerto Rico Cultural Parade, Tampa** The Puerto Rico Cultural Parade and Folklore Festival is held every April in the historic Ybor City district of Tampa. There are parades, music, dances, foods, and arts and crafts, with artists and musicians from all over the country.

# El arte

**Many Hispanic artists have made Florida their home. Their artwork reflects the styles, traditions, and concerns of their cultural heritage.**

▲ ***Fiestas de mi pueblo*** by Puerto Rican artist, Obed Gómez

◀ ***The Mask Maker Workshop*** by Peruvian craftsman, Nicario Jiménez

▲ **Shakira, Latin Grammy Awards** Colombian singer-songwriter Shakira has won several major awards at this ceremony, which has been held in Miami.

# La música

**Many of the biggest names in Spanish-language pop music have come to Miami to record their music.**

◀ **Emilio and Gloria Estefan** Two of the most influential people on the Miami music scene are Emilio and Gloria Estefan. Gloria is one of the most successful crossover singers (meaning that she sings in both Spanish and English) of all time. Her husband Emilio is an important recording producer who has helped many musicians get started.

◀ **Juanes at Premio Lo Nuestro, 2004** Since 1989, Miami has hosted the Premio Lo Nuestro Latin Music Awards. In this ceremony the biggest names in the Latin music industry come together for recognition. The broadcast has become the television program most watched by Hispanics in the United States.

◀ **Alejandro Sanz,** the all-time highest-selling Spanish pop artist, recorded "El alma al aire" at the Criteria studio in Miami.

## ¿Qué tanto sabes?

1. **Name three Latin musicians who regularly record their music in Miami.**
2. **When and where is the Festival de la Ocho held?**
3. **What cultural festivals are held in your community?**

# What's in your textbook?

## ¡Exprésate! for Florida

**Here are some special features in *¡Exprésate!* that will help you as you study Spanish and learn more about Florida. Any time you see [Florida symbol] you'll know there is special information in that section for Florida students.**

**Nota cultural** When you see a **Nota cultural** *(Culture Note)* with the Florida symbol, you will learn about aspects of Florida's unique history and culture—things that you may have seen or experienced yourself.

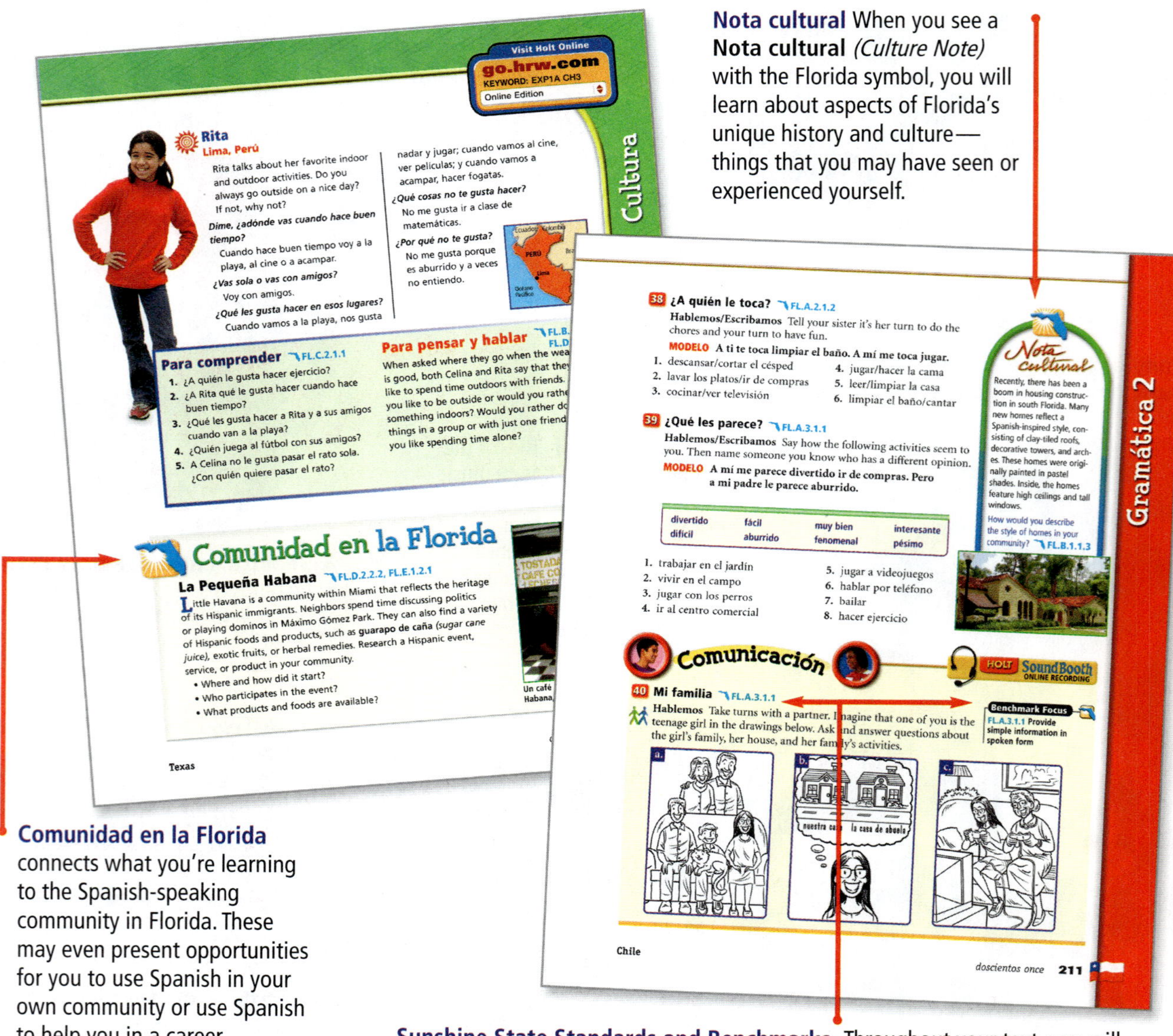

Visit Holt Online
go.hrw.com
KEYWORD: EXP1A CH3
Online Edition

Cultura

**Rita**
Lima, Perú

Rita talks about her favorite indoor and outdoor activities. Do you always go outside on a nice day? If not, why not?

***Dime, ¿adónde vas cuando hace buen tiempo?***
Cuando hace buen tiempo voy a la playa, al cine o a acampar.

***¿Vas sola o vas con amigos?***
Voy con amigos.

***¿Qué les gusta hacer en esos lugares?***
Cuando vamos a la playa, nos gusta nadar y jugar; cuando vamos al cine, ver películas; y cuando vamos a acampar, hacer fogatas.

***¿Qué cosas no te gusta hacer?***
No me gusta ir a clase de matemáticas.

***¿Por qué no te gusta?***
No me gusta porque es aburrido y a veces no entiendo.

**Para comprender** FL.C.2.1.1
1. ¿A quién le gusta hacer ejercicio?
2. ¿A Rita qué le gusta hacer cuando hace buen tiempo?
3. ¿Qué les gusta hacer a Rita y a sus amigos cuando van a la playa?
4. ¿Quién juega al fútbol con sus amigos?
5. A Celina no le gusta pasar el rato sola. ¿Con quién quiere pasar el rato?

**Para pensar y hablar** FL.B... FL.D...
When asked where they go when the wea... is good, both Celina and Rita say that they like to spend time outdoors with friends. Do you like to be outside or would you rathe... something indoors? Would you rather do things in a group or with just one friend... you like spending time alone?

**Comunidad en la Florida**

**La Pequeña Habana** FL.D.2.2.2, FL.E.1.2.1
Little Havana is a community within Miami that reflects the heritage of its Hispanic immigrants. Neighbors spend time discussing politics or playing dominos in Máximo Gómez Park. They can also find a variety of Hispanic foods and products, such as **guarapo de caña** *(sugar cane juice)*, exotic fruits, or herbal remedies. Research a Hispanic event, service, or product in your community.
- Where and how did it start?
- Who participates in the event?
- What products and foods are available?

Texas

**38 ¿A quién le toca?** FL.A.2.1.2
**Hablemos/Escribamos** Tell your sister it's her turn to do the chores and your turn to have fun.
**MODELO** **A ti te toca limpiar el baño. A mí me toca jugar.**
1. descansar/cortar el césped
2. lavar los platos/ir de compras
3. cocinar/ver televisión
4. jugar/hacer la cama
5. leer/limpiar la casa
6. limpiar el baño/cantar

**39 ¿Qué les parece?** FL.A.3.1.1
**Hablemos/Escribamos** Say how the following activities seem to you. Then name someone you know who has a different opinion.
**MODELO** **A mí me parece divertido ir de compras. Pero a mi padre le parece aburrido.**

| divertido | fácil | muy bien | interesante |
|---|---|---|---|
| difícil | aburrido | fenomenal | pésimo |

1. trabajar en el jardín
2. vivir en el campo
3. jugar con los perros
4. ir al centro comercial
5. jugar a videojuegos
6. hablar por teléfono
7. bailar
8. hacer ejercicio

**Nota cultural**
Recently, there has been a boom in housing construction in south Florida. Many new homes reflect a Spanish-inspired style, consisting of clay-tiled roofs, decorative towers, and arches. These homes were originally painted in pastel shades. Inside, the homes feature high ceilings and tall windows.
How would you describe the style of homes in your community? FL.B.1.1.3

Gramática 2

**Comunicación**

HOLT SoundBooth ONLINE RECORDING

**40 Mi familia** FL.A.3.1.1
**Hablemos** Take turns with a partner. Imagine that one of you is the teenage girl in the drawings below. Ask and answer questions about the girl's family, her house, and her family's activities.

**Benchmark Focus**
FL.A.3.1.1 Provide simple information in spoken form

a. b. c.
nuestra casa / la casa de abuela

Chile

doscientos once 211

**Comunidad en la Florida** connects what you're learning to the Spanish-speaking community in Florida. These may even present opportunities for you to use Spanish in your own community or use Spanish to help you in a career.

**Sunshine State Standards and Benchmarks** Throughout your text, you will see this symbol [Florida symbol] followed by a series of numbers. These references show you exactly which Florida Sunshine State Standards Benchmark you are working towards with each activity. You will find descriptions of the different benchmarks throughout your textbook. Knowing what these benchmarks are will help you get the most out of your Spanish class.

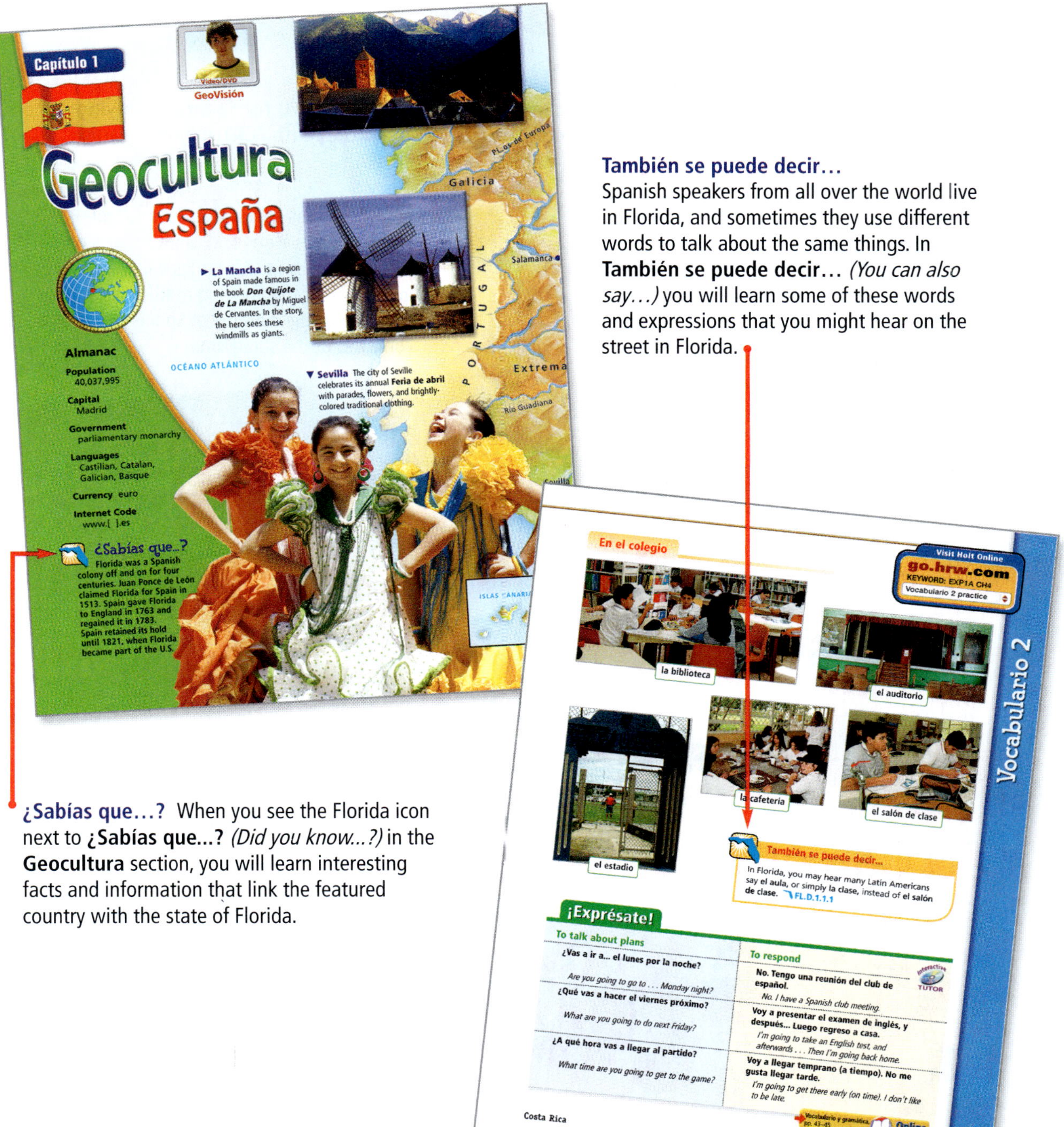


**También se puede decir…**
Spanish speakers from all over the world live in Florida, and sometimes they use different words to talk about the same things. In **También se puede decir…** *(You can also say…)* you will learn some of these words and expressions that you might hear on the street in Florida.

**¿Sabías que…?** When you see the Florida icon next to **¿Sabías que...?** *(Did you know...?)* in the **Geocultura** section, you will learn interesting facts and information that link the featured country with the state of Florida.

# FCAT *Preparation*

**Even though there is no Florida Comprehensive Assessment Test (FCAT) for Spanish, studying Spanish can help you prepare for the Language Arts FCAT and the Math FCAT. In your Spanish class, you will learn and practice different reading, writing, and math skills.**

In **Conexiones culturales,** look for the FCAT Reading Focus icons and Math Focus icons. The activities on these pages will help you improve your reading and math skills and learn about the cultures of Spanish-speaking countries at the same time.

In the **Leamos y escribamos** *(Let's Read and Write)* sections, you will read a short piece and then do some original writing—all in Spanish! In these sections, look for the FCAT Reading Focus and FCAT Writing Focus icons. All of the skills and strategies you use for reading and writing in Spanish can help you perfect your reading comprehension and writing skills in English, too!

In the **Literatura y variedades** *(Literature and other works)* section at the end of your textbook, you will find additional readings and strategies to help you perfect your language skills. In this section, you will also find FCAT Reading Focus icons.

# Búsqueda de tesoros

This **Búsqueda de tesoros** will help you become familiar with the different sections of your textbook, as well as give you a taste of what you'll be learning this year!

1. Where in each chapter will you find all the objectives for that chapter?
2. What Spanish-speaking country is featured in Chapter 4?
3. What sections do you have at the end of your textbook?
4. What is the Sunshine State Standards Benchmark Focus for page 163? Find one other page with the same Benchmark Focus.
5. What section can you find towards the end of the book, on page R15? What do you think that section is for?
6. Use the Table of Contents to find the pages where Weather Expressions are presented.
7. What kind of information will you find in the **También se puede decir** feature? What new words do you learn in the **También se puede decir** feature on page 141?
8. See whether you can find a feature called **¿Te acuerdas?** in Chapter 4. What do you think **¿Te acuerdas?** might mean? Can you find the same feature in other chapters? Where exactly within a chapter do you find them?
9. In what section at the end of the book will you find additional vocabulary in Spanish?
10. Where can you find and learn everyday conversational expressions to use in Spanish? Name the sections in your book where you could find this information.
11. Where do you find the **Repaso de vocabulario** section in each chapter?
12. What section in each chapter helps you prepare for the Chapter Test?

# Sunshine State Standards

## Spanish 1A Benchmarks

**The activities in *¡Exprésate!* will help you develop the skills outlined in each Foreign Language benchmark of the Florida Sunshine State Standards for M/J Spanish, Beginning. Each activity in your book correlates to one or more of the benchmarks.**

**1. Engage in conversation in Spanish to express feelings and ideas and exchange opinions.**

**FL.A.1.1.1** express likes and dislikes when asked simple questions (e.g., about toys or other objects).

**FL.A.1.1.2** greet others and exchange essential personal information (e.g., home address, telephone number, place of origin, and general health).

**FL.A.1.1.3** use appropriate gestures and expressions (i.e., body language) to complete or enhance verbal messages.

**FL.A.1.2.2** exchange information necessary to plan events or activities (e.g., picnics, birthday parties, science projects, and crafts).

**2. Demonstrate understanding of spoken and written Spanish on a variety of topics.**

**FL.A.2.1.1** follow and give simple instructions (e.g., instructions to participate in games or instructions provided by the teacher for classroom tasks).

**FL.A.2.1.2** restate and rephrase simple information from materials presented orally, visually, and graphically in class.

**FL.A.2.1.3** understand oral messages that are based on familiar themes and vocabulary (e.g., short conversations between familiar persons on familiar topics such as everyday school and home activities).

**FL.A.2.1.4** listen and read in the target language and respond through role playing, drawing, or singing.

3. **Present information and ideas to an audience through speaking and writing in Spanish.**

**FL.A.3.1.1** provide simple information in spoken form (e.g., descriptions of family members, friends, objects present in his or her everyday environment, or common school and home activities).

4. **Demonstrate understanding of social interaction patterns within Spanish culture(s) through participation in cultural activities.**

**FL.B.1.1.1** participate in age-appropriate cultural activities (e.g., games, songs, birthday celebrations, storytelling, dramatizations, and role playing).

**FL.B.1.1.2** recognize patterns of social behavior or social interaction in various settings (e.g., school, family, or immediate community).

**FL.B.1.1.3** recognize various familiar objects and norms of the target culture (e.g., toys, dresses, and typical foods).

5. **Apply knowledge of Spanish language and culture(s) to further knowledge of other disciplines.**

**FL.C.1.1.1** use simple vocabulary and phrases to identify familiar objects and concepts from other disciplines.

**FL.C.1.1.2** participate in an activity in the target-language class that is based on a concept taught in a content class (e.g., shapes or relationships).

**FL.C.2.1.1** use the target language to gain access to information that is only available through the target language or within the target culture (listen to a story told in the target language).

6. **Analyze and use different patterns of communication and social interaction appropriate to the setting.**

**FL.D.1.1.1** know examples of word borrowing from one language to another.

**FL.D.1.1.2** use simple vocabulary and short phrases in the target language.

**FL.D.1.2.1** identify examples and understand the significance of true and false cognates (i.e., words derived from a common original form).

**FL.D.2.1.1** know the similarities and differences between the patterns of behavior of the target culture related to recreation, celebration, holidays, customs, and the patterns of behavior of the local culture.

**FL.D.2.2.2** recognize forms of the target language evident in the local culture (e.g., signs, symbols, advertisements, packages, displays, murals, songs, and rhymes).

**7. Demonstrate knowledge of use of the Spanish language within and beyond the school setting.**

**FL.E.1.2.1** know that many people in the United States use languages other than English on a daily basis.

**FL.E.1.2.2** demonstrate an awareness of employment possibilities (and other applications) for those who are able to master the target language.

¡Exprésate!, The Florida Edition, Level 1A, © 2007
Front Matter Insert Photo Credits

Title page James Carmichael Jr./NHPA; FL2 (t, l), The Florida Center for Instructional Technology, University of South Florida/http://fcit.usf.edu/florida; FL2 (c), © Bettmann/CORBIS; FL3 (r), © Nik Wheeler/CORBIS; FL3 (tl, bl), The Florida Center for Instructional Technology, University of South Florida/ http://fcit.usf.edu/florida; FL4 (b), Don Couch Photography; FL5 (t, b), © Royalty-Free/CORBIS; FL5 (cr), © Jeff Greenberg/Alamy Photos; FL5 (cl), © Jeff Greenberg/PhotoEdit; FL6 (tl), Courtesy Ileana Ros-Lehtinen's Office; FL6 (tr), NASA Kennedy Space Center (NASA-KSC); FL6 (bl), Courtesy Mr. Ferdie Pacheco; FL6 (br), © Bob Gelberg/Courtesy Mr. Ferdie Pacheco; FL7 (t - all), Courtesy of The Florida State Spanish Conference; FL7 (b), Courtesy of the Orlando Ballet; FL8 (t), Courtesy of the Fiesta of Five Flags; FL8 (b), Courtesy of Puerto Rico Cultural Parade of Florida, Inc.; FL8 (cl), Photo by George Olsen/Viva Broward Hispanic Festival; FL8 (cr), David Adame/AP/Wide World Photos; FL9 (tl), Courtesy of Nicario Jiménez, Artist of the Andes; FL9 (tr), Courtesy of Mr. Obed Gómez; FL9 (cl), John Barrett/GLOBE PHOTOS; FL9 (c), © Photo by Alberto Tamargo/Getty Images; FL9 (cr), © Reuters/CORBIS; FL9 (b), © Ivan Garcia/AFP/Getty Images; FL13 (tr), © Image Source Limited/Index Stock Imagery, Inc.; FL13 (bl), Private Collection/Bridgeman Art Library; FL13 (br), Sam Dudgeon/HRW Photo; FL13 (bkgd), © Royalty Free/CORBIS; FL14-15 (b), © James Randklev Photography; FL16 (b), Photo © John Post/Panoramic Images, Chicago 1998

# ¡Exprésate!®

Nancy Humbach

Sylvia Madrigal Velasco

Ana Beatriz Chiquito

Stuart Smith

John McMinn

HOLT, RINEHART AND WINSTON

A Harcourt Education Company

Orlando • Austin • New York • San Diego • London

# Florida Teacher Contributors

We thank the following Florida educators who generously contributed their talent and time to help develop and review materials for the Florida Student Edition of *¡Exprésate!* **¡Muchísimas gracias!**

**Enrique Acosta**
Stoneman Douglas High School
Parkland, FL

**Alejandro Avendaño**
Eastside High School IB Program
Gainesville, FL

**Clementina Bassi**
Eastside High School
Gainesville, FL

**Maria Isabel Bentine**
Palm Beach Lakes Community High School
West Palm Beach, FL

**Vivian Bosque,** Ed. D.
Nova Southeastern University
Miami, FL

**Ana I. Carmona-Torres**
Winter Park High School
Winter Park, FL

**Debbie Chraibi**
William R. Boone High School
Orlando, FL

**Nitza Cochran**
Nathan B. Forrest High School
Jacksonville, FL

**Carmen Gómez**
George Washington Carver Middle School
Miami, FL

**Meruchy Haedo**
Eastside High School IB Program
Gainesville, FL

**Connie M. Heiselman**
William R. Boone High School
Orlando, FL

**Janice Karkis**
Estero High School
Estero, FL

**Rosa B. Leal**
Palm Beach Lakes Community High School
West Palm Beach, FL

**Rebekah Lindsey**
Campbell Middle School
Daytona Beach, FL

**Gudrun Martyny**
Timber Creek High School
Orlando, FL

**Antonio Román-Pérez**
River Ridge High School
New Port Richey, FL

**Vladimir Sanmiguel**
Palm Beach Lakes Community High School
West Palm Beach, FL

**Jessica Shrader**
Riverview High School
Sarasota, FL

# Holt Teacher Advisory Panel

As members of the **Holt World Languages Advisory Panel,** the following teachers made a unique and invaluable contribution to the *¡Exprésate!* Spanish program. They generously shared their experience and expertise in a collaborative group setting and helped refine early materials into the program design represented in this book. We wish to thank them for the many hours of work they put into the development of this program and for the many ideas they shared. **¡Muchísimas gracias a todos!**

**Erick Ekker**
Bob Miller Middle School
Henderson, NV

**Dulce Goldenberg**
Miami Senior High School
Miami, FL

**Beckie Gurnish**
Ellet High School
Akron, OH

**Bill Heller**
Perry High School
Perry, NY

**MilyBett Llanos**
Westwood High School
Austin, TX

**Rosanna Perez**
Communications Arts High School
San Antonio, TX

**Jo Schuler**
Central Bucks High School East
Doylestown, PA

**Leticia Schweigert**
Science Academy
Mercedes, TX

**Claudia Sloan**
Lake Park High School
Roselle, IL

**Judy Smock**
Gilbert High School
Gilbert, AZ

**Catriona Stavropoulos**
West Springfield High School
Springfield, VA

**Nina Wilson**
Burnet Middle School
Austin, TX

**Janet Wohlers**
Weston Middle School
Weston, MA

# Authors

## Nancy Humbach

Nancy Humbach is Associate Professor and Coordinator of Languages Education at Miami University, Oxford, Ohio. She has authored or co-authored over a dozen textbooks in Spanish. A former Fulbright-Hayes Scholar, she has lived and studied in Colombia and Mexico and has traveled and conducted research throughout the Spanish-speaking world. She is a recipient of many honors, including the Florence Steiner Award for Leadership in the Foreign Language Profession and the Nelson Brooks Award for the Teaching of Culture.

## Sylvia Madrigal Velasco

Sylvia Madrigal Velasco was born in San Benito, Texas. The youngest of four siblings, she grew up in the Rio Grande Valley, between two cultures and languages. Her lifelong fascination with Spanish has led her to travel in many Spanish-speaking countries. She graduated from Yale University in 1979 and has worked for over 20 years as a textbook editor and author at various publishing companies. She has written bilingual materials, video scripts, workbooks, CD-ROMs, and readers.

## Ana Beatriz Chiquito

Professor Ana Beatriz Chiquito is a native of Colombia. She teaches Spanish linguistics and Latin American culture at the University of Bergen, Norway, and conducts research and develops applications for language learning at the Center for Educational Computing Initiatives at the Massachusetts Institute of Technology. She has taught Spanish for more than thirty years and has authored numerous textbooks, CD-ROMs, videos, and on-line materials for college and high school students of Spanish.

## Stuart Smith

Stuart Smith began her teaching career at the University of Texas at Austin from where she received her degrees. She has been a professor of foreign languages at Austin Community College, Austin, Texas, for over 20 years and has been writing textbook and teaching materials for almost as long. She has given presentations on language teaching methodology at ACTFL, SWCOLT, and TCCTA.

## John McMinn

John McMinn is Professor of Spanish and French at Austin Community College, where he has taught since 1986. After completing his M.A. in Romance Linguistics at the University of Texas at Austin, he also taught Spanish and French at the secondary level and was a Senior Editor of World Languages at Holt, Rinehart and Winston. He is co-author of both Spanish and French textbooks at the college level.

# Contributing Writers

**Jeff Cole**
Tucson, AZ
Mr. Cole developed activities for **Taller del escritor.**

**JoDee Costello**
Gunnison, CO
Ms. Costello wrote activites for **Vocabulario, Integración**, and **Comunidad.**

**Jabier Elorrieta**
The University of Texas at Austin
Mr. Elorrieta wrote **Letra y sonido.**

**Karin Fajardo**
Englewood, CO
Ms. Fajardo wrote vocabulary activities and material for **También se puede decir.**

**Catherine Gavin**
New York City, NY
Ms. Gavin wrote material for **Geocultura** and **Cultura.**

**Pablo Muirhead**
Shorewood, WI
Mr. Muirhead wrote suggestions for the story sequence art.

**Gloria Munguía**
Austin, TX
Ms. Munguía wrote activities for **Integración.**

**Marci Reed**
Austin, TX
Ms. Reed contributed to the selection of and wrote material for **Literatura y variedades.**

**Mayanne Wright**
Austin, TX
Ms. Wright contributed to the selection of and wrote material for **Leamos.**

# Reviewers

**These educators reviewed one or more chapters of the Student Edition.**

**Elizabeth Baird**
Independence High School
Independence, OH

**Paula Camardella Twomey**
Ithaca High School
Ithaca, NY

**Johnnie Eng**
Alamo Heights High School
San Antonio, TX

**Patricia Gander**
Berkeley High School
Moncks Corner, SC

**Laura Grable**
Riverhead Central School District
Riverhead, NY

**Mani Hernández**
Presentation High School
San Jose, CA

**Yoscelina Hernández**
Montwood High School
El Paso, TX

**Jorge Muñoz**
St. Stephen's Episcopal School
Austin, TX

**Jessica Shrader**
Riverview High School
Sarasota, FL

**Sharlene Soto**
D.C. Everest Jr. and Sr. High Schools
Wausau, WI

**Nancy Walker de Llanas**
George C. Marshall High School
Falls Church, VA

**Thomasina I. White**
Lead Academic Coach
World Language Education
Philadelphia, PA

# Field Test Participants

**We thank the teachers and students who participated in the field test of *¡Exprésate!***

**Tim Burel**
West Middle School
Rockford, IL

**Liliana Camarena**
Gueillen Middle School
El Paso, TX

**Mariluz Julio**
Clover Junior High School
Clover, SC

**Patrice Kahn**
Noel Grisham Middle School
Austin, TX

**Rebekeh Lindsey**
Campbell Middle School
Daytona Beach, FL

**Estela Morel**
Corlears Middle School 56
New York, NY

**Linda Schell**
Landmark Middle School
Jacksonville, FL

**Sarah Taylor**
Richland Middle School
Richmond, VA

**Rebecca Taylor-Norton**
Beechwood Middle School
Cleveland, OH

**Amanda York**
George Washington Carver Academy
Waco, TX

# Contenido en breve

Table of Contents ..... vi
Páginas de referencia ..... xi
El español, ¿por qué? ..... xii
En la clase de español ..... xvi
Nombres comunes ..... xvii
Instrucciones ..... xviii
Sugerencias para aprender el español ..... xx

**España**
Geocultura ..... xxii
Capítulo 1 ..... 4
Integración Capítulo 1 ..... 40

**Puerto Rico**
Geocultura ..... 42
Capítulo 2 ..... 46
Integración Capítulos 1–2 ..... 86

**Texas**
Geocultura ..... 88
Capítulo 3 ..... 92
Integración Capítulos 1–3 ..... 132

**Costa Rica**
Geocultura ..... 134
Capítulo 4 ..... 138
Integración Capítulos 1–4 ..... 178

**Chile**
Geocultura ..... 180
Capítulo 5 ..... 184
Integración Capítulos 1–5 ..... 224

**Literatura y variedades**
España ..... 228
Puerto Rico ..... 230
Texas ..... 232
Costa Rica ..... 234
Chile ..... 236

**Mapas**
La Península Ibérica ..... R2
México ..... R3
Estados Unidos de América ..... R4
América Central y las Antillas ..... R5
América del Sur ..... R6

Vocabulario adicional ..... R7
Expresiones de ¡Exprésate! ..... R12
Síntesis gramatical ..... R15
Vocabulario español-inglés ..... R23
Vocabulario inglés-español ..... R41
Índice gramatical ..... R49
Agradecimientos ..... R52

# España

## Capítulo 1 ¡Empecemos!


Capítulo 1 ¡Empecemos! .......... 4


**OBJETIVOS**

In this chapter, you will learn to
- ask someone's name and give your name
- ask and say who someone is
- ask how someone is; say how you are
- introduce people and say where they are from
- ask for and give phone numbers
- say the time, the date, the day, and the season
- ask how words are spelled and give e-mail addresses

**Geocultura**


Mapas de España .......... 1, R2
Almanac .......... xxii
A conocer España .......... 2

Molinos de viento, España

**En video**

| | |
|---|---|
| Geocultura | GeoVisión |
| Vocabulario 1 y 2 | ExpresaVisión |
| Gramática 1 y 2 | GramaVisión |
| Cultura | VideoCultura |
| VideoNovela | ¿Quién será? |
| | Variedades |


Vocabulario en acción 1 .......... 6
- Greetings and goodbyes

Gramática en acción 1 .......... 12
- Using subjects and verbs in sentences
- Using subject pronouns

Cultura .......... 16
- **Comparaciones**
- **Comunidad**

Vocabulario en acción 2 .......... 18
- Numbers 0–31
- Telling time
- Days of the week and months of the year
- Alphabet

Gramática en acción 2 .......... 24
- Using the verb **ser**
- Punctuation marks and written accents

Conexiones culturales .......... 28
- **Ciencias sociales**
- **Matemáticas**

Novela .......... 30
**¿Quién será?** Episodio 1

Leamos y escribamos .......... 34
**Participa en el club de español** (Leamos)
**La página Web del club de español** (Escribamos)

Prepárate para el examen .......... 36

Repaso de gramática y de vocabulario .......... 38
- **Letra y sonido** • Trabalenguas • Dictado

Integración **(Repaso cumulativo)** Capítulo 1 .......... 40

Literatura y variedades
**El Museo del Prado** (folleto) .......... 228

# Puerto Rico

## Capítulo 2 A conocernos ............46


**Vocabulario en acción 1** ............48
- Describing friends
- Numbers 32–100

**Gramática en acción 1** ............54
- Using **ser** with adjectives
- Gender and adjective agreement
- Forming questions

**Cultura** ............60
- **Comparaciones**
- **Comunidad**

**Vocabulario en acción 2** ............62
- Likes and dislikes

**Gramática en acción 2** ............68
- Using nouns and definite articles
- Using **gustar**, **¿por qué?**, and **porque**
- Using the preposition **de**

**Conexiones culturales** ............74
- **Ciencias sociales**
- **Geografía**

**Novela** ............76

**¿Quién será?** Episodio 2

**Leamos y escribamos** ............80

**¿Qué color prefieres?** (Leamos)

**Mi personalidad** (Escribamos)

**Prepárate para el examen** ............82

**Repaso de gramática y de vocabulario** ............84
- **Letra y sonido** • Trabalenguas • Dictado

**Integración** **(Repaso cumulativo)** Capítulos 1–2 ............86

**Literatura y variedades**

**El coquí** (artículo) ............230


### OBJETIVOS

In this chapter, you will learn to
- ask what someone is like
- describe someone
- ask about someone's age and birthday
- tell someone your age and birthday
- talk about what you and others like
- describe things

## Geocultura


Mapas de Puerto Rico ...42, R5
Almanac ............42
A conocer Puerto Rico ............44

El Morro, San Juan, Puerto Rico

## En video

| | |
|---|---|
| Geocultura | **GeoVisión** |
| Vocabulario 1 y 2 | **ExpresaVisión** |
| Gramática 1 y 2 | **GramaVisión** |
| Cultura | **VideoCultura** |
| Video Novela | **¿Quién será?** |
| | **Variedades** |

# Texas

## Capítulo 3 ¿Qué te gusta hacer? ........ 92

### OBJETIVOS

In this chapter, you will learn to

- talk about what you and others like to do
- ask what a friend wants to do and answer
- talk about everyday activities
- ask how often someone does something and answer


Vocabulario en acción 1 ........ 94
- Sports and leisure activities

Gramática en acción 1 ........ 100
- Using **gustar** with infinitives
- Using pronouns after prepositions
- Using **querer** with infinitives

Cultura ........ 106
- **Comparaciones**
- **Comunidad**

Vocabulario en acción 2 ........ 108
- Weekend activities

Gramática en acción 2 ........ 114
- Using regular **-ar** verbs
- Using **ir** and **jugar**
- Using weather expressions

Conexiones culturales ........ 120
- **Música**
- **Ciencias naturales**

Novela ........ 122

**¿Quién será?** Episodio 3

Leamos y escribamos ........ 126

**Los cuatro elementos** (Leamos)

**Horario de actividades** (Escribamos)

Prepárate para el examen ........ 128

Repaso de gramática y de vocabulario ........ 130
- **Letra y sonido** • Trabalenguas • Dictado

Integración **(Repaso cumulativo)** Capítulos 1–3 ........ 132

Literatura y variedades

**Obras de Carmen Lomas Garza** (comentarios) ........ 232

### Geocultura


Mapas de Texas ........ 89, R4

Almanaque ........ 88

A conocer Texas ........ 90

Paisaje típico tejano

### En video

| | |
|---|---|
| Geocultura | GeoVisión |
| Vocabulario 1 y 2 | ExpresaVisión |
| Gramática 1 y 2 | GramaVisión |
| Cultura | VideoCultura |
| VideoNovela | ¿Quién será? |
| | Variedades |

# Costa Rica

## Capítulo 4 La vida escolar ....... 138


**Vocabulario** *en acción* **1** .................................. 140
- School supplies and items needed for school
- Classes

**Gramática** *en acción* **1** .................................. 146
- Using indefinite articles, **¿cuánto?, mucho,** and **poco**
- Using **tener** idioms
- Using **venir** and **a** with time

**Cultura** ........................................................ 152
- **Comparaciones**
- **Comunidad**

**Vocabulario** *en acción* **2** .................................. 154
- School events
- Places at school

**Gramática** *en acción* **2** .................................. 160
- Using **ir a** with infinitives
- Regular **-er** and **-ir** verbs and tag questions
- Using **-er** and **-ir** verbs with irregular **yo** forms

**Conexiones culturales** .................................. 166
- **Historia** • **Geografía** • **Matemáticas**

**Novela** ........................................................ 168
**¿Quién será?** Episodio 4

**Leamos y escribamos** .................................. 172
**Pepito, el niño precoz** (Leamos)
**Un recorrido con nuevos estudiantes** (Escribamos)

**Prepárate para el examen** .......................... 174

**Repaso de gramática y de vocabulario** ........ 176
- **Letra y sonido** • Trabalenguas • Dictado

**Integración** **(Repaso cumulativo)** Capítulos 1–4 ......... 178

**Literatura y variedades**
**La artesanía chorotega** (entrevista) ................................ 234


**OBJETIVOS**

In this chapter, you will learn to
- say what you have and what you need
- talk about school supplies and school subjects
- talk about plans and give invitations
- talk about school events and places

**Geocultura**


Mapas de Costa Rica ... 135, R5
Almanac ...................... 134
A conocer Costa Rica ........ 136

El volcán Arenal, Costa Rica

**En video**

| | |
|---|---|
| Geocultura | GeoVisión |
| Vocabulario 1 y 2 | ExpresaVisión |
| Gramática 1 y 2 | GramaVisión |
| Cultura | VideoCultura |
| Video Novela | ¿Quién será? |
| | Variedades |

# Chile

## Capítulo 5 En casa con la familia ................ 184

**OBJETIVOS**

In this chapter, you will learn to
- describe people and family relationships
- talk about where you and others live
- talk about responsibilities


Vocabulario en acción 1 ................ 186
- Family members
- Describing people (physical and personality)

Gramática en acción 1 ................ 192
- Possessive adjectives
- Stem-changing verbs **o → ue**
- Stem-changing verbs **e → ie**

Cultura ................ 198
- **Comparaciones** • **Comunidad**

Vocabulario en acción 2 ................ 200
- Rooms in the house
- Furniture and accessories
- Chores
- Where you live

Gramática en acción 2 ................ 206
- Using **estar** with prepositions
- Negation with **nunca, tampoco, nadie,** and **nada**
- Using **tocar** and **parecer**

Conexiones culturales ................ 212
- **Arte** • **Historia**

Novela ................ 214

**¿Quién será?** Episodio 5

Leamos y escribamos ................ 218

**Casas y apartamentos** (Leamos)

**¿Qué les toca hacer?** (Escribamos)

Prepárate para el examen ................ 220

Repaso de gramática y de vocabulario ....... 222
- **Letra y sonido** • Trabalenguas • Dictado

Integración **(Repaso cumulativo)** Capítulos 1–5 ......... 224

Literatura y variedades

**Las novelas de Isabel Allende** (comentario y fragmento) .......... 236

Mapas de Chile ......... 181, R6
Almanac ...................... 180
A conocer Chile .............. 182

Oficina de correos, Santiago, Chile

**En video**

| | |
|---|---|
| Geocultura | GeoVisión |
| Vocabulario 1 y 2 | ExpresaVisión |
| Gramática 1 y 2 | GramaVisión |
| Cultura | VideoCultura |
| VideoNovela | ¿Quién será? |
| | Variedades |

# Páginas de referencia


**Mapas**

La Península Ibérica .................................. R2

México .................................. R3

Estados Unidos de América .................................. R4

América Central y las Antillas .................................. R5

América del Sur .................................. R6

**Vocabulario adicional** .................................. R7

**Expresiones de ¡Exprésate!** .................................. R12

**Síntesis gramatical** .................................. R15

**Vocabulario español-inglés** .................................. R23

**Vocabulario inglés-español** .................................. R41

**Índice gramatical** .................................. R49

**Agradecimientos** .................................. R52

# El español, ¿por qué?
## Why Study Spanish?

## Por lo mundial *Because it's worldwide*

Spanish is the fourth most commonly spoken language in the world. You can visit any one of 21 countries in the world that speak Spanish and feel at home. Even in the United States, knowing Spanish can open doors to you.

So whether you're in Europe, North, Central, or South America, or even Africa, as a Spanish speaker you won't have to rely on someone else to watch television or read a newspaper. You'll learn things on your own. You'll truly be a citizen of the world.

## Por lo bello *Because it's beautiful*

You'll be amazed to discover how rich the Spanish-speaking world is in works of music, literature, science, religion, and art. The novels of Miguel de Cervantes or Isabel Allende, the paintings of Fernando Botero or Frida Kahlo, the poetry of Gabriela Mistral or Pablo Neruda: all these treasures and many more await you as you explore the Spanish-speaking world.

**Ceramic tiles form this mural by Dominican artist Said Musa.**

**Traditional painted carts in Costa Rica are a part of El Festival de las Carretas.**

**The fountain of Cibeles, named after the goddess Cybele, is one of Madrid's best-known landmarks.**

**These young Costa Ricans are wearing traditional dance costumes.**

# Por lo práctico *Because it's practical*

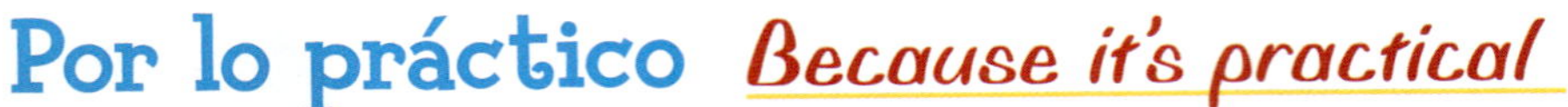

You're living in the country with the fifth-largest Hispanic population in the world, more than 33 million people. And whether they're originally from Mexico, Puerto Rico, or Cuba—or from any other part of Latin America or Spain—almost nine out of ten are Spanish speakers.

Businesses, government agencies, educational institutions, and other employers will be looking for more bilingual employees every year. Give yourself an edge in the job market with Spanish!

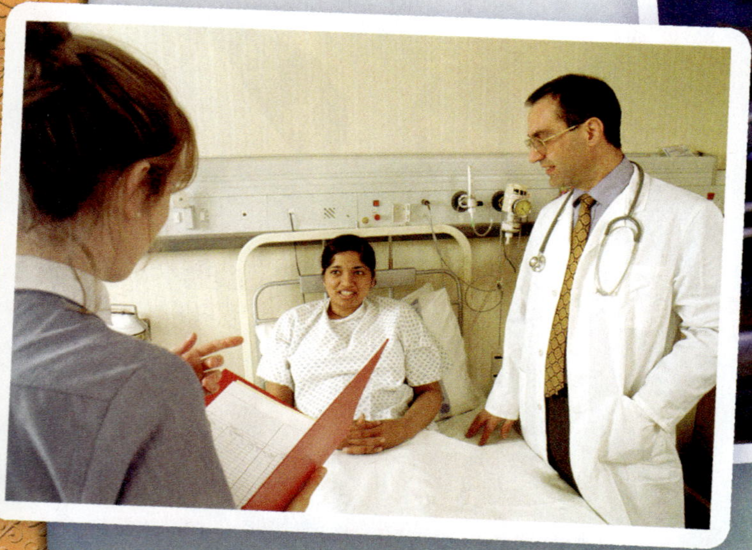

Bilingual doctors, nurses, and others in the field of medicine provide care for Spanish-speaking patients.

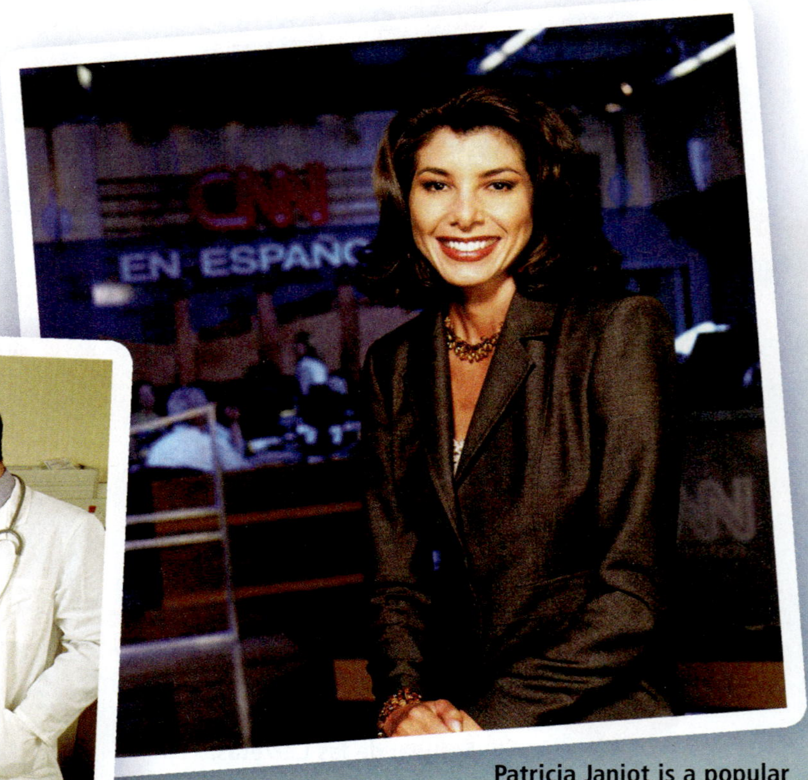

Patricia Janiot is a popular anchor at the Spanish language news department of CNN En Español.

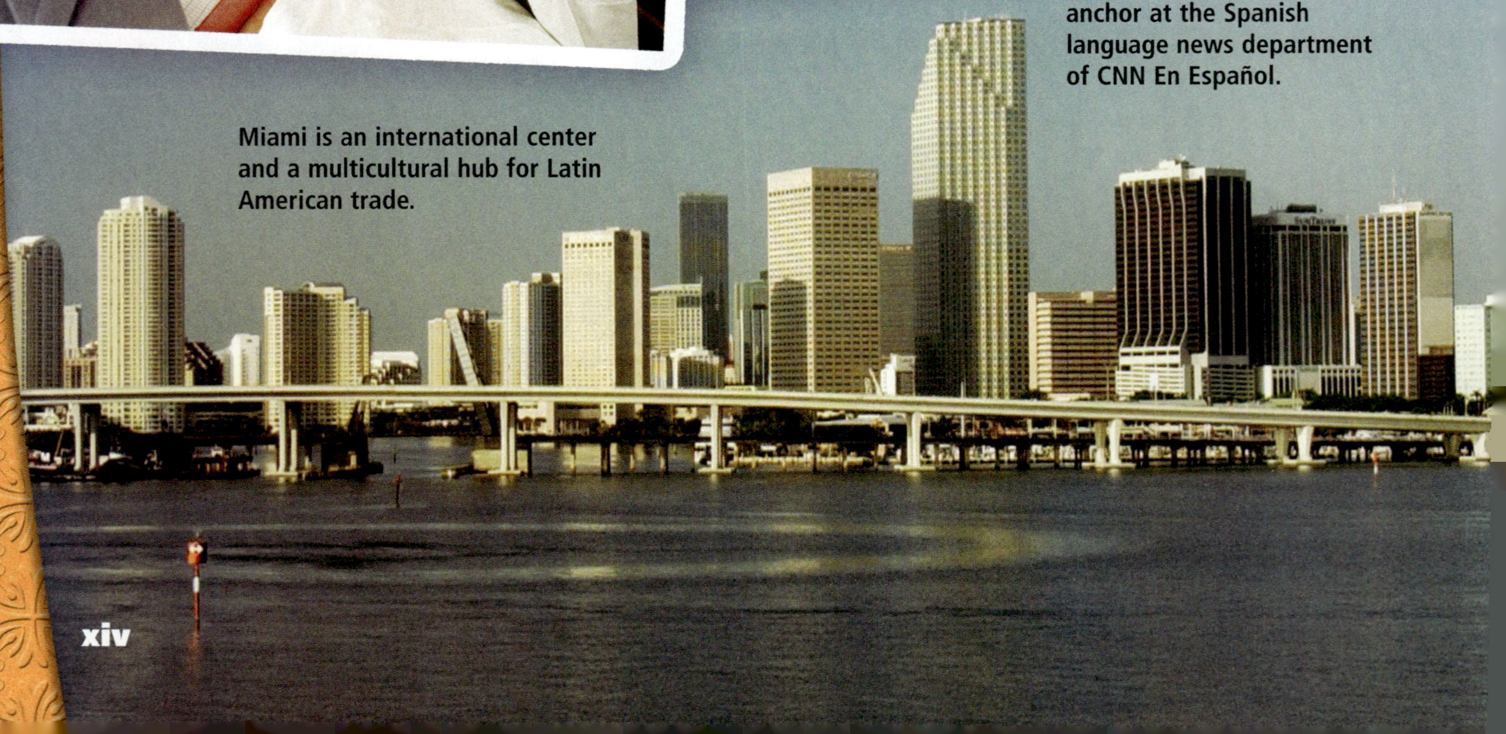

Miami is an international center and a multicultural hub for Latin American trade.

## ¡Porque puedes! *Because you can do it!*

Applying your learning skills to a new language will be challenging at first. But you have the tools you need to do the job. And you're lucky to be living at a time when there are almost no limits to your opportunities to practice Spanish. You can interact with Spanish speakers not just in your community but all over the world, via pen pal organizations, at the library, or through a multitude of resources and online networks.

**Bicyclists stop at a spot overlooking the historic city of Toledo, Spain.**

## En fin, porque sí *Finally, just because...*

The best reason of all to study Spanish is because you want to! You know better than anyone what motivated you to enroll for Spanish class. It might be one of the reasons given here, such as getting a job, learning about world issues, or enjoying works of art. Or it might be something more personal, like wanting to communicate with Spanish-speaking friends and family, or travel. So pat yourself on the back and **¡Exprésate!**

# En la clase de espanol

## In Spanish Class

*Here are some phrases you'll probably hear in your classroom, along with some responses.*

| Phrases: | Responses: |
|---|---|
| **Tengo una pregunta.**<br>*I have a question.* | **¿Sí? Dime.**<br>*Yes? What is it?* |
| **¿Cómo se dice...?**<br>*How do you say . . .?* | **Se dice...**<br>*You say . . .* |
| **¿Cómo se escribe...?**<br>*How do you spell . . .?* | **Se escribe...**<br>*It's spelled . . .* |
| **No entiendo. ¿Puede repetir?**<br>*I don't understand. Could you repeat that?*<br>**Más despacio, por favor.**<br>*More slowly, please.* | **Claro que sí.**<br>*Yes, of course.* |
| **¿Sabes qué significa (quiere decir)...?**<br>*Do you know what . . . means?* | **No, no sé.**<br>*No, I don't know.*<br>**Sí, significa (quiere decir)...**<br>*Yes, it means . . .* |
| **Gracias.**<br>*Thank you.* | **De nada.**<br>*You're welcome.* |
| **Perdón.**<br>*I'm sorry.* | **Está bien.**<br>*It's okay.* |

*Here are some things your teacher might ask you to do.*

**Levanten la mano.**
*Raise your hand.*

**Escuchen.**
*Listen.*

**¡Su atención, por favor!**
*Attention, please.*

**Silencio, por favor.**
*Silence, please.*

**Abran sus libros en la página...**
*Open your books to page . . .*

**Cierren los libros.**
*Close your books.*

**Estamos en la página...**
*We're on page . . .*

**Miren la pizarra (la transparencia).**
*Look at the board (transparency).*

**Saquen una hoja de papel.**
*Take out a sheet of paper.*

**Pasen la tarea (los papeles) al frente.**
*Pass the homework (the papers) to the front.*

**Levántense, por favor.**
*Stand up, please.*

**Siéntense, por favor.**
*Sit down, please.*

**Repitan después de mí.**
*Repeat after me.*

# Nombres comunes
## Common Names

*Here are some common names from Spanish-speaking countries.*

| Nombres de muchachas | | |
|---|---|---|
| Ana | Inés | Patricia |
| Bárbara | Irene | Pilar |
| Beatriz | Isabel | Rosalía |
| Cecilia | Josefina | Rosario |
| Cristina | Lourdes | Sonia |
| Dolores | María | Susana |
| Elena | Maribel | Tamara |
| Elisa | Marisol | Teresa |
| Emilia | Nuria | Vanesa |
| Fátima | Olga | Yolanda |

| Nombres de muchachos | | |
|---|---|---|
| Alfredo | Francisco | Óscar |
| Antonio | Gilberto | Pablo |
| Arturo | Héctor | Pedro |
| Bruno | Javier | Rafael |
| Carlos | Julio | Ramón |
| Daniel | Lorenzo | Roberto |
| Eduardo | Luis | Sergio |
| Enrique | Manuel | Tomás |
| Esteban | Marcos | Vicente |
| Fernando | Miguel | Víctor |

# Instrucciones
## Directions

*Throughout the book, many activities will have directions in Spanish. Here are some of the directions you'll see, along with their English translations.*

**Completa... con una palabra del cuadro.**
*Complete . . . with a word from the box.*

**Completa el párrafo con...**
*Complete the paragraph with . . .*

**Completa las oraciones con la forma correcta del verbo.**
*Complete the sentences with the correct form of the verb.*

**Con base en..., contesta cierto o falso. Corrige las oraciones falsas.**
*Based on . . ., respond with true or false. Correct the false sentences.*

**Con un(a) compañero(a), dramatiza...**
*With a classmate, act out . . .*

**Contesta las preguntas usando...**
*Answer the questions using . . .*

**Contesta (Completa) las siguientes preguntas (oraciones)...**
*Answer (Complete) the following questions (sentences) . . .*

**En parejas (grupos de tres), dramaticen...**
*In pairs (groups of three), act out . . .*

**Escoge el dibujo (la respuesta) que corresponde (mejor completa)...**
*Choose the drawing (the answer) that goes with (best completes) . . .*

**Escribe..., usando el vocabulario de la página...**
*Write . . ., using the vocabulary on page . . .*

**Escucha las conversaciones. Decide qué conversación (diálogo) corresponde a cada dibujo (foto).**
*Listen to the conversations. Decide which conversation (dialog) corresponds to each drawing (photo).*

**Mira las fotos (los dibujos) y decide (di, indica)...**
*Look at the photos (drawings) and decide (say, indicate) . . .*

**Pon en orden...**
*Put . . . in order.*

**Pregúntale a tu compañero(a)...**
*Ask your partner . . .*

**Sigue el modelo.**
*Follow the model.*

**Túrnense para...**
*Take turns . . .*

**Usa el vocabulario de... para completar...**
*Use the vocabulary from . . . to complete . . .*

**Usa una palabra o expresión de cada columna para escribir...**
*Use one word or expression from each column to write . . .*

**Usa los dibujos para decir lo que pasa.**
*Use the drawings to say what is happening.*

# Sugerencias para aprender el español
## Tips for learning Spanish

### Listen
Listen carefully in class and ask questions if you don't understand. You won't be able to understand everything you hear at first, but don't feel frustrated. You are actually absorbing a lot even when you don't realize it.

### Visualize
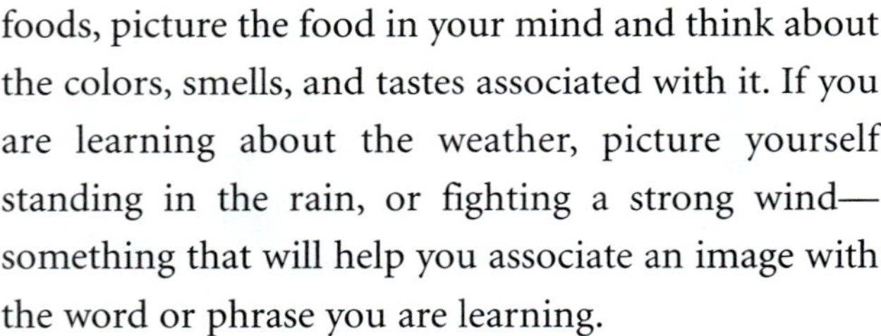

It may help you to visualize the words you are learning. Associate each new word, sentence, or phrase with a mental picture. For example, if you're learning words for foods, picture the food in your mind and think about the colors, smells, and tastes associated with it. If you are learning about the weather, picture yourself standing in the rain, or fighting a strong wind—something that will help you associate an image with the word or phrase you are learning.

### Practice
Short, daily practice sessions are more effective than long, once-a-week sessions. Also, try to practice with a friend or a classmate. After all, language is about communication, and it takes two to communicate.

### Speak
Practice speaking Spanish aloud every day. Don't be afraid to experiment. Your mistakes will help identify problems, and they will show you important differences in the way English and Spanish work as languages.

### Explore
Increase your contact with Spanish outside class in every way you can. Maybe someone living near you speaks Spanish. It's easy to find Spanish-language programs on TV, on the radio, or at the video store, and many magazines and newspapers in Spanish are published or sold in the United States and are on the Internet. Don't be afraid to read, watch, or listen, even if you don't understand every word.

### Connect
Making connections between what you learn in other subject areas and what you are learning in your Spanish class will increase your understanding of the new material, help you retain it longer, and enrich your learning experience.

### Have fun!
Above all, remember to have fun! Learn as much as you can, because the more you know, the easier it will be for you to relax—and that will make your learning easier and more effective.

**¡Buena suerte!** (Good luck!)

# Ven a conocer más del mundo hispanohablante y...

# ¡Exprésate!

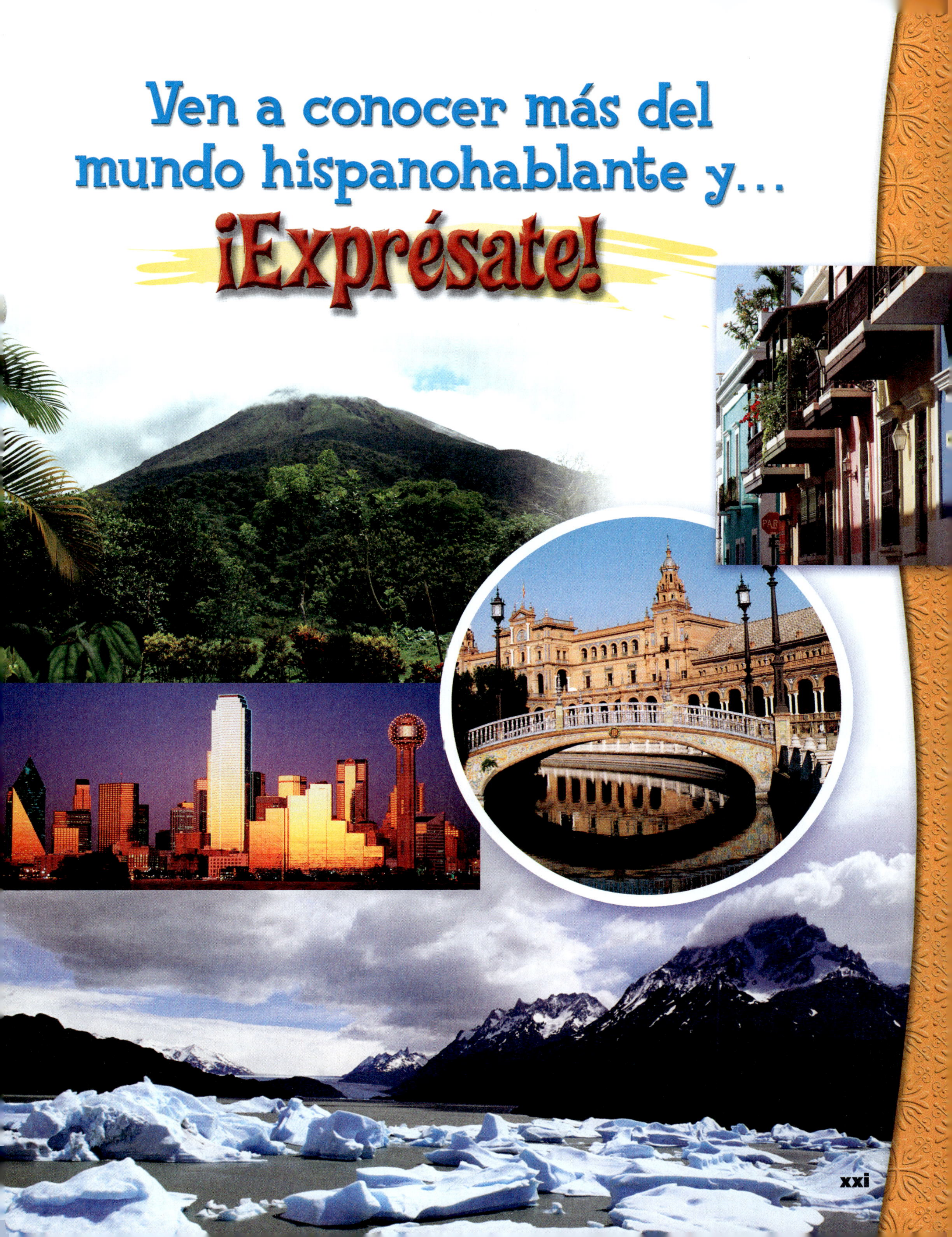

GeoVisión

# Geocultura España

▶ **La Mancha** is a region of Spain made famous in the book ***Don Quijote de La Mancha*** by Miguel de Cervantes. In the story, the hero sees these windmills as giants.

## Almanac

**Population**
40,037,995

**Capital**
Madrid

**Government**
parliamentary monarchy

**Languages**
Castilian, Catalan, Galician, Basque

**Currency** euro

**Internet Code**
www.[ ].es

OCÉANO ATLÁNTICO

▼ **Sevilla** The city of Seville celebrates its annual **Feria de abril** with parades, flowers, and brightly-colored traditional clothing.

Picos de Europ

Galicia

Salamanca

PORTUGAL

Extrem

Río Guadiana

Sevill

## ¿Sabías que...?

Florida was a Spanish colony off and on for four centuries. Juan Ponce de León claimed Florida for Spain in 1513. Spain gave Florida to England in 1763 and regained it in 1783. Spain retained its hold until 1821, when Florida became part of the U.S.

◀ **Los Pirineos** The Pyrenees mountain range forms a natural border between Spain and France.

▶ **Tossa de Mar** is a beach that attracts sunbathers from around the world.

FRANCIA
ANDORRA
Santillana
Bilbao
País Vasco
Los Pirineos
Cataluña
Tossa de Mar
COSTA BRAVA
Río Ebro
Barcelona
Castilla y León
Río Duero
MAR MEDITERRÁNEO
Segovia
Sierra de Guadarrama
Ávila
Aragón
MADRID
Sierra de Gredos
Río Tajo
Toledo
Valencia
ISLAS BALEARES
ura
ESPAÑA
Castilla-La Mancha
Alicante
COSTA BLANCA
Córdoba
Murcia
Río Guadalquivir
Granada
Sierra Nevada
Andalucía
Málaga
Gibraltar (RU)
Ceuta (ESP)
MARRUECOS

▲ **Madrid** This monument to the author Miguel de Cervantes is found in Madrid's **Plaza de España.** The monument includes two of his characters from ***Don Quijote de La Mancha,*** Don Quijote and Sancho Panza.

▼ **Andalucía** is a region of Spain that exports olive oil worldwide.

## ¿Qué tanto sabes?

**Which countries share a border with Spain? What bodies of water surround Spain?**

FL.C.1.1.1

# A conocer España

## Las celebraciones

▲ **Barcelona** The city of Barcelona is known for the **sardana,** a type of dance. Here people are dancing the **sardana** in the plaza in front of the cathedral.

▲ **Las castañuelas** Castanets are rhythm instruments used in traditional Spanish music.

▲ **Galicia** The region of Galicia in far northwest Spain was settled by Celtic peoples. These Celtic roots are reflected in the musical instruments and festivals of this Spanish province.

## La comida

◀ **La paella** **Paella** is a well-known Spanish dish made of rice, vegetables, seafood, chicken, and sausage.

▲ **La tortilla española** In Spain, a **tortilla** is an omelet made with eggs, onions, and potatoes. It is eaten cold as an appetizer.

# La arquitectura

Visit Holt Online
**go.hrw.com**
KEYWORD: EXP1A CH1
Photo Tour

▲ **El Museo de Guggenheim** The Guggenheim Museum in Bilbao is famous for its ultramodern architecture.

FL.B.1.1.3

## ¿Sabías que...?

**Did you know that there are five Guggenheim Museums? They are in Bilbao, New York, Las Vegas, Venice, and Berlin. How would you compare the architecture of the Bilbao museum with the city wall of Avila?**

▲ **Ávila** The city of Avila is surrounded by medieval walls that have stood for almost 1000 years.

# El arte

◀ **Las cuevas de Altamira** The Altamira Caves are famous for the colorful prehistoric art found on their walls. Which colors do you see in this cave painting?

◀ ***Personnages Oiseaux*** *(Bird People)* The Spanish artist **Joan Miró** lived from 1893 to 1983. Miró used bright, vivid colors in many of his paintings. Which colors does he use in this painting?

▲ **Joan Miró**

**rojo**

**azul**

**anaranjado**

**morado**

**café**

**verde**

**amarillo**

**gris**

**blanco**

**negro**

**Benchmark Focus**

**FL.C.1.1.1 Use simple vocabulary and phrases to identify familiar objects and concepts from other disciplines**

Capítulo 1

# ¡Empecemos!

## Objetivos

**In Part 1 you will learn to:**

- ask someone's name and give your name
- ask and say who someone is
- ask how someone is and say how you are
- introduce people and say where they are from
- use subjects and verbs in sentences
- use subject pronouns

**In Part 2 you will learn to:**

- ask for and give phone numbers
- say the time, the date, the day, and the season
- ask how words are spelled and give e-mail addresses
- use the verb **ser** in the present tense
- write Spanish punctuation marks and written accents

## ¿Qué ves en la foto?

- **How are these teenagers greeting each other?**
- **Based on the photo, what do you think Madrid is like?**

Look for the next to each activity and the **Benchmark Focus** to help you achieve the goals of the **Florida Sunshine State Standards,** found on pages FL14–FL16.

Amigos en el parque frente al Palacio Real, Madrid

**Objetivos**
- Asking someone's name
- Asking how someone is
- Introducing others
- Saying where you and others are from

# Vocabulario en acción 1

ExpresaVisión

## En Madrid

## ¡Exprésate!

| To ask a classmate or other young person's name *(familiar)* | To ask an adult's name *(formal)* | To give your name |
|---|---|---|
| **¿Cómo te llamas?**<br>*What's your name?* | **¿Cómo se llama usted?**<br>*What's your name?* | **Me llamo...**<br>*My name is . . .*<br>**Soy...**<br>*I'm . . .* |

Interactive TUTOR

| To ask who someone is | To say who someone is |
|---|---|
| **¿Quién es...?**<br>*Who is . . . ?* | **(Él/Ella) es...**<br>*He/She is . . .* |
| **¿Cómo se llama (él/ella)?**<br>*What is his/her name?* | **(Él/Ella) se llama...**<br>*His/Her name is . . .* |

Vocabulario y gramática, pp. 1–3 Online workbooks

▶ For **nombres comunes,** see page xvii.

Visit Holt Online
**go.hrw.com**
KEYWORD: EXP1A CH1
Vocabulario 1 practice

## 1 ¿Qué hacen? FL.A.2.1.3

**Escuchemos** As you listen, decide whether the people speaking are **a**) asking someone's name or **b**) giving a name.

## 2 ¿Cómo te llamas? FL.A.2.1.2

**Leamos** Decide if you would say these phrases in scene **a, b, c,** or **d.**

1. ¿Cómo te llamas?
2. Me llamo Margarita.
3. ¿Cómo se llama usted?
4. ¿Cómo se llama él?

A

B

C

D

## Nota cultural

Family members, friends, and teachers may add an ending such as **-ito** or **-ita** to a child's or friend's name to show affection. Rosa becomes **Rosita,** Teresa, **Teresita,** Juan becomes **Juanito,** and Miguel becomes **Miguelito.** How does your name change, adding **-ito** or **-ita** to the end? There are nicknames, **apodos,** associated with names that may be an abbreviation or part of a name. For example, Pilar, a very common girl's name in Spain, becomes **Pili,** and Santiago, a boy's name, becomes **Santi.**

Do we have similar nicknames in English? **FL.B.1.1.2**

## 3 Pareo FL.A.2.1.2

**Leamos** Match each question to the correct response. There may be more than one correct answer.

1. ¿Cómo se llama él?
2. ¿Cómo se llama ella?
3. ¿Cómo se llama usted?
4. ¿Cómo te llamas?

a. Me llamo Gustavo.
b. Se llama Pablo.
c. Soy Elena Rodríguez.
d. Se llama Josefina.

# Comunicación

## 4 Nombres y más nombres FL.A.1.1.2

**Hablemos** Get together with three classmates and ask them their names in Spanish. Then report their names to the class.

Vocabulario 1

## Más vocabulario...

### Greetings and Goodbyes

| | |
|---|---|
| **Buenos días, señor.** | *Good morning, sir.* |
| **Buenas tardes, señorita.** | *Good afternoon, miss.* |
| **Buenas noches, señora.** | *Good evening, ma'am.* |
| **Adiós.** | *Goodbye.* |
| **Buenas noches.** | *Good night.* |
| **Hasta luego.** | *See you later.* |
| **Hasta mañana.** | *See you tomorrow.* |
| **Hasta pronto.** | *See you soon.* |
| **Nos vemos.** | *See you.* |
| **Tengo que irme.** | *I have to go.* |

### También se puede decir...

In Florida, Cubans, Hondurans, Ecuadoreans, Colombians, and Argentineans may use **chao** instead of **adiós**.

## ¡Exprésate!

| To ask how a friend is | To ask how an adult is | To respond |
|---|---|---|
| **Hola, ¿cómo estás?**<br>*Hi, how are you?* | **¿Cómo está usted?**<br>*How are you?* | **Estoy bien/regular/mal.**<br>*I'm fine/all right/not so good.* |
| **¿Qué tal?**<br>*How's it going?* | | **Más o menos.**<br>*So-so.* |

Interactive TUTOR

Vocabulario y gramática, pp. 1–3 Online workbooks

## 5 ¿Qué dicen? FL.A.2.1.3

**Escuchemos** Are the people you hear
**a**) greeting each other or
**b**) asking each other how they are?

## 6 Adiós FL.A.3.1.1

**Hablemos** How would you say goodbye to someone . . .

**MODELO** you will see tomorrow?
**Hasta mañana.**

1. you will see again soon?
2. you will see again tomorrow in class?
3. when you don't know when you will see them next?
4. you will see in a few days?
5. wishing them a good night?
6. when you have to go?

## 7 Estoy bien, gracias. FL.A.1.1.2

**Hablemos** Work with a partner. Take turns deciding how you would greet these people and ask how they are. How would they respond? Base your answers on the pictures and times.

**MODELO** **—Buenos días, Señor Garza. ¿Cómo está usted?**
**—Estoy bien, gracias.**

8:00 A.M.
el señor Garza

11:00 A.M
Teresa

2:00 P.M.
Santi

9:00 P.M.
Maribel

## 8 Conversación FL.A.1.1.2

**Hablemos** Create a conversation with a classmate. Greet each other, find out each other's name, ask how it's going, and say goodbye.

**Benchmark Focus**
FL.A.1.1.2 Greet others and exchange essential personal information

## ¡Exprésate!

| To introduce someone | To respond | To say that you are also pleased to meet someone |
|---|---|---|
| **Éste es Juan. (Él) es un compañero de clase.** *This is Juan. He is a classmate.* | **Encantado(a). Mucho gusto.** *Pleased/Nice to meet you.* | **Igualmente.** *Likewise.* |
| **Éste es el señor Vega. (Él) es mi profesor de español.** *This is Mr. Vega. He is my Spanish teacher.* | | |
| **Ésta es Rosa. (Ella) es una compañera de clase.** *This is Rosa. She is a classmate.* | | |
| **Ésta es la señora (la señorita) Talavera. (Ella) es mi profesora de ciencias.** *This is Mrs. (Miss) Talavera. She is my science teacher.* | | |

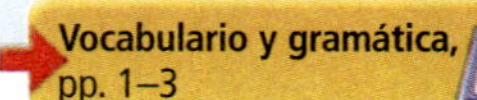
Vocabulario y gramática, pp. 1–3 Online workbooks

### Más vocabulario...

**¿Quién es el muchacho?**
*Who is the boy?*
**(Él) es mi mejor amigo.**
*He is my best friend.*
**(Él) es estudiante.**
*He is a student.*
**¿Quién es la muchacha?**
*Who is the girl?*
**(Ella) es mi mejor amiga.**
*She is my best friend.*
**(Ella) es estudiante.**
*She is a student.*

### 9 Tus amigos FL.A.3.1.1

**Hablemos/Escribamos** How would you introduce these people?

**MODELO** **your classmate Antonio**
**Éste es Antonio. Él es mi compañero de clase.**

1. your best friend Ana
2. your best friend Juan
3. your classmate Enrique
4. your classmate Luisa
5. your Spanish teacher
6. yourself

# ¡Exprésate!

| To ask where someone is from | To say where you and others are from |
|---|---|
| **¿De dónde eres?**<br>*Where are you from? (familiar)* | **Soy de Estados Unidos.**<br>*I'm from the United States.* |
| **¿De dónde es usted?**<br>*Where are you from? (formal)* | **Soy de España.**<br>*I'm from Spain.* |
| **¿De dónde es...?**<br>*Where is . . . from?* | **Es de Cuba.**<br>*He (She) is from Cuba.* |

Interactive TUTOR

Vocabulario y gramática, pp. 1–3 Online workbooks

## 10 ¿De dónde son? FL.A.2.1.3

**Escuchemos** As you listen, match the name of the person with the place he or she is from.

1. Javier
2. Angélica
3. la profesora Gutiérrez
4. Rafael
5. Fernando

a. Es de Cuba.
b. Es de México.
c. Es de España.
d. Es de Estados Unidos.
e. Es de Puerto Rico.

## 11 Es de... FL.A.3.1.1

**Hablemos** Using the photos, introduce these people and tell where they are from.

**MODELO** **Ésta es mi amiga Carolina. Ella es de España.**

Carolina, España

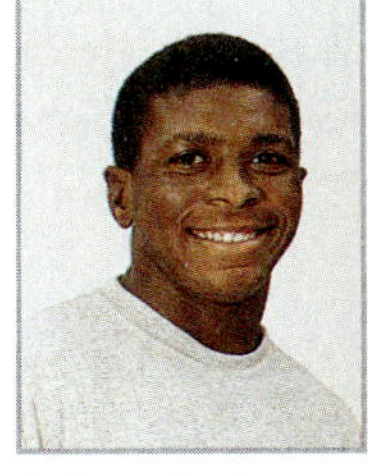
1. Juan José, la República Dominicana

2. María, Cuba

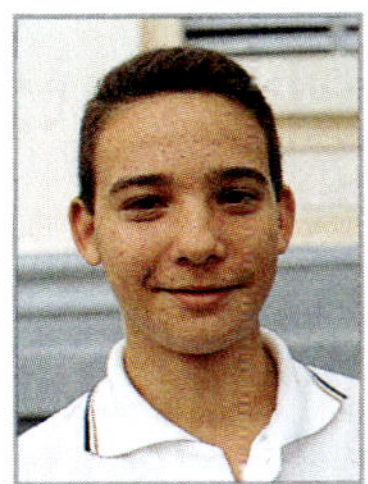
3. Blas, Puerto Rico

4. Irma, México

5. Alberto, Estados Unidos

# Comunicación

## 12 El club de español FL.A.1.1.2, FL.A.3.1.1

**Hablemos** Imagine you and your partner have joined the Spanish Club. Greet each other, ask each other's name and where each other is from. Then introduce each other to a classmate.

**Benchmark Focus**
**FL.A.3.1.1** Provide simple information in spoken form (e.g., descriptions of friends)

Vocabulario 1

## Objetivos

- Using subjects and verbs in sentences
- Using subject pronouns

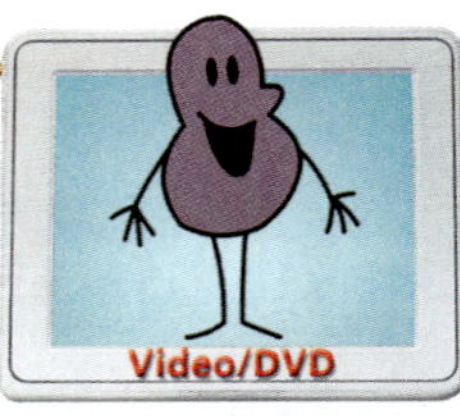


GramaVisión

## Subjects and verbs in sentences

**1** In English, sentences have a **subject** and a **verb**. The **subject** is the noun (person or thing) that is doing something or being described. The **verb** is the action word like **run** or **sing**, or a word like **am**, **is**, or **are** that links the subject to a description.

*subject* **Mrs. Pérez is** my teacher. *verb*
**She is** from Madrid.

**2** In Spanish, sentences also have a **subject** and a **verb**.

*subject* **La señora Pérez es** mi profesora. *verb*
**Ella es** de Madrid.

**3** Both English and Spanish use nouns as subjects. Nouns can be replaced with **pronouns**. Some examples of Spanish **pronouns** you have seen are **él**, **ella**, **tú** and **usted**.

*Él stands for Juan.*

**Juan es** un compañero de clase. — **Él es** mi mejor amigo.
*Juan is a classmate.* — *He is my best friend.*

**4** English sentences always have a subject. But in Spanish the **subject** or the **subject pronoun** can be left out if everyone knows who you're talking about.

**Maria** is my friend. — **María** es mi amiga.
**She** is from Spain. — Es de España. *Ella can be left out.*

### Nota cultural

Students in Spanish-speaking countries address teachers in several ways. Women may be called by their title and first name **(señorita Rosa)** or by title and last name **(señora García)**. If the teacher is older, she may be addressed as **doña** with her first name, such as **doña Josefina.** Similarly, men may be addressed as **don Pablo** (title and first name) or **señor Gómez** (title and last name).

How does this compare to the way you address your teachers? **FL.D.2.1.1**

Plaza de Zocodover en Toledo

Vocabulario y gramática, pp. 4–6
Actividades, pp. 1–4

### 13 Mis amigos de Toledo **FL.A.2.1.2, FL.D.1.1.2**

**Leamos** Identify the subjects and verbs. If there is no subject or subject pronoun, state who you think the subject is.

1. Luisa is my friend.
2. She is from Spain.
3. Mrs. García is my teacher.
4. She is from Toledo.
5. Luisa es mi amiga.
6. Es de España.
7. La señora García es mi profesora.
8. Es de Toledo.

Visit Holt Online
**go.hrw.com**
KEYWORD: EXP1A CH1
Gramática 1 practice

## 14 ¿Quién más? FL.A.2.1.2

**Leamos** Identify the subject and the verb in the following sentences.

1. Susana es de Perú.
2. Pablo es estudiante.
3. Ella es mi mejor amiga.
4. El muchacho es de México.

## 15 ¿Quién es quién? FL.A.2.1.2

**Leamos** Identify the subjects and verbs in the following sentences. Then say whether you would use **él** or **ella** in place of each subject.

1. Laura es de Madrid. Es una compañera de clase.
2. Juan es mi mejor amigo. Es estudiante.
3. La señora Ayala es mi profesora de ciencias. Es de Perú.
4. El señor Garza es mi profesor de español. Es de España.
5. El muchacho es un compañero de clase. Es mi amigo.

# Comunicación

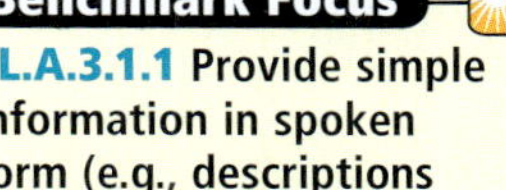


## 16 ¿De quién hablas? FL.A.1.1.2, FL.A.3.1.1

**Escribamos/Hablemos** Use at least three sentences from the word box to write a description of one of the people pictured below. Read your description aloud to your partner. He or she will guess which person you have just described. Then switch roles.

**Benchmark Focus**
**FL.A.3.1.1** Provide simple information in spoken form (e.g., descriptions of friends)

| | |
|---|---|
| Éste es el señor Madero. | Ella es mi profesora de español. |
| Él es mi mejor amigo. | Es de Estados Unidos. |
| Es de España. | Ella es mi mejor amiga. |
| Ésta es Rosaura. | Él es un compañero de clase. |
| Éste es Mario. | Ella es una compañera de clase. |
| Él es mi profesor de ciencias. | Ésta es la señora Matute. |

1

2

3

4

## Subject pronouns

**En inglés**

**In English,** the subject pronoun *you* is used with anyone, no matter their age or relationship to you.

**In Spanish,** the choice of the pronoun **tú** or **usted** is based on your relationship to the person.

In English, is *you* used to talk to one person, more than one person, or both? How does this compare with Spanish usage of **usted** and **ustedes**? FL.D.1.1.2

**1** These are the **subject pronouns** in Spanish.

| | |
|---|---|
| **yo** *I* | **nosotros** *we* |
| | **nosotras** *we (all female)* |
| **tú** *you* | **vosotros** *you* |
| | **vosotras** *you (all female)* |
| **usted** *you* | **ustedes** *you* |
| **él** *he* | **ellos** *they* |
| **ella** *she* | **ellas** *they (all female)* |

**2** The subject pronouns **tú** and **usted** both mean *you* when you're talking to one person. However, they are used in different situations.

| | Familiar | Formal | |
|---|---|---|---|
| *friend, relative, someone your age* | **tú** | **usted** | *teacher, adult you've just met, someone you show respect to* |

Although subject pronouns are often left out, the pronoun **usted** is commonly stated when addressing someone to show respect.

¿Cómo está **usted**? *How are you?*

**3** The subject pronouns **ustedes** and **vosotros** mean *you* when talking to more than one person. They are also used in different situations.

| | Familiar (in Spain) | Formal and Familiar | |
|---|---|---|---|
| *friends, relatives, people your age* | **vosotros** | **ustedes** | *any group* |

**4** The pronouns **nosotros, vosotros,** and **ellos** have feminine forms.

| | Masculine | Feminine | |
|---|---|---|---|
| *group of all males, group of males and females* | **nosotros** | **nosotras** | *group of all females* |
| | **vosotros** (Spain) | **vosotras** (Spain) | |
| | **ellos** | **ellas** | |

Vocabulario y gramática, pp. 4–6
Actividades, pp. 1–3

**Nota cultural**

Spanish influence in Florida dates to 1513, when Ponce de León claimed the territory for Spain. In 1565, Pedro Menéndez de Avilés founded St. Augustine, the oldest city in the U.S. In the 19th century, there were two major migrations from Cuba (still a Spanish colony at that time) to Florida—the first to Key West in the 1860s and the second to Tampa in the 1890s. How is Florida's Spanish-speaking heritage reflected in the names of places in your community? FL.D.2.2.2

### 17 ¿Cómo le(s) dices para hablarles? FL.B.1.1.2, FL.D.1.1.2

**Hablemos** What pronouns would you use to speak to these people?

1. two or more teachers
2. a group of female students (in Spain)
3. your best friend
4. a school principal
5. two or more males
6. a group of male and female students (in Spain)

## 18 ¿Con quién habla Javier? FL.A.2.1.3, FL.D.1.1.2

**Escuchemos** Listen as Javier, a teenager from Spain, talks to his friends and teachers. Match each statement with the correct picture. Remember that Javier uses **vosotros** and **vosotras.**

**Benchmark Focus**
FL.D.1.1.2 Use simple vocabulary and short phrases in the target language

A

B
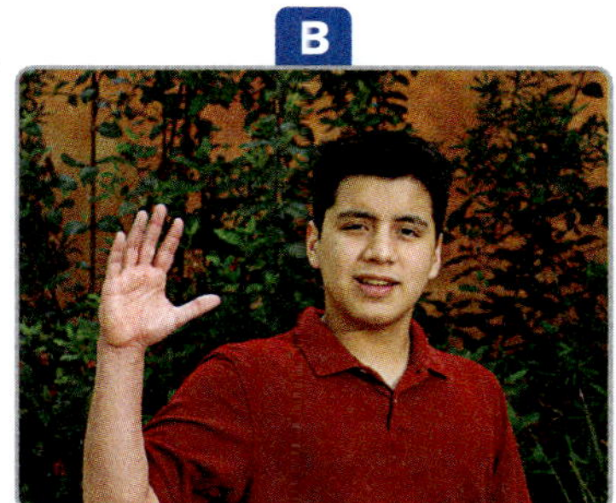

C

D

E

F

## 19 Nuevos amigos FL.A.2.1.2

**Leamos/Escribamos** Complete this conversation using the correct subject pronouns.

—Hola. __1__ *(I)* soy Rosalinda Chávez. Y __2__ *(he)* es mi amigo Juan. ¿Cómo te llamas __3__ *(you)?*

—__4__ *(I)* me llamo Antonia. Y __5__ *(she)* es mi amiga Talía. __6__ *(We–Talía and I)* somos de Estados Unidos. Juan y tú, ¿de dónde son __7__ *(you, plural)?*

## Comunicación

## 20 Eres reportero(a) FL.A.1.1.2

**Hablemos** Imagine that you are a reporter interviewing new students and teachers for the school paper. With a partner, role-play one interview with a student and one with a teacher. Use the cues below.

1. Greet the person you are interviewing.
2. Ask what his or her name is.
3. Ask where he or she is from.
4. Say goodbye.

Gramática 1

# Cultura

**Benchmark Focus**

**FL.A.1.1.3** Use appropriate gestures and expressions (i.e., body language) to complete or enhance verbal messages

**VideoCultura**

## Comparaciones

Buenos amigos, Madrid

### ¿Cómo saludas a tus amigos, familiares y profesores? FL.B.1.1.2, FL.D.2.1.1

Spanish speakers usually greet each other with a handshake or a kiss depending on the situation. Here, you will see several people greet each other in different situations. See if you can find any similarities to the greetings and goodbyes you use with your friends, family, and teachers.

### Saludos informales

In Spain, friends and family members may greet each other with two kisses, one on each cheek. In Latin America, friends and family members kiss each other on only one cheek. Men and boys greet each other with a hug, a pat on the back, or a handshake. In some Latin American countries, men who have not seen each other in a long time greet with a handshake, followed by a hug, followed by a second handshake.

—Hola, madrina, ¿cómo estás?

—¡Hola amigo! ¡Tanto tiempo!

—¿Cómo estás?

—Mucho gusto.
—Igualmente.

## Saludos formales

In professional or school settings, or when meeting someone for the first time, the usual greeting in Spain and Latin America is a handshake.

—Es un compañero de clase.
—Encantado.

### Para comprender FL.B.1.1.2

1. How would a young girl greet her grandparents in Spain?
2. How would a young girl greet her grandparents in Latin America?
3. How would a businessman and a businesswoman greet each other in Spain or Latin America?
4. In Latin America, how might a boy greet his uncle if they haven't seen each other in a long time?

### Para pensar y hablar FL.A.1.1.3

Among family and close friends, hugs and kisses are common greetings throughout the Spanish-speaking world. Do family and close friends in your community greet each other with hugs, kisses, or handshakes? With a partner, model how two people might greet each other with a handshake.

# Comunidad en la Florida

## Hispanos famosos de la Florida FL.C.2.1.1, FL.E.1.2.2

Hispanics in Florida have been influential at state, national, and international levels since Florida's earliest history as a U.S. territory. Use Spanish and English resources from the library or the Internet to learn more about one of the following famous Floridians. Present your research to the class.

- Joseph Marion Hernández, Congressman, 1822
- Desi Arnaz, entertainer
- Gloria Estefan, singer and songwriter
- Fernando Caldeiro, astronaut
- Alberto Ibargüen, former publisher of *The Miami Herald*, 1998–2005

Alberto Ibargüen, editor de *The Miami Herald*, 1998–2005

## Objetivos

- Giving phone numbers, the time, the date, and the day
- Spelling words and giving e-mail addresses

ExpresaVisión

### Los números

0 cero | 1 uno | 2 dos | 3 tres | 4 cuatro

5 cinco | 6 seis | 7 siete | 8 ocho | 9 nueve | 10 diez

#### Más vocabulario...

| | |
|---|---|
| 11 | once |
| 12 | doce |
| 13 | trece |
| 14 | catorce |
| 15 | quince |
| 16 | dieciséis |
| 17 | diecisiete |
| 18 | dieciocho |
| 19 | diecinueve |
| 20 | veinte |
| 21 | veintiuno |
| 22 | veintidós |
| 23 | veintitrés |
| 24 | veinticuatro |
| 25 | veinticinco |
| 26 | veintiséis |
| 27 | veintisiete |
| 28 | veintiocho |
| 29 | veintinueve |
| 30 | treinta |
| 31 | treinta y uno |

### 21 Contando FL.A.3.1.1

**Hablemos** What numbers do you think of for the following things? Say the number in Spanish.

1. hours in a day
2. a rectangle
3. the English alphabet
4. a volleyball team
5. an octopus
6. a quarter
7. a driver's license
8. a carton of eggs
9. a trio
10. days in a week

### 22 ¿Qué números faltan? FL.A.3.1.1

**Escribamos/Hablemos** Complete these series of numbers logically. Then read them aloud.

1. 1, 3, ____, 7, 9, ____, 13, 15
2. 2, 4, ____, 8, ____, 12, ____
3. 16, 17, ____, 19, ____, ____
4. 31, 25, ____, ____, ____, 1
5. 19, 18, ____, 16, 15, ____, 13, 12
6. 20, 22, ____, 26, ____, 30
7. 3, 6, ____, 12, ____, ____
8. 5, 10, ____, 20, ____, ____

## ¡Exprésate!

| To ask for phone numbers | To give phone numbers |
|---|---|
| **¿Cuál es tu teléfono?** *What's your telephone number?* | **Es tres-dos-cinco-uno-dos-tres-uno.** *It's 3-2-5-1-2-3-1.* |
| **¿Cuál es el teléfono de Rosita?** *What's Rosita's telephone number?* | **Es seis-uno-nueve-uno-cinco-dos-ocho.** *It's 6-1-9-1-5-2-8.* |

Interactive TUTOR

Vocabulario y gramática, pp. 7–9 — Online workbooks

### 23 Números de teléfono FL.A.2.1.3

**Escuchemos** You and your friend Elena are double-checking phone numbers for some of the students in your class. Listen to what Elena says and fill in the missing numbers.

1. Beatriz 3-___-___-1-9-___-___
2. Jorge 2-___-___-___-___-2-8
3. Rosaura ___-1-3-___-___-3-1
4. Ángel 7-1-8-___-___-___-___
5. Gladys ___-2-8-1-5-___-___

### 24 Directorio telefónico FL.A.1.1.2

**Leamos/Hablemos** Pick a person from the school directory and ask a classmate if you have the right number for him or her. When you give the number, get one digit wrong. Your partner should correct the number.

**MODELO** —**¿El teléfono de Teresa Benavides es uno-uno-cuatro-siete-ocho-dos-dos?**
—**No, es uno-uno-cuatro-uno-ocho-dos-dos.**

28

| | | |
|---|---|---|
| **BENAVIDES**, Teresa | Núñez de Cáceres 11 | 1-14-18-22 |
| **GÓMEZ**, Emilia | Santo Tomás de Aquino 27 | 2-13-25-17 |
| **GONZÁLEZ**, Rocío | Avenida Juárez 18 | 6-15-29-17 |
| **MARTÍNEZ**, Elena | Camino Real 25 | 4-11-16-28 |
| **ORTEGA**, Jaime | Avenida Mella 31 | 3-31-13-27 |
| **RODRÍGUEZ**, Alberto | Calle Constitución 12 | 6-27-19-12 |
| **TORRES**, Federico | Carretera Simón Bolívar 13 | 9-21-15-10 |

### 25 Número secreto FL.A.1.1.3, FL.B.1.1.1

**Hablemos** Try to guess the secret number between 0 and 31 that your partner has written down. If you are wrong, your partner will point up or down to indicate a higher or lower number. Keep trying until you guess right. Then switch roles and play again.

**Benchmark Focus**
**FL.A.1.1.3** Use appropriate gestures and expressions (i.e., body language) to complete or enhance verbal messages

Vocabulario 2

# ¿Qué hora es?

Es mediodía.
*It's noon.*

Son las dos y trece de la tarde.
*It's 2:13 in the afternoon.*

Son las diez menos diez de la noche.
*It's 9:50 at night.*

Son las siete menos cuarto.
*It's 6:45.*

Es la una en punto.
*It's one o'clock on the dot.*

Es medianoche.
*It's midnight.*

Son las seis y cuarto de la mañana.
*It's 6:15 in the morning.*

Son las seis y media de la tarde.
*It's 6:30 in the evening.*

## 26 ¿Son las dos? FL.A.2.1.2

**Leamos** Choose the correct time.

**1.** 3:00
- **a.** Son las tres en punto.
- **b.** Son las tres y media.

**2.** 9:15
- **a.** Son las nueve menos cuarto.
- **b.** Son las nueve y cuarto.

**3.** 7:25
- **a.** Son las siete y media.
- **b.** Son las siete y veinticinco.

**4.** 1:30
- **a.** Es la una y cuarto.
- **b.** Es la una y media.

**5.** 11:40
- **a.** Son las doce menos veinte.
- **b.** Son las once y veinte.

**6.** 8:10
- **a.** Son las ocho en punto.
- **b.** Son las ocho y diez.

**7.** 2:50
- **a.** Son las tres menos diez.
- **b.** Son las tres y diez.

**8.** 4:05
- **a.** Son las cuatro y cinco.
- **b.** Son las cuatro y cuarto.

**Benchmark Focus** 
FL.A.2.1.2 Restate and rephrase simple information from materials presented orally, visually and graphically in class

## 27 ¿Qué hora es? FL.A.3.1.1

**Hablemos/Escribamos** Say and write what time it is.

**1.** 4:00 P.M. **3.** 4:45 A.M. **5.** 6:10 A.M.

**2.** 12:00 P.M. **4.** 1:15 P.M. **6.** 9:05 A.M

# ¡Exprésate!

| To ask someone the date and day of the week | To respond |
|---|---|
| **¿Qué fecha es hoy?** *What's today's date?* | **Es el primero (dos, tres...) de enero.** *It's the first (second, third . . .) of January.* |
| **¿Qué día es hoy?** *What day is today?* | **Hoy es lunes.** *Today is Monday.* |

Interactive TUTOR

Vocabulario y gramática, pp. 7–9 Online workbooks

## Los días de la semana

## Los meses del año

## Las estaciones

| | | | |
|---|---|---|---|
| **la primavera** | *spring* | **el otoño** | *fall* |
| **el verano** | *summer* | **el invierno** | *winter* |

### 28 ¿Sabes? FL.A.2.1.2

**Escribamos/Hablemos** Complete the following series logically.

1. lunes, ___, miércoles, ___
2. viernes, ___, ___, lunes
3. enero, ___, marzo, ___
4. mayo, junio, ___, ___
5. primavera, ___, otoño, ___
6. invierno, ___, ___, otoño

### 29 ¿Cuándo es tu cumpleaños? FL.A.1.1.2

**Hablemos** Work in groups of three to guess one another's birthday. Guide your classmates by saying **antes** *(before)* or **después** *(after)* until they guess correctly. Guess the month first, then try for the date.

## El alfabeto

*Another way to say *W* in Spanish is **doble ve.**

## ¡Exprésate!

| To ask how words are spelled and give e-mail addresses | To respond |
|---|---|
| **¿Cómo se escribe...?**<br>*How do you spell . . . ?* | **Se escribe...**<br>*It's spelled . . .* |
| **¿Cuál es el correo electrónico de Marisa?**<br>*What is Marisa's e-mail address?* | **Es eme punto ge-o-ene-zeta-a-ele-o arroba ere-e-de punto hache-ere-uve doble punto a-ere.**<br>*It's m.gonzalo@red.hrw.ar.* |
| **¿Cuál es tu correo electrónico?**<br>*What's your e-mail address?* | **Es...**<br>*It's . . .* |

Interactive TUTOR

Vocabulario y gramática, pp. 7–9 Online workbooks

### 30 Dictado FL.A.2.1.3

**Escuchemos/Escribamos** Listen as several speakers say and spell out the Spanish words for some animals. On a separate sheet of paper, write the words in Spanish as you hear them.

**Benchmark Focus**
**FL.A.2.1.3** Understand oral messages that are based on familiar themes and vocabulary

### 31 ¿Cómo se escribe...? FL.A.2.1.2, FL.A.3.1.1

**Hablemos/Escribamos** Spell each item below aloud in Spanish while your classmates write it out.

**MODELO** **eme-e-ere-ce-e-de-e-ese (Mercedes)**

1. your name
2. your e-mail address
3. the city or town where you were born
4. your best friend's full name
5. your best friend's e-mail address
6. your favorite actor's name

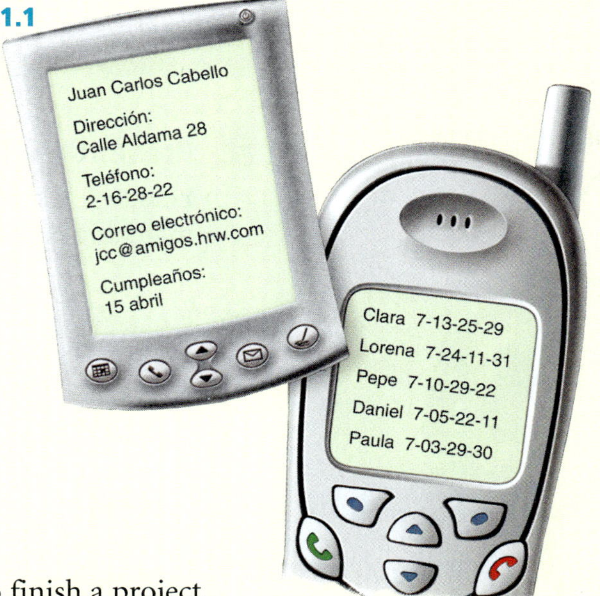


### 32 El proyecto FL.A.1.2.2

**Hablemos** You and several classmates have to finish a project outside of class. Work with three partners to create a conversation in which you ask one another's names (spell them out if you need to), phone numbers, and e-mail addresses.

**Objetivos**
- Using the verb **ser**
- Punctuation marks and written accents

GramaVisión

## The verb ser

Interactive TUTOR

**1** In Spanish, a verb has different forms to tell you who the subject is. Changing a verb form so that it matches its subject is called **conjugating.** This is the conjugation of the verb **ser** *(to be)*.

| | | | | | |
|---|---|---|---|---|---|
| yo | **soy** | *I am* | nosotros(as) | **somos** | *we are* |
| tú | **eres** | *you are* | vosotros(as) | **sois** | *you are* |
| usted | **es** | *you are* | ustedes | **son** | *you are* |
| él | **es** | *he is* | ellos | **son** | *they are* |
| ella | **es** | *she is* | ellas | **son** | *they are* |

With nouns and names of people, use the same form of the verb as for **él/ella** or **ellos/ellas.**

**Mi profesora es de Cuba.** **Juan y Carlos son de España.**

**2** To make a sentence negative, place **no** in front of the verb.

Hoy **no es** martes, **es** jueves.

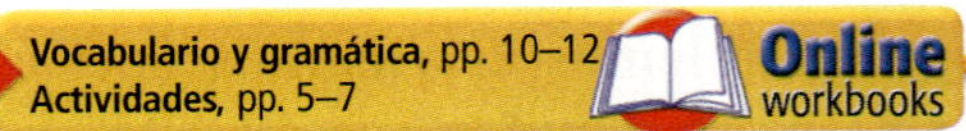


## ¿Te acuerdas?

You've used forms of the verb **ser** to say who someone is or where you or others are from, to give your telephone number, and to say the date, the day, and the time.

Éste **es** un compañero de clase.
Yo **soy** de Perú.
Mi teléfono **es** 555-5555.
Hoy **es** el diez de febrero.
Hoy **es** jueves.
**Son** las tres de la tarde.

### 33 Presentaciones FL.A.2.1.2

**Leamos** What is Maribel saying? Complete her statements by matching elements from the two columns.

1. Hola. Yo
2. Y ella
3. Nosotras
4. Y tú, ¿de dónde
5. Juan y tú, ¿de dónde
6. Jorge y Carlos
7. Juan, ¿cuál
8. Carla, ¿qué hora
9. No, Carla, no es la una,
10. Juan, ¿qué día
11. Y la señora Tan, ¿de dónde

a. son de Cuba.
b. somos de México.
c. eres?
d. son ustedes?
e. es mi amiga Carla.
f. soy Maribel Gómez.
g. es?
h. es hoy?
i. es tu teléfono?
j. es ella?
k. son las dos y media.

Visit Holt Online
**go.hrw.com**
Keyword: EXP1A CH1
Gramática 2 practice

## 34 Nuestro club FL.A.2.1.2

**Leamos/Escribamos** Miguel has written a description of the International Spanish Club. Complete the paragraph with the correct forms of the verb **ser.**

Nosotros ___1___ estudiantes y profesores del club internacional de español. Yo ___2___ de Puerto Rico. Juan Emilio ___3___ de la República Dominicana. Lisa y Rebeca ___4___ de Estados Unidos. El teléfono del club ___5___ 5-24-11-21. El correo electrónico del club ___6___ club.internacional.deespañol@school.hrw.org. Nosotros ___7___ el club internacional. ¡Hasta pronto!

# Comunicación

## 35 Charla FL.A.1.1.2

**Escribamos/Hablemos** Work with two classmates to write out the following conversation in Spanish. Then take turns playing the roles.

*Hi, where are you from?*

*I'm from the United States.*

*This is Juana, she's a classmate.*

*Pleased to meet you, Juana. Where are you from?*

*Likewise. I'm from Mexico. What time is it?*

*It's three thirty. See you tomorrow!*

## 36 No es correcto FL.A.1.1.2, FL.A.3.1.1

**Hablemos** Take turns with a partner giving information about the people in the pictures, but include at least one detail that is not correct. Your partner should then say **no** to disagree, and provide the correct information.

**MODELO** **—Ana es de Guatemala. El teléfono de Ana es 3-20-16-04.**
**—No, el teléfono de Ana no es 3-20-16-04. Es 3-29-16-04.**

**Benchmark Focus** 
**FL.A.1.1.2** Greet others and exchange essential personal information (e.g., telephone number)

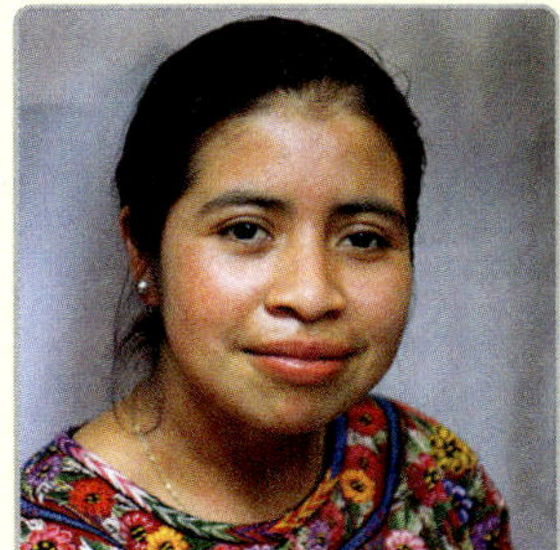

Ana, Guatemala
3-29-16-04

Juan, Puerto Rico
5-14-07-21

Lupe, México
7-20-11-05

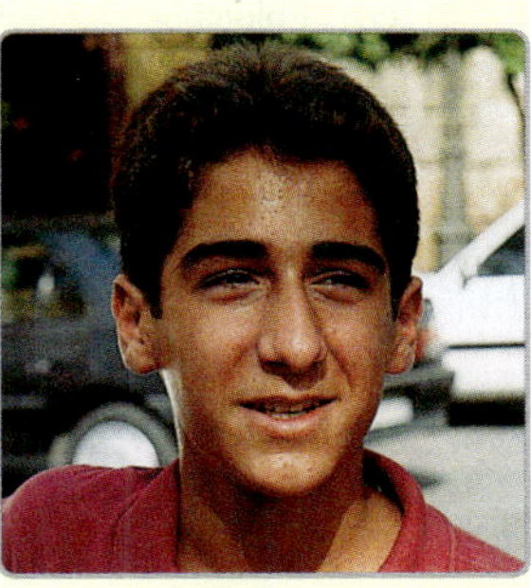

Ricardo, España
2-23-01-16

Gramática 2

## Punctuation marks and written accents

**FL.E.1.2.1** Know that many people in the United States use languages other than English on a daily basis

**1** In Spanish, upside-down **punctuation marks** such as **(¿)** and **(¡)** are placed at the beginning of a phrase to signal a question or an exclamation. These are used along with those that come at the end of phrases.

**¡Hasta luego!**
**¿Cómo se llama ella?**

**2** In Spanish, some words have written **accent marks**. An accent mark is a tilted line **(´)** placed over a vowel. Putting accent marks over vowels is part of spelling words correctly. When learning new words, memorize where the accent marks are.

**Adiós.**
**¿Cuál?**

**3** The wavy line in the letter **ñ** is called a **tilde.** The **ñ** is pronounced similarly to the *ny* in the word *canyon.*

**señor**
**compañero**

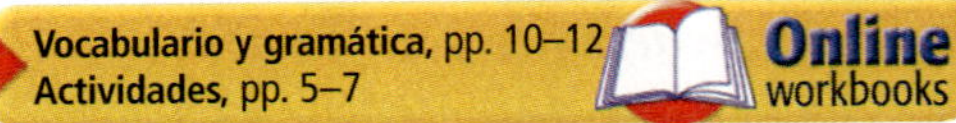


### Nota cultural

Florida is home to a growing and diverse Hispanic population. Many Cubans moved to south Florida in the 1960s, particularly to Miami. Cubans are still the largest Spanish-speaking group in Florida, but other groups, notably Puerto Ricans, Mexicans, Colombians, Nicaraguans, and Dominicans, have also chosen to come to Florida in search of political or economic stability. In addition to settling in south Florida, these and other groups are increasingly found in other parts of the state.

What groups of Hispanics live in your area of Florida?

**FL.E.1.2.1**

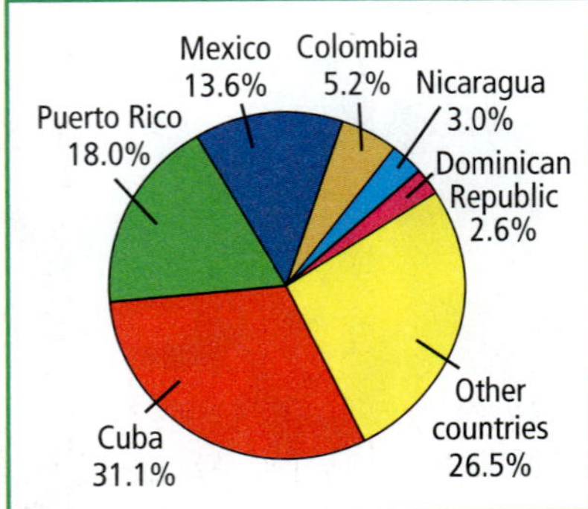


Origins of Florida's Hispanics

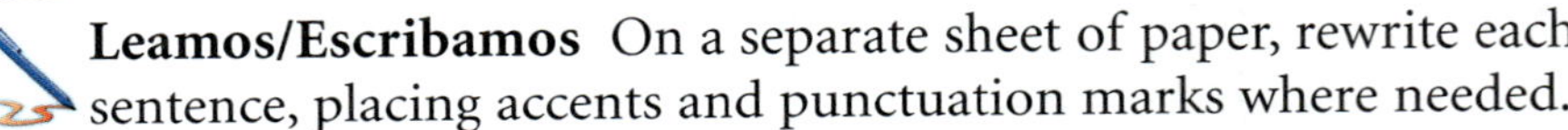

### 37 ¡Cuidado con los acentos! FL.A.2.1.2

**Leamos/Escribamos** On a separate sheet of paper, rewrite each sentence, placing accents and punctuation marks where needed.

1. Buenos dias senorita
2. Como esta usted senor
3. Que tal
4. Mucho gusto
5. Que hora es
6. De donde eres
7. Cual es tu telefono
8. Me llamo Pedro
9. Hola Como te llamas
10. El es un companero de clase
11. Quien es la profesora de ciencias
12. Como estas
13. Que fecha es hoy
14. Estoy bien gracias

Una carnicería *(butcher shop)* en Segovia, España

## 38 En contacto FL.A.2.1.2

**Leamos/Escribamos** When people write e-mails in Spanish, they sometimes leave out punctuation or written accents. On a separate piece of paper rewrite these two messages including the missing accent marks, tildes, and punctuation.

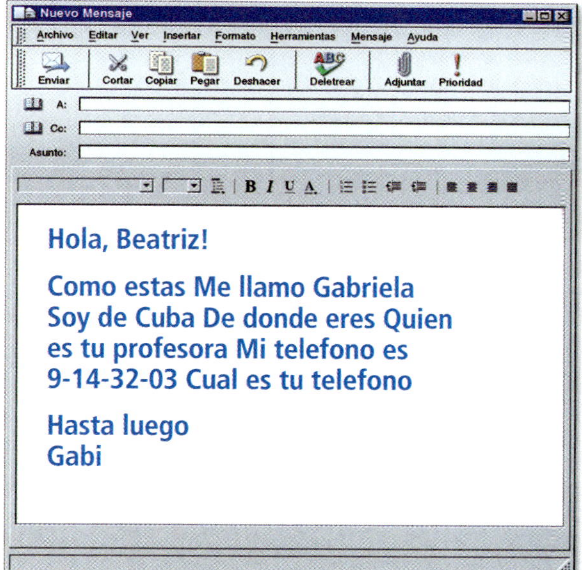

Hola, Beatriz!

Como estas Me llamo Gabriela Soy de Cuba De donde eres Quien es tu profesora Mi telefono es 9-14-32-03 Cual es tu telefono

Hasta luego
Gabi

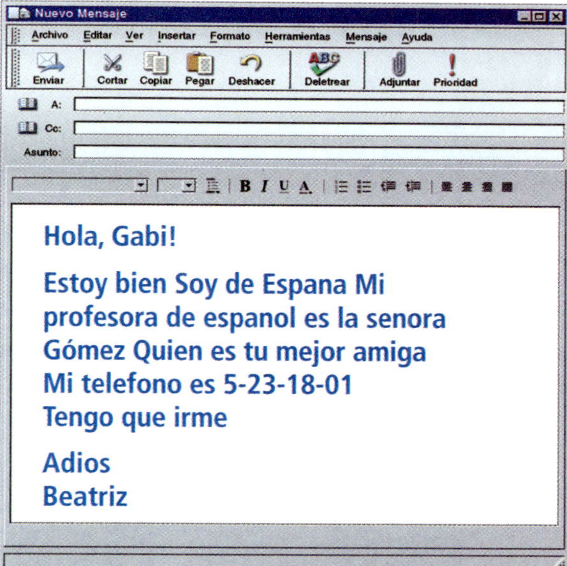

Hola, Gabi!

Estoy bien Soy de Espana Mi profesora de espanol es la senora Gómez Quien es tu mejor amiga Mi telefono es 5-23-18-01 Tengo que irme

Adios
Beatriz

# Comunicación

## 39 En la clase FL.A.2.1.4

**Hablemos** Today is the first day of school. With a partner, create brief conversations for each picture below. Choose the best conversation to perform for the class. Your classmates will guess which scene you role-played.

a.

b.

c.

# Conexiones culturales

FCAT Mathematics Focus 

**MA.A.1.3.4.7.4**

Convert a number expressed in one form to its equivalent in another form

## Conexión Ciencias sociales

LOS CALENDARIOS Most of the words for days of the week in Spanish come from Latin. Look at the chart to see the roots of the Spanish words. Then answer the questions that follow.

| lunes | martes | miércoles | jueves | viernes | sábado | domingo |
|---|---|---|---|---|---|---|
| **Latin:** *lunae* | **Latin:** *Martis* | **Latin:** *Mercurii* | **Latin:** *Jovis* | **Latin:** *Veneris* | **Hebrew:** *shabbat* | **Latin:** *dominus* |
| moon | Mars: Roman god of war | Mercury: Roman messenger of the gods | Jupiter: Roman king of the gods | Venus: Roman goddess of love | sabbath | Lord's day |

### 1 Los planetas FL.C.1.1.1

What planet corresponds to each day of the week?

**1.** viernes
**2.** miércoles
**3.** jueves
**4.** martes

**a.** Júpiter
**b.** Venus
**c.** Mercurio
**d.** Marte

### 2 El calendario azteca FL.C.1.1.2

The Aztec Sun Calendar, the **xihuitl** (shee-wee-TAL) or "count of the years," is similar to ours. Both are 365 days long, the number of days it takes the earth to orbit the sun. The **xihuitl,** however, has 18 months of 20 days each, with extra "unlucky days" at the end of the year.

1. Can you find the ring on the Sun Calendar that represents the twenty days?
2. Since 18 months of 20 days each do not add up to 365 days, what is the Spanish word for the number of "unlucky days" at the end of the year?

# Conexiones culturales

HOW THE 24-HOUR SYSTEM WORKS: Many countries around the world use schedules based on a 24-hour clock. Travelers can look at schedules and know the difference between 9:00 A.M. and 9:00 P.M. For example, using a 24-hour clock for a train schedule, a morning train would leave at 9:00 and a night train would leave at 21:00.

## 3 Convertir a 24 horas FL.B.1.1.2

Write the following times using the 24-hour system. For P.M. hours, add 12:00 to the hour. For A.M. hours, write the same hour but without using the abbreviation "A.M."

1:05 P.M.
+ 12:00
**13:05**

**MODELO** **2:35 A.M. 2:35**

1. 7:20 A.M.
2. 3:15 P.M.
3. 9:25 P.M.
4. 4:30 P.M.
5. 11:00 A.M.
6. 8:15 P.M.

## 4 Convertir de 24 horas FL.B.1.1.2

Rewrite these times using A.M. and P.M. For times before 12:00, add A.M. to the end. For times after 12:59, subtract 12:00 from the hour and add P.M. at the end of the result.

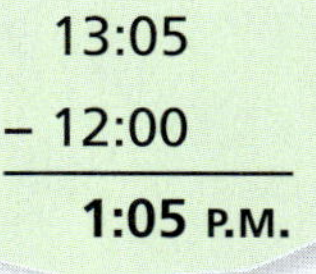


**MODELO** **2:35 2:35 A.M.**

1. 23:40
2. 17:55
3. 1:15
4. 15:25
5. 20:39
6. 5:42

## 5 Horario de aviones FL.C.2.1.1

Answer the following questions using the 12-hour system (A.M. and P.M.).

1. What time does flight AO 444 to Madrid leave?
2. If you got to the airport at 2:00 P.M., would you have enough time to catch the flight to Barcelona? Why or why not?

| VUELO FLIGHT | SALIDAS DESTINO TO | HORA TIME |
|---|---|---|
| IB 346 | MADRID | 1250 |
| AO 444 | MADRID | 1310 |
| IB 834 | BARCELONA | 1405 |
| AO 452 | P.MALLORCA | 1445 |
| AAN106 | P.MALLORCA | 1450 |
| IB 387 | MELILLA | 1500 |
| IB 397 | MELILLA | 1615 |

Novela en video

# ¿Quién será?

## Episodio 1

**Benchmark Focus**

**FL.C.2.1.1** Use the target language to gain access to information that is only available through the target language or within the target culture

ESTRATEGIA

**Making connections** Sometimes, as a story unfolds on screen, things happen in different parts of the world at the same time. Although the connection between those events may not be immediately obvious, as an experienced viewer, you know that one probably exists. In this episode, you will see things going on at the same time in Spain, Mexico, and Puerto Rico. Look for clues that help explain the connection among the events in all three locations. **FL.C.2.1.1**

### En España

***In Madrid, Spain, la profesora is studying the files of a Mexican student and a Puerto Rican student. She calls her assistant, Marcos, and makes an appointment to meet with him.***

1

**La profesora** Y tú, Sofía Corona Ramírez, eres de México, ¿no es así?

Hmmm... Nicolás Ortega García, el artista puertorriqueño.

2

**La profesora** Sí, Marcos. Necesito hablar contigo. Sí, pronto. Es urgente. A ver, mañana es domingo. Bien, el lunes, en mi casa. Sí, a las diez de la mañana.

Oye, ¿cuál es tu e-mail? Te quiero enviar unos documentos. Bien. Nos vemos el lunes.

Visit Holt Online
**go.hrw.com**
KEYWORD: EXP1A CH1
Online Edition

## En México

***In Mexico City, Mexico, a girl named Sofía is having breakfast before going to school. Both her father and her little brother interrupt her.***

3 **Sr. Corona** Buenos días, Sofía. Hola, Sofía, buenos días.

4 **Quique** Sofía, Sofía, ¡cara de tortilla!

### A. Contesta

What is happening in the **Novela**? Check your understanding by answering these questions in English. Don't be afraid to guess!

1. Who are the people in the **Novela**? Make a list of their names and where they are from.
2. What do you know about Sofía and her family? FL.A.2.1.2

## En Puerto Rico

***In San Juan, Puerto Rico, a boy named Nicolás is in a rush on his way home from school. He bumps into some people.***

5

**Sra. Ortiz** ¡Buenas tardes, Nico!

**Nicolás** ¡Buenas tardes, Señora Ortiz!

6

**Nicolás** ¡Uy, perdone, don Pablo! ¿Cómo está usted?

**Don Pablo** Estoy bien, gracias, Nico. ¿Y tú? ¿Cómo estás tú?

### B. Contesta

1. Who are the people Nicolás is talking to?
2. Where do you think Nicolás is going in such a hurry?

FL.A.2.1.2

# Actividades

## 1 Expresiones de cortesía FL.A.2.1.2

Match the English phrases to the Spanish phrases used by some characters in the **Novela.**

1. Hello.
2. Goodbye.
3. My name is . . .
4. How are you? (to an adult)
5. How are you? (to a young person)
6. I'm fine, thanks.

**a.** Me llamo...
**b.** ¿Cómo estás tú?
**c.** Estoy bien, gracias.
**d.** Hola.
**e.** Adiós.
**f.** ¿Cómo está usted?

## 2 ¿Cierto o falso? FL.A.2.1.2

Tell whether each statement is **cierto** *(true)* or **falso** *(false),* based on **la profesora's** phone call to her assistant.

1. She urgently needs to talk with him.
2. They will meet on Sunday.
3. The meeting will be at her house at 10 A.M.
4. She asks him for his mailing address.

## 3 ¿Comprendes la Novela? FL.A.2.1.2

Check your understanding of the events in the story by answering these questions.

1. What do you learn in Frame 3 on page 31 about Sofía and things she likes?
2. What do you think Nicolás is carrying under his arm? What does this tell you about him? Is there anything else to support your conclusion?
3. Who do you think Marcos is?
4. Why do you think **la profesora** is looking at photos of students?

**Próximo episodio**
*Marcos goes to visit la profesora. Can you predict what she might ask him to do?*
PÁGINAS 76–79

Novela en video

# Leamos y escribamos

**FCAT Reading Focus** 
**LA.A.1.3.2**
Use a variety of strategies to analyze words and text; use context and word structure clues

**ESTRATEGIA**

**para leer Recognizing cognates** Cognates are words that look alike and have similar meanings in two languages. Recognizing these words will help you get a general idea of what a reading passage is about.

## A Antes de leer FL.D.1.2.1

Look at the homepage for one school's Spanish Club. To get an idea of what the club has to offer, write all the cognates you can find on a separate sheet of paper. Compare your list with a classmate's and try to guess what each word means. If you are not sure, look the word up in a dictionary.

Archivo Editar Ver Herramientas Ayuda

Atrás Adelante Actualizar Detener Página Inicial Buscar Favoritos Correo Imprimir

Dirección:

### Participa en el club de español

**¿INTERESANTE? ¡CLARO QUE SÍ!**
Programas de inmersión en Cádiz, España. Clases de español, excursiones turísticas y mucho más. Del 26 de mayo al 10 de junio y del 22 de julio al 6 de agosto. Más información en http://www.spprogramsabroad.hrw.com

**¡Y DIVERTIDO[2]! RITMOS DEL MOMENTO**
Escuchen la música favorita de muchos estudiantes hispanos y diviértanse bailando[3]. Clases de salsa y merengue. Martes y jueves en el gimnasio. Hora: 4:30 a 5:30 Más música en http://morelatinmusic.hrw.com

**EVENTOS DEPORTIVOS**
Gran partido[4] de fútbol. Viernes 19 de septiembre. En el estadio local. Hora: 7:00 p.m. Más información en el teléfono 2-17-22-08 o en http://schoolevents.hrw.edu

LUIS MIGUEL
Mis Boleros Favoritos
Edición Especial

Nuevo Mensaje

Correspondencia con estudiantes de España y Latinoamérica

To: clubesp@exchange.hrw.com
From: Camim@exchange.hrw.com

Hola, ¿qué tal? Me llamo Camilo Medina. Soy de Guanajuato, México. Soy estudiante del Colegio Benito Juárez y participo en el Club de español. Escríbanme[1].

1. write to me 2. fun 3. have fun dancing 4. game

Visit Holt Online
**go.hrw.com**
KEYWORD: EXP1A CH1
Online Edition



## B Comprensión FL.C.2.1.1

Based on the reading, say if the following statements are true (**cierto**) or false (**falso**). Correct the false statements.

1. The Spanish Club offers a variety of fun and interesting activities.
2. The club sponsors summer trips to Spanish-speaking countries.
3. If you join the club, you will be able to correspond with students from Asia.
4. The club offers **salsa** and **merengue** classes on Fridays.
5. The club homepage provides you with links to other sites.

## C Después de leer FL.A.3.1.1

Would you like to become a member of this club? Why or why not? Which activity seems the most interesting to you? What other activities would you suggest if you were a member?

**FCAT Writing Focus** 
**LA.B.1.3.1**
Organize information before writing according to the type and purpose of writing

Interactive TUTOR

# Taller del escritor

Nombre
Número de teléfono
Correo electrónico
Soy de ...

**ESTRATEGIA** FL.A.2.1.2

**para escribir** Jot down a list of ideas to include in your writing before starting to write sentences. List all your ideas even if you don't know how to say something in Spanish. Get help later from the dictionary if you need to find a specific word or phrase.

### La página Web del club de español

Imagine you have joined the Spanish Club. Write a short paragraph about yourself to be posted on the club's Web site. In your paragraph, include

- your name
- where you are from
- your e-mail address

### 1 Antes de escribir

Make a list of the information you will need for the Web site. You may use English or Spanish for this step.

### 2 Escribir y revisar

Write your information in complete sentences in Spanish. Read your sentences at least twice. Make sure you have included all the information you want to post on the site. Then check your spelling and punctuation.

### 3 Publicar

Post your completed paragraph on the bulletin board or your class Web site.

Capítulo 1
Repaso

# Prepárate para el examen

Interactive TUTOR

1 Pretend you are introducing the following people to a classmate. Greet your classmate and ask how he or she is, then introduce each person, and say where he or she is from. FL.A.3.1.1

1. Beatriz, México

2. el señor Huang, Estados Unidos

3. Antonio, España

2 For each pair of sentences, identify the subject and verb in the first sentence. Then choose the correct subject pronoun in the second sentence. FL.A.2.1.2

1. Rosa es mi mejor amiga. (Ella/Él) es de Segovia, España.
2. La señora Cortez es mi profesora de español. (Ellos/Ella) es de Estados Unidos.
3. El muchacho es de México. (Él/Ustedes) es un compañero de clase.
4. El profesor Muñoz es de la República Dominicana. (Nosotros/Él) es mi profesor de ciencias.

3 Choose the correct subject pronoun to complete the following short conversations. FL.A.2.1.2

1. —Alicia y Laura, ¿de dónde son ____ *(you, plural)*?
   —____ *(We)* somos de Costa Rica.
2. —Hola, Señor Martínez. ¿Cómo está ____ *(you, formal)*?
   —Bien, gracias, Jorge. ¿Y ____ *(you, familiar)*?
3. —¿De dónde son Juan y Susana?
   —____ *(They)* son de Bolivia.

4 Answer the following questions. FL.A.2.1.2, FL.A.3.1.1

1. ¿Cuál es tu correo electrónico?
2. ¿Cuál es tu teléfono?
3. ¿Cómo se escribe tu nombre?
4. ¿Qué hora es?
5. ¿Qué día es hoy?
6. ¿Qué fecha es hoy?

**1 Vocabulario 1**
- asking someone's name and who someone is
- asking how someone is
- introducing others
- saying where you and others are from

**pp. 6–11**

**2 Gramática 1**
- subjects and verbs in sentences

**pp. 12–13**

**3 Gramática 1**
- subject pronouns
- **tú, usted,** and **ustedes**

**pp. 14–15**

**4 Vocabulario 2**
- numbers 0–31
- asking for and giving phone numbers
- telling time
- giving the date and day of the week
- the alphabet
- spelling words and giving e-mail addresses

**pp. 18–23**

**5** On a separate piece of paper, copy the following conversation. Use the correct form of **ser** and add the correct punctuation and accent marks. FL.A.2.1.2

—Me llamo Pilar (Yo) ____ tu companera de clase

—De donde ____ (tu) Pilar

—(Yo) ____ de Espana Y tu, ____ de Miami

—Si, (yo) ____ de Miami Que hora ____

— ____ las cuatro en punto

**5 Gramática 2**
- the verb **ser**
- punctuation marks and written accents

**pp. 24–27**

**6** Answer the following questions. FL.B.1.1.2

1. In Spanish, how do people change their friends' names to show affection for them? Give at least two examples.
2. Name four ways that a teacher might be addressed in a Spanish-speaking country.

**6 Cultura**
- **Comparaciones** **pp. 16–17**
- **Notas culturales** **pp. 7, 12**
- **Geocultura** **pp. xxii–3**

**7** Listen to the following conversations. For each one, decide whether the speakers are **a**) telling time, **b**) greeting each other, **c**) introducing someone, or **d**) exchanging phone numbers. FL.A.2.1.3

**8** Use the drawings to create a conversation for what is happening. Give as many details as you can. FL.A.3.1.1

**Benchmark Focus**

FL.B.1.1.2 Recognize patterns of social behavior or social interaction in various settings (e.g., school, family, or immediate community)

a.

b.

c.

d.

**Gramática 1**
- subjects and verbs in sentences **pp. 12–13**
- subject pronouns **pp. 14–15**
- **tú, usted** and **ustedes** **pp. 14–15**

# Repaso de Gramática 1

Every sentence has a **subject** and a **verb.** The verb tells what the **subject** does or links the **subject** to a description.

**La señora Pérez es mi profesora.**

The **subject pronouns** in Spanish are

| | |
|---|---|
| **yo** | **nosotros(as)** |
| **tú** | **vosotros(as)** |
| **usted/él/ella** | **ustedes/ellos/ellas** |

The subject pronouns **tú** and **usted** both mean *you.* Use **tú** when you're talking to a friend. Use **usted** to show respect towards elders and teachers. When talking to a group of people, use **ustedes** to say *you.* In Spain only, use **vosotros(as)** to say *you* to a group of friends, family members, or children.

**¿De dónde es usted? ¿De dónde eres tú?**

**Gramática 2**
- the verb **ser** **pp. 24–25**
- punctuation marks and written accents **pp. 26–27**

# Repaso de Gramática 2

This is the conjugation of **ser** *(to be).*

| | | | |
|---|---|---|---|
| yo **soy** | *I am* | nosotros(as) **somos** | *we are* |
| tú **eres** | *you are* | vosotros(as) **sois** | *you are* |
| Ud./él/ella **es** | *you are/ he/she is* | Uds./ellos/ellas **son** | *you/they are* |

| **Question marks** | **Exclamation points** | **Accent marks** |
|---|---|---|
| **¿ ... ?** | **¡ ... !** | **á, é, í, ó, ú, ñ** |
| ¿Cuál es tu teléfono? | ¡Hola! | cuál, qué, sí, cómo, tú, mañana |

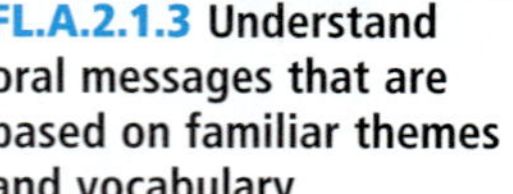
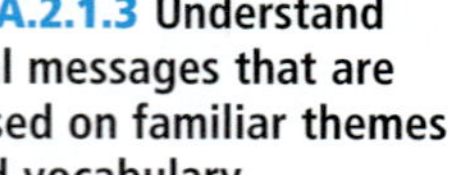
**Benchmark Focus**
**FL.A.2.1.3 Understand oral messages that are based on familiar themes and vocabulary**

## Letra y sonido a e i o u

### Las vocales *(The Vowels)*

The five vowels in Spanish are always pronounced clearly and fully no matter where they are in a word.

- **a:** between the ***a*** of *cat* and *father*: **a**migo, hol**a**
- **e:** as in *they,* but shorter: **e**n**e**ro, corr**e**o
- **i:** as in *police,* but shorter: **i**gualmente, abr**i**l
- **o:** as in *low,* but shorter: **o**nce, c**ó**m**o**
- **u:** as in *sue,* but shorter: **u**no, est**u**diante

### Trabalenguas

La a, la e, la i—son fáciles para mí.
La a, la e, la i—las puedo hacer así.
A, e, i, o, u—aprende a hacerlas tú.

### Dictado **FL.A.2.1.3**

Escribe las oraciones de la grabación.

# Repaso de Vocabulario 1

### Asking someone's name and saying yours

| | |
|---|---|
| **¿Cómo se llama él (ella)?** | *What's his (her) name?* |
| **¿Cómo se llama usted?** | *What's your name? (formal)* |
| **¿Cómo te llamas?** | *What's your name? (familiar)* |
| **Él (Ella) es...** | *He (She) is . . .* |
| **Él (Ella) se llama...** | *His (Her) name is . . .* |
| **Me llamo...** | *My name is . . .* |
| **¿Quién es...?** | *Who is . . .?* |
| **Soy...** | *I'm . . .* |
| **¿Y tú?** | *And you? (familiar)* |

### Asking and saying how you are

| | |
|---|---|
| **Adiós.** | *Goodbye.* |
| **Buenas noches.** | *Good evening, good night.* |
| **Buenas tardes.** | *Good afternoon.* |
| **Buenos días.** | *Good morning.* |
| **¿Cómo está usted?** | *How are you?* |
| **Estoy bien, gracias.** | *I'm fine, thanks.* |
| **Estoy regular/mal.** | *I'm all right/not so good.* |
| **Hasta luego.** | *See you later.* |
| **Hasta mañana.** | *See you tomorrow.* |
| **Hasta pronto.** | *See you soon.* |
| **Hola, ¿cómo estás?** | *Hi, how are you?* |
| **Más o menos.** | *So-so.* |
| **Nos vemos.** | *See you.* |
| **¿Qué tal?** | *How's it going?* |
| **señor** | *sir, Mr.* |
| **señora** | *ma'am, Mrs.* |
| **señorita** | *Miss* |
| **Tengo que irme.** | *I have to go.* |
| **¿Y usted?** | *And you? (formal)* |

### Introducing others

| | |
|---|---|
| **Encantado(a).** | *Pleased/Nice to meet you.* |
| **Ésta es Rosa/la señora...** | *This is Rosa/Mrs. . . .* |
| **Éste es Juan/el señor...** | *This is Juan/Mr. . . .* |
| **el/la estudiante** | *student (male or female)* |
| **Igualmente.** | *Likewise.* |
| **mi mejor amiga** | *my best friend (female)* |
| **mi mejor amigo** | *my best friend (male)* |
| **mi profesora** | *my teacher (female)* |
| **mi profesor** | *my teacher (male)* |
| **...de ciencias** | *science . . .* |
| **...de español** | *Spanish . . .* |
| **la muchacha** | *the girl* |
| **el muchacho** | *the boy* |
| **Mucho gusto.** | *Pleased/Nice to meet you.* |
| **una compañera de clase** | *a (female) classmate* |
| **un compañero de clase** | *a (male) classmate* |

### Saying where you and others are from

| | |
|---|---|
| **¿De dónde eres?** | *Where are you from? (familiar)* |
| **¿De dónde es...?** | *Where is . . . from?* |
| **¿De dónde es usted?** | *Where are you from? (formal)* |
| **Es de...** | *He (She) is from . . .* |
| **ser** | *to be* |
| **Soy de...** | *I'm from . . .* |

# Repaso de Vocabulario 2

### Exchanging phone numbers

| | |
|---|---|
| **¿Cuál es el teléfono de...?** | *What's . . . telephone number?* |
| **¿Cuál es tu teléfono?** | *What's your telephone number?* |

**Los números 0–31** . . . . . . . . . . . . . . . . . . . . *See p. 18.*

### Telling time

| | |
|---|---|
| **de la mañana** | *in the morning, A.M.* |
| **de la noche** | *at night, P.M.* |
| **de la tarde** | *in the afternoon, P.M.* |
| **en punto** | *on the dot* |
| **Es la una.** | *It's one o'clock.* |
| **medianoche** | *midnight* |
| **mediodía** | *midday, noon* |
| **menos cuarto** | *a quarter to* |
| **¿Qué hora es?** | *What time is it?* |
| **Son las...** | *It's . . . o'clock.* |
| **y cuarto** | *a quarter past* |
| **y media** | *half past* |

### Giving the date and the day

| | |
|---|---|
| **Es el primero (dos, tres) de...** | *It's the first (second, third) of . . .* |
| **Hoy es lunes.** | *Today is Monday.* |
| **¿Qué día es hoy?** | *What day is today?* |
| **¿Qué fecha es hoy?** | *What's today's date?* |

**Los días de la semana** . . . . . . . . . . . . . . . . . *See p. 21.*

**Los meses y las estaciones del año** . . . . . . *See p. 21.*

**El alfabeto** . . . . . . . . . . . . . . . . . . . . . . . . . . *See p. 22.*

**Spelling words and giving e-mail addresses** . . . . . . . . . . . . . . . . . . . . *See p. 23.*

# Integración capítulo 1

**1** Listen to each conversation and match it with the appropriate picture. FL.A.2.1.3

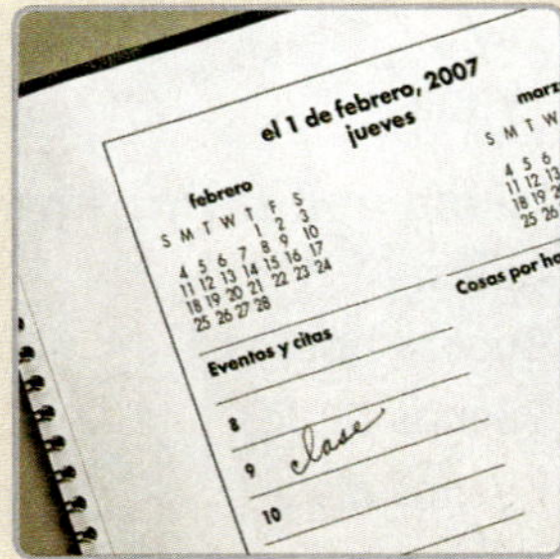


**2** Read the following conversation between Marisa and Sonia and decide if the statements are **cierto** or **falso.** FL.A.2.1.2

| | |
|---|---|
| MARISA | Hola Sonia. ¿Cómo estás? |
| SONIA | Bien. ¿Y tú? |
| MARISA | Más o menos. Dime, ¿cuál es el correo electrónico de Pilar, Alicia y Jorge? |
| SONIA | No sé el correo electrónico de Pilar. El correo electrónico de Alicia es a-ele-i arroba be-ese-te punto hache-ere-uve doble ce-o-eme y el correo electrónico de Jorge es jota-uno-tres-seis arroba a-te-ene punto hache-ere-uve doble punto ce-o-eme. |
| MARISA | Gracias. ¿Cuál es el teléfono de Pilar? |
| SONIA | Es dos-treinta y uno-veintinueve-doce. |
| MARISA | Muchas gracias. ¿Sabes *(do you know)* qué hora es? |
| SONIA | Sí, son las dos menos cuarto de la tarde. |
| MARISA | Uy, tengo que irme. Hasta luego. |
| SONIA | Adiós. |

1. Marisa y Sonia son amigas.
2. Marisa está mal.
3. El correo electrónico de Alicia es ali@bst.hrw.com.
4. El correo electrónico de Jorge es j136@atn.hrw.com.
5. El teléfono de Pilar es 2-31-19-12.
6. Son las 2:15.

**3** Salvador Dalí was born in Figueras, Spain, on May 11, 1904. He died on January 23, 1989. He was a leader of the painters called 'surrealists', who liked to show dream-like images in their work. Study the painting and write the following in Spanish. **FL.A.2.1.2**

1. a sentence that tells where the artist is from
2. his birth date
3. a question: *What time is it?*
4. an answer to the time question based on the large clock face
5. names of numbers you see in the painting
6. names of colors you see in the painting
7. the date of the artist's death

**Benchmark Focus** 

**FL.A.2.1.2** Restate and rephrase simple information from materials presented orally, visually, and graphically in class

***La persistencia de la memoria,*** **de Salvador Dalí (1904–1989)**

**4**

**Situación**

Imagine that you have just joined the Spanish Club and are meeting a new friend. Work with a partner. Have a conversation where you: **FL.A.1.1.2, FL.A.1.1.3**

- greet each other using appropriate gestures
- exchange names
- ask and tell each other how you are doing
- ask and tell each other where you are from
- spell out your e-mail addresses and phone numbers for each other
- close the conversation and say you'll see each other soon

Capítulo 2

GeoVisión

# Geocultura
# Puerto Rico

▲ **El Viejo San Juan** The buildings and streets of Old San Juan reflect the Spanish colonial period.

▼ **San Juan** The capital of Puerto Rico, San Juan, is on the northeastern coast of the island.

Isabela

Rincón

Río Grande de Añasco

Mayagüez

## Almanac

**Population**
3,937,316

**Capital** San Juan

**Government**
commonwealth associated with the United States

**Official Languages**
Spanish, English

**Currency** U.S. dollar

**Internet Code**
www.[ ].pr

### ¿Sabías que...?

**Did you know that the Okeechobee Hurricane of 1928, one of the deadliest weather disasters in U.S. history, also hit Puerto Rico? The storm is called the San Felipe Hurricane in Puerto Rico because it struck on San Felipe Day, September 13.**

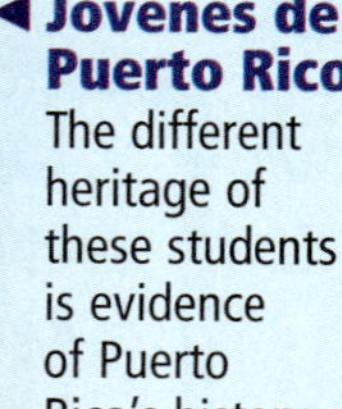

◀ **Jóvenes de Puerto Rico** The different heritage of these students is evidence of Puerto Rico's history.

▲ **Isabela** Large waves make the beaches of Isabela, a town in the rural northwest part of Puerto Rico, an ideal spot for surfers.

▲ **El Yunque** The Caribbean National Forest, **El Yunque,** is the largest forested area in Puerto Rico at 113 square kilometers. You can see many species of plants and animals while hiking in **El Yunque.**

OCÉANO ATLÁNTICO
SAN JUAN
Arecibo
Cavernas del Río Camuy
Río Grande de Arecibo
Lago Dos Bocas
Lago Caonillas
Río Grande de Manatí
Río de la Plata
Bayamón
Carolina
Río Grande de Loíza
Embalse Río Grande de Loíza
Caguas
El Toro
Parque Nacional El Yunque
Sierra de Luquillo
PLAYA SARDINERA
ISLA DE CULEBRA
ISLA DE VIEQUES
PUERTO RICO
Cordillera Central
Coamo
Río Coamo
Ponce
ISLA CAJA DE MUERTOS
BAHÍA DE RINCÓN
MAR CARIBE

▼ **La Cordillera Central** The **Cordillera Central,** Puerto Rico's central mountain range, is one of the places where the red-flowered poinciana tree grows.

▲ **El coquí** The tiny **coquí,** named for the loud sound it makes, is a symbol of Puerto Rico.

**¿Qué tanto sabes?**

What two major bodies of water surround Puerto Rico?

FL.C.1.1.2

# A conocer a Puerto Rico

## La comida

▲ **El pollo frito con tostones** Fried chicken with fried plantains is a typical dish in Puerto Rico.

▲ **Las habichuelas** **Habichuelas** are beans, a Puerto Rican staple often eaten with rice and chicken or beef.

## El arte

▼ ***Retrato de un oficial del Regimento Fijo* (1790)** This portrait was painted by José Campeche, one of Puerto Rico's most famous artists. It hangs in the Ponce Museum of Art.

► **Las máscaras de vejigante** **Vejigante** masks can be made out of a dried coconut shell. They sometimes have horns and are often painted black or red.

► **La cultura taína** The Taino culture was the dominant culture of Puerto Rico before the arrival of Christopher Columbus in 1493. Puerto Rico's pre-Columbian heritage can be seen in Taino art.

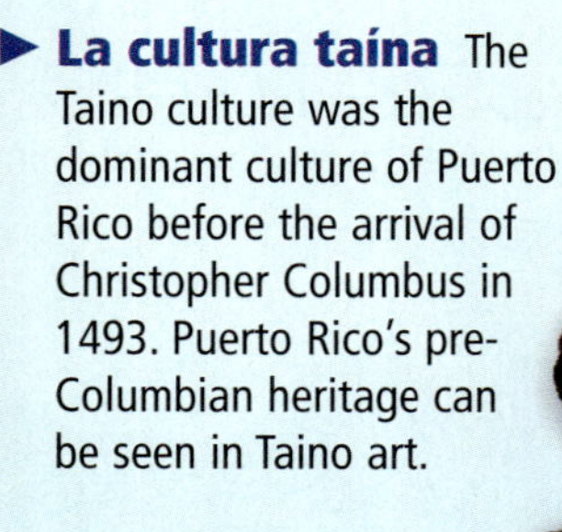

# Las celebraciones

Visit Holt Online
**go.hrw.com**
KEYWORD: EXP1A CH2
Photo Tour


◄ **La Fiesta de Santiago** The Festival of St. James is celebrated in the town of **Loíza** with traditional music, such as the **bomba** and the **plena**.

FL.B.1.1.2, FL.B.1.1.3

## ¿Sabías que...?

**Did you know that the culture of Puerto Rico is a mixture of Taino, African, and European influences? What evidence of these cultures do you see in the music and architecture of Puerto Rico?**

► **El Festival Casals** The Casals Festival in San Juan, a celebration of classical music, was founded in 1957 by the famous cellist Pablo Casals.

# La arquitectura

**Benchmark Focus**
**FL.B.1.1.3 Recognize various familiar objects and norms of the target culture**

▲ **El Parque de Bombas** The unique **Parque de Bombas** in Ponce was a fire station from 1883 until 1989. Today it is a museum dedicated to the Ponce fire department.

◄ **El Morro** Construction of this Spanish fortress began in 1539. Its outer walls are six meters thick. The circular sentry boxes, or **garitas,** have become the architectural symbol of Puerto Rico.

# Capítulo 2

# A conocernos

## Objetivos

**In Part 1 you will learn to:**

- ask what someone is like
- describe someone
- ask about someone's age and birthday
- tell someone your age and birthday
- use **ser** with adjectives
- use gender and adjective agreement
- form questions

**In Part 2 you will learn to:**

- talk about what you and others like
- describe things
- use singular and plural forms of nouns
- use definite articles
- use the verb **gustar**
- use the words **¿por qué?** and **porque**
- use **de** in different ways

## ¿Qué ves en la foto?

- **¿De dónde es el muchacho?**
- **¿Cómo son las muchachas?**
- **¿Cómo eres tú ?**

Look for the next to each activity and the **Benchmark Focus** to help you achieve the goals of the **Florida Sunshine State Standards,** found on pages FL14–FL16.

El parque Antonia S. Quiñones, Condado, Puerto Rico

**Objetivos**
- Describing people
- Asking someone's age and birthday

# Vocabulario en acción 1

ExpresaVisión

## En un colegio de San Juan

### Mi amigo es...

pelirrojo, intelectual, serio

moreno, bajo, romántico

moreno, alto, tímido

moreno, atlético, gracioso

rubio, guapo, perezoso

**Más vocabulario...**

| | |
|---|---|
| **aburrido** | *boring* |
| **activo** | *active* |
| **antipático** | *unfriendly* |
| **extrovertido** | *outgoing* |
| **inteligente** | *intelligent* |
| **simpático** | *friendly* |
| **tonto** | *silly, foolish* |
| **trabajador** | *hard-working* |

▶ **Vocabulario adicional,** Palabras descriptivas, p. R10

## Mi amiga es...

pelirroja | morena | morena | morena | rubia

bonita | perezosa

intelectual | baja | alta | atlética

seria | romántica | tímida | graciosa

### También se puede decir...

In Florida, you may hear Ecuadoreans say **tocho(a)** instead of **bajo(a),** while Hondurans and Mexicans might use **chaparro(a).** A Peruvian might say **chato(a),** and some Colombians prefer **chiquito(a).**

### Más vocabulario...

| | |
|---|---|
| **aburrida** | *boring* |
| **activa** | *active* |
| **antipática** | *unfriendly* |
| **extrovertida** | *outgoing* |
| **inteligente** | *intelligent* |
| **simpática** | *friendly* |
| **tonta** | *silly, foolish* |
| **trabajadora** | *hard-working* |

## ¡Exprésate!

| To ask what someone is like | To describe someone |
|---|---|
| **¿Cómo es Paco?**<br>*What's Paco like?* | **Paco es moreno. También es inteligente y un poco tímido.**<br>*Paco has dark hair/a dark complexion. He's also intelligent and a little shy.* |
| **¿Cómo eres? ¿Eres cómico(a)?**<br>*What are you like? Are you funny?* | **Sí, soy bastante cómico(a).**<br>*Yes, I'm pretty funny.* |

Interactive TUTOR

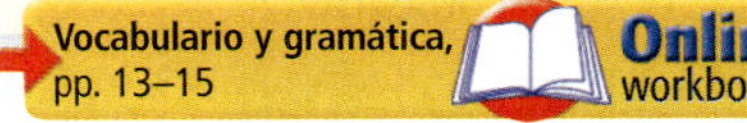

Vocabulario y gramática, pp. 13–15 Online workbooks

## Nota cultural

In many Latin American countries, someone with dark hair and skin shaded from very light brown to darker shades of brown is described as **moreno(a)** or **trigueño(a).** The word **rubio(a)** in most Spanish-speaking countries, or **güero(a)** in Mexico, may be used to describe someone with fairly light skin and blond to light brown hair.

How are these descriptions similar to or different from the ones used in English?

**FL.D.1.1.2, FL.D.2.1.1**

**Benchmark Focus** 

**FL.A.2.1.2** Restate and rephrase simple information from materials presented orally, visually, and graphically in class

### 1 Jimena y Daniel FL.A.2.1.3

**Leamos** Jimena and Daniel are complete opposites. Based on Jimena's description, choose the word in parentheses that best describes Daniel.

**MODELO** **Jimena es perezosa. Daniel es ____. (antipático/trabajador)**
**Daniel es trabajador.**

1. Jimena es tímida. Daniel es ____. (extrovertido/guapo)
2. Jimena es morena. Daniel es ____. (alto/rubio)
3. Jimena es graciosa. Daniel es ____. (atlético/serio)
4. Jimena es baja. Daniel es ____. (alto/pelirrojo)
5. Jimena es atlética. Daniel es ____. (moreno/intelectual)

### 2 Luis y Marta son... FL.A.2.1.2

**Leamos/Hablemos** Complete each description with the most logical choice.

1. Luis no es moreno. Es...
   **a.** bajo **b.** rubio **c.** perezoso
2. Marta no es antipática. Es...
   **a.** tímida **b.** activa **c.** simpática
3. Luis no es perezoso. Es...
   **a.** trabajador **b.** inteligente **c.** pelirrojo
4. Marta no es tímida. Es...
   **a.** extrovertida **b.** morena **c.** atlética
5. Luis no es bajo. Es...
   **a.** romántico **b.** gracioso **c.** alto
6. Marta no es pelirroja. Es...
   **a.** morena **b.** perezosa **c.** bonita

### 3 ¿Cómo es cada uno? FL.A.2.1.2

**Escuchemos** For each picture, you will hear two descriptions. Write the letter of the description that best matches the picture.

1. Roberto

2. Magda

3. Geraldo

4. Julieta

## 4 ¿Cómo es? FL.A.2.1.2

**Leamos/Escribamos** Read the statements about the picture and respond with **cierto** *(true)* or **falso** *(false)*. Rewrite any false statements so they are true.

1. Lucía es baja.
2. La abuela es rubia.
3. Panchito es moreno y activo.
4. Oso es perezoso.
5. El señor Medina es moreno.
6. Lupita Reyes es bonita.
7. El señor Medina es antipático.

## 5 ¿Quién es? FL.A.1.1.2

**Hablemos** With a partner, take turns describing the characters in the picture above. Have your partner guess who you are describing.

**MODELO** —**Es bonita y morena.**
—**Es Lupita Reyes.**

## Más vocabulario...

32 treinta y dos
33 treinta y tres
40 cuarenta
50 cincuenta
60 sesenta
70 setenta
80 ochenta
90 noventa
100 cien

Recently, some girls of Hispanic background in south Florida have started celebrating their 15th birthday in a very creative manner, with a **quince** cruise, usually to the Caribbean. The birthday girl or **quinceañera** invites her friends and their parents to an on-board celebration with Latin music. She starts the party by dancing a waltz with her father.

Have you been to a **quince** party? How does it compare to other birthday celebrations you have attended?

FL.D.2.1.1

Quinceañera en la Florida

## ¡Exprésate!

| To ask someone's age and birthday | To respond |
|---|---|
| **¿Cuántos años tienes?**<br>*How old are you?* | **Tengo quince años.**<br>*I'm 15 years old.* |
| **¿Cuántos años tiene María?**<br>*How old is Maria?* | **Ella tiene veintiún años.**<br>*She's 21 years old.* |
| **¿Cuándo es tu cumpleaños?**<br>*When is your birthday?* | **Es el 6 de mayo.**<br>*It's May 6th.* |
| **¿Cuándo es el cumpleaños de Ana?**<br>*When is Ana's birthday?* | **Es el 24 de noviembre.**<br>*It's November 24th.* |

Interactive TUTOR

Vocabulario y gramática, pp. 13–15 Online workbooks

### 6 Respuesta lógica FL.A.2.1.2

**Leamos** Choose the best response to each question.

1. ¿Cuántos años tienes?
2. ¿Cómo eres?
3. ¿Cuándo es tu cumpleaños?
4. ¿Quién es tu mejor amigo?
5. ¿Cómo es?
6. ¿Cuántos años tiene?
7. ¿Cuándo es el cumpleaños de Ana?

a. Es Juan.
b. Mi cumpleaños es el dos de mayo.
c. El cumpleaños de ella es el once de marzo.
d. Soy tímido y serio.
e. Tengo doce años.
f. Tiene trece años.
g. Es rubio(a) y activo(a).

### 7 Edades y cumpleaños FL.A.2.1.2

**Escribamos** Using the prompts, write questions that ask for the required information. Then write the answers.

**MODELO** **Luisa/13 years old/January 17**
**—¿Cuántos años tiene Luisa?**
**—Tiene trece años.**
**—¿Cuándo es el cumpleaños de Luisa?**
**—Es el 17 de enero.**

1. Mr. López/85 years old/July 15
2. Mrs. García/79 years old/December 12
3. Carmen/26 years old/April 30
4. Francisco/2 years old/September 25
5. you/12 years old/May 6

## 8 ¿Quién es? FL.A.2.1.2

**Leamos** Daniel has written these notes abcut family members. Match each description with a picture.

1. El cumpleaños de Carlitos es el 13 de octubre; él tiene dos años.
2. El cumpleaños de Diego es el 24 de marzo y tiene doce años.
3. El cumpleaños de Martina es el 15 de junio. Ella tiene diez años.
4. Todos los primos tienen *(cousins have)* cumpleaños en febrero.
5. El cumpleaños de tía *(aunt)* Juanita es el 31 de agosto; ella tiene treinta y tres años.

A

B

C

D

E

Comunicación

## 9 Presentaciones FL.A.1.1.2, FL.A.3.1.1

**Hablemos** Take turns with two classmates introducing yourselves to each other. First exchange greetings, then ask each other's names, ages, and birthdays. Be prepared to introduce each other to the class and report the information that you just learned.

**MODELO** **—Hola, ¿cómo te llamas?**
**—Me llamo...**
**—¿Cuántos años tienes?**
**—Tengo... años.**
**—¿Cuándo es tu cumpleaños?**
**—Es el... de...**

**Objetivos**
- Using **ser** with adjectives
- Gender and adjective agreement
- Forming questions

**GramaVisión**

## Ser with adjectives

Interactive TUTOR

**1** **Adjectives** are words that describe people or things. You can use the verb **ser** with **adjectives** to describe what someone is like.

Carlos **es simpático**. Pedro **es pelirrojo**.
Ana **es simpática**. Rosa y Julio **son inteligentes**.

**2** In Spanish, you don't usually need the subject pronoun if it's clear who the subject is.

¿Cómo **es** el profesor? **Es bajo** y **gracioso**.
¿Cómo **son** Leticia y Diego? **Son simpáticos**.

**3** To say what someone is not like, put **no** in front of the verb.

**No soy** tonto. **Soy** inteligente.

**Vocabulario y gramática**, pp. 16–18
**Actividades**, pp. 11–13

### ¿Te acuerdas?

Remember that **ser** means *to be.*

| | |
|---|---|
| yo **soy** | nosotros(as) **somos** |
| tú **eres** | vosotros(as) **sois** |
| usted **es** | ustedes **son** |
| él/ella **es** | ellos/ellas **son** |

### 10 ¿Cómo son...? FL.A.2.1.2

**Leamos** Complete these sentences about your classmates, your friends, your teacher, and yourself.

1. Yo ______ muy alto(a).
   **a.** soy **b.** no soy
2. Profesor(a), usted ______ moreno(a).
   **a.** es **b.** no es
3. Tú ______ tímido(a).
   **a.** eres **b.** no eres
4. Mi mejor amigo ______ cómico.
   **a.** es **b.** no es
5. Mis amigos(as) y yo ______ serios(as).
   **a.** somos **b.** no somos
6. Los estudiantes ______ tontos.
   **a.** son **b.** no son
7. Mis compañeros de clase ______ perezosos.
   **a.** son **b.** no son

Visit Holt Online
**go.hrw.com**
KEYWORD: EXP1A CH2
Gramática 1 practice

### 11 Una persona simpática FL.A.2.1.2

**Escribamos/Hablemos** Roberto always says good things about everyone. What does he say about the following people?

**MODELO** **yo/guapo → Soy guapo.**
**tú/tonta → No eres tonta.**

1. yo/perezoso
2. tú/bonita
3. mi amigo Carlos/inteligente
4. Profesor Garza, usted/aburrido
5. nosotros/simpáticos
6. Mari y Gisela/graciosas
7. mis compañeras de clase/antipáticas
8. ustedes/activos

**Benchmark Focus**
**FL.A.2.1.2** Restate and rephrase simple information from materials presented orally, visually, and graphically in class

### 12 ¿Quién es...? FL.A.2.1.2

**Escribamos/Hablemos** Look at the photos below, and say who is described by each adjective.

**MODELO** **simpático(a)**
**Felipe es simpático.**

Felipe

Gladys

Juan

Rebeca

1. rubio(a)
2. atlético(a)
3. moreno(a)
4. serio(a)
5. intelectual
6. tímido(a)
7. bonita
8. pelirrojo(a)
9. extrovertido(a)

### 13 Yo soy... ¿Y tú? FL.A.3.1.1

**Hablemos** Write down three adjectives that describe you. If you're male, use the words on page 48. If you're female, use the words on page 49. Then get together in small groups. Record how many students in your group used the same adjectives that you used.

**MODELO** **atlético(a)**
**—¿Eres atlético(a)?**
**—Sí, soy atlético(a)./—No, no soy atlético(a).**

Gramática 1

## Gender and adjective agreement

**1** Nouns and pronouns in Spanish are divided into genders. Nouns for men and boys are **masculine**. Nouns for women and girls are **feminine**.

**Masculine:** amigo, él, Juan **Feminine:** amiga, ella, María

**2** Adjectives describe nouns. They have different forms that match, or agree with, the noun or pronoun in gender. The **masculine** form of most adjectives ends in **-o**, while the **feminine** form ends in **-a**.

**Raúl** es romántic**o**. **Mari** es romántic**a**.

Adjectives that end in **-e** have the same **masculine** and **feminine** forms.

**Rafael** es inteligent**e**. **Carmen** es inteligent**e**.

Adjectives ending in **consonants** do not add an **-a**,unless they end in **-or** or are adjectives of nationality.

**Lorenzo** es españo**l**, intelectua**l** y trabajad**or**. **Gloria** es españo**la**, intelectua**l** y trabajador**a**.

**3** Adjectives also agree with nouns in number. An adjective that describes one person or thing is in **singular** form. When it describes more than one person or thing, its form is **plural**. If the singular form ends in a vowel, add **-s** to make it plural. If it ends in a consonant, add **-es**.

Joaquín es alt**o**. Paco y Luis son alto**s**.
Rosa es intelectua**l**. Mis amigos son intelectual**es**.

To describe a mixed group of men and women, boys and girls, use the **masculine plural** forms of the adjective:

**Carlos** y **Ana** son romántic**os**.

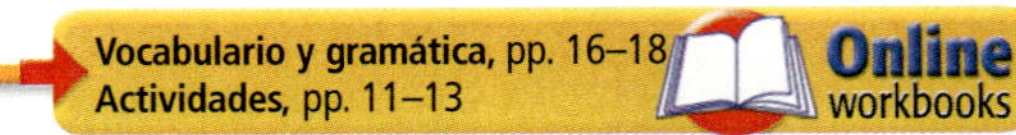

*Nota cultural*

New York State has the highest population of Puerto Ricans living in the U.S. mainland, but since the 1990s, great numbers of **boricuas,** or **puertorriqueños,** have moved to Florida, giving this state the country's second largest population of Puerto Ricans. They have settled primarily in Orlando, Broward County, and Tampa.

Why do you think some Puerto Ricans prefer to live in Florida instead of New York? Find out from a Puerto Rican in your school or community the reasons why he/she moved to Florida. **FL.E.1.2.1**

**Festival anual de puertorriqueños en Tampa**

### 14 ¿Cómo son los gemelos? FL.A.2.1.2

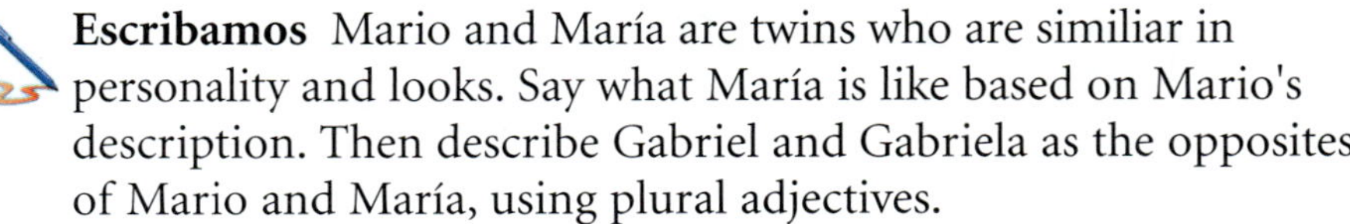

**Escribamos** Mario and María are twins who are similiar in personality and looks. Say what María is like based on Mario's description. Then describe Gabriel and Gabriela as the opposites of Mario and María, using plural adjectives.

**MODELO** **Mario es moreno. María es morena también. Gabriel y Gabriela son rubios.**

1. Mario es bajo.
2. Mario es intelectual.
3. Mario es perezoso.
4. Mario es simpático.
5. Mario es tímido.
6. Mario es serio.

## 15 Mi clase favorita FL.A.2.1.2

**Leamos/Escribamos** A student has only good things to say about her favorite class. Complete her description with the correct forms of the most logical adjective in parentheses.

La clase es muy interesante y la profesora es __1__ (simpático, antipático). Los estudiantes son __2__ (perezoso, trabajador). Mis amigas Marta y Gabi son muy __3__ (tonto, intelectual) y mi amigo Ricardo es muy __4__ (gracioso, aburrido). ¿Y yo? Soy __5__ (tonto, inteligente) y __6__ (activo, perezoso).

**Benchmark Focus**

**FL.A.2.1.2** Restate and rephrase simple information from materials presented orally, visually, and graphically in class

## 16 ¿Cómo son? FL.A.2.1.2, FL.A.3.1.1

**Escribamos/Hablemos** Describe yourself and people you know by combining words from each column. Use the correct forms of the verb **ser** and the adjectives listed.

**MODELO** **Mis amigas y yo somos graciosas.**

| 1 | 2 | 3 | |
|---|---|---|---|
| yo | eres | simpático | activo |
| mi mejor amigo(a) | es | inteligente | perezoso |
| mis amigos y yo | son | atlético | interesante |
| tú (una compañera de clase) | somos | gracioso | trabajador |
| profesor(a), usted | soy | tímido | serio |
| ustedes | | | |

# Comunicación

HOLT SoundBooth ONLINE RECORDING

## 17 Nuestros compañeros FL.A.3.1.1

**Hablemos** With a partner, take turns describing someone from the picture below and guessing who is being described.

Gramática 1

## Question formation

**1** To ask a question that may be answered **sí** or **no**, just raise the pitch of your voice at the end of the question. The **subject,** if included, can go before or after the **verb**.

| | |
|---|---|
| ¿**Eres** extrovertido? | *Are you outgoing?* |
| ¿**La profesora es** simpática? | *Is the teacher nice?* |
| ¿**Es** simpática **la profesora**? | *Is the teacher nice?* |

**2** You can answer a question like this with **sí** or **no.** You say the word **no** twice in your answer: once to mean ***no*** and another time to mean ***not***.

| | |
|---|---|
| —¿Eres atlético? | *Are you athletic?* |
| —**Sí**, soy atlético. | *Yes, I'm athletic.* |
| —**No**, **no** soy atlético. | *(No, I'm not athletic.)* |

**3** You can ask for more information by using **question words**. Notice that all question words are written with an accent mark.

| | |
|---|---|
| ¿**Cómo** es Paco? | *What's Paco like?* |
| ¿**Cuándo** es tu cumpleaños? | *When is your birthday?* |
| ¿**Quién** es? | *Who is he (she)?* |
| ¿**Quiénes** son? | *Who are they?* |
| ¿**Qué** día es hoy? | *What day is today?* |
| ¿**De dónde** eres? | *Where are you from?* |
| ¿**Cuál** es tu teléfono? | *What's your phone number?* |

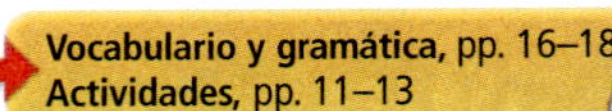

### ¿Te acuerdas?

Remember that **¿Cómo está?** asks how someone is feeling. To ask what someone is like, say **¿Cómo es?**

¿**Cómo está** usted?

Estoy bien, gracias.

¿**Cómo es** tu amigo?

Él es guapo.

### 18 ¿Pregunta o no? FL.A.2.1.3

**Escuchemos** Decide if what you hear is a question or statement.

### 19 ¡Muchas preguntas! FL.A.2.1.2

**Hablemos** María is full of questions for her new neighbor, Jorge. Fill in her questions with the best question word. Use Jorge's answers as cues.

1. ¿ ______ estás? (Estoy bien, gracias.)
2. ¿ ______ te llamas? (Me llamo Jorge.)
3. ¿ ______ eres? (Soy de Puerto Rico.)
4. ¿ ______ es tu cumpleaños? (Es el 10 de enero.)
5. ¿ ______ es tu teléfono? (Es 809-1212.)
6. ¿ ______ son ellos? (Son mis amigos Luisa y Óscar.)
7. ¿ ______ es? (Son las tres. Tengo que irme.)

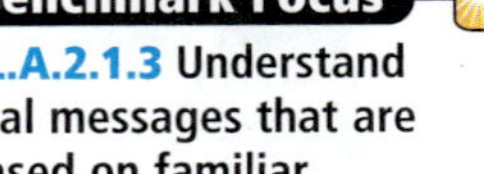


**FL.A.2.1.3** Understand oral messages that are based on familiar themes and vocabulary

## 20 ¿Qué tal? FL.A.2.1.2

**Leamos/Escribamos** Read the e-mail and then answer the questions.

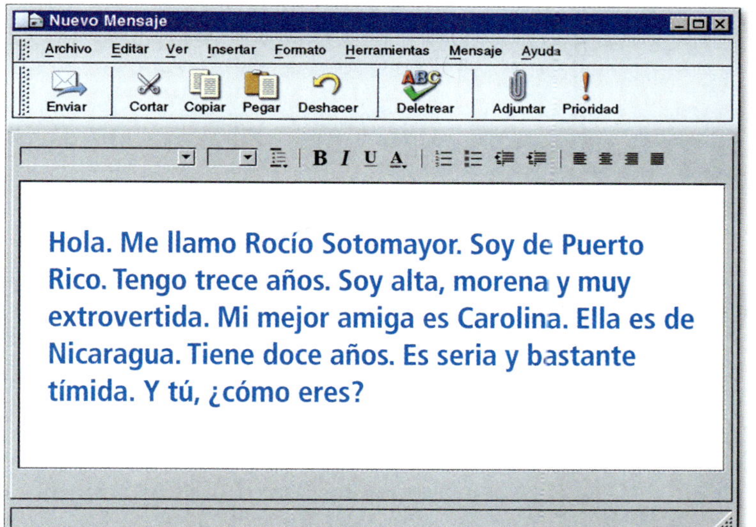

Rocío y Carolina en San Juan

1. ¿De dónde es Rocío?
2. ¿Cuántos años tiene?
3. ¿Es rubia o morena?
4. ¿Cómo es Rocío?
5. ¿De dónde es Carolina?
6. ¿Cómo es ella?

### Nota cultural

In the United States, a person's 16th and 18th birthdays are important milestones. In most Spanish-speaking countries, the legal driving and voting age is 18. Since Puerto Ricans are U.S. citizens, they can vote when they are 18 years old. They can get their driver's license at age 18 or at 16 with parental consent.

How would your 18th birthday be different if you lived in Puerto Rico?

FL.B.1.1.2, FL.D.2.1.1

## 21 Entrevista a Gisela FL.A.2.1.2

**Hablemos/Escribamos** On a separate piece of paper, write the missing questions to complete the interview.

**MODELO** **—¿Cómo estás?**
**—Muy bien, gracias.**

1. ¿ ___ ? —Me llamo Gisela Ríos Perales.
2. ¿ ___ ? —Soy de Burgos, España.
3. ¿ ___ ? —No, no soy tímida. Soy extrovertida.
4. ¿ ___ ? —Son inteligentes, simpáticos y atléticos.
5. ¿ ___ ? —Tengo once años.
6. ¿ ___ ? —Mi cumpleaños es el quince de marzo.

## 22 Veinte preguntas FL.A.2.1.3

**Hablemos** Ask your partner to think of a classmate. Guess who he or she is by asking questions that can be answered with **sí** or **no**. Keep trying until you guess correctly. Switch roles.

Gramática 1

# Cultura

VideoCultura

**Benchmark Focus**

**FL.D.2.1.1** Know the similarities and differences between the patterns of behavior of the target culture and the local culture

## Comparaciones

Un grupo de amigos, San Juan

### ¿Cómo eres? FL.B.1.1.2, FL.D.2.1.1

There's a saying in Spanish, **"Dime con quién andas y te diré quién eres."** *(Tell me who you spend time with and I'll tell you who you are.)* This saying is like the English expressions "Birds of a feather flock together" and "You're known by the company you keep." These sayings stem from the belief that we choose as friends those who are much like ourselves. Why do you think both English and Spanish have these sayings? Do you think they are true? Why or why not?

### Luis
#### San Juan, Puerto Rico

Luis talks about the interests that he and his best friend have in common. Do you and your best friend have common interests?

***Dime, ¿cómo eres tú?***

Bueno, pues, yo me considero una persona simpática, graciosa, alegre, un buen amigo y una buena persona.

***¿Y qué cosas te gustan?***

Me gusta el deporte. Me gusta la música. Me gusta la escuela.

***¿Cómo es tu mejor amigo?***

Pues, es una persona que es simpática también, amigable, alegre, atleta. Él es moreno. Es bien activo. Me gusta ser amigo de él.

***¿Qué cosas le gustan a él?***

Le gusta también la música, el deporte. Le gusta la escuela. Y como es una persona alegre, pues no le gusta estar aburrido.

***¿Cómo son ustedes?***

Pues, tenemos muchos gustos como lo de la música y pues además nos llevamos bien y nos comprendemos en todo.

***¿Qué significa la expresión "Dime con quién andas y te diré quién eres"?***

Yo pienso que, que es con quien tú te pasas, según esa persona, pues, va a ser tu personalidad.

***¿La expresión se aplica en su caso?***

Sí.

Visit Holt Online
**go.hrw.com**
KEYWORD: EXP1A CH2
Online Edition

## Andrea

**Ciudad de México, México**

Andrea talks about what she and her friends have in common. Do you and your friends have similiar personalities?

***¿Cómo eres tú?***

Yo soy alegre, inteligente y divertida.

***¿Qué cosas te gustan a ti?***

Pues, me gusta el cine, me gustan los libros, la música.

***¿Cómo es tu mejor amigo o amiga?***

Es alegre también, es divertida y muy inteligente.

***¿Qué cosas le gustan a ella?***

Le gusta el cine, los libros, bailar.

***¿Cómo son ustedes?***

Somos muy parecidas.

***¿Qué cosas les gustan?***

Nos gusta el cine, bailar, cantar.

***¿La expresión se aplica en este caso?***

Sí, porque somos muy parecidas. Salimos mucho juntas.

Cultura

### Para comprender FL.A.3.1.1

1. ¿Qué cosas le gustan a Luis?
2. ¿Qué cosas le gustan a Andrea?
3. ¿A quién le gustan las películas?
4. ¿El amigo de Luis es atlético?
5. ¿Quién es más como su amigo(a), Luis o Andrea?

### Para pensar y hablar FL.A.2.1.2

Both Luis and Andrea say that the expression **"Dime con quién andas y te diré quién eres"** applies to them and their friends. Based on what they say, do you agree? What are two advantages and disadvantages of being like your friends?

# Comunidad en la Florida

## Conexiones culturales FL.C.2.1.1, FL.E.1.2.2

Florida sponsors programs that develop cultural and educational connections with Latin America and Spain. The state provides money to pair up Florida cities with sister cities in Spanish-speaking countries. For example, there is an annual regatta (sailboat race) from St. Petersburg, Florida to Isla Mujeres, Mexico. This event has become a multi-day festival featuring art shows, parades, and films.

- Find other sister cities in Florida and Spanish-speaking countries by using English and Spanish Internet resources.
- What types of cultural exchanges are involved?
- Present your findings to the class.

**Regata de St. Petersburg a Isla Mujeres, México**

**Objetivos**
- Talking about what you and others like
- Describing things

# Vocabulario en acción 2

Video/DVD
ExpresaVisión

## Me gusta...

▶ **Vocabulario adicional** — Comida, p. R7

## Me gustan...

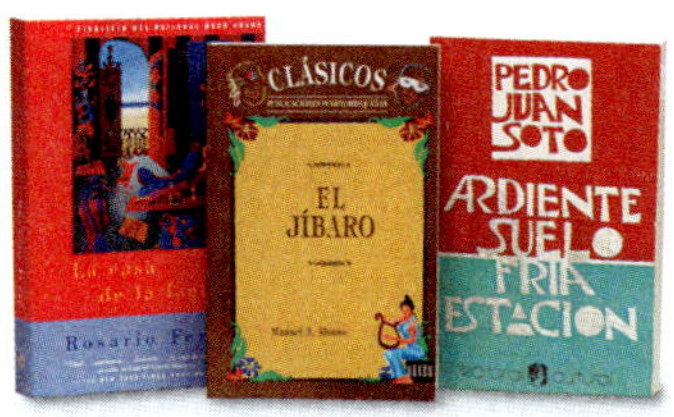


los libros (de aventuras, de amor)

las películas (de ciencia ficción, de terror, de misterio)

los carros

las fiestas

las hamburguesas

las verduras

las frutas

los deportes

los videojuegos

los animales

## ¡Exprésate!

| To ask someone what he or she likes | To respond |
|---|---|
| **¿Te gusta(n)...?**<br>*Do you like . . . ?* | **Sí, me gusta(n) mucho...**<br>*Yes, I like . . . a lot.*<br>**No, no me gusta(n)...**<br>*No, I don't like . . .* |
| **¿Te gusta(n) más...o...?**<br>*Do you like . . . or . . . more?* | **Me gusta(n) más...**<br>*I like . . . more.*<br>**Me da igual.**<br>*It's all the same to me.* |

Interactive TUTOR

Vocabulario y gramática, pp. 19–21 Online workbooks

▶ Vocabulario adicional — Deportes y pasatiempos, p. R8

## 23 Dime cómo eres FL.A.2.1.2

**Leamos/Hablemos** Based on the descriptions, which item in parentheses would these people say they like or don't like?

**MODELO** **Me llamo Carlos. Soy muy atlético. Me gustan ___ (los libros/los deportes).**
**Me gustan los deportes.**

1. ¿Qué tal? Soy Marta y soy muy extrovertida. Me gustan ___ (las fiestas/los libros).
2. Soy Juan y me gusta la pizza. Me gusta ___ (la comida mexicana/la comida italiana).
3. Buenas tardes. Me llamo Javier y soy muy romántico. Me gustan ___ (las películas de ciencia ficción/las películas de amor).
4. Hola. Yo soy Samuel y soy intelectual. Me gustan ___ (los videojuegos/los libros).
5. Soy Carlota y no soy muy activa. Me gustan ___ (los videojuegos/los deportes).
6. Hola, me llamo Celia. No soy muy atlética. No me gustan ___ (los deportes/las fiestas).
7. Soy Enrique y soy muy tímido. No me gustan mucho ___ (los carros/las fiestas).

### Nota cultural

Many Latin American families like to play games such as baseball and dominoes. They also enjoy books, TV and radio soap operas **(novelas)**, and movies. In Puerto Rico, as in many other countries, middle and high school students love music and enjoy live performances and dancing.

How would your pastimes be similiar or different if you lived in Puerto Rico?

FL.D.2.1.1

**Benchmark Focus**

**FL.D.2.1.1 Know the similarities and differences between the patterns of behavior of the target culture and the local culture**

## 24 ¿Quiénes hablan? FL.A.2.1.3

**Escuchemos** You will hear four conversations. Decide which conversation goes with each photo.

A

B

C

D

## 25 ¿Qué te gusta? FL.A.2.1.2

**Escribamos** Write complete sentences to answer these questions.

1. ¿Te gusta el helado?
2. ¿Te gustan los carros?
3. ¿Te gusta más la comida mexicana o la comida italiana?
4. ¿Te gustan más las frutas o las verduras?
5. ¿Te gustan las hamburguesas?
6. ¿Te gustan más los deportes o los videojuegos?

## 26 ¿Qué les gusta? FL.A.2.1.4

**Escribamos** Imagine that you are working in the cafeteria and you are asking Ana, Gloria, and Beto what they like. Write their answers to the following questions.

**MODELO** **—¿Qué te gusta, Gloria?**
**—Me gusta la pizza.**

1. ¿Qué te gusta, Beto?
2. Gloria, ¿te gusta la fruta?
3. Ana, ¿te gustan las verduras?
4. Beto, ¿te gusta la comida mexicana?
5. ¿Qué te gusta, Ana?

## 27 ¡Entrevista! FL.A.1.1.2, FL.A.3.1.1

**Hablemos** Interview a classmate. Find out your partner's name, age, birthday, and where he or she is from. Also find out at least three things your partner likes and doesn't like. Be prepared to present your interview to the class.

| ¿Cómo te llamas? | ¿Cuántos años tienes? | ¿Qué te gusta? |
|---|---|---|
| ¿Qué no te gusta? | ¿De dónde eres? | ¿Cuándo es tu cumpleaños? |

**Benchmark Focus**
**FL.A.3.1.1** Provide simple information in spoken form

Vocabulario 2

## ¡Exprésate!

| To describe something | |
|---|---|
| **¿Cómo es...?** *What's . . . like?* | **Es (muy) delicioso(a)/horrible.** *It's (really) delicious/horrible.* |
| | **Es pésimo(a)/fenomenal/formidable.** *It's awful/awesome/great.* |
| | **Es algo divertido(a)/interesante.** *It's kind of fun/interesting.* |
| | **Es bastante bueno(a)/malo(a).** *It's quite good/bad.* |

Interactive TUTOR

Vocabulario y gramática, pp. 19–21 Online workbooks

### 28 ¿Qué dice? FL.A.2.1.2

**Leamos** Look at the pictures and choose the word that best completes each of the following sentences.

1. 2. 3. 4.

1. La música es aburrida/divertida.
2. Los libros de amor son muy románticos/no son interesantes.
3. Los videojuegos son pésimos/fenomenales.
4. Las verduras son deliciosas/horribles.

### 29 En tu opinión FL.A.2.1.2

**Escribamos/Hablemos** Say whether or not you agree with the description of each item. Make sure adjectives agree with the nouns they modify.

**MODELO** **la pizza/bueno**
**Sí, la pizza es buena. /No, la pizza no es buena.**

1. el helado/delicioso
2. la comida china/bueno
3. las verduras/delicioso
4. las películas de terror/horrible
5. los libros de misterio/pésimo
6. los deportes/divertido

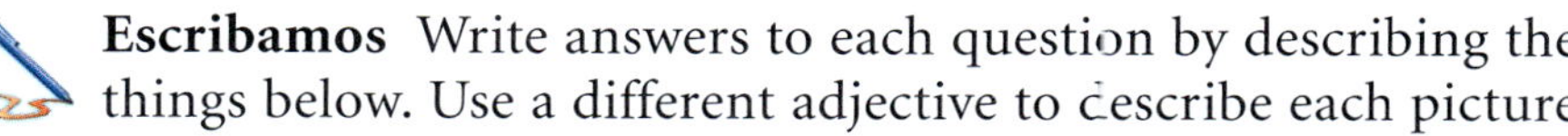

## 30 Descripciones FL.A.2.1.2

**Escribamos** Write answers to each question by describing the things below. Use a different adjective to describe each picture.

1. ¿Cómo es el libro de amor?
2. ¿Cómo son los deportes?
3. ¿Cómo son Chato y Salchicha?
4. ¿Cómo es el videojuego?
5. ¿Cómo es el libro?
6. ¿Cómo es el cumpleaños de Lupe?

1.

2.

3.

4.

5.

6.

## 31 ¿Te gustan o no? FL.A.1.1.1, FL.A.3.1.1

**Hablemos** Work with a partner. Find out whether or not your classmate likes the things listed below. Take turns.

**MODELO** **—¿Te gustan los videojuegos?**
**—Sí, me gustan. Son fenomenales. (No, no me gustan. Son aburridos.)**

| | | |
|---|---|---|
| los videojuegos | los animales | las películas de aventuras |
| los libros de amor | los deportes | las fiestas |

**Benchmark Focus**
FL.A.3.1.1 Provide simple information in spoken form

**Objetivos**

- Using nouns with definite articles
- Using **gustar, ¿por qué?** and **porque**
- The preposition **de**

GramaVisión

Interactive TUTOR

## Nouns and definite articles

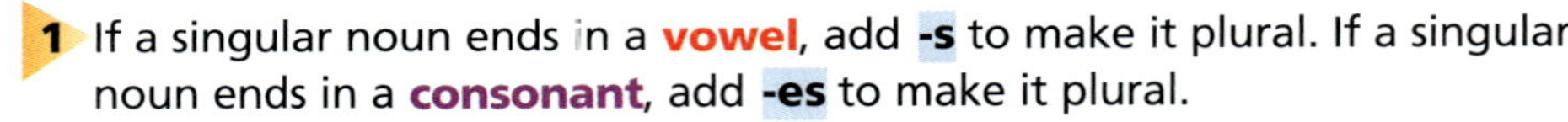

**1** If a singular noun ends in a **vowel**, add **-s** to make it plural. If a singular noun ends in a **consonant**, add **-es** to make it plural.

estudiant**e** *student* — estudiant**es** *students*
anima**l** *animal* — anima**les** *animals*

**2** Adjectives must agree with the **gender** and **number** of the nouns they describe, just as they do when describing people.

La comid**a** mexican**a** es delicios**a**.

**3** The **definite articles** can be used to say *the* with a specific noun. They have different forms that agree with the noun in gender and number.

| | Masculine | Feminine |
|---|---|---|
| SINGULAR | el | la |
| PLURAL | los | las |

¿Cómo es **el** profesor? *What is the teacher like?* — **El** profesor es simpático. *The teacher is nice.*

**4** Use **definite articles** to talk about a noun as a general category or when saying what you like with **gustar**.

¿Cómo es **la** pizza? *What's pizza (in general) like?* — Es deliciosa. Me gusta **la** pizza. *It's delicious. I like pizza.*

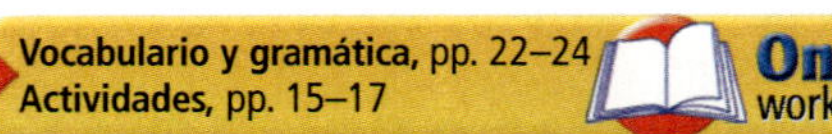
**Vocabulario y gramática**, pp. 22–24
**Actividades**, pp. 15–17
Online workbooks

### En inglés

**In English,** people and animals are masculine or feminine, but things are always neuter in gender.

The book? It's good!
Ana? She's pretty!

**In Spanish,** all nouns have gender. With some exceptions, nouns ending in **-o** are **masculine**, and nouns ending in **-a** are **feminine**.

**el libro**
**la pizza**

Does the English definite article *the* show gender? How do the Spanish definite articles show gender?

FL.D.1.1.2

### 32 Los gustos de Luisa FL.A.2.1.2

**Leamos** Luisa wrote a note describing what she likes. Choose the correct answer for each item.

Me gusta __1__ (el/la) helado porque es __2__ (delicioso/deliciosa). También me gustan __3__ (los/las) frutas porque son __4__ (buenos/buenas). Me gusta mucho __5__ (el/la) pizza y ¡la comida italiana es __6__ (fenomenal/fenomenales)! Mi mejor amiga, Juana, es __7__ (divertido/divertida). Yo soy bastante __8__ (atlético/atlética). Me gustan mucho __9__ (los/las) deportes porque son __10__ (formidable/formidables). Mis amigos y yo somos __11__ (activos/activas).

Visit Holt Online
**go.hrw.com**
KEYWORD: EXP1A CH2
Gramática 2 practice

## 33 Son así... FL.A.2.1.2

**Escribamos** Write sentences using words from each column. Remember that articles and adjectives must agree.

| 1 | 2 | 3 | 4 | |
|---|---|---|---|---|
| El | estudiantes de español | es | serio | aburrido |
| La | deportes | son | interesante | atlético |
| Los | helado | somos | bueno | divertido |
| Las | música mexicana | | malo | fenomenal |
| | fiestas | | gracioso | delicioso |

## 34 ¿Te gusta? FL.A.2.1.2

**Escribamos** Write a sentence saying what you think each item pictured is like.

**MODELO** **Las frutas son muy deliciosas.**

**Benchmark Focus**
**FL.A.2.1.2** Restate and rephrase simple information from materials presented orally, visually, and graphically in class

1.

2.

3.

4.

5.

6.

7.

8.

## 35 Entrevista FL.A.1.1.1

**Hablemos** Ask three classmates their opinions about the things in Activity 34. How are their opinions different from yours?

**MODELO** —**¿Cómo son los libros?**
—**Los libros son horribles/divertidos.**

Gramática 2

## The verb gustar, ¿por qué?, and porque

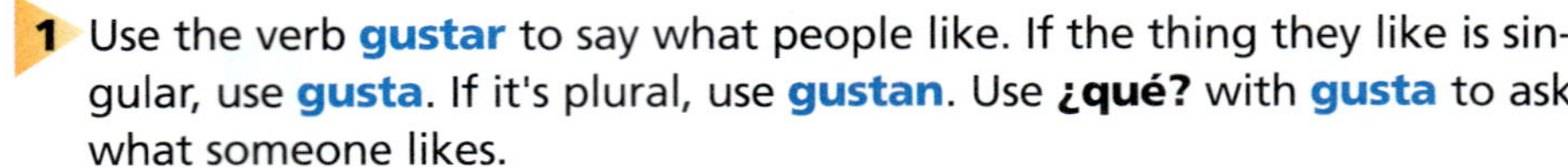

**En inglés**

**In English,** the definite article *the* is not used when talking about general likes and dislikes.

I like pizza.

How does using *the* change the meaning of a sentence about likes and dislikes?

**In Spanish,** the definite articles **el, la, los,** and **las** are always used when talking about things you like or dislike.

**Me gusta *la* pizza.**

FL.D.1.1.2

**1** Use the verb **gustar** to say what people like. If the thing they like is singular, use **gusta**. If it's plural, use **gustan**. Use **¿qué?** with **gusta** to ask what someone likes.

| | |
|---|---|
| —¿Te **gusta** la pizza?<br>*Do you like pizza?* | —¿**Qué** te **gusta**?<br>*What do you like?* |
| —Sí, y me **gustan** las verduras.<br>*Yes, and I like vegetables.* | —Me **gustan** los carros.<br>*I like cars.* |

**2** Put one of these **pronouns** before **gustar** to say who likes something.

| | | | |
|---|---|---|---|
| **me** gusta(n) | *I like* | **nos** gusta(n) | *we like* |
| **te** gusta(n) | *you* (tú) *like* | **os** gusta(n) | *you* (vosotros) *like* |
| **le** gusta(n) | *you* (usted) *like, he, she, it likes* | **les** gusta(n) | *you* (ustedes) *like, they like* |

**3** Notice that **le** can stand for *you* **(usted),** *he, she* or *it;* and **les** can stand for *you* **(ustedes)** or *they.* To ask who is being talked about, use **a quién** or **a quiénes**. To clarify who is being talked about, use **a** + **name(s)**.

| | |
|---|---|
| —¿**A quién le** gusta la pizza?<br>*Who likes pizza?* | —¿**A quiénes les** gusta la pizza?<br>*Who likes pizza?* |
| —**A Juan le** gusta la pizza.<br>*Juan likes pizza.* | —**A Juan** y **a Sara les** gusta la pizza.<br>*Juan and Sara like pizza.* |

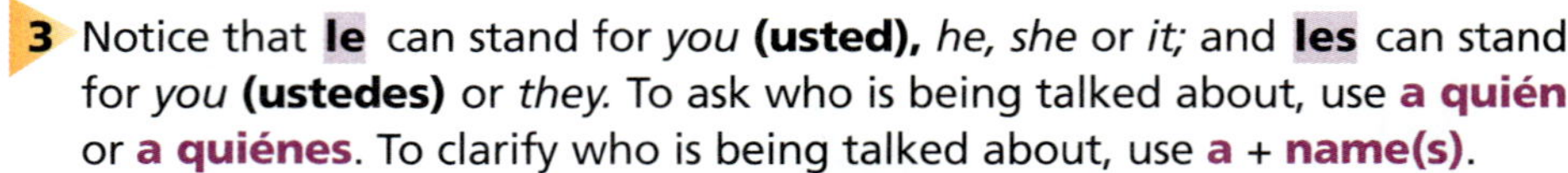

**4** Put the word **no** before the pronoun to say *don't* or *doesn't.*

| | |
|---|---|
| —¿Te gusta la fruta?<br>*Do you like fruit?* | —No, **no me** gusta la fruta.<br>*No, I don't like fruit.* |

**5** To ask *why,* say **¿por qué?** Answer with **porque** *(because).*

| | |
|---|---|
| —**¿Por qué** te gusta el helado?<br>*Why do you like ice cream?* | —Me gusta **porque** es delicioso.<br>*I like it because it's delicious.* |

Vocabulario y gramática, pp. 22–24
Actividades, pp. 15–17

### 36 El festival de Ponce FL.A.2.1.3

**Escuchemos** Listen to Mari and Josué as they talk about the festival. Decide if the following statements are **cierto** or **falso.**

1. A Mari y a Josué les gusta la fiesta.
2. A Juan no le gusta la fiesta porque no le gusta la comida.
3. A Ana y a Silvia no les gusta la música.
4. A los amigos de Mari les gusta la música.

El festival de Ponce

## 37 ¿Qué les gusta más? FL.A.2.1.2

**Escribamos** Based on the following people's personalities, which things do they like more?

**MODELO** **Somos muy románticos.**
**(películas de amor/películas de terror)**
**Nos gustan más las películas de amor.**

1. Eres muy intelectual. (libros/videojuegos)
2. Mis amigos Juan y Beti son atléticos. (música/deportes)
3. Teresa es muy extrovertida. (fiestas/libros)
4. No soy muy atlético. (videojuegos/deportes)
5. Ustedes son bastante serios. (películas de amor/libros de misterio)
6. No somos muy activos. (deportes/películas de aventuras)

## 38 La fiesta FL.A.1.2.2, FL.A.3.1.1

**Hablemos** You're throwing a party and you want to find out what your guests like. Ask four classmates if they like each of these things. Be prepared to report your findings to the class.

**1.** ice cream **2.** videogames **3.** hamburgers **4.** fruit **5.** music by . . .

**Benchmark Focus**
FL.A.1.1.1 Express likes and dislikes when asked simple questions

## 39 ¿Por qué te gusta(n)? FL.A.1.1.1, FL.A.3.1.1

**Hablemos** With a partner, take turns asking each other if you like the things pictured. Then tell why you like them or not. Be prepared to report to the class what you both like as well as what you disagree about.

**MODELO** **—¿Te gustan los deportes?**
**—Sí, me gustan los deportes porque son divertidos.**

## The preposition de

**1** The word **de** is used to tell where someone is from.

Julio es **de** Costa Rica. — *Julio is from Costa Rica.*

**2** In addition, **de** can be used to indicate what type of thing you're describing.

los libros **de** aventuras — *adventure books*
las películas **de** misterio — *mystery movies*

**3** **De** is also used to show possession or relationship.

Es el carro **de** Ernesto. — *It's Ernesto's car.*
Son los amigos **de** la profesora. — *They're the teacher's friends.*

**4** The preposition **de** followed by **el** makes the contraction **del**.

el correo electrónico **del** profesor
*the teacher's e-mail address*

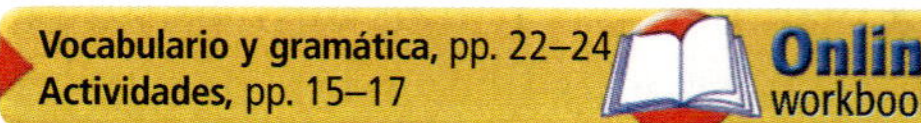


### En inglés

**In English,** we add **'s** or just an apostrophe **(')** to show ownership.

Chris**'s** class
the teacher**'s** book

How does English use *of* to show possession?

**In Spanish,** use **de** to show possession.

**la clase de Carlos**
**los libros de la profesora**

**FL.D.1.1.2**

### 40 ¿Cómo son? FL.A.2.1.2

**Escribamos/Hablemos** Complete the statements with **de, del, de la, de los,** or **de las.** Then, decide whether or not each statement is true. Correct the false statements.

**MODELO** **Los animales de los amigos son malos.**
**No, los animales de los amigos son buenos.**

1. El carro ____ profesora es fenomenal.

2. La pizza ____ Roberto es deliciosa.

3. La fiesta ____ amiga de Ana es pésima.

4. El carro ____ profesor es bueno.

5. Los videojuegos ____ amigas son divertidos.

6. El libro ____ profesor es horrible.

## 41 ¿De o del? FL.A.2.1.2

**Escribamos** Decide whether each blank should be filled with **de, del, de los, de la,** or **de las.**

**MODELO** **Los muchachos son de México.**

1. La profesora ____ María es ____ Puerto Rico.
2. A María le gustan los libros ____ aventuras.
3. Las fiestas ____ cumpleaños son fenomenales.
4. Los libros ____ profesora son interesantes.
5. Las películas ____ ciencia ficción son interesantes.
6. El correo electrónico ____ profesor es profesor@xpgs.hrw.edu.
7. Mis compañeros ____ clase son simpáticos.
8. Los libros son ____ estudiantes.

**Benchmark Focus**

FL.A.2.1.2 Restate and rephrase simple information from materials presented orally, visually, and graphically in class

Gramática 2

## 42 La preposición de FL.A.2.1.3

**Escuchemos** As you listen to each sentence, decide how the preposition **de** is being used.

**a)** to ask about ownership
**b)** to tell ownership
**c)** to ask where someone is from
**d)** to tell where someone is from
**e)** to describe something

## Comunicación

## 43 Gustos FL.A.1.1.1, FL.A.3.1.1

**Hablemos** Work with a partner. Use the drawings to describe Alicia and Rodrigo. Say what they like and dislike.

# Conexiones culturales

**FCAT Mathematics Focus** 

**MA.E.1.3.1.7.2**
Interpret and analyze data presented in a variety of forms, including box-and-whisker graphs and scatter plots

## 1 ¿De dónde son? FL.C.1.1.2, FL.C.2.1.1

Did you know that over 30 million people of Spanish-speaking origin live in the United States? What countries do they come from? Use the information in the pie chart to complete these sentences.

**Países de origen de los hispanohablantes en Estados Unidos**

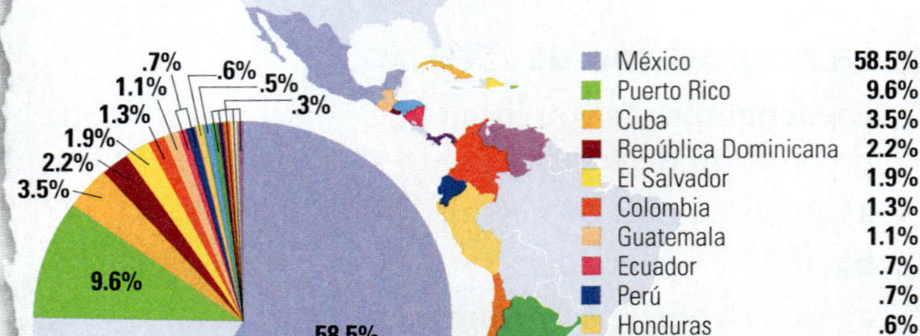


*Hispanic respondents who did not give a detailed answer in the 2000 census. Due to rounding, sum does not equal 100%

1. Most Spanish speakers in the United States are from ______.
2. The three largest Spanish-speaking groups in the United States come from ______, ______, and ______.
3. The largest group of Central American Spanish speakers comes from ______.
4. The largest group of South American Spanish speakers comes from ______.

## 2 ¿De dónde somos? FL.A.1.1.2, FL.C.1.1.1

Work in small groups. Write down what countries each student and his or her father and mother **(padre y madre),** grandparents **(abuelos),** or great-grandparents **(bisabuelos)** came from. Take turns asking and answering in Spanish. You may use a Spanish-English dictionary for additional countries.

**MODELO** —¿De dónde eres/es...?
—Soy de Estados Unidos. Mi padre es de China. Mi madre es de Estados Unidos. Mis bisabuelos son de China.

| | | | |
|---|---|---|---|
| **Alemania** | *Germany* | **Japón** | *Japan* |
| **Australia** | *Australia* | **Kenia** | *Kenya* |
| **Corea** | *Korea* | **Paquistán** | *Pakistan* |
| **China** | *China* | **Polonia** | *Poland* |
| **Francia** | *France* | **Portugal** | *Portugal* |
| **Grecia** | *Greece* | **Rusia** | *Russia* |
| **India** | *India* | **Sudáfrica** | *South Africa* |
| **Inglaterra** | *England* | **Tanzanía** | *Tanzania* |
| **Irlanda** | *Ireland* | **Turquía** | *Turkey* |
| **Italia** | *Italy* | **Vietnam** | *Vietnam* |

## Conexión Geografía

### 3 En el mapa FL.C.1.1.2, FL.C.2.1.1

Read the clues below aloud to your partner. Identify where each Spanish-speaking student lives. Use the maps at the end of the book on pages R2 through R6 to figure out what country each student is describing. Use Spanish to tell your partner where each student is from.

*Norte*

*Oeste* *Este*

*Sur*

I'm from South America. My country doesn't have a border next to an ocean. Peru and Chile are to the west and to the east is Brazil. To the south is Argentina.

Me llamo Carolina. Vivo en América del Sur. ¿De dónde soy?

I'm from a country in Central America. To the north is Mexico and to the east, Belize. To the south are El Salvador and the Pacific Ocean.

Me llamo Alberto. Vivo en Centroamérica. ¿De dónde soy?

I'm from the Spanish-speaking half of an island between Cuba and Puerto Rico. It's in the Caribbean Sea. Haiti is the other half of the island.

Me llamo Graciela. Vivo en el Caribe. ¿De dónde soy?

Me llamo Paloma. Vivo en Europa. ¿De dónde soy?

I'm from Europe. They speak Portuguese in the country to the west. To the east is the Mediterranean Sea.

Novela en video

# ¿Quién será?

## Episodio 2

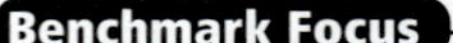
**Benchmark Focus**

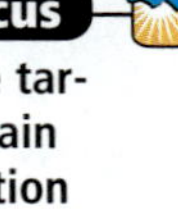

**FL.C.2.1.1** Use the target language to gain access to information that is only available through the target language or within the target culture

**ESTRATEGIA**

**Drawing conclusions** Drawing logical conclusions based on information you have gathered is an important skill. You draw conclusions about events in a story. Even if things turn out differently than you thought, that does not mean that your conclusion was illogical. Maybe you did not have all the information. As you read the **Novela** or watch the video, gather all the information you can, so that you can draw conclusions about the story and the characters as events unfold. **FL.C.2.1.1**

## En España

***Marcos meets with la profesora in her office. He reviews Nicolás's files. She describes Nicolás to him, and gives him an assignment.***

1

**La profesora** Nicolás Ortega García. Le gusta el arte. Es un chico muy simpático. Es de San Juan, Puerto Rico.

2

## En Puerto Rico

*An art professor and a gym coach compare notes about a student they each have in their class.*

3

**Profesora de arte** ¿Tienes buenos estudiantes este año?

**Entrenador** Sí, tengo unos estudiantes muy atléticos este año, y unos que son un poco perezosos.

4

**Profesora de arte** Yo tengo un estudiante que es muy trabajador. Siempre hace las tareas a tiempo. Es un poco serio y también un poco tímido. Pero creo que va a ser muy buen artista.

**Entrenador** ¿Quién es?

**Profesora de arte** Se llama Nicolás Ortega García.

5

**Entrenador** ¿Nicolás? Dime, ¿cómo es?

**Profesora de arte** Es alto y rubio.

**Entrenador** ¿Cuántos años tiene?

**Profesora de arte** Tiene quince años.

### A. Contesta

Check your understanding of the **Novela** by answering these questions.

1. Where does the meeting between **la profesora** and her assistant take place?
2. Where is the assistant going to go?
3. What does the art teacher think of the Nicolás Ortega García in her class? **FL.A.2.1.2**

**6** **Entrenador** Yo también tengo un Nicolás Ortega García en mi clase de educación física.

**Profesora de arte** ¿Ah, sí?

**Entrenador** Sí, pero este Nicolás no es trabajador. Es perezoso.

**7** **Entrenador** No, este Nicolás no es serio. Es cómico.

**8** **Profesora de arte** No es el mismo Nicolás.

**Entrenador** No, es verdad. Hay dos Nicolás de apellido Ortega García en este colegio, ¿no crees?

**Profesora de arte** Sí. Así es.

## B. Contesta

1. What does the gym teacher think of the Nicolás Ortega García in his class?
2. What conclusion do the teachers draw about Nicolás Ortega García?

FL.A.2.1.2

# Actividades

## 1 Correspondencias FL.A.2.1.2

Use the **Novela** to help you match each sentence in English to its corresponding sentence in Spanish.

1. Good morning.
2. He likes art.
3. Who is it?
4. What's he like?
5. It's true.

a. Le gusta el arte.
b. Es verdad.
c. Buenos días.
d. ¿Quién es?
e. ¿Cómo es?

## 2 ¿Qué dicen? FL.A.2.1.2

Find the following sentences in the **Novela** and rewrite the conversation on a separate piece of paper with the missing words.

| | |
|---|---|
| ENTRENADOR | ¿Nicolás? Dime, ¿ __1__ ? |
| PROFESORA DE ARTE | Es __2__ y rubio. |
| ENTRENADOR | ¿ __3__ años tiene? |
| PROFESORA DE ARTE | Tiene __4__ años. |

## 3 ¿Comprendes la Novela? FL.A.2.1.2

Check your understanding of the events in the story by answering these questions.

1. What information does **la profesora** give Marcos about Nicolás?
2. What do you think Marcos is about to do? Why do you think that?
3. Is the conclusion the two teachers draw about Nicolás logical? Is it correct?
4. What is your conclusion about Nicolás? Which class does he prefer? Why does he act so differently in the two classes?

**Próximo episodio**

*Can you predict whether Marcos might be going to Puerto Rico? Why?*

PÁGINAS 122–125

# Leamos y escribamos

**FCAT Reading Focus**
**LA.A.1.3.2**
Use a variety of strategies to draw conclusions

**ESTRATEGIA**

**para leer** Inferring is drawing conclusions based on what is only hinted at in what you read. To make inferences, connect what the author writes with your own knowledge and experience. Then draw conclusions based on a combination of the two.

**A Antes de leer** FL.C.1.1.1

Do you think that there is a relationship between someone's personality and the colors he or she likes? On a separate sheet of paper, write two personality traits in Spanish that you would associate with each of the colors blue, red, green, yellow, orange, and black.

## ¿QUÉ COLOR PREFIERES?

**Mi color favorito es el verde.**

Si te gusta el color verde, eres una persona muy inteligente, inventiva y lógica. No eres muy extrovertido(a) y no te gusta la rutina. Para ti[1], la naturaleza[2] es importante. Personas famosas: Sócrates, Sherlock Holmes y Thomas Edison.

**Mi color preferido es el ANARANJADO.**

Si te gusta el anaranjado, eres una persona simpática, graciosa y espontánea. Tienes mucha energía y te fascinan las cosas nuevas, interesantes y diferentes. Para ti, la acción y la diversión[3] son muy importantes. Personas famosas: Winston Churchill y Lucille Ball.

**¿Te gusta el color AZUL?**

Si te gusta el azul, eres una persona creativa y artística. Eres romántico(a) y sincero(a). Para ti, la armonía entre[4] las personas es muy importante. Personas famosas: Mozart, Indira Gandhi y Thomas Jefferson.

**Me fascina el color negro.**

Si te gusta el negro, eres una persona seria, elegante y algo misteriosa. También[5] eres disciplinado(a), eficiente y muy independiente. No eres muy extrovertido(a) y no te gustan las personas expresivas. Personas famosas: Cervantes y Abraham Lincoln.

**Me gusta el rojo.**

Si te gusta el color rojo, eres una persona apasionada, enérgica y activa. Eres muy extrovertido(a) y sociable. Te fascina ser[7] el centro de atención. Personas famosas: Ernest Hemingway, Elizabeth Peña y F. Scott Fitzgerald.

**A mí me encanta el color amarillo.**

Si te gusta el amarillo, eres intelectual, metódico(a) y analítico(a). Eres tímido(a) y tienes pocos[6] pero buenos amigos. Eres un líder formidable, organizado, eficiente y puntual. Para ti, la familia y las tradiciones son muy importantes. Personas famosas: George Washington y la Madre Teresa.

1. for you 2. nature 3. fun 4. harmony between 5. also 6. few 7. you love being

Visit Holt Online
go.hrw.com
KEYWORD: EXP1A CH2
Online Edition

## B Comprensión FL.C.2.1.1

Based on the reading, match the colors from Column A with the personality types from Column B. Then draw your own inferences and say what someone might like or dislike based on his or her personality.

| A | B | Te gusta(n).../No te gusta(n)... |
|---|---|---|
| 1. el azul | a. Eres tímido(a). | las personas |
| 2. el amarillo | b. Eres muy inteligente. | los videojuegos |
| 3. el anaranjado | c. Eres romántico(a). | los animales |
| 4. el rojo | d. Eres extrovertido(a). | los libros |
| 5. el verde | e. Eres serio(a). | las fiestas |
| 6. el negro | f. Eres simpático(a). | la música |

## C Después de leer FL.C.2.1.1

1. Did the personality traits you listed for the various colors in **Antes de leer** agree with the reading?
2. Does your favorite color match your own personality? Explain why or why not.

**FCAT Writing Focus** 
**LA.B.1.3.1**
Organize information before writing according to the type and purpose of writing

Interactive TUTOR

# Taller del escritor

**ESTRATEGIA**

**para escribir** Cluster diagrams can help you organize and see how your ideas go together.

### Mi personalidad FL.C.1.1.2

Write a paragraph in which you describe yourself and say what you like and don't like. Tell which "personality color" comes closest to your description of yourself.

### 1 Antes de escribir

Draw four circles. Label the first one **Yo soy...**, the second **Yo no soy...**, the third **Me gusta(n)...**, and the fourth **No me gusta(n)...** Connect other circles to these four and label the new circles with words that describe you, words that do not describe you, things you like, and things you don't like.

### 2 Escribir y revisar

Use your cluster diagram to organize the information for your paragraph. Include information from each part of the diagram. Read your sentences at least twice. Make sure the paragraph describes you well. Then check spelling and punctuation.

### 3 Publicar

Get together with three or four classmates. Each member of the group takes someone else's paragraph from the stack and reads it aloud without telling who wrote it. See if the group can guess who wrote each paragraph.

Capítulo 2
Repaso

# Prepárate para el examen

Interactive TUTOR

1 **Vocabulario 1**
- asking what someone is like
- describing people
- asking how old someone is

**pp. 48–53**

**1** Write descriptions of each person. Give each person a name and an age, then describe his or her appearance. Write some sentences as questions. **FL.A.2.1.2**

1. Leo 2. Mario 3. Paco 4. Eva 5. Ana 6. Luz 7. Pili

2 **Gramática 1**
- using **ser** with adjectives
- gender and adjective agreement
- question formation

**pp. 54–59**

**2** Complete the following conversations using adjectives, **ser,** and question words. Remember to use the correct adjective and verb forms. **FL.A.2.1.2**

1. —¿_____ es tu mejor amigo(a)?
   —_____ Paco.
2. —¿_____ día es hoy?
   —_____ sábado.
3. —¿Cómo _____ tu mejor amigo(a)?
   —Es _____. No es _____.
4. —¿_____ eres tú?
   — _____ _____.
5. —¿_____ es tu cumpleaños?
   —_____ el _____.

3 **Vocabulario 2**
- talking about what you and others like
- describing things

**pp. 62–67**

**3** Ask your partner if he or she likes the following things and why. Then ask which things he or she likes more. Switch roles. **FL.A.1.1.1**

1. 2. 3. 4.

FL.A.2.1.2

**4** Complete the paragraph, using the correct word in parentheses.

___1___ (El/La) cumpleaños ___2___ (de/del) Fernando y Maribel es ___3___ (el/la) catorce de diciembre. A ellos ___4___ (les gusta/les gustan) mucho las fiestas ___5___ (de/del) cumpleaños. A Maribel ___6___ (le gustan/les gustan) los libros ___7___ (de/de las) aventuras más que ___8___ (los/las) películas. A Fernando ___9___ (le gusta/le gustan) los videojuegos más que ___10___ (el/la) música de Los Hidalgos.

**5** Answer the following questions. FL.B.1.1.2

1. How do Latin Americans describe someone with dark or light-brown hair and skin?
2. Why are ages sixteen and eighteen important to young people in Puerto Rico?

**6** Listen as Patricia reads the e-mail message from Yoli. Then say whether the statements that follow are **cierto** or **falso**. FL.A.2.1.3

1. A Yoli no le gustan las clases porque son aburridas.
2. Los compañeros de clase son antipáticos.
3. El cumpleaños de Yoli es el 16 de agosto.
4. A Yoli le gusta la comida china.

**7** Describe Alicia and her friends, and tell what they like. FL.A.3.1.1

a.

b.

c.

d.

Visit Holt Online
**go.hrw.com**
KEYWORD: EXP1A CH2
Chapter Self-test

**4 Gramática 2**
- nouns and definite articles
- **gustar, ¿por qué?** and **porque**
- the preposition **de**

**pp. 68–73**

**5 Cultura**
- **Comparaciones** **pp. 60–61**
- **Notas culturales** **pp. 50, 59, 64**
- **Geocultura** **pp. 42–44**

**Benchmark Focus**
**FL.B.1.1.2** Recognize patterns of social behavior or social interaction in various settings

**Gramática 1**
- using **ser** with adjectives **pp. 54–55**
- gender and adjective agreement **pp. 56–57**
- question formation **pp. 58–59**

# Repaso de Gramática 1

You can use adjectives with the verb **ser** to describe people. Adjectives should agree with the nouns they describe in number and gender. Adjectives are either singular or plural, **masculine** or **feminine**.

**Carlos es alto.** **Lupe es alta.** **Carlos y Lupe son altos.**

Form questions by changing your tone of voice or using question words such as **qué, cómo, cuándo, quién, de quiénes, cuál** and **de dónde.**

**Gramática 2**
- nouns and definite articles **pp. 68–69**
- **gustar, ¿por qué?,** and **porque** **pp. 70–71**
- the preposition **de** **pp. 72–73**

# Repaso de Gramática 2

Nouns can be singular or plural, masculine or feminine.

| | Masculine | Feminine |
|---|---|---|
| SINGULAR | carro | fiesta |
| PLURAL | carros | fiestas |

Use definite articles to say *the* or with a noun used as a general category. Definite articles agree with the nouns they describe in gender and number.

| | Masculine | Feminine |
|---|---|---|
| SINGULAR | el libro | la pizza |
| PLURAL | los libros | las pizzas |

The verb **gustar** is used to talk about likes and dislikes.

**Me gusta la comida italiana. No te gustan los deportes.**

The preposition **de** is used to indicate possession, relationship, or where someone is from. It can also describe a type of thing.

**Es el libro de Juan.** **Paco es de Perú.** **Es el amigo del Sr. Tan.**

## Letra y sonido

### La sílaba tónica

- Words ending in a vowel, **-n**, or **-s** are normally stressed on the next-to-last syllable: **in-te-li-GEN-te, mo-RE-nos, bas-TAN-te.**
- Words ending in a consonant other than **-n** or **-s** are normally stressed on the last syllable: **us-TED, se-ÑOR, es-TOY.**
- All words whose pronunciation doesn't follow these rules are written with an accent mark over the vowel that is stressed: **ca-FÉ, pe-LÍ-cu-la, a-ten-CIÓN.**

### Trabalenguas

Tres tristes tigres tragaban trigo en un trigal en tres tristes trastos.

### Dictado

Escribe las oraciones de la grabación.

**Benchmark Focus**

**FL.A.2.1.3** Understand oral messages based on familiar themes and vocabulary

## Repaso de Vocabulario 1

### Describing people

| | |
|---|---|
| aburrido(a) | *boring* |
| activo(a) | *active* |
| alto(a) | *tall* |
| antipático(a) | *unfriendly* |
| atlético(a) | *athletic* |
| bajo(a) | *short* |
| bastante | *quite, pretty* (+ adjective) |
| bonito(a) | *pretty* |
| cómico(a) | *funny* |
| ¿Cómo eres? | *What are you like?* |
| ¿Cómo es...? | *What is . . . like?* |
| ¿Eres...? | *Are you . . .?* |
| Es... | *He (She, It) is . . .* |
| extrovertido(a) | *outgoing* |
| gracioso(a) | *witty* |
| guapo(a) | *good-looking* |
| intelectual | *intellectual* |
| inteligente | *intelligent* |
| moreno(a) | *dark-haired; dark-skinned* |
| muy | *very* |
| pelirrojo(a) | *redheaded* |
| perezoso(a) | *lazy* |
| romántico(a) | *romantic* |
| rubio(a) | *blond* |
| serio(a) | *serious* |
| simpático(a) | *friendly* |
| Soy... | *I'm . . .* |
| también | *also* |
| tímido(a) | *shy* |
| tonto(a) | *silly, foolish* |
| trabajador(a) | *hard-working* |
| un poco | *a little* |

### Asking and saying how old someone is

| | |
|---|---|
| ¿Cuándo es el cumpleaños de...? | *When is . . . 's birthday?* |
| ¿Cuándo es tu cumpleaños? | *When is your birthday?* |
| ¿Cuántos años tiene...? | *How old is . . .?* |
| ¿Cuántos años tienes? | *How old are you?* |
| Él (Ella) tiene ... años. | *He (She) is . . . years old.* |
| Es el... de... | *It's the . . . of . . .* |
| Tengo ... años. | *I'm . . . years old.* |

**Numbers 32–100** . . . . . . . . . . . . . . *See p. 52.*

## Repaso de Vocabulario 2

### Describing things

| | |
|---|---|
| el ajedrez | *chess* |
| los animales | *animals* |
| los carros | *cars* |
| la comida china (italiana, mexicana) | *Chinese (Italian, Mexican) food* |
| los deportes | *sports* |
| Es algo divertido(a). | *It's kind of fun.* |
| Es bastante bueno(a). | *It's quite good.* |
| Es delicioso(a). | *It's delicious.* |
| Es pésimo(a). | *It's awful.* |
| fenomenal | *awesome* |
| las fiestas | *parties* |
| formidable | *great* |
| las frutas | *fruit* |
| las hamburguesas | *hamburgers* |
| el helado | *ice cream* |
| horrible | *horrible* |
| interesante | *interesting* |
| los libros (de aventuras, de amor) | *(adventure, romance) books* |
| malo(a) | *bad* |
| la música (de...) | *music (of/by . . .)* |
| las películas (de ciencia ficción, de terror, de misterio) | *(science fiction, horror, mystery) movies* |
| la pizza | *pizza* |
| las verduras | *vegetables* |
| los videojuegos | *videogames* |

### Talking about what you and others like

| | |
|---|---|
| Me da igual. | *It's all the same to me.* |
| Me gusta(n)... mucho. | *I like . . . a lot.* |
| Me gusta(n) más... | *I like . . . more.* |
| No, no me gusta(n)... | *No, I don't like . . .* |
| ¿Te gusta(n)...? | *Do you like . . . ?* |
| ¿Te gusta(n) más... o ...? | *Do you like . . . or . . . more?* |

Repaso cumulativo

# Integración
## capítulos 1-2

**1** Listen to these statements and match them with the appropriate picture. FL.A.2.1.3

A

B

C

D

**2** You want to find an Internet pen pal. Read the ads for **Ciberamigos,** and then answer the questions that follow. FL.A.2.1.2, FL.A.3.1.1

**Andrés Vallejo**
14 años
**avall123@mailmex.hrw.com**
Soy cómico y activo. Me gustan las computadoras y las películas de terror. No me gusta la comida italiana. Me gustan las hamburguesas.

**Yasmín Herrera**
15 años
**yazz@telecom.hrw.com.es**
¿Qué tal? Soy inteligente y extrovertida. No me gusta la televisión, pero sí me gustan los libros de aventuras y las fiestas.

**Liliana Caraval**
13 años
**lilcar@correo.hrw.com.pr**
¡Hola! Soy simpática y seria. No soy aburrida. Me gustan los videojuegos y la música rock. No me gusta la pizza.

1. How old is Andrés? Yasmín? Liliana?
2. What does Liliana like to do? What doesn't she like?
3. Who likes hamburgers? adventure books? videogames?
4. Who is the most active? outgoing? funny?
5. Who would you most like as your pen pal? Why?
6. Based only on the e-mail address, can you guess where each person lives?

Visit Holt Online
go.hrw.com
KEYWORD: EXP1A CH2
Cumulative Self-test



**3** Imagine that you know the family under the umbrella in the painting. Choose words from the word box to complete the description of these people. Use each word only once. FL.A.2.1.2

**Benchmark Focus**

**FL.A.2.1.2** Restate and rephrase simple information from materials presented orally, visually, and graphically in class

| azul | bajo | sesenta | tiene | tímidas |
|---|---|---|---|---|
| llama | alto | abril | dos | animales |

Es el 12 de ___1___ y el día en San Juan es algo lluvioso *(rainy)*. El paraguas *(umbrella)* del señor es ___2___. Son las ___3___ de la tarde. El señor se ___4___ don Fernando. Tiene ___5___ años. Él es ___6___. El muchacho, Pablo, ___7___ nueve años y no es alto, es ___8___. Las muchachas son Benita y Maribel. Ellas son ___9___ y bajas. A los muchachos les gustan los ___10___.

Día lluvioso en El Viejo San Juan *(Rainy Day in Old San Juan)* by Orlando Santiago Correa courtesy of Patrick Santiago

***Día lluvioso en El Viejo San Juan,*** **de Orlando Santiago Correa**

**4** Situación

Work with a partner to role-play an interview with a famous person. One person is the interviewer, the other is the celebrity. Ask questions to get the following information. Make up any facts that you don't know for sure.

- name, age, and birthday
- where he or she is from
- physical description
- likes and dislikes (food, music, books, and so on)

Take turns playing both roles, and be prepared to present your interviews to the class. FL.A.1.1.2, FL.A.3.1.1

Capítulo 3

GeoVisión

# Geocultura
## Texas

▼ **El Valle de Texas** The Rio Grande valley is where red grapefruit is grown. It's the official state fruit of Texas.

▼ **El Parque Nacional Big Bend** The name "Big Bend" in Big Bend National Park comes from the large "U" formed by the Rio Grande.

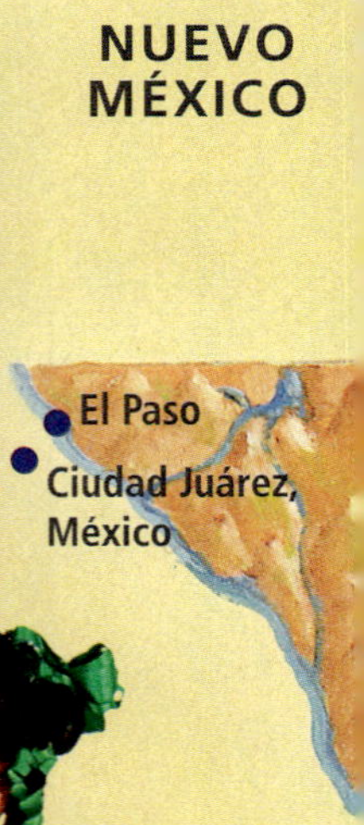

NUEVO MÉXICO

El Paso

Ciudad Juárez, México

► **El Paso** The traditional costumes of these dancers show the influence of neighboring Mexico.

### Almanac

**Population**
20,851,820

**Capital**
Austin

**Area**
266,807 square miles ($691,030 \text{ km}^2$)

**Economy**
chemicals, foodstuffs, vehicles, petroleum products, computers, livestock, fruit

### ¿Sabías que...?

**Did you know that the mockingbird is the state bird of both Florida and Texas? The mockingbird can mimic the songs of up to 30 different birds and is fiercely protective of its nest.**

▲ **Dallas** is a center of international business.

▲ **San Antonio** is a multicultural city famous for its Riverwalk.

▲ **Houston** The port of Houston handles nearly 200 million tons of cargo every year, much of it from Mexico and Venezuela.

▼ **La isla del Padre** The coast of Texas has many scenic areas such as Padre Island, which stretches for 113 miles (182 kilometers).

## ¿Qué tanto sabes?

What is the name of the Rio Grande in Mexico? Where is the state fruit of Texas grown?
FL.C.1.1.1

# A conocer Texas

## La arquitectura

▼ **La biblioteca central de San Antonio** San Antonio's Central Library was designed by Ricardo Legorreta, a famous Mexican architect.

▲ **La capilla de San Elceario** San Elceario Mission, near El Paso, is a fine example of Spanish mission architecture in Texas.

## El arte

▲ ***Tamalada*** was painted by Carmen Lomas Garza (1948–), a Mexican American artist. Many of her paintings show scenes of Mexican American daily life in South Texas.

► ***Vaquero*** is a fiberglass sculpture in front of the El Paso Museum of Art. It was created by Texas artist Luis Jiménez (1940-2006).

# La comida

**Benchmark Focus**
FL.B.1.1.3 Recognize various familiar objects and norms of the target culture

Visit Holt Online
**go.hrw.com**
KEYWORD: EXP1A CH3
Photo Tour

▲ **Barbacoa al estilo tejano** Barbecue is a typical Texas food.

◀ **Tostaditas con salsa** Chips and salsa is the official state snack of Texas.

FL.B.1.1.2, FL.B.1.1.3
## ¿Sabías que...?

**Did you know that over the course of history, Texas has been ruled by six different governments? Can you name some of them? What influences of these cultures do you see in Texas today?**

# Las celebraciones

◀ **El rodeo** Rodeo is a sport that grew out of the cowhand culture in Texas. Rodeo contestants demonstrate their skills in horseback riding and working with livestock.

▲ **El Cinco de Mayo** The celebration of **Cinco de Mayo** commemorates the Battle of Puebla in 1862, when Mexican troops defeated a French army. Mexican Americans all over Texas celebrate **Cinco de Mayo** with parades, street festivals, and cultural events.

Capítulo 3

# ¿Qué te gusta hacer?

## Objetivos

**In Part 1 you will learn to:**

- talk about what you and others like to do
- ask what a friend wants to do and answer
- use the verb **gustar** with infinitives
- place pronouns after prepositions
- use the verb **querer** with infinitives

**In Part 2 you will learn to:**

- talk about everyday activities
- ask how often someone does something and answer
- form and use regular **-ar** verbs
- use the present tense of **ir** and **jugar**
- talk about the weather

## ¿Qué ves en la foto?

- **¿Cómo son las muchachas?**
- **¿Cómo es el muchacho?**
- **¿Qué te gusta hacer los fines de semana?**

Look for the [Florida icon] next to each activity and the **Benchmark Focus** to help you achieve the goals of the **Florida Sunshine State Standards,** found on pages FL14–FL16.

Visit Holt Online
go.hrw.com
KEYWORD: EXP1A CH3
Online Edition

Amigos mirando hacia El Paso y Juárez desde las montañas Franklin

**Más vocabulario...**

| | | | |
|---|---|---|---|
| alquilar videos | *to rent videos* | ir al cine | *to go to the movies* |
| cantar | *to sing* | nadar | *to swim* |
| comer | *to eat* | navegar por Internet | *to surf the Internet* |
| escribir cartas | *to write letters* | pasar el rato solo(a) | *to spend time alone* |
| hacer la tarea | *to do homework* | ver televisión | *to watch television* |

Visit Holt Online
go.hrw.com
KEYWORD: EXP1A CH3
Vocabulario 1 practice



## Me gusta jugar...

al básquetbol

al béisbol

al fútbol americano

a juegos de mesa

al volibol

al fútbol

al tenis

### Más vocabulario...

| | |
|---|---|
| **¿Con quién?** | ***With whom?*** |
| conmigo | *with me* |
| contigo | *with you* |
| con mis amigos(as) | *with my friends* |
| con mi familia | *with my family* |

### También se puede decir...

In Florida, many Cubans and Puerto Ricans may refer to **el béisbol** as **la pelota** and say **el balompié** instead of **el fútbol.** FL.D.1.1.1

## ¡Exprésate!

| To ask what others like to do | To respond |
|---|---|
| **¿Qué te gusta hacer?**<br>*What do you like to do?* | **A mí me gusta salir con amigos.**<br>*I like to go out with friends.* |
| **¿A Juan y a Pablo les gusta ir al centro comercial?**<br>*Do Juan and Pablo like to go to the mall?* | **Sí, porque les gusta ir de compras.**<br>*Yes, because they like to go shopping.* |

Vocabulario y gramática, pp. 25–27

▶ Vocabulario adicional, Deportes y pasatiempos, p. R8

## Nota cultural

Unlike in the United States, Latin American middle and high schools typically do not sponsor organized sports teams. Students who may want to take a more active part in sports can do so by joining clubs and associations outside of school.

How is this similar to or different from your school sports program?

FL.D.2.1.1

### 1 Les gusta... FL.A.2.1.3

**Escuchemos/Leamos** Choose the most logical description based on the sentences you hear.

1. Es (extrovertida/tímida).
2. Es (muy activo/perezoso).
3. Es (trabajador/perezoso).
4. Son (atléticos/intelectuales).
5. Es (activa/seria).
6. Son (divertidas/serias).

### 2 Me gusta... FL.A.3.1.1

**Hablemos** Say whether or not you like to do the things pictured.

**MODELO** **Me gusta jugar al béisbol.**
**(No me gusta jugar al béisbol.)**

1

2

3

4

5

6

7

8

**Benchmark Focus**

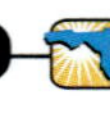

**FL.D.2.1.1** Know the similarities and differences between the patterns of behavior of the target culture related to customs and the patterns of behavior of the local culture

### 3 ¿Qué les gusta hacer? FL.A.2.1.2, FL.A.3.1.1

**Escribamos/Hablemos** Complete the following sentences.

*¿Se te olvidó?* Gustar, p. 70

1. Me gusta...
2. No me gusta...
3. A mi mejor amigo(a) le gusta...
4. A mi familia y a mí nos gusta...
5. A mis amigos les gusta...
6. A mis amigos y a mí nos gusta...
7. Me gusta salir con...
8. Me gusta ir al cine con...

## 4 Les gusta jugar... FL.A.2.1.2

**Leamos/Escribamos** Read the questions and write answers in complete sentences based on the pictures.

1. ¿A los amigos les gusta jugar al fútbol?
2. ¿A quiénes les gusta jugar al tenis?
3. A Paco le gusta jugar al béisbol, ¿verdad?
4. ¿Qué les gusta hacer a las hermanas Núñez?
5. ¿A quién le gusta jugar al béisbol?
6. ¿A Lili y a Ana les gusta jugar al volibol?
7. ¿Qué les gusta hacer a José y a Raúl?
8. ¿Qué te gusta hacer?

## 5 Actividades FL.A.1.1.1, FL.A.3.1.1

**Hablemos** Take turns with a partner telling whether or not you like the activities in **Vocabulario 1**. Take notes. Then report to the class one activity that your partner likes and one that he or she does not like.

**MODELO** **—Susana, ¿te gusta escuchar música?**
**—Sí, me gusta mucho escuchar música.**
**—A Susana le gusta mucho escuchar música.**

## ¡Exprésate!

| To ask what a friend wants to do | To respond |
|---|---|
| **¿Qué quieres hacer hoy?**<br>*What do you want to do today?* | **Ni idea.**<br>*I have no idea.* |
| **¿Quieres ir al cine conmigo?**<br>*Do you want to go to the movies with me?* | **Está bien.**<br>*All right.*<br>**No, gracias. No quiero ir al cine hoy.**<br>*No, thanks. I don't want to go to the movies today.* |

Interactive TUTOR

Vocabulario y gramática, pp. 25–27 Online workbooks

**Benchmark Focus**

**FL.A.2.1.2** Restate and rephrase simple information from materials presented orally, visually, and graphically in class

### 6 Una conversación FL.A.2.1.2

**Leamos/Escribamos** Complete the following conversation.

**montar jugar gustar ir alquilar hacer**

GERARDO ¿Quieres ___1___ al centro comercial?
MARÍA No, no quiero. ¿Quieres ___2___ videos?
GERARDO No, no quiero. Quiero ___3___ ejercicio.
MARÍA ¿Quieres ___4___ al básquetbol?
GERARDO No, no me gusta el básquetbol. ¿Quieres ___5___ en bicicleta?
MARÍA Está bien. Buena idea.

### 7 ¿Qué quieres hacer? FL.A.2.1.2

**Escribamos** Write a question for each picture asking if someone likes the activity. Then write a second question asking if that person wants to do the activity with you. Write their answer.

**MODELO** **—¿Te gusta jugar al fútbol? ¿Quieres jugar al fútbol conmigo?**
**—Sí, quiero jugar al fútbol.**

1

2

3

4

5

## 8 Entre amigos FL.A.2.1.2

**Leamos/Escribamos** Rewrite the conversation on a separate sheet of paper, putting the sentences in the correct order.

Yo también quiero salir. ¿Quieres comer en el centro comercial?

No me gusta ir al cine. ¿Quieres hacer ejercicio?

Hola, Raúl. ¿Quieres ir al cine conmigo?

¡Está bien!

Sí, me gusta pasear.

No, no quiero alquilar videos. Quiero salir.

¡Hacer ejercicio! No, gracias. ¿Quieres alquilar unos videos?

Sí, quiero comer. ¿Y quieres pasear?

## 9 Entrevista FL.A.1.2.2, FL.A.3.1.1

**Hablemos/Escribamos** Interview three classmates to learn what they want to do with their friends this Saturday. Report your findings to the class.

**MODELO** —**Roberto, ¿qué quieres hacer este *(this)* sábado?**
—**Quiero ir al centro comercial.**
—**¿Con quién?**
—**Con Javier.**

## Objetivos

- Using **gustar** with infinitives
- Using pronouns after prepositions
- Using **querer** with infinitives

GramaVisión

## Gustar with infinitives

Interactive TUTOR

**1** An **infinitive** tells the meaning of the verb without naming any subject or tense. There are three kinds of **infinitives** in Spanish: those ending in **-ar**, those ending in **-er**, and those ending in **-ir**.

| **-ar** infinitives | **-er** infinitives | **-ir** infinitives |
|---|---|---|
| **cantar** *to sing* | **comer** *to eat* | **escribir** *to write* |

**2** Like **nouns**, **infinitives** can be used after a verb like **gustar** to say what you and others like *to do.*

Me **gusta la música.**
*I like music.*

Me **gusta cantar**.
*I like to sing.*

**3** Always use **gusta** (not **gustan**) with **infinitives**.

Me **gustan los deportes.**
*I like sports.*

Me **gusta jugar** al tenis.
*I like to play tennis.*

Vocabulario y gramática, pp. 28–30
Actividades, pp. 21–23
Online workbooks

### En inglés

**In English, infinitives** do not have any special endings, but they almost always have the word **to** in front of them.

**to play** **to run** **to write**

**In Spanish, infinitives** always end in **-ar**, **-er**, or **-ir**.

**cantar** **comer** **escribir**

In the following sentences, find the infinitive.

**¿Qué te gusta hacer?**
*What do you like to do?*

**FL.D.1.1.2**

### 10 Gustos FL.A.2.1.2

**Hablemos/Escribamos** Based on the things Carlos and his friends like, what activities do you think they like to do?

*¿Se te olvidó?* Gustar, p. 70

**MODELO** **A Roberto le gustan las películas.**
**Le gusta ir al cine.**

| | | |
|---|---|---|
| ir al cine | ver televisión | escuchar música |
| jugar al tenis | comer comida italiana | jugar a los videojuegos |

1. A mis amigos les gustan los deportes.
2. Me gusta la televisión.
3. A Paco le gusta la música.
4. A mi familia y a mí nos gusta la pizza.
5. Te gustan las películas.
6. A mis amigos y a mí nos gustan los videojuegos.

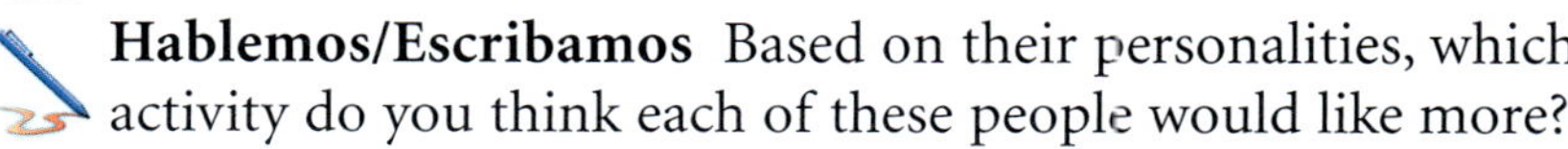

Visit Holt Online
**go.hrw.com**
KEYWORD: EXP1A CH3
Gramática 1 practice

## 11 Más gustos FL.A.2.1.2

**Hablemos/Escribamos** Based on their personalities, which activity do you think each of these people would like more?

**MODELO** **Raúl es muy activo. (patinar/ver televisión)**
**Le gusta más patinar.**

1. Diego es perezoso. (hacer ejercicio/ver televisión)
2. Mis amigos son atléticos. (nadar y correr/alquilar videos)
3. Elena es trabajadora. (hacer la tarea/escuchar música)
4. Mario es tímido. (ir a fiestas/pasar el rato solo)
5. Mis amigas son románticas. (leer novelas de amor/leer novelas de terror)
6. Soy muy seria. (hacer la tarea/ir a fiestas)
7. Eres muy extrovertido. (salir con amigos/pasar el rato solo)

## 12 Preguntas y respuestas FL.A.2.1.2

**Leamos/Escribamos** Read the answers that Andrés gave during his interview. Then write the missing questions.

*¿Se te olvidó?* Question words, p. 58

**MODELO** **¿______? Me gusta leer revistas.**
**¿Qué te gusta hacer?**

1. ¿______? Soy de Chile.
2. ¿______? Tengo trece años.
3. ¿______? Soy extrovertido y gracioso.
4. ¿______? Me gusta ir al cine y hacer deportes.
5. ¿______? Me gusta ir al cine con mis amigos.

# Comunicación

HOLT SoundBooth ONLINE RECORDING

## 13 Preferencias FL.A.1.1.1, FL.A.3.1.1

**Hablemos** Ask whether your partner likes to do each of the following things. Switch roles. Then tell the class what you found out.

**Benchmark Focus**

**FL.A.3.1.1** Provide simple information in spoken form

# Pronouns after prepositions

**1** Pronouns can stand for the same noun yet still have different forms, depending on how they're being used in the sentence.

*Both stand for Javier*

**Yo** soy Javier. Tengo quince años y **me** gusta dibujar.

**2** You already know subject pronouns and the pronouns used with **gustar.** After prepositions such as **a** *(to)*, **de** *(of, from, about)*, **con** *(with)* and **en** *(in, on, at)*, **pronouns** have a different form.

| Subject | With **gustar** | After **preposition** |
|---|---|---|
| yo | me | **mí** |
| tú | te | **ti** |
| usted<br>él<br>ella | le | **usted**<br>**él**<br>**ella** |
| nosotros(as) | nos | **nosotros(as)** |
| vosotros(as) | os | **vosotros(as)** |
| ustedes<br>ellos<br>ellas | les | **ustedes**<br>**ellos**<br>**ellas** |

**3** The pronouns **mí** and **ti** combine with **con** to make the special forms **conmigo** and **contigo**.

**4** With **gustar,** the phrase formed by **a** and a pronoun can be added to a sentence to clarify or emphasize who likes something.

*adds emphasis* — **¿A ti** te gusta dibujar?

*adds emphasis* — **A mí** no me gusta. *clarifies* — **A ella** le gusta.

Vocabulario y gramática, pp. 28–30
Actividades, pp. 21–23

## ¿Te acuerdas?

**Pronouns** take the place of nouns. They can stand for the person talking, the person being talked to, or someone or something that has already been named.

—¿Cuántos años tienes **tú**?
—¿**Yo**? Tengo once años.

Juan es mi amigo.
**Él** tiene trece años.

## 14 María y los amigos FL.A.2.1.2

**Leamos/Escribamos** On a separate piece of paper, rewrite María's letter choosing the correct prepositions and pronouns.

**MODELO** **Mi amigo Felipe es muy inteligente. A mí me gusta hacer la tarea con él.**

Soy extrovertida. **1.** (A mí/A ellos) me gusta pasar el rato con amigos. Mis amigos son muy divertidos. Me gusta mucho salir **2.** (a ellos/con ellos). Mi amigo Jorge es muy activo. **3.** (A él/A mí) no le gusta ver televisión. Mi amiga Laura es muy tímida. **4.** (A ti/A ella) no le gusta ir a fiestas. **5.** (A ellas/A nosotras) nos gusta ir al cine. Juan y Carlos son mis amigos también. **6.** (A ellos/A mí) les gusta jugar a los videojuegos. Y **7.** (a nosotras/a ti), ¿qué te gusta hacer?

## 15 ¿Te gusta...? FL.A.2.1.2

**Hablemos** Look at the photos and say whether you like to do these activities. Also say what friends you do each activity with.

**MODELO** **Me gusta ir de compras con mi amiga Mari.**

1.

2.

3.

4.

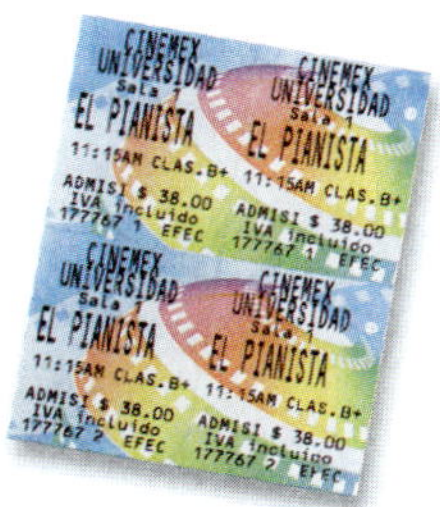


5.

## 16 ¿Qué les gusta? FL.A.2.1.2

**Leamos/Escribamos** Read the description of each person and tell what he or she likes or doesn't like to do.

**MODELO** **Juan es muy activo. Le gustan los deportes. A él le gusta jugar al béisbol. (A él no le gusta jugar a los videojuegos.)**

1. Sara es muy intelectual. Le gustan los juegos de mesa.
2. Pablo es muy gracioso. Le gustan las fiestas.
3. Lupe es muy extrovertida. No le gusta pasar el rato sola.
4. Alonso es muy serio y tímido. Le gusta pasar el rato solo.
5. A Cristina le gustan las películas. No le gusta salir. Es tímida.
6. Carlos es extrovertido. Le gusta salir con amigos y ver películas.
7. Alicia es muy atlética. Le gusta pasar el rato con amigos.
8. Miguel es muy inteligente y trabajador. Le gustan los libros.

**Benchmark Focus**

**FL.A.2.1.2** Restate and rephrase simple information from materials presented orally, visually, and graphically in class

## 17 Los sábados y los domingos FL.A.1.1.1

**Escribamos/Hablemos** First, write a list of three things you like to do on weekends. Then discuss what you like to do with a small group of classmates and find out what you have in common.

**MODELO** **—Me gusta jugar al fútbol. No me gusta jugar a los videojuegos.**

**—A mí me gusta jugar a los videojuegos. También me gusta escuchar música.**

**—Me gustan las fiestas. ¿Les gusta ir a fiestas?**

**—Sí, nos gusta ir a fiestas.**

## Present tense of querer with infinitives

**1** To say what you or others *want* or *want to do,* use a form of the verb **querer**. The form you use depends on the subject.

| | | | |
|---|---|---|---|
| yo | qu**ie**ro | nosotros(as) | queremos |
| tú | qu**ie**res | vosotros(as) | queréis |
| Ud., él, ella | qu**ie**re | Uds., ellos, ellas | qu**ie**ren |

**2** Just as with **gustar**, you can use a **noun** or an **infinitive** after a form of **querer** to say what you and others want or want to do.

**Quiero fruta.**
*I want some fruit.*

**Quiero comer.**
*I want to eat.*

¿Qué **quieres hacer**?
*What do you want to do?*

**Quiero escuchar** música.
*I want to listen to music.*

Vocabulario y gramática, pp. 28–30
Actividades, pp. 21–23

In Latin America many teens must introduce their friends to their parents before they go out with them. When inviting a friend out, teens are often expected to tell the friend's parents where they are going and when they will return. While this custom may be changing, it is still common in many places.

Is this similar to or different from your parents' rules?
**FL.B.1.1.2, FL.D.2.1.1**

### 18 ¿Quién quiere? FL.A.2.1.2

**Leamos/Escribamos** Choose the correct form of **querer** to complete the sentences.

1. Marta y yo (quieren/queremos) comer.
2. Yo (quieres/quiero) salir.
3. Pablo (queremos/quiere) hacer ejercicio.
4. ¿Tú (quieres/quieren) ir al centro comercial?
5. Marco y Felipe (quieren/quiero) navegar por Internet.
6. ¿Ustedes (quieren/queremos) jugar al béisbol?
7. ¿(Quiero/Quiere) usted pasar el rato solo?
8. Juan y Sandra (quieres/quieren) pasear.
9. Tú eres trabajador. (Quieres/Queremos) hacer la tarea.

### 19 Queremos ir FL.A.2.1.2

**Leamos/Escribamos** Complete the conversation with the correct forms of **querer.**

—Hola, Carla. ¿Qué __1__ hacer hoy?
—Ni idea. ¿Qué __2__ hacer tú?
—Bueno, mi familia y yo __3__ ir al cine.
—¿Y tu amigo Paco no __4__ ir al cine con ustedes?
—No, Paco y unos amigos __5__ ir de compras y __6__ alquilar videos. ¿Y tú? ¿__7__ ir al cine con nosotros?
—Sí, gracias. Yo __8__ ver una película con ustedes.

## 20 ¿Qué quieren hacer? FL.A.2.1.2

**Leamos/Escribamos** Say what Juanita and her friends want to do this weekend based on what they like. Use the expressions in the box.

**MODELO** **A mis amigos les gusta la televisión. Quieren ver televisión.**

| ver televisión | jugar al ajedrez | comer pizza | leer |
|---|---|---|---|
| comer comida china | alquilar videos | jugar al tenis | escuchar música |

1. A mis amigos les gusta la comida china.
2. A ti te gustan los deportes.
3. A mi mejor amigo le gusta la comida italiana.
4. A mí me gustan las novelas.
5. A nosotros nos gustan los juegos de mesa.
6. A mi amiga le gustan las películas.

## 21 Vamos al centro comercial FL.A.2.1.3

**Escuchemos** Listen to the conversation between Juan and Sofía and decide which photos show what they both want to do.

A

B

C

D

E

# Comunicación

## 22 Actividades FL.A.1.2.2, FL.A.3.1.1

**Hablemos/Escribamos** Imagine that your class is going to have a party. Using the activities listed on pages 94–95, ask three classmates what they want to do at the party. Then write their answers in two lists showing what they want to do and what they don't want to do. Be prepared to share your answers with the class.

**MODELO** **—¿Qué quieres hacer en la fiesta?**
**—Quiero escuchar música pero no quiero nadar.**

**Benchmark Focus**
**FL.A.1.2.2** Exchange information necessary to plan events or activities

# Cultura

VideoCultura

**Benchmark Focus**

**FL.D.2.1.1** Know the similarities and differences between the patterns of behavior of the target culture and the local culture

## Comparaciones

Amigos en el Paseo del Río, San Antonio, Texas

### ¿Qué les gusta hacer a ti y a tus amigos los fines de semana? FL.B.1.1.2, FL.D.2.1.1

It is common in Spain and Latin America for young people to get together and do things in large groups. Often they will meet up with their friends in a plaza, park, or café to hang out and eat before going shopping or dancing. Many young people also spend a fair amount of time with their families, especially on Sundays, when it is typical to eat a large family meal together. What do you like to do on the weekends, and how is it different from what these people do?

### Celina
**El Paso, Texas**

Celina talks about what she and her friends like to do on a nice day. What do you and your friends like to do when the weather is good?

***Dime, ¿adónde vas cuando hace buen tiempo?***

Me gusta salir al parque.

***¿Vas sola o vas con amigos?***

Me gusta ir con amigos.

***¿Qué les gusta hacer en el parque?***

Nos gusta ir a correr o jugar fútbol; si no, a platicar.

***¿Qué no te gusta hacer?***

No me gusta pasar el tiempo sola.

***¿Por qué no te gusta?***

Porque me gusta estar acompañada... con familia y amigos.

Visit Holt Online
go.hrw.com
KEYWORD: EXP1A CH3
Online Edition

Cultura

## Rita
**Lima, Perú**

Rita talks about her favorite indoor and outdoor activities. Do you always go outside on a nice day? If not, why not?

***Dime, ¿adónde vas cuando hace buen tiempo?***

Cuando hace buen tiempo voy a la playa, al cine o a acampar.

***¿Vas sola o vas con amigos?***

Voy con amigos.

***¿Qué les gusta hacer en esos lugares?***

Cuando vamos a la playa, nos gusta nadar y jugar; cuando vamos al cine, ver películas; y cuando vamos a acampar, hacer fogatas.

***¿Qué cosas no te gusta hacer?***

No me gusta ir a clase de matemáticas.

***¿Por qué no te gusta?***

No me gusta porque es aburrido y a veces no entiendo.

### Para comprender FL.C.2.1.1

1. ¿A quién le gusta hacer ejercicio?
2. ¿A Rita qué le gusta hacer cuando hace buen tiempo?
3. ¿Qué les gusta hacer a Rita y a sus amigos cuando van a la playa?
4. ¿Quién juega al fútbol con sus amigos?
5. A Celina no le gusta pasar el rato sola. ¿Con quién quiere pasar el rato?

### Para pensar y hablar FL.B.1.1.2, FL.D.2.1.1

When asked where they go when the weather is good, both Celina and Rita say that they like to spend time outdoors with friends. Do you like to be outside or would you rather do something indoors? Would you rather do things in a group or with just one friend? Do you like spending time alone?

## Comunidad en la Florida

### La Pequeña Habana FL.D.2.2.2, FL.E.1.2.1

Little Havana is a community within Miami that reflects the heritage of its Hispanic immigrants. Neighbors spend time discussing politics or playing dominos in Máximo Gómez Park. They can also find a variety of Hispanic foods and products, such as **guarapo de caña** *(sugar cane juice)*, exotic fruits, or herbal remedies. Research a Hispanic event, service, or product in your community.

- Where and how did it start?
- Who participates in the event?
- What products and foods are available?

**Un café cubano, La Pequeña Habana, Miami**

**Objetivos**
- Talking about everyday activities
- Saying how often you do things

# Vocabulario en acción 2

ExpresaVisión

## Los fines de semana me gusta...

estudiar

descansar

trabajar

practicar deportes

tocar el piano

hablar por teléfono

bailar

a la piscina

a la iglesia

al gimnasio

a la playa

**Más vocabulario...**

| | |
|---|---|
| **al baile** | *to the dance* |
| **a la casa de...** | *to . . . 's house* |
| **al colegio** | *to school* |
| **al ensayo** | *to rehearsal* |
| **al entrenamiento** | *to (sports) practice* |
| **al gimnasio** | *to the gym* |
| **a la reunión** | *to the meeting* |
| **al trabajo** | *to work* |

**También se puede decir...**

In Florida, you may hear Mexicans say **la alberca** instead of **la piscina.** Argentineans may call it **la pileta.**

## ¡Exprésate!

| To ask about everyday activities | To respond |
|---|---|
| **¿Qué haces los fines de semana?** *What do you do on weekends?* | **Los sábados, cuando hace buen tiempo, voy con mis amigos al parque.** *On Saturdays, when the weather is nice, I go with my friends to the park.* |
| **¿Qué hace Luis cuando hace mal tiempo?** *What does Luis do when the weather is bad?* | **Le gusta escuchar música. No va a ninguna parte.** *He likes to listen to music. He doesn't go anywhere.* |

Interactive TUTOR

Vocabulario adicional — Deportes y pasatiempos, p. R8

## Nota cultural

In Spanish-speaking countries, the person who invites friends to go out with him or her will usually pay for everything. If the person inviting wants everyone to pay their own way, then he or she invites **a la americana.** Young people may also pool all their money and split the expenses evenly.

Who pays when you invite friends to go out?

FL.D.2.1.1

Un restaurante de Austin, Texas

**Benchmark Focus**

**FL.D.2.1.1** Know the similarities and differences between the patterns of behavior of the target culture related to customs and the patterns of behavior of the local culture

## 23 El fin de semana FL.A.2.1.2

**Leamos** Alberto's cousin Margarita is coming for a weekend visit and has asked Alberto what they will be doing. Complete his letter to her by choosing the correct words.

| descansar | deportes | baile | gimnasio |
|---|---|---|---|
| iglesia | playa | tiempo | casa |

Hola Margarita,

El sábado, si hace buen __1__ quiero ir a la __2__ a nadar. Si hace mal tiempo, quiero ir al __3__ a hacer ejercicio y practicar unos __4__ . El domingo quiero ir a la __5__ a las 12:00 y de las 4:00–6:00 de la tarde quiero __6__. El domingo a las 8:00 P.M. hay un __7__ en la __8__ de Juan con música muy buena.

Chao, Alberto

## 24 ¿Qué planes tienes? FL.A.2.1.2

**Hablemos/Escribamos** Using the pictures, complete these sentences.

**MODELO** **Hoy quiero ir...**

Hoy quiero ir a la piscina.

1. Me gusta...

2. Quiero...

3. Mañana voy...

4. Cuando hace buen tiempo, quiero ir...

5. ¿Te gusta ir...?

6. Cuando hace mal tiempo, ¿te gusta...?

## 25 Una conversación telefónica FL.A.2.1.2

**Leamos/Escribamos** Jaime and Gabi are deciding what to do this afternoon. Rewrite their conversation in the correct order on a separate piece of paper.

¡Sí! Me gusta nadar.

Jaime, ¿qué haces hoy? Hace muy buen tiempo.

Hola, Jaime. ¿Qué tal?

Hasta pronto.

Voy a la piscina. ¿Quieres ir conmigo?

Hola, Gabi. Estoy bien.

Está bien. Nos vemos en la piscina.

## 26 ¿Adónde vas los fines de semana? FL.A.2.1.2, FL.A.3.1.1

**Hablemos** Take turns with a partner asking and answering whether you go to these places on weekends. Why or why not?

**MODELO** **al parque**
**—¿Vas al parque los fines de semana?**
**—Sí, voy al parque porque quiero correr.**
**(No, no voy al parque porque quiero descansar.)**

1. a la playa
2. al gimnasio
3. al ensayo
4. al colegio
5. al trabajo
6. al cine
7. a la casa de...
8. al entrenamiento
9. a la piscina

Vocabulario 2

## ¡Exprésate!

| To ask how often | To respond |
|---|---|
| **¿Con qué frecuencia vas a la playa?** *How often do you go to the beach?* | **Casi nunca. No me gusta nadar.** *Hardly ever. I don't like to swim.* |
| **¿Te gusta salir con amigos?** *Do you like to go out with friends?* | **Sí. Después de clases, casi siempre vamos al parque. A veces vamos también a la piscina.** *Yes. After classes, we almost always go to the park. Sometimes we also go to the swimming pool.* |

Interactive TUTOR

Vocabulario y gramática, pp. 31–33 Online workbooks

**Más vocabulario...**

| | |
|---|---|
| **los...** | *on . . .* |
| **lunes** | *Mondays* |
| **martes** | *Tuesdays* |
| **miércoles** | *Wednesdays* |
| **jueves** | *Thursdays* |
| **viernes** | *Fridays* |
| **sábados** | *Saturdays* |
| **domingos** | *Sundays* |
| **fines de semana** | *weekends* |
| **todos los días** | *every day* |
| **siempre** | *always* |
| **nunca** | *never* |

### 27 Un programa de radio FL.A.2.1.3

**Escuchemos** Complete the sentences based on what you hear.

1. La estudiante se llama (Susana Parra/Alicia Hernández).
2. Los jueves le gusta (ir a la casa de amigas/trabajar).
3. Susana va al cine (los sábados y domingos/los lunes).
4. Los sábados Susana va a (nadar/patinar).
5. Los domingos, a Susana le gusta (leer/tocar el piano).
6. A Susana (le gusta/no le gusta) bailar.

### 28 A mí me gusta... FL.A.2.1.2

**Escribamos** Write about what you like to do. Replace the underlined activities with ones that apply to you.

**MODELO** **Me gusta alquilar videos todos los fines de semana.**
**Me gusta bailar todos los fines de semana.**

1. Todos los días me gusta ir al parque.
2. Nunca quiero trabajar los viernes.
3. Los fines de semana después de hacer la tarea me gusta salir con amigos.
4. Los domingos quiero descansar.
5. No me gusta salir los martes.
6. Los sábados me gusta ir al centro comercial con mis amigos Pablo y Maribel.
7. A veces, los viernes me gusta ir al cine.
8. Nunca quiero tocar el piano los fines de semana.
9. Los viernes después de clases me gusta hablar por teléfono con Ricardo.
10. Después de clases siempre quiero estudiar.

## 29 Mi agenda FL.A.2.1.4

**Escribamos** Imagine that this is your schedule. Write at least five sentences telling what you like to do and when.

### AGENDA

| | | |
|---|---|---|
| lunes: | practicar el piano | (9:30) |
| martes: | trabajar en el cine | (4:00) |
| miércoles: | bailar con amigos en el gimnasio | (7:30) |
| jueves: | ir a la reunión del Club de español | (8:15) |
| viernes: | practicar el piano | (9:00) |
| sábado: | trabajar en el cine | (3:00) |
| domingo: | ir a la iglesia con mis abuelos | (2:00) |

**Benchmark Focus** 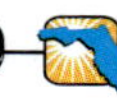

**FL.A.2.1.4** Listen and read in the target language and respond through role-playing, drawing, or singing

## Comunicación

## 30 ¿Con qué frecuencia vas...? FL.A.1.1.1

**Hablemos** Work with a partner. Take turns asking how often you each go the following places. Include information about why you go there and what you do there in your answers.

**MODELO** **—¿Con qué frecuencia vas a la playa?**
**—Nunca voy a la playa. No me gusta nadar.**

1.

2.

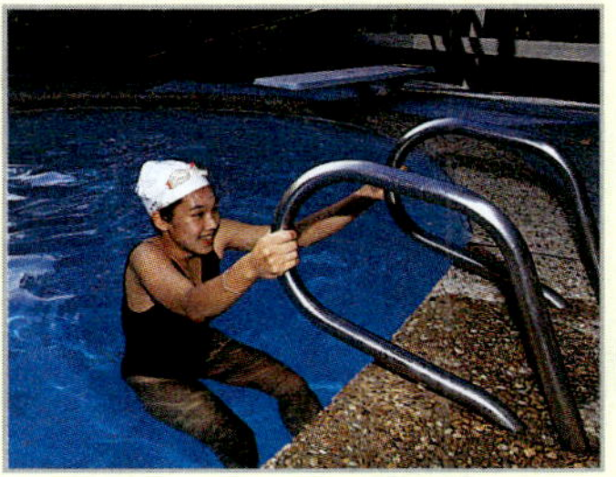
3.

4.

5.

6.

Vocabulario 2

**Objetivos**
- Regular **-ar** verbs
- **Ir** and **jugar**
- Weather expressions

GramaVisión

## Present tense of regular -ar verbs

**1** Every verb has a **stem** followed by an ending. The stem tells the verb's meaning. An **infinitive ending** doesn't name a subject.

| *verb stems* | | | *infinitive endings* |
|---|---|---|---|
| | **habl** | **-ar** | |
| | **com** | **-er** | |
| | **escrib** | **-ir** | |

**2** To give the verb a subject you **conjugate** it. To conjugate a regular **-ar** verb in the present tense, drop the **-ar** ending of the infinitive and add these **endings**. Each ending goes with a particular subject.

| | | | |
|---|---|---|---|
| yo | cant**o** | nosotros(as) | cant**amos** |
| tú | cant**as** | vosotros(as) | cant**áis** |
| Ud., él, ella | cant**a** | Uds., ellos, ellas | cant**an** |

—¿Te gusta **cantar**?
*Do you like to sing?*

—Sí, **canto** todos los días.
*Yes, I sing every day.*

—¿**Nadan** ustedes mucho?
*Do you swim a lot?*

—No, casi nunca **nadamos**.
*No, we hardly ever swim.*

**3** Since usually the ending of the verb tells the subject, the **subject pronoun** is normally left out. Use **subject pronouns** to add emphasis, or when it wouldn't otherwise be clear who the subject is.

—¿Patinan **ustedes** mucho?
*Do you skate a lot?*

—**Ellos** patinan. **Yo** nunca patino.
*They skate. I never skate.*

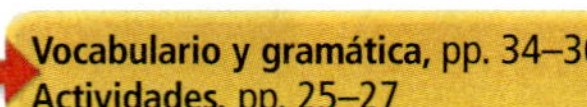

**Vocabulario y gramática**, pp. 34–36
**Actividades**, pp. 25–27

### En inglés

**In English**, most verbs in the present tense have only two forms. The **subject pronouns** are not left out.

| | |
|---|---|
| **I** sing | **we** sing |
| **you** sing | **you** sing |
| **he, she, it** sing**s** | **they** sing |

**In Spanish**, the verb ending tells you who the subject is.

When do both Spanish and English verb forms change their endings?

FL.D.1.1.2

### 31 En el parque FL.A.2.1.2

**Leamos** Complete the sentences that Marcos wrote.

1. Los sábados yo (paso/pasas) el rato con amigos.
2. Y tú, ¿cómo (pasas/pasa) el rato con amigos?
3. Ana (patinan/patina) en el parque con José.
4. Javi y yo (nadan/nadamos) en la piscina.
5. Maribel y Florencia (patinan/patinas) con nosotros.

Unos amigos montan en bicicleta en un parque en Texas.

Visit Holt Online
**go.hrw.com**
KEYWORD: EXP1A CH3
Gramática 2 practice

## 32 Los fines de semana FL.A.2.1.2

**Hablemos/Escribamos** Based on the pictures, say what each person does on weekends.

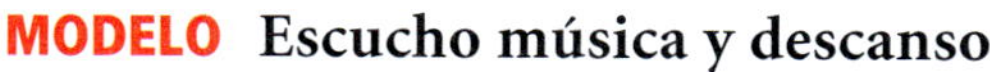

**MODELO** **Escucho música y descanso.**

yo

1. nosotros

2. Juan

3. ellas

4. mi mejor amiga

## 33 ¿Cuándo? FL.A.2.1.2

**Escribamos** Write sentences using words from each column to tell what you and your friends do or don't do at certain times during the week.

**MODELO** **Mi mejor amigo (no) descansa los domingos.**

| | | |
|---|---|---|
| mi mejor amigo(a) | practicar deportes | los lunes |
| mis amigos | pasear | los jueves |
| ustedes *(to your classmates)* | tocar el piano | los viernes |
| mis amigos y yo | escuchar música | los sábados |
| yo | estudiar | los fines de semana |
| tú *(to a classmate)* | trabajar | todos los días |
| | navegar por Internet | después de clases |
| | hablar por teléfono | |

## 34 ¿Con qué frecuencia vas al cine? FL.A.1.1.2, FL.D.1.1.2

**Hablemos** Take turns with a partner talking about how often each of you does the activities in **Vocabulario 2.**

**MODELO** **—¿Con qué frecuencia practicas deportes?**
**—Practico deportes todos los fines de semana. ¿Y tú?**
**—¿Con qué frecuencia tocas el piano?**
**—Casi nunca toco el piano. ¿Y tú?**

**Benchmark Focus**

**FL.D.1.1.2** Use simple vocabulary and short phrases in the target language

Gramática 2

## Present tense of ir and jugar

**1** The **-ar** verbs you have learned are called regular verbs because their conjugations all follow a predictable pattern. Some verbs such as **ir** *(to go)* are called irregular, because they do not follow a clear pattern.

| | | | |
|---|---|---|---|
| yo | **voy** | nosotros(as) | **vamos** |
| tú | **vas** | vosotros(as) | **vais** |
| Ud., él, ella | **va** | Uds., ellos, ellas | **van** |

—¿Adónde **vas** los sábados? —**Voy** a la piscina.

**2** The verb **jugar** *(to play a sport or game)* has regular **-ar** endings, but the vowel **u** in the stem changes to **ue** in all but the **nosotros** and **vosotros** forms.

| | | | |
|---|---|---|---|
| yo | j**ue**go | nosotros(as) | jugamos |
| tú | j**ue**gas | vosotros(as) | jugáis |
| Ud., él, ella | j**ue**ga | Uds., ellos, ellas | j**ue**gan |

—¿**Juegan** ustedes en el colegio? —No, no **jugamos** mucho.

**3** The preposition **a** is used after **ir** to mean *to.* Use **¿adónde?** to ask *where to.* **A** is also used after **jugar** with a sport. When **a** is followed by **el**, the two words combine to form the contraction **al**.

—¿**Adónde van** los domingos? **—Vamos al** gimnasio. **Jugamos al** básquetbol.

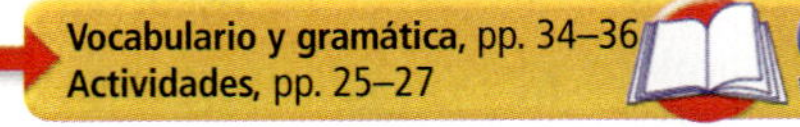

When **de** is followed by **el**, the two words combine to form the contraction **del**.

**el teléfono del profesor**
**el libro del estudiante**

### 35 Sitios FL.A.2.1.2

**Escribamos** Write complete sentences using the correct word or words from the box. Then say whether or not you like the activity and how often you do it. *¿Se te olvidó?* Definite articles, p. 68

**MODELO** **Me gusta ir a la playa los sábados.**
**(No me gusta ir a la playa. Nunca voy a la playa.)**

| al | a los | a las | a la |
|---|---|---|---|

1. ir ____ piscina
2. jugar ____ béisbol
3. ir ____ cine
4. ir ____ iglesia
5. ir ____ entrenamiento
6. ir ____ casas de mis amigos
7. jugar ____ ajedrez
8. jugar ____ videojuegos

## 36 Pasatiempos FL.A.2.1.2

**Escribamos/Hablemos** Based on the pictures, say where these people go in their free time and what game they play there. Use the verbs **ir** and **jugar**.

**MODELO** **Sonia va al parque. Juega al tenis.**

Sonia

1. yo

2. tú

3. mi amigo(a)

4. nosotros

5. ellos

## 37 ¿Con qué frecuencia? FL.A.2.1.2

**Leamos/Escribamos** How often do you, your family, and your friends go to the following places on weekends?

**MODELO** **yo/playa**
**Casi nunca voy a la playa los fines de semana.**

| siempre | a veces | (casi) nunca |
|---|---|---|

1. mi familia y yo/cine
2. mis amigos/piscina
3. mi mejor amigo(a)/iglesia
4. mis amigos y yo/fiestas
5. yo/clase de español
6. los profesores/colegio

**Benchmark Focus**

FL.A.2.1.2 Restate and rephrase simple information from materials presented orally, visually, and graphically in class

**Nota cultural**

Florida is a popular destination for Spanish speakers coming to the United States on vacation. They go to the state's many well-known theme parks. They also visit beautiful beaches and fine restaurants on both the Atlantic and Gulf coasts.

How does what you like to do on vacation compare to what Spanish-speaking tourists in Florida often do? FL.D.2.1.1

## 38 ¿Qué haces? FL.A.1.1.2, FL.A.2.1.2

**Escribamos/Hablemos** Complete the questions with the correct form of the verb. Then use them to interview a partner.

1. ¿A qué deportes ____ (jugar) tú?
2. ¿Quién ____ (jugar) contigo?
3. ¿Tu mejor amigo y tú ____ (jugar) al ajedrez?
4. ¿Adónde ____ (ir) tú los sábados?
5. ¿Tu mejor amigo(a) y tú ____ (ir) de compras?
6. ¿Adónde ____ (ir) ustedes de compras?

## Weather expressions

### Nota cultural

Florida, the Sunshine State, is often sunny, but the temperatures can vary considerably depending on latitude and distance from the ocean. In the winter, the Panhandle and central Florida often experience temperatures in the 30s. Cold weather is particularly hard on the orange groves that need to be kept from freezing.

How do temperatures vary from summer to winter in your area? How does very cold weather affect your community?

FL.C.1.1.2

**1** Many expressions for the weather begin with the word **hace**, a form of the verb **hacer**.

| | |
|---|---|
| ¿Qué tiempo **hace**? | *What's the weather like?* |
| **Hace** buen/mal tiempo. | *The weather is nice/bad.* |
| **Hace** fresco. | *It's cool.* |

Hace calor.

Hace frío.

Hace sol.

Hace viento.

**2** The verb **llover** means *to rain* and the verb **nevar** means *to snow*. Use **llueve** to say *it rains* and **nieva** to say *it snows*.

Llueve.

Nieva.

—¿Adónde vas cuando **llueve**?
—Cuando **llueve**, no voy a ninguna parte.
—¿Qué haces cuando **nieva**?
—Cuando **nieva**, juego con los amigos.

Vocabulario y gramática, pp. 34–36
Actividades, pp. 25–27

### 39 ¿Qué tiempo hace? FL.A.2.1.2

**Leamos/Hablemos** Look at the photo. For each set of expressions, choose the one that better describes the photo.

1. **a.** Nieva. **b.** No nieva.
2. **a.** Hace calor. **b.** Hace fresco.
3. **a.** Llueve. **b.** No llueve.
4. **a.** Hace mal tiempo. **b.** Nieva.
5. **a.** Hace sol. **b.** No hace sol.
6. **a.** Hace buen tiempo. **b.** No hace buen tiempo.

## 40 ¿Cuál? FL.A.2.1.3

**Escuchemos** Listen to six descriptions of the weather. Decide if each one describes picture A, picture B, or neither picture.

A

B

## 41 ¿Qué haces? FL.A.2.1.2

**Hablemos** Say what the weather is usually like in these places during the given months.

**MODELO** **en Texas en abril**
**En Texas en abril hace muy buen tiempo.**

1. en Alaska en enero
2. en Florida en julio
3. en Arizona en mayo
4. en Seattle en febrero
5. en California en mayo
6. en Illinois en diciembre
7. en Texas en agosto
8. en Louisiana en noviembre
9. en Nueva York en abril
10. en Colorado en octubre

**Benchmark Focus**

**FL.A.2.1.2** Restate and rephrase simple information from materials presented orally, visually, and graphically in class

## Comunicación

HOLT SoundBooth ONLINE RECORDING

## 42 ¿Adónde van? FL.A.1.2.2, FL.A.3.1.1

**Hablemos** With a partner, use the drawings to say what Miguel and Alicia do on the weekends. Give as many details as you can.

a.

b.

c.

# Conexiones culturales

**FCAT Mathematics Focus** 
**MA.E.1.3.1.7.3**
Construct, interpret, and explain displays of data, such as tables and graphs

## 1 Los instrumentos FL.C.1.1.1

People in Spanish-speaking countries play many different musical instruments. Some of these instruments are described here. Look at the photographs as you read the descriptions.

1. La **flauta** azteca es un instrumento muy bonito. Es parecida a *(it looks like)* la flauta dulce *(recorder).*
2. El **charango** es popular en los Andes. Es parecido a la guitarra.
3. El **güiro** es un instrumento percusivo *(percussion instrument)*. ¡Pero es muy diferente al tambor *(drum)*!
4. En muchos países el **arco** se usa *(is used)* para tocar el violín. En Centroamérica el **arco** es un instrumento musical.

la flauta

el charango

el güiro

el arco

## 2 ¿Cómo lo harías *(would you do it)*? FL.B.1.1.3

People have always made musical instruments from materials that are readily available. For example, people have made pottery flutes from clay and percussion instruments from gourds. If you had to make your own musical instrument from materials you have around your classroom, what materials would you use? What instrument would you make? Share your answers with a partner.

**Músicos en la región de Asturias, España, tocando gaitas *(bagpipes)***

## Conexión Ciencias naturales

**El huracán** Hurricanes are violent tropical thunderstorms with extremely heavy rains and high wind speeds of up to 186 mph. Hurricanes usually occur in the Atlantic Ocean, the Gulf of Mexico, and the Caribbean Sea between June 1 and November 30. During the worst hurricanes, streets become rivers, whole cities lose their electricity, and people must sometimes leave their homes and go to higher ground. The word hurricane comes from *hurakán,* the storm god of the Caribbean Taino Indians. FL.D.1.1.1

**Sección de puente destrozada después del huracán Ivan cerca de Pensacola, Florida**

### 3 ¿Dónde está el huracán? FL.C.1.1.2

Use the information in the table to track Hurricane Charley on graph paper. Draw a line connecting the points of the hurricane's path. Put a dot on the map where the latitudes and longitudes listed cross on your graph. Find out which countries it hit. See the example of Hurricane Frances drawn on the map.

**Hurricane Charley**

| Day | Latitude | Longitude |
|---|---|---|
| 1 | 17° N | 77° W |
| 2 | 19° N | 81° W |
| 3 | 26° N | 82.5° W |
| 4 | 32° N | 80° W |

### 4 ¿Cómo se llama? FL.C.1.1.1

Each tropical storm of the season is given a name. The names are chosen ahead of time, and they alternate between female and male names in alphabetical order. For example, the first storm would be Alex, the next Brenda, and so on. Write Spanish names for the first ten tropical storms of the season. Would a hurricane named Rosa be early or late in the hurricane season?

**Daño ocasionado por el huracán Charley en Port Charlotte, Florida**

Conexiones culturales

Novela en video

# ¿Quién será?

## Episodio 3

**Benchmark Focus**

**FL.A.2.1.2** Restate and rephrase simple information from materials presented orally, visually, and graphically in class

**ESTRATEGIA**

**Understanding subtext** People do not always say what they mean. When someone asks, "How are you?," the **text** of your answer (what you say) might be, "I'm just fine." But your **subtext** (what you really mean) may be, "I feel awful, but I don't want to talk about it." As you read the **Novela** or watch the video, listen for Sra. Corona's and Sofía's subtexts. **FL.C.2.1.1**

## En México

**En casa de Sofía** ***Sofía and her mother talk about Sofía's interests.***

**1**

**Sra. Corona** Sofía, a ti te gusta mucho la música, ¿verdad, hija?

**Sofía** Claro, mamá.

**Sra. Corona** Y te gusta bailar, ¿no es así, hija?

**Sofía** Claro, mamá, me gusta mucho bailar.

**2**

**Sra. Corona** Vas a tomar clases de ballet los lunes y los viernes en la Academia de Danza Clásica.

**Sofía** Pero, mamá, ¡no quiero tomar clases de ballet!

**Sra. Corona** El ballet es música y es baile, hija, las dos cosas que más te gustan en todo el mundo.

**3**

**Sofía** ¿Viernes? Mamá, ¡hoy es viernes!

**Sra. Corona** Sí, hija. Hoy vas a la clase de ballet a las cinco en punto. ¡Adiós, cariño!

**4**

**Sofía** ¿Ballet? ¿Yo? ¿Bailarina? ¡Nunca!

Visit Holt Online
**go.hrw.com**
KEYWORD: EXP1A CH3
Online Edition 

5

**Roque** Hace muy buen tiempo hoy. ¿Por qué no vamos a la piscina a nadar?

**Celeste** No, no quiero nadar. Quiero ir al cine. Hay una película formidable en el Cineplex que quiero ver.

**Sofía** Pero, no quiero ir a la piscina. Y tampoco quiero ir al cine.

6

**Roque** ¡Pero, Sofía! ¡Es viernes! ¡Siempre hacemos algo juntos los viernes!

**Sofía** Ya lo sé. Pero hoy no quiero hacer nada hoy. Voy a casa a estudiar.

**Celeste** ¿Qué te pasa, Sofía? ¡Tú casi nunca estudias los viernes por la noche!

7

**Celeste** Hay algo muy raro aquí.

**Roque** Sí, muy raro. Es viernes y ¡no quiere salir con sus amigos!

## A. Contesta

Check your understanding of the **Novela** by answering these questions.

1. What does Sofía's mother want her to do after school on Friday? How does Sofía feel about it?
2. Who are Celeste and Roque?
3. What do Celeste and Roque want to do after school on Friday?
4. Why do they find Sofía's behavior odd? **FL.A.2.1.2**

## En España

*La profesora calls Marcos in Puerto Rico to tell him where he's going next.*

8

**La profesora** Tengo otra candidata. Es una chica de Texas. Después de Puerto Rico, vas a Texas. A El Paso, Texas.

Cuatro candidatos... Sólo nos faltan seis.

## En Puerto Rico

*Marcos arrives in Puerto Rico.*

9

### B. Contesta

1. Where is **la profesora's** assistant supposed to go after this episode?
2. How many **candidatos** have been located? How many are yet to be found? FL.A.2.1.2

# Actividades

## 1 ¿Cierto o falso? FL.A.2.1.2

Based on the story, tell whether each statement is **cierto** or **falso**.

1. A Sofía le gusta la música.
2. Sofía quiere tomar clases de ballet.
3. Celeste quiere nadar.
4. Sofía no quiere nadar, y tampoco quiere ver una película.
5. El asistente habla por teléfono celular.

## 2 ¿Listos? FL.A.2.1.2

Complete the following sentences with words from the story that la señora Corona says to Sofía.

| viernes | cinco | tomar | colegio |
|---|---|---|---|

Hija, vas a __1__ clases de ballet los lunes y __2__. Hoy vas a la clase de ballet a las __3__ en punto.

## 3 ¿Comprendes la Novela? FL.A.2.1.2

In **Estrategia** for this episode, you learned that people sometimes say one thing but mean another. What would you say about the following people? Do they mean what they say, or are they saying one thing but meaning another?

1. Sofía's mother, when she talks to Sofía about ballet lessons
2. Sofía, when she answers her mother
3. Sofía, when she is talking to her friends about Friday afternoon

**Próximo episodio**
***Can you predict what Marcos will find out about Nicolás?***
PÁGINAS 168–171

Novela en video

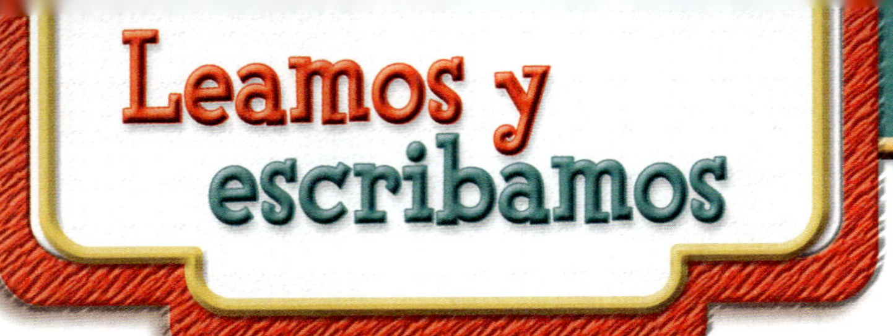


**FCAT Reading Focus** 

**LA.A.2.3.1**
Determine the main idea or essential message in a text and identify relevant details and facts

**ESTRATEGIA**

**para leer** Predicting what will happen in a story is a helpful strategy. You will be able to read a story more quickly and easily if you focus your attention on what you expect to happen.

## A Antes de leer FL.C.2.1.1

The following story is a myth from the southwestern United States. Read the title and the first paragraph of the text and use what you know about myths to predict what will happen in this one.

# Los cuatro elementos

Existen cuatro elementos en el mundo[1]: el agua[2], el fuego[3], el viento y el honor. Son amigos inseparables. Son inteligentes, divertidos y graciosos. Siempre pasan el rato juntos y les gusta hablar por horas y horas. Pero un día, el día de la creación, los amigos saben que tendrán que separarse[4]. En una reunión, en la casa del agua, se dicen adiós[5].

**El agua dice así:** —Vamos a lugares diferentes. En el futuro, si me quieren encontrar[6], búsquenme[7] en los lugares[8] donde llueve. ¡Nado con los océanos!

**El fuego dice así:** —Ustedes son mis mejores amigos. En el futuro, si me quieren encontrar, búsquenme en los lugares donde hace calor. ¡Paseo con el sol!

**El viento dice así:** —¡Amigos! No quiero separarme de ustedes. En el futuro, si me quieren encontrar, búsquenme en el aire, en los lugares donde hace mal tiempo. ¡Corro con los tornados y los huracanes!

**El honor, el último[9] en hablar, dice así:** —Compañeros. ¡Escuchen con atención! En el futuro, si me pierden[10] a mí, ¡no me busquen! ¡No me van a encontrar!

**1** world **2** water **3** fire **4** will have to part **5** say goodbye
**6** if you want to find me **7** look for me **8** places **9** the last one
**10** if you lose me

Visit Holt Online
go.hrw.com
KEYWORD: EXP1A CH3
Online Edition



**B Comprensión** FL.C.2.1.1

Complete the following sentences.

1. Los cuatro elementos en el mundo son...
2. Los elementos son amigos inseparables y les gusta...
3. El día de la creación, los amigos se dicen adiós en...
4. En el futuro el agua, el fuego y el viento se pueden encontrar en los lugares donde...
5. El último elemento dice: "...no me busquen" porque...

**C Después de leer** FL.B.1.1.2, FL.D.2.1.1

What is the moral of the story? What does this myth tell you about the cultural values of people in the Southwest? Do the people in your community share similar values?

**FCAT Writing Focus** 

**LA.B.1.3.3**

Produce final documents that have been edited for correct spelling and punctuation

Interactive TUTOR

## Taller del escritor

**ESTRATEGIA** FL.A.1.2.2, FL.A.2.1.2

**para escribir** When describing things that happen in a certain order, or scheduling activities, it helps first to arrange your ideas. You can use lists, timelines, or charts.

| viernes | sábado | febrero domingo |
|---|---|---|
| | | |

### Horario de actividades

Imagine a friend is coming to visit for a week and you need to plan activities. Write your friend a letter:

- explain your plans
- describe a few of them
- ask what he or she wants to do.

### 1 Antes de escribir

Divide a sheet of paper into seven columns, one for each day of the week. Jot down what you want to do with your friend for each day.

### 2 Escribir y revisar

Using your chart, write a letter to your friend. When and where will the activities take place? Tell your friend why you like these activities. Ask what he or she likes or wants to do. Read your draft at least two times, comparing it with your chart. Did you explain your plans? Are some activities described? Did you ask what your friend likes to do? Check spelling and punctuation.

### 3 Publicar

Post your letter along with those of your classmates on the bulletin board. Which letter sounds like the best week?

Capítulo 3
Repaso

# Prepárate para el examen

Interactive TUTOR

**1 Vocabulario 1**
- talking about what you and others like to do
- talking about what a friend wants to do

**pp. 94–99**

**1** Using the pictures below to guide you, say what you like or what you want to do. **FL.A.1.1.1**

A

B

C

D

E

F

**2 Gramática 1**
- **gustar** with infinitives
- pronouns after prepositions
- **querer** with infinitives

**pp. 100–105**

**2** Choose the correct word in parentheses. **FL.A.2.1.2**

Yo soy Diana. Mi mejor amiga se llama Maribel. Ella es muy atlética y le __1__ (gustan/gusta) jugar al volibol y al básquetbol. A mí __2__ (me/te) gusta más navegar por Internet o ver películas. Me __3__ (gusta/gustan) las películas románticas. A Maribel __4__ (le/me) gustan las películas románticas también. Me gusta ir al cine con __5__ (ella/usted). Pero a nuestras amigas Ana y Rita no __6__ (les/le) gusta ir al cine. Ellas __7__ (quiero/quieren) alquilar videos o ver televisión.

**3 Vocabulario 2**
- talking about everyday activities
- saying how often you do things

**pp. 108–113**

**3** Complete the sentences with logical answers. **FL.A.2.1.2**

1. Me gustan los deportes. Los sábados me gusta ____.
2. Soy introvertida. Después de clases me gusta ____.
3. Me gusta la música; me gusta ____ el piano.
4. ¿Te gusta ____ por teléfono con amigos todos los días?
5. Cuando hace mal tiempo nos gusta ____.
6. Me gustan las películas. No me gusta ir al cine. Me gusta ____ videos.

**4** Complete the paragraph with the correct verb forms. FL.A.2.1.2

Yo __1__ (jugar) al fútbol con amigos los domingos. Me gusta jugar cuando __2__ (hacer) sol. Después, ellos y yo __3__ (pasear) y __4__ (ir) a la piscina. A mí me gusta el cine, y los sábados __5__ (ir) al cine con mi amigo Leo. A él le gusta la música. Él __6__ (tocar) el piano y __7__ (cantar). Cuando __8__ (hacer) mal tiempo, mis amigos y yo __9__ (jugar) al básquetbol en el gimnasio. Yo __10__ (descansar) los lunes y los martes __11__ (ir) al entrenamiento de fútbol.

**5** Answer the following questions. FL.B.1.1.2, FL.D.2.1.1

1. How can Latin American students participate in sports?
2. When do parents expect to meet their teenager's friends? Is this true for you and your parents too?
3. Who pays the bill when friends go out **a la americana?**

**6** Marta is interviewing students for an article for her journalism class. Listen to her interview with Paco. List the days of the week and write what Paco does during the week. FL.A.2.1.3

**7** Use the drawings to describe what is happening or to tell a story. FL.A.3.1.1

a.

b.

c.

d.

Visit Holt Online
**go.hrw.com**
KEYWORD: EXP1A CH3
Chapter Self-test

**4 Gramática 2**
- regular **-ar** verbs
- **ir** and **jugar**
- weather expressions

**pp. 114–119**

**5 Cultura**
- **Comparaciones** **pp. 106–107**
- **Notas culturales** **pp. 96, 104, 110**
- **Geocultura** **pp. 88–91**

**Benchmark Focus**
**FL.B.1.1.2** Recognize patterns of social behavior or social interaction in various settings

**Gramática 1**
- **gustar** with infinitives **pp. 100–101**
- pronouns after prepositions **pp. 102–103**
- **querer** with infinitives **pp. 104–105**

# Repaso de Gramática 1

Use **gustar** with an **infinitive** to say what you and others like to do.

A mí **me gusta hablar** por teléfono contigo.
Use these pronouns after the prepositions **a, de, en,** and **con.**

| | | |
|---|---|---|
| mí | (conmigo) | nosotros(as) |
| ti | (contigo) | vosotros(as) |
| usted, él, ella | | ustedes, ellos, ellas |

Use **querer** with an **infinitive** to say what you and others want to do.

| | |
|---|---|
| qu**ie**ro | queremos |
| qu**ie**res | queréis |
| qu**ie**re | qu**ie**ren |

**Queremos ir** a la playa.

**Gramática 2**
- regular **-ar** verbs **pp. 114–115**
- **ir** and **jugar** **pp. 116–117**
- weather expressions **pp. 118–119**

# Repaso de Gramática 2

| hablar | | ir | | jugar | |
|---|---|---|---|---|---|
| habl**o** | habl**amos** | **voy** | **vamos** | **jue**go | jugamos |
| habl**as** | habl**áis** | **vas** | **vais** | **jue**gas | jugáis |
| habl**a** | habl**an** | **va** | **van** | **jue**ga | **jue**gan |

Use the verb **hacer** to talk about the weather.

¿Qué tiempo **hace**?
**Hace** buen/mal tiempo.
**Hace** frío. **Hace** calor.
**Hace** sol. **Hace** fresco.
**Hace** viento.

Use the words **llueve** and **nieva** to say *it rains* and *it snows.*

**Benchmark Focus** 
**FL.A.2.1.3 Understand oral messages that are based on familiar themes and vocabulary**

## Letra y sonido h j g

### Las letras h, j, g

- The letter **h** in Spanish is silent. It is not pronounced: **h**ola, **h**ora, **h**ablar, **h**acer **h**oy.
- The letter **j** is pronounced much like the English *h,* though sometimes it sounds harsher, a little like the *h* in *hue.* The letter **g** before the vowels **e** and **i** **(ge, gi)** has the same pronunciation: **j**ugar, **j**ueves, **J**osé, **g**eografía, **g**imnasio, e**j**ercicio, pelirro**j**a, inteli**g**ente, a**g**itar.

### Trabalenguas

El hipopótamo Hipo
está con hipo.
Me trajo Tajo tres trajes,
tres trajes me trajo Tajo.

### Dictado FL.A.2.1.3

Escribe las oraciones de la grabación.

# Repaso de Vocabulario 1

### Talking about what you and others like to do

| | |
|---|---|
| A ellos(as) les gusta... | *They like to . . .* |
| A mis amigos y a mí nos gusta... | *My friends and I like to . . .* |
| alquilar videos | *to rent videos* |
| el básquetbol | *basketball* |
| el béisbol | *baseball* |
| cantar | *to sing* |
| el centro comercial | *mall* |
| el cine | *movie theater* |
| comer | *to eat* |
| correr | *to run* |
| dibujar | *to draw* |
| escribir cartas | *to write letters* |
| escuchar música | *to listen to music* |
| el fútbol | *soccer* |
| el fútbol americano | *football* |
| hacer ejercicio | *to exercise* |
| hacer la tarea | *to do homework* |
| ir al cine | *to go to the movies* |
| ir de compras | *to go shopping* |
| los juegos de mesa | *board games* |
| jugar (ue) | *to play* |
| leer revistas y novelas | *to read magazines and novels* |
| Me gusta... | *I like to . . .* |
| montar en bicicleta | *to ride a bike* |
| nadar | *to swim* |
| navegar por Internet | *to surf the Internet* |
| pasar el rato solo(a) | *to spend time alone* |
| pasear | *to go for a walk* |
| patinar | *to skate* |
| ¿Qué te gusta hacer? | *What do you like to do?* |
| salir con amigos | *to go out with friends* |
| el tenis | *tennis* |
| ver televisión | *to watch television* |
| el volibol | *volleyball* |

### Talking about what you want to do

| | |
|---|---|
| con mis amigos(as) | *with my friends* |
| con mi familia | *with my family* |
| conmigo | *with me* |
| contigo | *with you* |
| Está bien. | *All right.* |
| Ni idea. | *I have no idea.* |
| ¿Qué quieres hacer hoy? | *What do you want to do today?* |
| querer (ie) | *to want* |
| Quiero ir... | *I want to go . . .* |

# Repaso de Vocabulario 2

### Talking about everyday activities

| | |
|---|---|
| ¿Adónde vas...? | *Where do you go . . .?* |
| bailar | *to dance* |
| el baile | *dance* |
| la casa de... | *. . . 's house* |
| el colegio | *school* |
| ...cuando hace buen tiempo... | *. . . when the weather is good . . .* |
| ...cuando hace mal tiempo... | *. . . when the weather is bad . . .* |
| descansar | *to rest* |
| el ensayo | *rehearsal* |
| el entrenamiento | *practice* |
| estudiar | *to study* |
| el gimnasio | *gym* |
| hablar por teléfono | *to talk on the phone* |
| la iglesia | *church* |
| Le gusta... | *He/She likes . . .* |
| No va a ninguna parte. | *He/She doesn't go anywhere.* |
| el parque | *park* |
| la piscina | *pool* |
| la playa | *beach* |
| practicar deportes | *to play sports* |
| ¿Qué hace...? | *What does . . . do?* |
| ¿Qué haces...? | *What do you do . . .?* |
| la reunión | *meeting* |
| tocar el piano | *to play the piano* |
| trabajar | *to work* |
| el trabajo | *work* |

### Saying how often

| | |
|---|---|
| a veces | *sometimes* |
| (casi) nunca | *(almost) never* |
| (casi) siempre | *(almost) always* |
| ¿Con qué frecuencia vas...? | *How often do you go . . .?* |
| después de clases | *after class* |
| todos los días | *every day* |

**To say on which day something happens** *See p. 112.*

Repaso cumulativo

# Integración

## capítulos 1-3

**1** Listen to each conversation and match it with the appropriate picture. FL.A.2.1.3

A

B

C

D

**2** Marisol wants to find an e-mail pen pal. Read her e-mail and then answer the questions. FL.A.2.1.2, FL.A.3.1.1

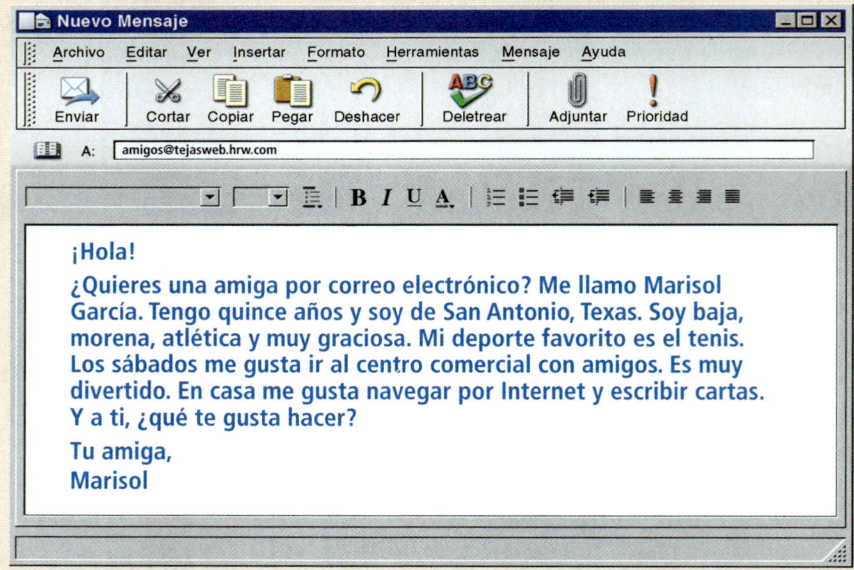


¡Hola!

¿Quieres una amiga por correo electrónico? Me llamo Marisol García. Tengo quince años y soy de San Antonio, Texas. Soy baja, morena, atlética y muy graciosa. Mi deporte favorito es el tenis. Los sábados me gusta ir al centro comercial con amigos. Es muy divertido. En casa me gusta navegar por Internet y escribir cartas. Y a ti, ¿qué te gusta hacer?

Tu amiga,
Marisol

1. ¿Cuántos años tiene Marisol y de dónde es?
2. ¿Cómo es Marisol?
3. ¿Qué deporte le gusta más?
4. ¿Cuándo le gusta salir con amigos? ¿Adónde van?
5. ¿Qué le gusta hacer a Marisol cuando pasa el rato sola?

Visit Holt Online
**go.hrw.com**
KEYWORD: EXP1A CH3
Cumulative Self-test

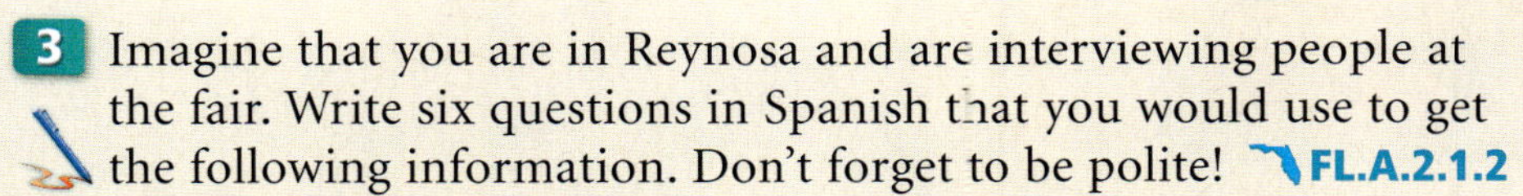

**3** Imagine that you are in Reynosa and are interviewing people at the fair. Write six questions in Spanish that you would use to get the following information. Don't forget to be polite! **FL.A.2.1.2**

1. the name of an adult
2. the age of a child
3. a child's birthday
4. where an adult is from
5. a description of a child
6. if a child likes Mexican food

*La feria en Reynosa,* **de Carmen Lomas Garza (n. 1948)**



**4** With a partner, take turns role-playing interviewer and one of the people in the painting above. Ask questions similar to those you wrote for Activity 3. Switch roles. Be prepared to tell the class what you learned about your partner. **FL.A.2.1.4, FL.A.3.1.1**

**Benchmark Focus**
**FL.A.3.1.1** Provide simple information in spoken form

**5**

**Situación**

The Student Council is planning an outdoor teen camp for the summer and wants to have activities ready for whatever weather condition might occur. In groups of three, discuss in Spanish what you like to do in the following weather conditions. **FL.A.1.2.2, FL.A.3.1.1**

- hot and sunny
- rainy
- cool and windy
- cold

List everyone's ideas on the board. With the rest of the class, decide on two activities to plan for each weather condition.

Capítulo 4

Video/DVD

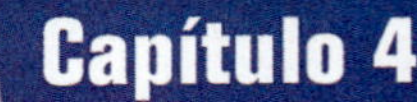

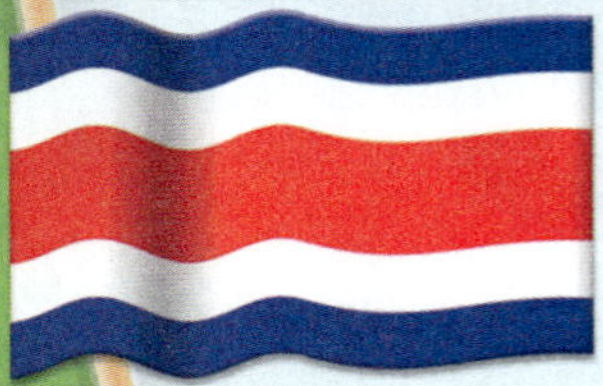

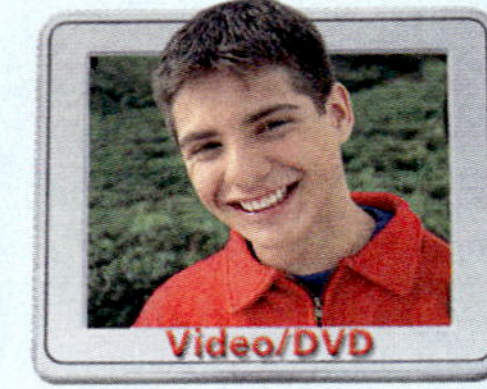

GeoVisión

# Geocultura
# Costa Rica

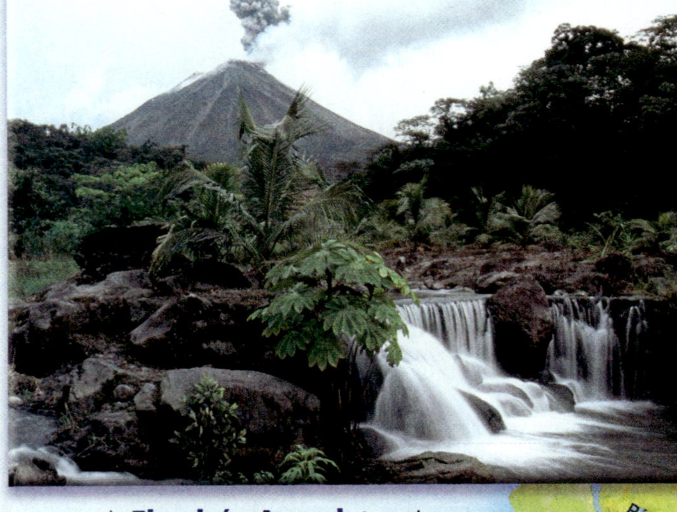

▲ **El volcán Arenal** Arenal Volcano, dormant until 1968, is the most active volcano in Costa Rica. It sits near Lake Arenal.

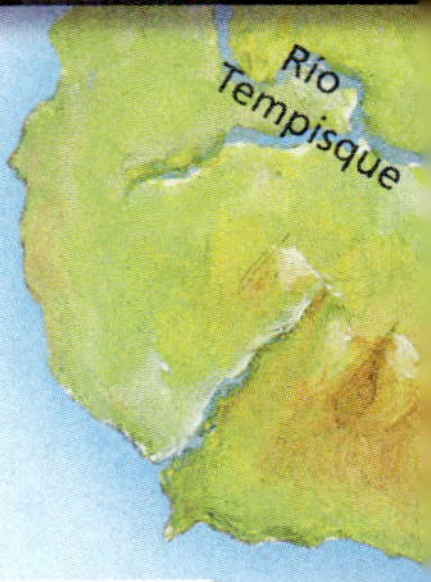

Río Tempisque

▼ **San José** The capital of Costa Rica lies in the Central Valley. The region around **San José** is the most populated in the country. There are several volcanoes nearby.

◀ **Ticos** People in Costa Rica call themselves **ticos**. Here you can see a young **tico** and **tica** wearing traditional dance costumes.

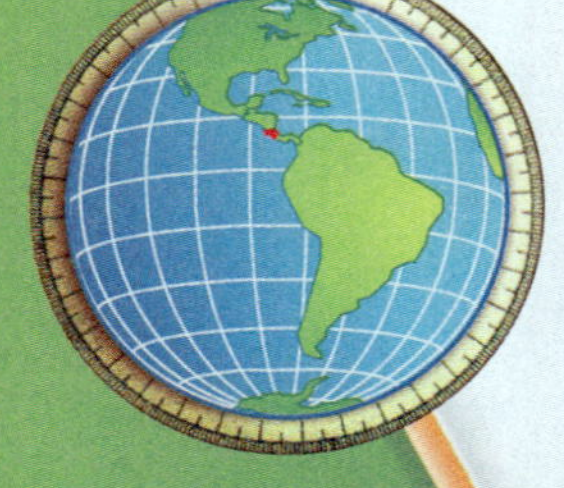

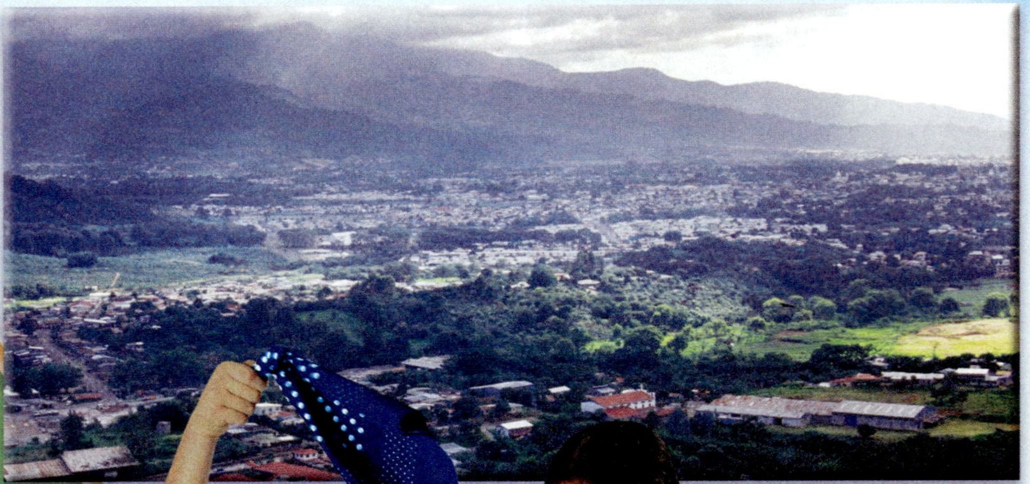

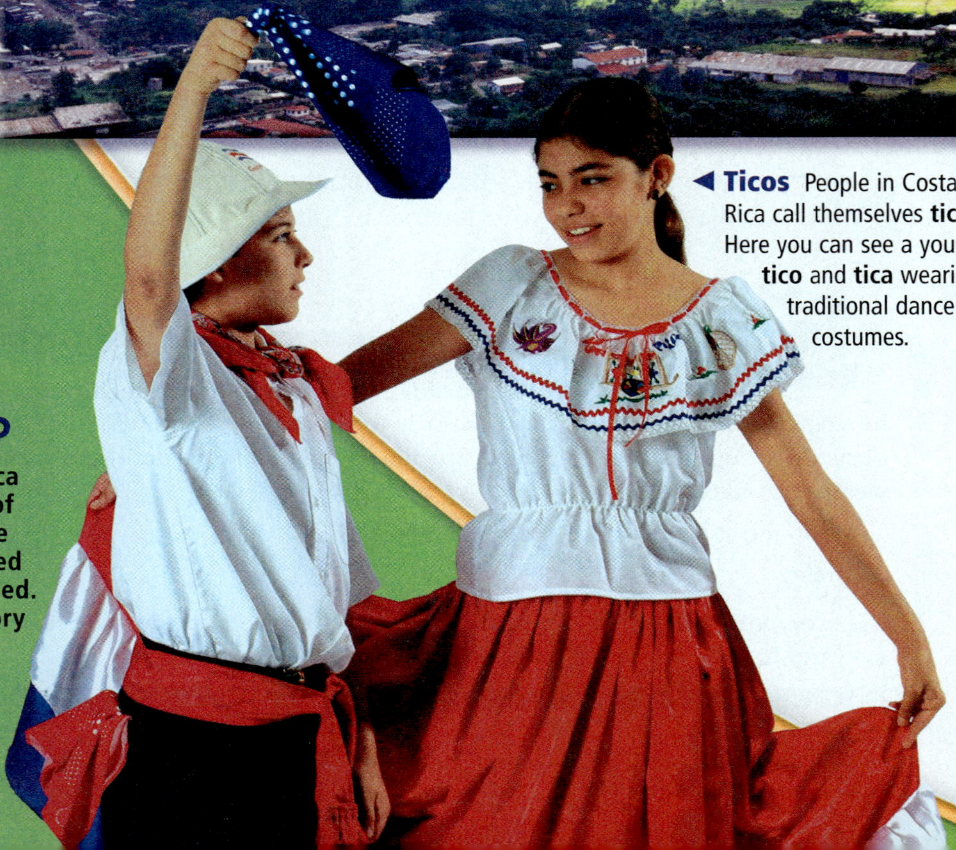

## Almanac

**Population**
3.8 million

**Capital** San José

**Government**
democratic republic

**Official Language**
Spanish

**Currency** colón

**Internet code**
www.[ ].cr

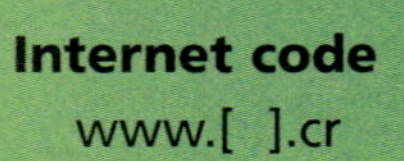

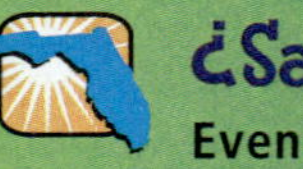

### ¿Sabías que...?

**Even though Costa Rica is only one-third the size of Florida in area, it has more bird species than the United States and Canada combined. Many tropical and migratory birds are found in both Florida and Costa Rica.**

NICARAGUA
Río San Juan
Río San Carlos
Volcán Arenal
Laguna Arenal
Reserva Biológica del Bosque Nuboso de Monteverde
Río Chirripó
Parque Nacional Tortuguero
MAR CARIBE
Volcán Poás
Volcán Barva
Volcán Irazú
Río Reventazón
Limón
Alajuela
Valle Central
Puntarenas
GOLFO DE NICOYA
Escazú
SAN JOSÉ
Cartago
Cordillera Central
PENÍNSULA DE NICOYA
Río Telire
OCÉANO PACÍFICO
Cerro Chirripó (3819 m)
Cordillera de Talamanca
Río General
COSTA RICA
Parque Nacional Corcovado
GOLFO DULCE

► **El perezoso de tres dedos** The three-toed sloth moves very slowly and spends most of its time in forest treetops.

▲ **El café** Coffee beans are the main crop in Costa Rica's Central Valley.

▲ **El Parque Nacional Tortuguero** Tortuguero National Park is on the Caribbean coast of Costa Rica. The park is home to endangered green sea turtles, jaguars, and howler monkeys.

◄ **El Parque Nacional Corcovado** Corcovado National Park is located on the rugged Osa Peninsula. Its tropical rain forest gets almost six meters of rain per year.

**¿Qué tanto sabes?**
Which volcanoes are found near **San José**? FL.C.1.1.1

# A conocer Costa Rica

## Las celebraciones

◄ **Las fiestas patronales**
On patron saints' days you can see young people dressed up in **payaso** costumes, dancing to live music.

► **El Día de Juan Santamaría**
On April 11, Costa Rica celebrates the memory of national hero **Juan Santamaría,** a drummer boy who died bravely in 1856 during the Battle of Rivas against the invader William Walker.

## El arte

◄ **Jorge Jiménez Deredia (1954–)**
This modern artist is world famous for his harmonious sculptures in marble and bronze. He is the first Latin American artist to have a work displayed at St. Peter's Basilica in Rome. The marble sculpture you see here is displayed in **San José**.

▼ **El Día del Boyero** A festival for oxcart drivers, or **boyeros,** is celebrated in **San Antonio de Escazú** on the second Sunday in March. The festival includes a parade of beautifully painted carts pulled by oxen.

## La comida

► **Olla de carne** Costa Ricans make a traditional stew called **olla de carne** out of meat with vegetables such as sweet potatoes, chayote squash, corn, and potatoes.

**Benchmark Focus**

FL.B.1.1.2 Recognize patterns of social behavior or social interaction in various settings

### ¿Sabías que...?

**The quetzal is endangered across Central America because its habitat is being destroyed. How are animals and their habitats being protected in Costa Rica?**

▼ **La mariposa "el perro de los naranjos"** The giant swallowtail butterfly is commonly seen in March and April.

## Los animales

► **La lapa roja** The scarlet macaw can be seen on the Osa Peninsula.

◄ **El mono congo** You can easily find the howler monkey in the forest by listening for its loud yell.

► **El quetzal** The quetzal lives in cloud forests. This bird is famous for its beautiful green feathers.

# Capítulo 4

# La vida escolar

## Objetivos

**In Part 1 you will learn to:**

- say what you have and what you need
- talk about school supplies and school subjects
- use indefinite articles and **¿cuánto?, mucho,** and **poco**
- form **tener** and some of its idioms
- use **venir** and **a** + time

**In Part 2 you will learn to:**

- talk about plans and give invitations
- talk about school events and places
- use **ir a** + infinitive
- form **-er** and **-ir** verbs in the present
- use the tag questions **¿no?** and **¿verdad?**
- use **hacer, poner, saber, traer,** and **ver**
- use **de** with **salir** and **saber**

## ¿Qué ves en la foto?

- **¿Dónde están los muchachos?**
- **¿Qué hacen?**
- **¿Qué haces tú cuando vas al zoológico?**

Look for the next to each activity and the **Benchmark Focus** to help you achieve the goals of the **Florida Sunshine State Standards,** found on pages FL14–FL16.

Jóvenes en el parque Zoo Ave de San José, Costa Rica

Objetivos
• Saying what you have and what you need
• Talking about classes
Vocabulario en acción 1
Video/DVD
ExpresaVisión
En Costa Rica
Tengo muchas cosas, pero...
todavía necesito unos útiles esclares.
unos cuadernos
unos lápices (un lápiz, sing.)
una regla
papel (m.)
También necesito...
unas carpetas
unos bolígrafos
una mochila
un diccionario
una computadora
zapatos (m.)
un reloj (unos relojes, pl.)
ropa (f.)

Visit Holt Online
**go.hrw.com**
KEYWORD: EXP1A CH4
Vocabulario 1 practice

| Horas | Clases |
|---|---|
| 8:00 | *matemáticas* |
| 8:50 | *arte* |
| 9:40 | *biología* |
| 10:30 | *español* |
| 11:20 | *educación física* |
| 12:10 | *almuerzo* |
| 13:00 | *historia* |
| 13:50 | *inglés* |

# Vocabulario 1

## Más vocabulario...

| **las materias** | ***school subjects*** |
|---|---|
| **el alemán** | *German* |
| **las ciencias** | *science* |
| **la computación** | *computer science* |
| **el francés** | *French* |
| **la química** | *chemistry* |
| **el taller** | *shop, workshop* |

## También se puede decir...

In Florida, you may hear Cubans say **un bolígrafo** for **una pluma.** Mexicans and Venezuelans might use **un lapicero.** Ecuadoreans usually say both **bolígrafo** and **pluma,** while for Colombians **un bolígrafo** may be either **un esfero** or **un plumero.**

## ¡Exprésate!

| To ask what others have or need | To respond |
|---|---|
| **¿Necesitas algo para el colegio?**<br>*Do you need anything for school?*<br>**¿Necesitas algo para la clase de arte?**<br>*Do you need anything for art class?* | **Sí, necesito muchas cosas.**<br>*Yes, I need a lot of things.*<br>**No, no necesito nada.**<br>*No, I don't need anything.* |
| **¿Necesitas una calculadora?**<br>*Do you need a calculator?* | **Sí, necesito una calculadora.**<br>*Yes, I need a calculator.* |
| **¿Tienes carpetas?**<br>*Do you have folders?* | **Sí, tengo un montón./No, no tengo.**<br>*Yes, I have a ton of them./No, I don't have any.* |

Interactive TUTOR

Vocabulario y gramática, pp. 37–39
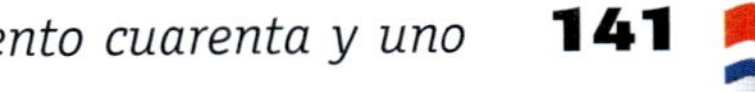


▶ Vocabulario adicional — Materias, p. R7

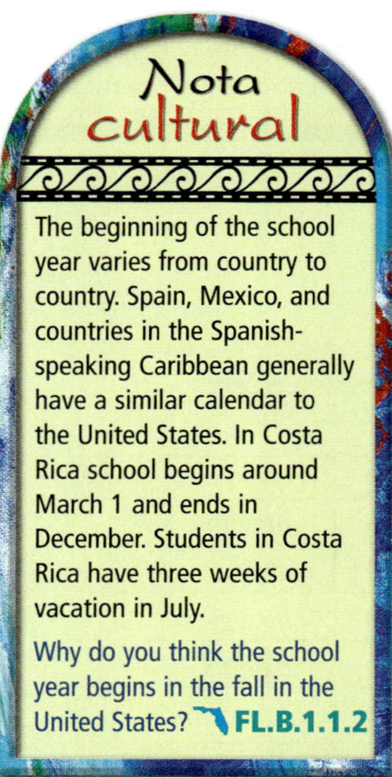

## Nota cultural

The beginning of the school year varies from country to country. Spain, Mexico, and countries in the Spanish-speaking Caribbean generally have a similar calendar to the United States. In Costa Rica school begins around March 1 and ends in December. Students in Costa Rica have three weeks of vacation in July.

Why do you think the school year begins in the fall in the United States? **FL.B.1.1.2**

## 1 ¿Qué necesitas y qué tienes? FL.A.2.1.3

**Escuchemos** Listen as Óscar and his mom talk about what school supplies he needs and already has. Choose the picture that shows what they're going to buy.

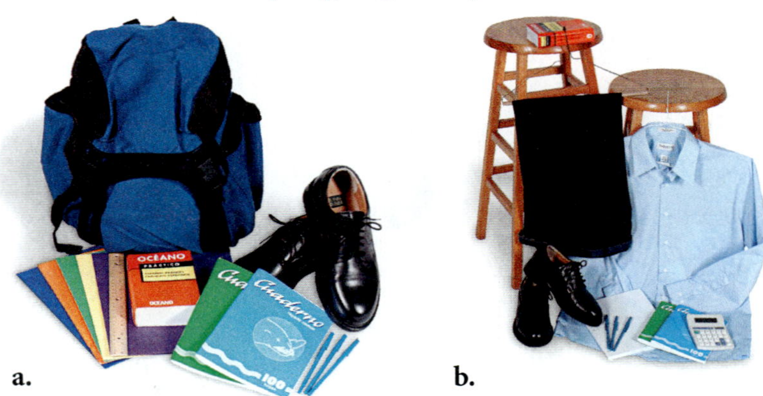


**a.** **b.**

## 2 Una carta electrónica FL.A.2.1.2

**Leamos** Lupe wrote to tell Francisco of some supplies he'll need for school. Read the e-mail and answer the questions that follow.

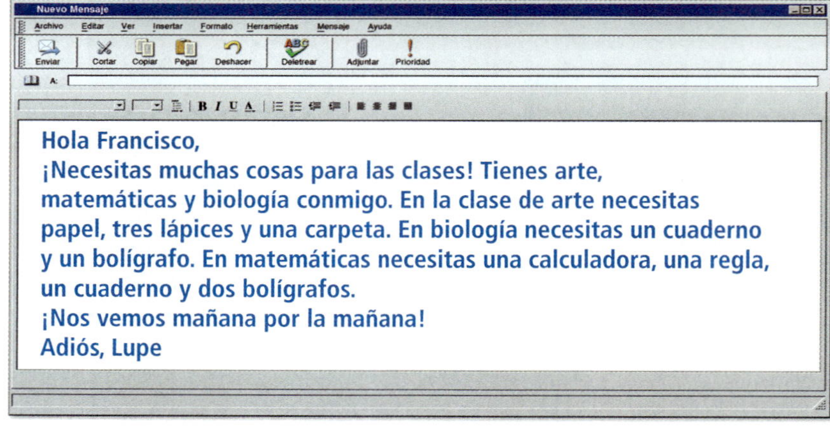

Nuevo Mensaje

Hola Francisco,
¡Necesitas muchas cosas para las clases! Tienes arte, matemáticas y biología conmigo. En la clase de arte necesitas papel, tres lápices y una carpeta. En biología necesitas un cuaderno y un bolígrafo. En matemáticas necesitas una calculadora, una regla, un cuaderno y dos bolígrafos.
¡Nos vemos mañana por la mañana!
Adiós, Lupe

**Benchmark Focus** 

**FL.A.2.1.2** **Restate and rephrase simple information from materials presented orally, visually, and graphically in class**

1. What classes do Lupe and Francisco have together?
2. For which class do they need pencils and paper?
3. What supplies do they need for math class?
4. What do they need to bring for biology?
5. When will Lupe and Francisco see each other next?
6. For which classes do they need a pen?
7. For which class do they need a folder?
8. For which classes do they need a notebook?

## 3 Necesito muchas cosas FL.A.3.1.1

**Hablemos** Di *(Say)* cuatro cosas que tienes y cuatro cosas que necesitas para el colegio.

**MODELO** **Tengo una mochila. Necesito ropa.**

## 4 Necesito mucho para las clases FL.A.2.1.2, FL.A.3.1.1

**Escribamos/Hablemos** Use the model and one word from each box to make logical sentences.

**MODELO** **Para la clase de arte, necesito unos lápices. No necesito una calculadora.**

| | |
|---|---|
| matemáticas | inglés |
| español | computación |
| arte | historia |

| | |
|---|---|
| un diccionario | una computadora |
| unos lápices | unas carpetas |
| papel | una calculadora |

## 5 ¿Qué tiene Ricardo? FL.A.2.1.2

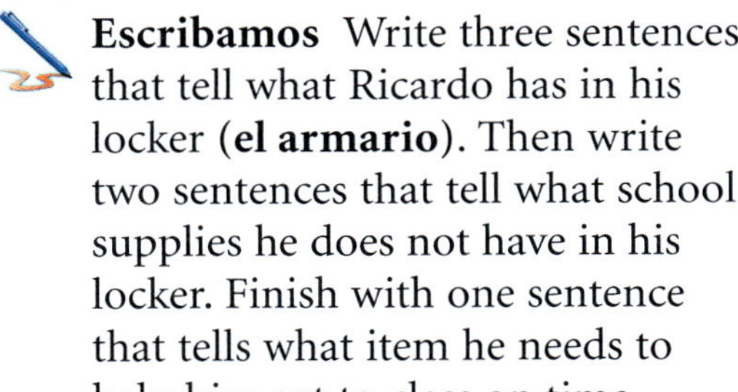

**Escribamos** Write three sentences that tell what Ricardo has in his locker (**el armario**). Then write two sentences that tell what school supplies he does not have in his locker. Finish with one sentence that tells what item he needs to help him get to class on time.

## 6 ¿Qué necesitas? FL.A.1.2.2

**Hablemos** What school supplies do you need for your classes? With a partner, take turns asking each other what you need for the following classes. Name at least two items.

**MODELO** la clase de arte **—¿Qué necesitas para la clase de arte?**
**—Necesito unos lápices y papel.**

1. la clase de español
2. la clase de matemáticas
3. la clase de inglés
4. la clase de ciencias
5. la clase de computación

## ¡Exprésate!

| To ask about classes | To respond |
|---|---|
| **¿Qué clases tienes esta tarde/después del almuerzo?**<br>*What classes do you have this afternoon/ after lunch?* | **Primero tengo español y después tengo computación.**<br>*First I have Spanish and afterwards I have computer science.* |
| **¿Cuál es tu materia preferida?**<br>*What's your favorite subject?* | **Mi materia preferida es matemáticas. Es fácil. No me gusta la clase de inglés porque es difícil.**<br>*My favorite subject is math. It's easy. I don't like English because it's hard.* |

Interactive TUTOR

Vocabulario y gramática, pp. 37–39 — Online workbooks

### Nota cultural

Students in public schools in some Spanish-speaking countries have fewer elective classes than students in the United States. In Costa Rica, high school students take the same classes for the first three years. In their third year, they take a national exam to see if they will continue a college preparatory program, or attend a technical or vocational program for their last two years.

How is this different from your school? FL.D.2.1.1

**Benchmark Focus**

**FL.D.2.1.1** Know the similarities and differences between the patterns of behavior of the target culture and the local culture

### 7 Muchas materias FL.A.2.1.4, FL.C.2.1.1

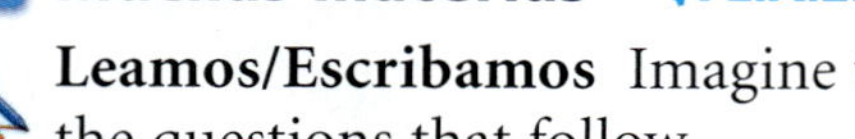

**Leamos/Escribamos** Imagine this is your class schedule. Answer the questions that follow.

LUX ET LEX
400 mts Oeste del Beneficio La Meseta, San Juan de Santa Barbara Heredia, Telfax 506.265.5393 Tel 506.265.7934

| Día | lunes | martes | miércoles | jue |
|---|---|---|---|---|
| Horario | | | | |
| 8:45 | *historia* | *biología* | *historia* | *bio* |
| 9:40 | *matemáticas* | *computación* | *matemáticas* | *com* |
| 10:35 | *ed. física* | *arte* | *ed. física* | *arte* |
| 11:30 | *español* | *ciencias* | *español* | *cie* |
| 12:25 | *almuerzo* | *almuerzo* | *almuerzo* | *alm* |
| 12:55 | *química* | *inglés* | *química* | *ing* |
| 1:50 | *taller* | *francés* | *taller* | *fran* |

1. ¿Qué clases tienes los lunes por la mañana?
2. ¿Qué tienes primero los martes?
3. ¿Qué días tienes educación física?
4. ¿Qué clase tienes después de química los miércoles?
5. ¿Qué clases tienes por la tarde los martes?

### 8 Mis clases FL.A.2.1.2

**Leamos/Escribamos** Complete the paragraph, describing your own schedule.

Por la mañana tengo __1__ clases. Primero, tengo la clase de __2__. Después, tengo __3__ y __4__. Me gusta la clase de __5__ porque es __6__. Después de __7__ tengo el almuerzo. Por la tarde tengo la clase de __8__. La profesora es __9__. Para la clase de español, necesito __10__ y para la clase de matemáticas, necesito __11__. Mi materia preferida es __12__.

# Comunicación

## 9 ¿Qué clases tienes? FL.A.1.2.2

**Hablemos** Work with a partner. Take turns asking if your partner has the classes indicated below. Answer with the day of week and the time of day (morning or afternoon).

**MODELO** arte —**¿Tienes clase de arte?**
**—Sí, tengo arte los lunes y miércoles por la mañana.**
**(No, no tengo clase de arte.)**

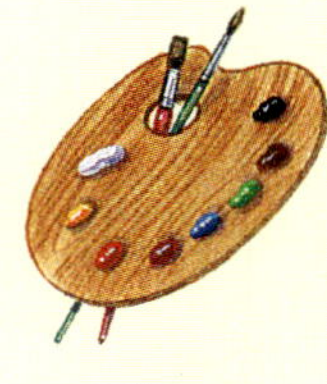
arte

francés

computación

almuerzo

historia

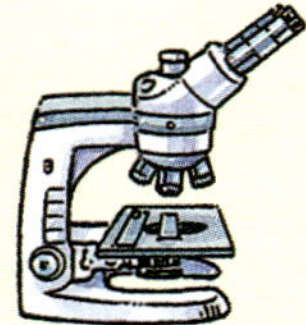
ciencias

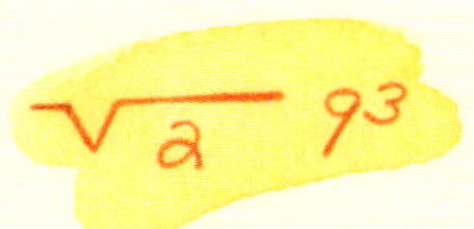
matemáticas

alemán

educación física

taller

inglés

español

## 10 ¿Cómo es tu horario? FL.A.1.1.1

**Hablemos** Write your school schedule. Include the days, times, and classes. With a partner, talk about your classes, using the schedules you've created. Mention at least three classes and say why you like or dislike them.

**MODELO** **—¿Qué clase tienes primero los jueves?**
**—Primero, tengo la clase de... Me gusta porque...**

GramaVisión

## Objetivos

- Using indefinite articles, **¿cuánto?**, **mucho** and **poco**
- **Tener** and some **tener** idioms
- **Venir** and **a la/las** with time

## Indefinite articles; ¿cuánto?, mucho, and poco

Interactive TUTOR

**1** The **indefinite articles un** and **una** are used to say *a* or *an* before a singular noun, while **unos** and **unas** are used to say *some* before a plural noun. The indefinite articles can sometimes be left out, especially when the noun is plural.

Necesito **un** diccionario. — *I need a dictionary.*
¿Tienes (**unos**) lápices? — *Do you have (some) pencils?*

**2** The indefinite articles agree with the noun in gender and number.

| | Masculine | Feminine |
|---|---|---|
| SINGULAR | **un** libr**o** | un**a** mochil**a** |
| PLURAL | un**os** libr**os** | un**as** mochil**as** |

**3** To talk about amounts of things, use the following adjectives. These words also agree with the nouns they describe in gender and number.

| | | | |
|---|---|---|---|
| SINGULAR | ¿cuánto(a)? how much? | mucho(a) a lot of, much | poco(a) little, not much |
| PLURAL | ¿cuántos(as)? how many? | muchos(as) a lot of, many | pocos(as) few, not many |

—¿**Cuánta** tare**a** tienes? — *How much homework do you have?*
—Tengo **mucha**. — *I have a lot.*

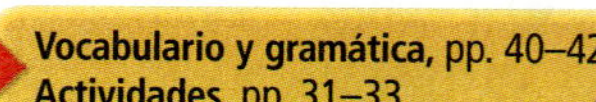

Vocabulario y gramática, pp. 40–42
Actividades, pp. 31–33
Online workbooks

### En inglés

**In English,** adjectives generally go before the nouns they modify.

It's an **awful** book.

Think of an example in English where the adjective follows the noun it modifies.

**In Spanish,** adjectives like **¿cuánto(a)?**, **mucho(a)** and **poco(a)** go before the noun.

**¿Cuánta tarea tienes?**

**Tengo muchas mochilas.**

**Hay poca tarea hoy.**

However, most other adjectives follow the noun they modify.

Es un libro **pésimo.**

FL.D.1.1.2

### 11 ¿Tienes o necesitas? FL.A.2.1.2

**Hablemos** Give the correct indefinite article for the following nouns. Then say whether you need these items or whether you already have them.

**MODELO** **<u>una</u> regla**
**Necesito una regla. (Tengo una regla.)**

| | | |
|---|---|---|
| 1. ____ cuaderno | 4. ____ bolígrafos | 7. ____ diccionario |
| 2. ____ calculadora | 5. ____ carpetas | 8. ____ computadora |
| 3. ____ lápices | 6. ____ mochila | 9. ____ reloj |

Gramática 1

## 12 ¿Cuánto? FL.A.2.1.2

**Hablemos** Ask a friend how many of these items he or she has. Use **cuánto, cuántos, cuánta,** or **cuántas.**

**MODELO** **¿Cuántas mochilas tienes?**

1. ¿____ ropa tienes?
2. ¿____ lápices tienes?
3. ¿____ relojes tienes?
4. ¿____ reglas tienes?
5. ¿____ cuadernos tienes?
6. ¿____ carpetas tienes?
7. ¿____ papel tienes?
8. ¿____ libros tienes?

## 13 ¿Mucho o poco? FL.A.2.1.2, FL.A.3.1.1

**Escribamos/Hablemos** Now answer the questions from Activity 12, using the correct forms of **mucho** and **poco.**

**MODELO** **Tengo muchas (pocas) mochilas.**

**Benchmark Focus**
**FL.A.2.1.3** Understand oral messages based on familiar themes and vocabulary

## 14 Útiles escolares FL.A.2.1.3

**Escuchemos** Gabi is helping her younger sister, Verónica, figure out what school supplies she still needs. Look at the picture and decide if what she says is **cierto** or **falso**.

## Comunicación

## 15 ¿Qué necesitamos? FL.A.1.2.2

**Hablemos** You and your partner need to prepare a report that includes pictures, graphs, and mathematical calculations. Talk about the supplies you have and make a list of the supplies you need.

**MODELO** **—¿Necesitamos papel?**
**—No, tengo mucho papel pero** *(but)* **necesitamos revistas.**

## Present tense of tener and some tener idioms

**1** Use the verb **tener** to tell what someone *has.* To conjugate the **yo** form, drop the **-er** ending and add **-go.** To conjugate all the other forms except **nosotros(as)** and **vosotros(as),** change the **-e** in the stem of **tener** to **-ie.**

| | | | |
|---|---|---|---|
| **yo** | ten**go** | nosotros(as) | tenemos |
| tú | t**ie**nes | vosotros(as) | tenéis |
| Ud., él, ella | t**ie**ne | Uds., ellos, ellas | t**ie**nen |

—¿T**ie**nes un bolígrafo? *Do you have a pen?*

—No. Ten**go** un lápiz. *No. I have a pencil.*

**2** Use **tener que** + **infinitive** to talk about what you have to do.

**Tengo que ir** a un ensayo. *I have to go to a rehearsal.*

**Some other commom tener idioms**

| | |
|---|---|
| **tener ganas de** + infinitive | *to feel like doing something* |
| **tener prisa** | *to be in a hurry* |
| **tener (mucha) hambre** | *to be (very) hungry* |
| **tener (mucha) sed** | *to be (very) thirsty* |

Vocabulario y gramática, pp. 40–42
Actividades, pp. 31–33
Online workbooks

### En inglés

**In English,** we use the verb *to be* to say how old we are, or to say we're hungry or thirsty.

**I am** 15 years old.

**We are** hungry and thirsty.

**In Spanish,** use a form of **tener** *(to have)* with a noun for these expressions.

**Tengo** 15 años.

**Tenemos** hambre y sed.

Give examples where **ser** means *to be* and **tener** means *to have.*

FL.D.1.1.2

### 16 ¿De quién habla? FL.A.2.1.3

**Escuchemos** Listen as Ana Mari talks about some of her friends. Match each picture to each statement she makes.

a. c. b. d.

## 17 ¿Qué planes tienes? FL.A.2.1.2

**Leamos** Complete the conversation between Elena and her friend with the correct forms of **tener** and **tener que.**

—Elena, necesito un favor. ¿ ___1___ un diccionario?

—No, pero la señora López ___2___ muchos diccionarios en el salón de clase.

—Buena idea. ___3___ irme. ¿Nos vemos por la tarde?

—¿Hoy? ¿Qué ___4___ hacer (tú)?

—Nosotras ___5___ un examen de alemán mañana y ___6___ estudiar.

—Está bien. Nos vemos a las 4:00.

**Benchmark Focus**

**FL.A.2.1.2** Restate and rephrase simple information from materials presented orally, visually, and graphically in class

## 18 Rompecabezas FL.A.2.1.2

**Escribamos** Use the correct form of **tener** and a phrase from each puzzle piece to form six logical sentences.

**1**
Quiero salir. ¿(Tú)...?
Es tarde y el profesor...
Hace calor. (Yo)...
Y ustedes, ¿qué clases...?

**2**
tener
tener que
tener ganas de

**3**
pasear conmigo
hoy por la tarde
prisa
nadar
sed
los lunes

# Comunicación

HOLT SoundBooth ONLINE RECORDING

## 19 Planes FL.A.1.2.2

**Hablemos** Look at the pictures. With a partner, take turns asking each other if you either want to or have to do these things today.

**MODELO** **—¿Tienes ganas de ir al baile hoy por la noche?**
**—Sí, tengo ganas de bailar.**

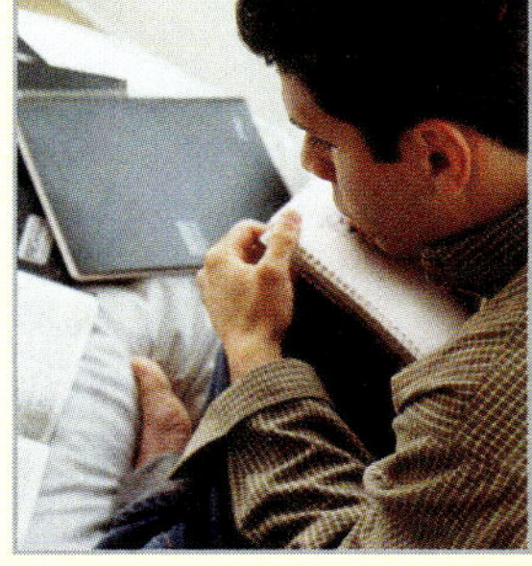

Gramática 1

## The verb venir and a + time

**1** The verb **venir** means *to come.* In the present tense its endings are like those of **tener,** except for the **nosotros** and **vosotros** forms.

| | | | |
|---|---|---|---|
| **yo** | ven**go** | nosotros(as) | venimos |
| tú | v**ie**nes | vosotros(as) | venís |
| Ud., él, ella | v**ie**ne | Uds., ellos, ellas | v**ie**nen |

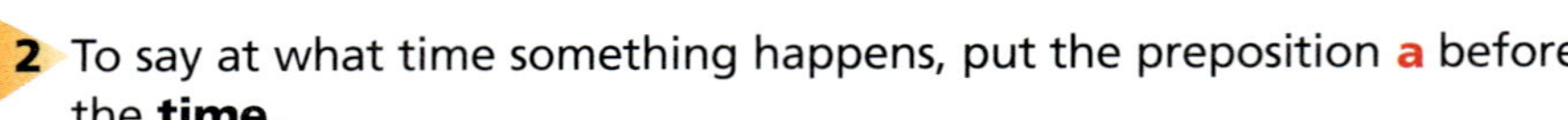

**2** To say at what time something happens, put the preposition **a** before the **time.**

—**¿A qué hora** vienes al colegio?
—Vengo **a las ocho en punto.**

—**¿A qué hora** es la clase de álgebra?
—Es **a la una de la tarde.**

**Vocabulario y gramática,** pp. 40–42
**Actividades,** pp. 31–33 **Online** workbooks

## Nota cultural

Instead of taking the school bus at a nearby stop, many students in the Miami-Dade area have the option of being picked up at their homes by private bus companies. Before and after school, one can often see students riding these buses or vans with the names of the owners, such as Carlos and Susana or Conchita's.

How does the way you and your friends get to school compare to this system?

FL.D.2.1.1

**Servicio particular de transporte para estudiantes de un colegio de Miami-Dade**

### 20 Mi fiesta FL.A.2.1.3

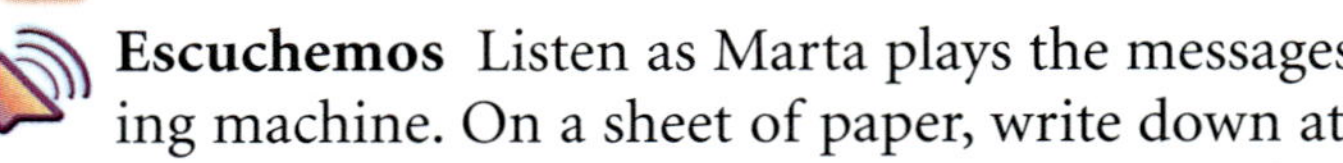

**Escuchemos** Listen as Marta plays the messages on her answering machine. On a sheet of paper, write down at what time Marta's friends are coming to her party tonight.

1. Jorge
2. Juliana
3. Anabel
4. Valentín
5. Marisol y Chema
6. Gabi

### 21 ¿Vienes conmigo? FL.A.2.1.2

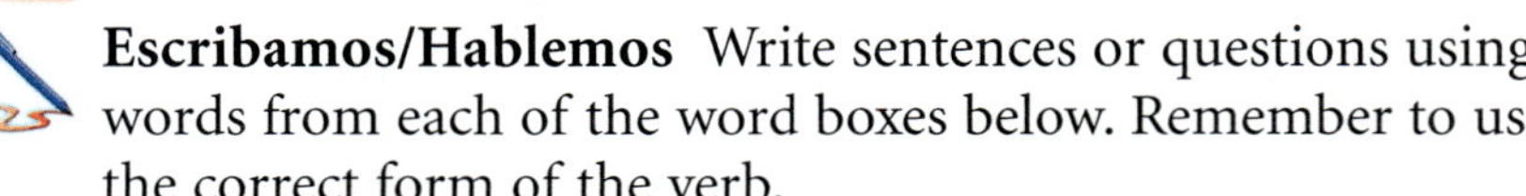

**Escribamos/Hablemos** Write sentences or questions using words from each of the word boxes below. Remember to use the correct form of the verb.

**MODELO** **(tú) ¿Vienes a la clase de español esta tarde?**

| | | | |
|---|---|---|---|
| yo<br>tú<br>nosotros<br>el profesor<br>(la profesora)<br>ustedes<br>usted | (no) venir | a la clase de español<br>al colegio<br>a la clase de...<br>a la reunión de... | los fines de semana<br>los lunes y...<br>los...<br>a veces<br>todos los días |

## 22 ¿A qué hora viene el autobús? FL.C.2.1.1

**Escribamos/Hablemos** Given the situations below, use the bus schedule to find the earliest bus that goes to Chirripó National Forest. Follow the model.

**MODELO** **Son las once y veinte. Roberto está en San Isidro.**
**El autobús cincuenta y seis viene a las once y media.**

1. Es mediodía. Juan está en San Isidro.
2. Son las nueve en punto. Ángela está en Cartago.
3. Es la una y cuarto. Mónica está en San Isidro.
4. Son las ocho y diez. Antonio está en San José.
5. Son las diez y cinco. Carlos está en Cartago.
6. Son las once menos cuarto. Jorge está en Cartago.
7. Son las nueve y treinta y cinco. Amalia está en San José.
8. Son las nueve y veinticinco. Raúl está en San José.

Autobuses, San José

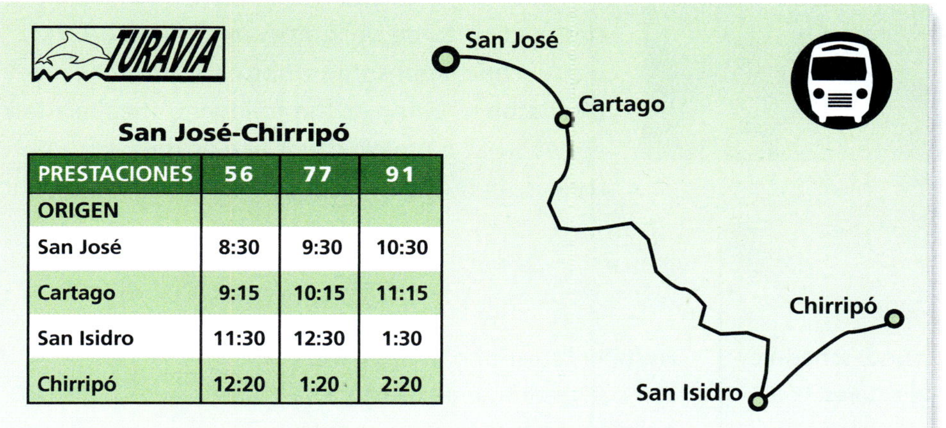



**San José-Chirripó**

| PRESTACIONES | 56 | 77 | 91 |
|---|---|---|---|
| ORIGEN | | | |
| San José | 8:30 | 9:30 | 10:30 |
| Cartago | 9:15 | 10:15 | 11:15 |
| San Isidro | 11:30 | 12:30 | 1:30 |
| Chirripó | 12:20 | 1:20 | 2:20 |

**Benchmark Focus** 

**FL.C.2.1.1** Use the target language to gain access to information that is only available through the target language or within the target culture

## 23 En el colegio FL.A.1.1.2

**Hablemos** Ask your classmate when he or she comes to school, what classes he or she has, and at what time. Then switch roles.

**MODELO** **—¿A qué hora vienes al colegio?**
**—Vengo a las ocho y media.**
**—¿Qué clases tienes?**
**—Tengo español, matemáticas, historia...**
**—¿A qué hora es la clase de...?**
**—Es a las...**

# Cultura

VideoCultura

**Benchmark Focus**
FL.E.1.2.2 Demonstrate an awareness of employment possibilities (and other applications) for those who master the target language

## Comparaciones

En el Colegio de Santa Ana, Costa Rica

### ¿Cómo es un día típico en tu colegio? FL.B.1.1.2, FL.D.2.1.1

Students in the United States usually have certain classes they must take, as well as a few elective classes such as choir, drama, shop, and so on. Most schools have after-school activities as well, such as sports or band. In Spain and Latin America, all classes tend to be obligatory, and there aren't many school-sponsored clubs or teams that meet after school. Listen as the following speakers talk about what a typical day is like at their schools. How is their day similar to or different from yours?

### Julio
**San José, Costa Rica**

Julio talks about his school schedule, required classes, and electives.

***¿A qué colegio asistes?***

Yo asisto al colegio de Santa Ana.

***¿Cómo es un día típico en tu colegio?***

Un día típico es entrar a las siete de la mañana, salir a las once y veinte de la mañana, ir a almorzar, regresar de nuevo a las doce y de ahí hasta las cuatro y veinte de la tarde. Luego ya retorna uno a la casa de uno.

***¿Qué materias tienes?***

A nosotros nos dan matemáticas, inglés, francés, español, estudios sociales.

***¿Son materias obligatorias u opcionales?***

Hasta el tercer año inglés y francés son obligatorias y de cuarto a quinto, uno puede escoger entre inglés y francés.

***¿Cuál es tu materia favorita y por qué?***

Mi materia favorita es matemáticas. Es más fácil para mí desarrollarla.

Visit Holt Online
**go.hrw.com**
KEYWORD: EXP1A CH4
Online Edition

Cultura

## Jasna
**Santiago, Chile**

***¿A qué colegio asistes?***
Asisto al Colegio Carmen Macfi.

***¿Cómo es un día típico en tu colegio?***
Bueno, entro en la mañana, ocho y media, y bueno, tenemos distintas materias durante los días y tenemos recreo, luego el almuerzo y después salgo a las tres. Y me voy a mi casa y estudio.

***¿Qué materias tienes?***
Tengo castellano, historia, matemáticas, inglés, los electivos y ciencias que es química, física y biología.

***¿Son materias obligatorias u opcionales?***
Los electivos son opcionales. Yo en mi caso tomé ciudad contemporánea y problemas del conocimiento. Y cuando estás en cuarto medio, con ciencias puedes eliminar una que en mi caso yo eliminé física.

### Para comprender FL.A.2.1.2

1. ¿A qué hora va Julio al colegio?
2. ¿Estudia Julio ciencias?
3. ¿Qué hace Jasna después de ir a casa?
4. ¿Jasna estudia ciencias?
5. ¿Te gusta más el día escolar de Julio o Jasna? ¿Por qué?

### Para pensar y hablar FL.B.1.1.2, FL.D.2.1.1

Make a list of three classes that Julio and Jasna have in common. Do you also have these classes? Why or why not? Both Julio and Jasna are required to study English as a foreign language. Does your school require you to study a foreign language, or is it an elective? Do you think requiring a foreign language is a good idea? Why or why not?

# Comunidad en la Florida

## Al servicio de la educación FL.E.1.2.2

The Hispanic community in Florida benefits from educational services provided by schools and libraries, such as Spanish storytelling, tutoring, and English classes. Work with your school library to organize a storytelling time in Spanish for children in elementary school.

- Make a list of Spanish-language books in your library.
- Send letters to elementary classrooms.
- Arrange times to read Spanish stories to classes.
- Practice reading the stories before visiting the classes.

**Estudiante de español ayuda a su compañero en un colegio de Miami-Dade.**

**Objetivos**
- Talking about plans
- Inviting someone to do something

# Vocabulario en acción 2

ExpresaVisión

## En Costa Rica

un partido

un concierto

una clase de baile

**Más vocabulario...**

| | |
|---|---|
| esta semana | *this week* |
| este fin de semana | *this weekend* |
| mañana | *tomorrow* |
| pasado mañana | *day after tomorrow* |
| la próxima semana | *next week* |

## En el colegio

la biblioteca

el auditorio

el estadio

la cafetería

el salón de clase

**También se puede decir...**

In Florida, you may hear many Latin Americans say **el aula,** or simply **la clase,** instead of **el salón de clase.** FL.D.1.1.1

## ¡Exprésate!

| To talk about plans | To respond |
|---|---|
| **¿Vas a ir a... el lunes por la noche?**<br>*Are you going to go to . . . Monday night?* | **No. Tengo una reunión del club de español.**<br>*No. I have a Spanish club meeting.* |
| **¿Qué vas a hacer el viernes próximo?**<br>*What are you going to do next Friday?* | **Voy a presentar el examen de inglés, y después... Luego regreso a casa.**<br>*I'm going to take an English test, and afterwards . . . Then I'm going back home.* |
| **¿A qué hora vas a llegar al partido?**<br>*What time are you going to get to the game?* | **Voy a llegar temprano (a tiempo). No me gusta llegar tarde.**<br>*I'm going to get there early (on time). I don't like to be late.* |

Interactive TUTOR

Vocabulario y gramática, pp. 43–45 Online workbooks

## Nota cultural

In Costa Rica, if a student fails a course, it must be made up during vacation. If a student fails two classes and also fails the exams offered at the end of vacation, he or she must repeat the whole semester.

How does this compare to the grading system and to state exams in the United States? FL.B.1.1.2, FL.D.2.1.1

**VALORACIÓN DE LOS APRENDIZAJES Y DE LA CONDUCTA**

| PERÍODOS / ASIGNATURAS | I | II | III | PROMEDIO ANUAL | CONDICIÓN |
|---|---|---|---|---|---|
| Estudios Sociales | 80 | 84 | 86 | 83 | Aprobado |
| Cívica | | | | | |
| Matemática | 83 | $75^{6}$ | 72 | 77 | Aprobado |
| Español | 89 | 87 | 93 | 90 | Aprobado |
| Biología | 86 | 74 | 88 | 83 | Aprobado |
| Química | 79 | 89 | 88 | 85 | Aprobado |
| Física | | | | | |
| Inglés | 82 | 80 | 79 | 80 | Aprobado |
| Educación Física | 78 | 85 | 93 | 85 | Aprobado |
| Educación Musical | 80 | 96 | 100 | 92 | Aprobado |
| Psicología Ética Profesional | 65 | 85 | 81 | 77 | Aprobado |
| Educación Religiosa | 100 | 95 | 98 | $97^{60}$ | Aprobado |
| Conducta | $91^{64}$ | 99 | 99 | 97 | Aprobado |

ESPECIALIDAD: Secretariado

| Sub área* | I | II | III | PROMEDIO ANUAL | CONDICIÓN |
|---|---|---|---|---|---|
| [illegible] | 89 | 97 | 95 | 94 | Aprobado |
| [illegible] | | | | | |
| [illegible] | 96 | 93 | 100 | 96 | Aprobado |
| [illegible] | 79 | [illegible] | [illegible] | 83 | Aprobado |

* Consignar el nombre de cada sub área

Libreta de calificaciones de un colegio de Costa Rica

### 24 ¿Dónde están? FL.A.2.1.3

**Escuchemos** Escucha las conversaciones. Para cada conversación decide dónde están las personas.

**a.** en el salón de clase
**b.** en la biblioteca
**c.** en la cafetería
**d.** en el auditorio
**e.** en el estadio
**f.** en el club de computación

### 25 Tengo que hacer muchas cosas FL.A.2.1.2

**Leamos** Usa las palabras del cuadro para completar el párrafo.

| | | | |
|---|---|---|---|
| luego | partido | tarde | presentar |
| auditorio | regresar | club | pasado |

Esta semana voy a hacer muchas cosas. Hoy por la ___1___, a las 2:30, voy a ___2___ el examen de química y ___3___ voy a ir a la reunión del ___4___ de alemán. Mañana a las 5:00 tengo un ___5___ de béisbol. ___6___ mañana voy a ir al ensayo de piano en el ___7___ del colegio. Voy a ___8___ a casa tarde.

### 26 ¿Qué haces? FL.A.2.1.2

**Hablemos** Use **hay** *(there is, there are)* and the photos to say where these things are at your school.

**MODELO** **partidos de fútbol**
**Hay partidos de fútbol en el estadio.**

1. exámenes

2. conciertos

3. muchos libros

4. partidos de béisbol

5. el piano

6. ensayos

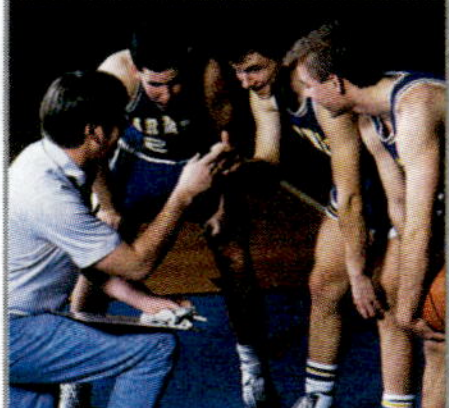
7. partido de básquetbol

8. comida

9. computadoras

10. bailes

## 27 ¿Adónde tienen que ir? FL.A.2.1.4

**Escribamos** You're helping some students figure out where to go for different activities. Based on what you read in each item, write a sentence telling where each person has to go. For item 7, think of what you want to do and tell where you have to go.

**MODELO** **Martín quiere hablar con el profesor de ciencias.**
**Martín tiene que ir al salón de clase.**

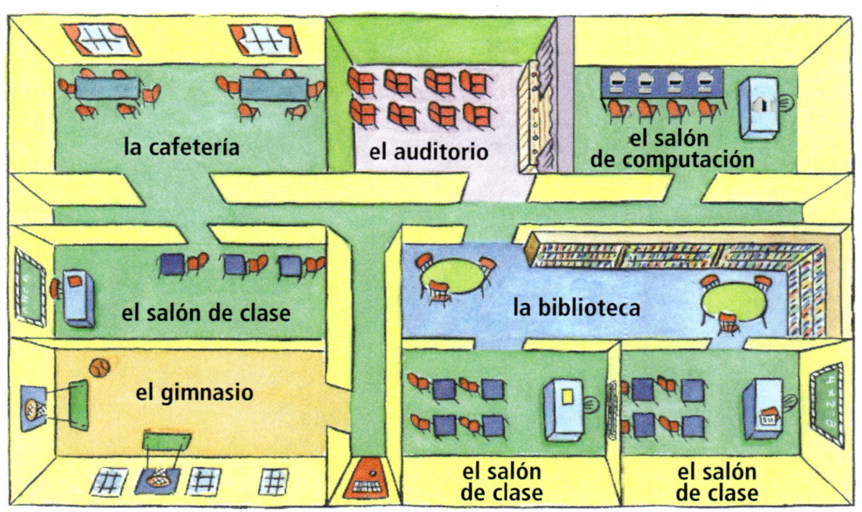


1. Quiero jugar al básquetbol.
2. Blanca y Ángel quieren estudiar.
3. Paula necesita ir a un ensayo.
4. Paco y David tienen hambre.
5. Marisol quiere hacer la tarea en la computadora.
6. Luis Miguel necesita presentar el examen de química.
7. ¿Tú?

**Benchmark Focus**
**FL.A.2.1.4** Listen and read in the target language and respond through role playing, drawing, or singing

Comunicación

## 28 ¿Vas a la biblioteca? FL.A.1.2.2

**Hablemos** Take turns with a partner asking if he or she is going to go to the places or events listed. Answers should include when you are going to that place or event and your reason for going.

**MODELO** la biblioteca —**¿Vas a la biblioteca?**
—**Sí, voy a las 5:00 de la tarde. Tengo que estudiar.**

1. la cafetería
2. el auditorio
3. el estadio
4. el concierto
5. el gimnasio
6. la reunión del club de español

Vocabulario 2

## ¡Exprésate!

| To invite someone to do something | To respond |
|---|---|
| **¿Qué tal si vamos al partido de fútbol?**<br>*How about if we go to the soccer game?* | **No sé. ¿Sabes qué? No tengo ganas.**<br>*I don't know. You know what? I don't feel like it.* |
| **Vienes conmigo a la cafetería, ¿no?**<br>*You're coming with me to the cafeteria, aren't you?* | **¡Claro que sí! Tengo mucha hambre.**<br>*Yes, of course! I'm very hungry.* |
| **Hay un concierto. Vas a ir, ¿verdad?**<br>*There's a concert.*<br>*You're going to go, right?* | **No, no voy a ir. Tengo que estudiar.**<br>*No, I'm not going to go.*<br>*I have to study.* |

Interactive TUTOR

Vocabulario y gramática, pp. 43–45 Online workbooks

### 29 Invitaciones FL.A.2.1.3

**Escuchemos/Escribamos** Listen to the conversations. On a separate piece of paper, write down what each person is invited to do, then tell whether the invitation is accepted or not.

**1.** Raquel **2.** Andrés **3.** Silvia **4.** Marta

### 30 Esta noche FL.A.2.1.2

**Leamos** Marta and Fernando are deciding what to do tonight. Read their conversation and choose the correct word for each sentence.

FERNANDO ¿Qué vas a (hacer/hablar) esta noche?
MARTA No sé. ¿No hay un (practicar/partido) de fútbol en el estadio?
FERNANDO Sí hay, pero no tengo (ganas/hambre) de ir.
MARTA ¿Quieres ir (a la clase/al concierto) en el auditorio?
FERNANDO Está bien, yo (voy/vienes) contigo. Pero, ¿sabes qué? ¡Tengo hambre!
MARTA Vamos primero a la (biblioteca/cafetería.)
FERNANDO ¡Buena idea!

## 31 ¿Qué tal si...?  FL.A.2.1.2

**Hablemos/Escribamos** Use the expressions below to invite a friend to each event.

**MODELO** **¿Qué tal si vamos al gimnasio el martes por la tarde?**

| 1 | 2 | 3 |
|---|---|---|
| ¿Qué tal si vamos...? | al gimnasio | el martes por la tarde |
| ¿Quieres ir conmigo...? | a la cafetería | el sábado próximo |
| Vas a ir... ¿verdad? | al concierto de piano | pasado mañana a las 4:30 |
| Vienes conmigo...¿no? | al baile del colegio | el viernes por la noche |
| | al partido de volibol | el miércoles a las 12:00 |
| | a la reunión del club de alemán | el lunes próximo por la mañana |

## 32 ¿Sabes qué? FL.A.2.1.2

**Hablemos** Now turn down your friend's invitations from Activity 31 by saying you have to do what is pictured.

**MODELO** **¿Sabes qué? Tengo que ir al partido de fútbol.**

A

B

C

D

## Comunicación

## 33 ¿Viernes conmigo? FL.A.1.2.2

**Hablemos** Choose three school events you'd like to attend, and then invite three different classmates to each of them. They will accept or turn down the invitation.

**MODELO** **—Hay un baile el viernes por la noche en el colegio. ¿Quieres ir conmigo?**

**—¡Claro que sí! Me gustan los bailes.**

**Benchmark Focus** 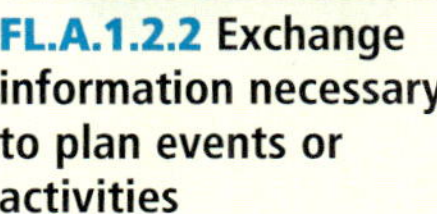

**FL.A.1.2.2** Exchange information necessary to plan events or activities

Vocabulario 2

**Objetivos**
- Using **ir a** with infinitives
- **-er** and **-ir** verbs, tag questions
- **-er** and **-ir** verbs with irregular **yo** forms

GramaVisión

## Ir a with infinitives

Interactive TUTOR

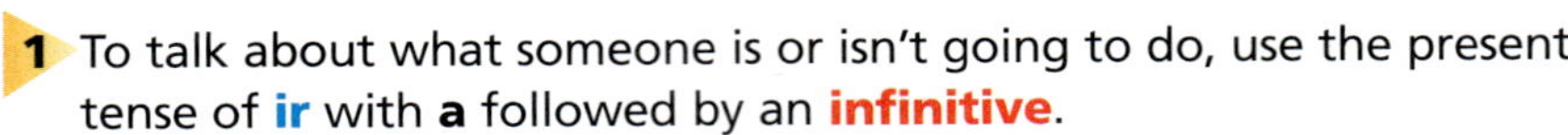

**1** To talk about what someone is or isn't going to do, use the present tense of **ir** with **a** followed by an **infinitive**.

—¿**Vas a estudiar**?
*Are you going to study?*

—No, **voy a descansar**.
*No, I'm going to rest.*

—¿**Van a salir**?
*Are you going to go out?*

—Sí, **vamos a comer**.
*Yes, we're going to eat.*

**2** To say that you are going to do something on a certain day of a particular week, use **el** before the **weekday**.

**El sábado** voy a ir de compras.
*On Saturday I'm going to go shopping.*

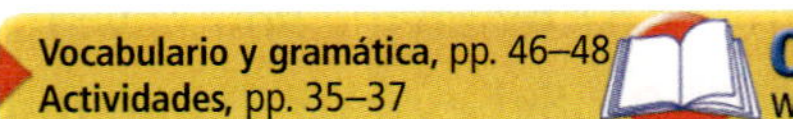


**¿Te acuerdas?**

Use **los** and a **plural form of the day of the week** to say you do something on that day every week.

**¿Qué haces los sábados?**
*What do you (usually) do on Saturdays?*

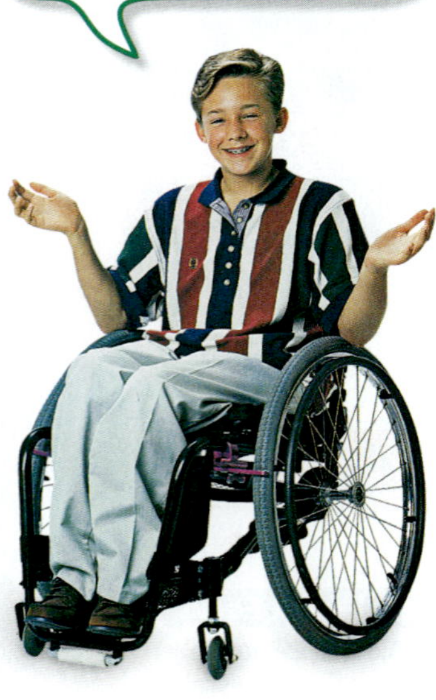

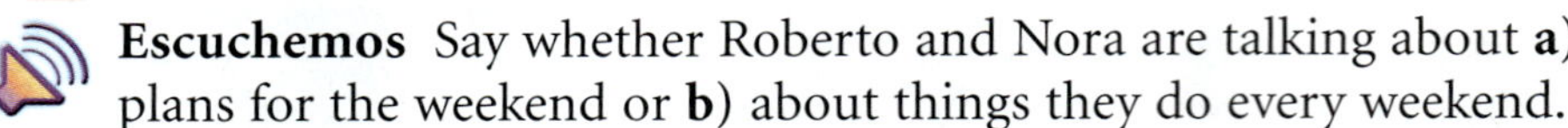

### 34 Planes diferentes FL.A.2.1.3

**Escuchemos** Say whether Roberto and Nora are talking about **a**) plans for the weekend or **b**) about things they do every weekend.

### 35 ¿Qué van a hacer? FL.A.2.1.2

**Leamos/Escribamos** Complete the sentences with the correct form of (**no**) **ir a** based on the cues.

**MODELO** **Yo ═══ descansar el sábado. Tengo que trabajar.**
**Yo no voy a descansar el sábado.**

1. Mi mejor amigo casi siempre quiere pasar el rato conmigo. Él ═══ comer conmigo este fin de semana.
2. Mis amigos y yo ═══ salir el viernes por la noche. Nos gusta salir.
3. Mi familia y yo ═══ ir al cine el domingo. Tenemos que ir a una reunión el domingo.
4. Yo ═══ comer en la cafetería hoy. No tengo hambre.
5. Los estudiantes de la clase de español ═══ estudiar mucho esta tarde. Van a presentar un examen mañana.
6. Mi mejor amiga ═══ ir de compras el domingo. Siempre va de compras los sábados.

## 36 ¿Cuándo vas a...? FL.A.2.1.2, FL.A.3.1.1

**Hablemos** Use the pictures to say what these people are going to do and when. Then say whether or not you're going to do the same things and when.

**MODELO** **Sara va a estudiar mañana.**
**Yo no. Voy a estudiar pasado mañana.**

Sara
mañana

1. Lucía/ el sábado próximo

2. Enrique/ el domingo

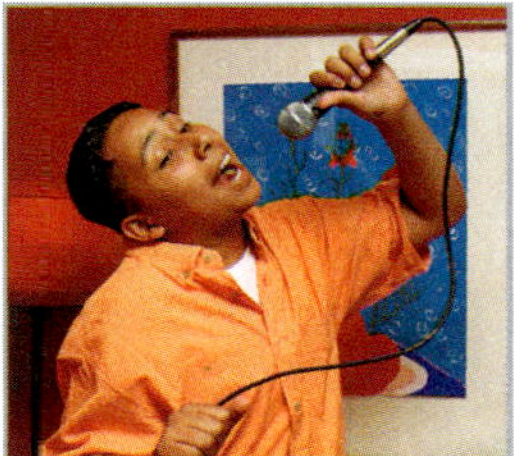
3. Andrés/ el viernes próximo

4. Mario y Lola/ el lunes

## 37 ¿Sabes qué van a hacer? FL.A.2.1.2

**Escribamos/Hablemos** Say whether the following people are going to do the activities listed. For items 4 and 5, guess what another student and your teacher are going to do.

**MODELO** **yo (salir con amigos esta noche, ver televisión)**
**No voy a salir con amigos esta noche.**
**Voy a ver televisión.**

1. yo (hacer ejercicio hoy, tocar el piano después de clases)
2. mis amigos y yo (salir este fin de semana, ir al cine el sábado)
3. mi mejor amigo(a) (pasar el fin de semana conmigo, jugar al básquetbol esta semana)
4. tú (llegar temprano al colegio mañana, ir a una reunión hoy)
5. usted (venir al colegio mañana, alquilar un video esta noche)

**Benchmark Focus** 

**FL.A.2.1.2** Restate and rephrase simple information from materials presented orally, visually, and graphically in class

## Comunicación

## 38 ¡Cuántos planes! FL.A.1.2.2

**Hablemos** Ask your classmate what he or she is going to do on Friday, Saturday, and Sunday. After he or she invites you along, say whether you want to go or do something else. Switch roles.

**MODELO** **—¿Qué vas a hacer el viernes por la noche?**
**—El viernes por la noche voy a bailar. ¿Quieres venir conmigo?**
**—Sí. Me gusta bailar. (No. El viernes voy a nadar.)**

## -er and -ir verbs; tag questions

**1** To conjugate a regular **-er** or **-ir** verb in the present tense, drop the **-er** or **-ir** of the infinitive and add these **endings**.

| | **comer** *to eat* | **escribir** *to write* |
|---|---|---|
| yo | com**o** | escrib**o** |
| tú | com**es** | escrib**es** |
| Ud., él, ella | com**e** | escrib**e** |
| nosotros(as) | com**emos** | escrib**imos** |
| vosotros(as) | com**éis** | escrib**ís** |
| Uds., ellos, ellas | com**en** | escrib**en** |

**2** A **tag question** is attached to the end of a sentence to make it a question. If you expect someone to answer *yes,* use **¿no?** or **¿verdad?** When the expected answer is *no,* use **¿verdad?**

—Vienes a la fiesta, **¿no? (¿verdad?)**
*You're coming . . . aren't you?*

—**Sí**, voy a ir.
*Yes, I'm going to go.*

—No vas al partido, **¿verdad?**
*You're not going . . . right?*

—**No**, no voy.
*No, I'm not going.*

**Some -er and -ir verbs**

| | |
|---|---|
| **abrir** | *to open* |
| **asistir (a)** | *to attend* |
| **beber (algo)** | *to drink (something)* |
| **interrumpir** | *to interrupt* |

**Vocabulario y gramática**, pp. 46–48
**Actividades**, pp. 35–37

Private schools in Costa Rica start in the morning and run until early afternoon, similar to what happens in U.S. schools. On the other hand, public schools in Costa Rica have three sessions: **el turno matutino** is four hours of classes in the morning, **el turno vespertino** is four hours in the afternoon, and **el turno nocturno** is four hours in the evening.

How would your life be different if you had classes in the evenings?
**FL.B.1.1.2, FL.D.2.1.1**

### 39 ¿Cierto o falso? FL.A.2.1.2

**Leamos/Escribamos** Complete each sentence with the correct verb from the box.

| | | | | |
|---|---|---|---|---|
| comen | asistimos | lee | escriben | corro |
| escribimos | bebes | abre | corres | abro |

1. Mis amigas y yo ═══ al colegio en julio.
2. Mis compañeros de clase ═══ muchas cartas en español.
3. Yo casi nunca ═══ en la clase de educación física.
4. Mis amigos ═══ conmigo en la cafetería.
5. El (La) profesor(a) ═══ revistas interesantes en clase.
6. Tú a veces ═══ algo en la clase.
7. La biblioteca ═══ a las 9:00 de la mañana.

## 40 En la clase de español FL.A.3.1.1

**Escribamos/Hablemos** Using the words from each word box, say whether or not these things happen in your school. Remember to conjugate the verbs.

**Benchmark Focus**

**FL.A.3.1.1** Provide simple information in spoken form

**MODELO** **Muchos estudiantes leen muchas cartas en español.**

| | | |
|---|---|---|
| muchos (pocos) estudiantes | comer | muchas (pocas) cartas en español |
| el profesor (la profesora) | beber | algo (nada) en clase |
| yo | interrumpir | temprano (tarde) los viernes |
| nosotros | (no) leer | pocas (muchas) revistas |
| tú | escribir | al colegio en diciembre |
| ustedes | asistir | a los estudiantes/al profesor/a la profesora |
| la cafetería (la biblioteca) | abrir | en la cafetería |

Gramática 2

## 41 Un día típico en el colegio FL.A.2.1.2

**Leamos/Escribamos** Complete the sentences with an activity pictured below.

**MODELO** **A veces los profesores comen en la cafetería.**

1. Yo nunca...
2. Con frecuencia el (la) profesor(a)...
3. Mis compañeros de clase y yo...
4. La biblioteca siempre...
5. Todos los días mi mejor amigo(a)...
6. Cuando tienen educación física, los estudiantes...

Comunicación

## 42 En nuestra escuela FL.A.1.2.2

**Hablemos** Ask a classmate questions using the pictures in Activity 41 and tag questions. Have your partner answer the questions. Switch roles.

**MODELO** **—La biblioteca del colegio abre a las 10:00, ¿verdad?**

**—No, la biblioteca abre a las 9:00.**

## Some -er/-ir verbs with irregular yo forms

**1** The following **-er** and **-ir** verbs have irregular **yo** forms.

| | **hacer** *to do, to make* | **poner** *to put* | **traer** *to bring* |
|---|---|---|---|
| yo | ha**go** | pon**go** | trai**go** |
| tú | haces | pones | traes |
| Ud., él, ella | hace | pone | trae |
| nosotros(as) | hacemos | ponemos | traemos |
| vosotros(as) | hacéis | ponéis | traéis |
| Uds., ellos, ellas | hacen | ponen | traen |
| | **saber** *to know information* | **ver** *to see* | **salir** *to go out* |
| yo | **sé** | v**eo** | sal**go** |
| tú | sabes | ves | sales |
| Ud., él, ella | sabe | ve | sale |
| nosotros(as) | sabemos | vemos | salimos |
| vosotros(as) | sabéis | veis | salís |
| Uds., ellos, ellas | saben | ven | salen |

**2** The preposition **de** is used after **salir** to talk about leaving a place. It is used after **saber** to say how much someone knows about something.

**Salgo de** mi casa a las siete. *I leave my house at seven.*
No **sé** mucho **de** arte. *I don't know much about art.*

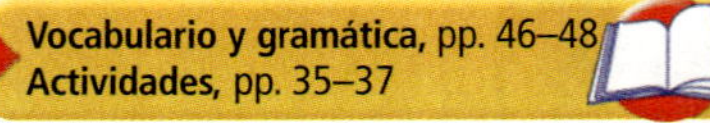

### Nota cultural

Students in south Florida, just like students everywhere, enjoy cultural school programs. Since many of the students in the Miami-Dade area have Caribbean roots, their school-related cultural activities reflect their Caribbean heritage. Many teenagers keep up with the Latin music scene and contribute in the special school programs, performances that are reflective of their background.

How are cultural programs similar or different in your school? **FL.B.1.1.2**

Carnaval juvenil caribeño de *Mardi Gras* en Ft. Lauderdale

### 43 Y tú, ¿qué haces? FL.A.2.1.2

**Leamos** Complete these sentences with the correct verb.

1. ¿Tú ___ del colegio a las 5:30?
   **a.** hago **b.** sales **c.** salgo
2. Yo ___ mis papeles en mi mochila.
   **a.** pongo **b.** vemos **c.** salgo
3. Mi amigo ___ su tarea por la noche.
   **a.** ponen **b.** pone **c.** hace
4. A veces mis amigas ___ su almuerzo de casa.
   **a.** traigo **b.** ponen **c.** traen
5. Nosotros nunca ___ películas en la cafetería.
   **a.** sé **b.** sabemos **c.** vemos
6. Yo no ___ mucho de computadoras.
   **a.** salgo **b.** sé **c.** hace

## 44 Un amigo de Internet FL.A.2.1.2

**Leamos/Escribamos** Rogelio posts this e-mail on a pen pal Web site. Read the e-mail and decide if the statements that follow are **cierto** or **falso.** Then write Rogelio and tell him about your interests.

1. Rogelio sale con amigos los fines de semana.
2. Rogelio lee libros de misterio.
3. Rogelio hace ejercicio a veces.
4. A Rogelio no le gusta el Internet.
5. A veces, Rogelio tiene conciertos.
6. A Rogelio le gusta ir al cine.

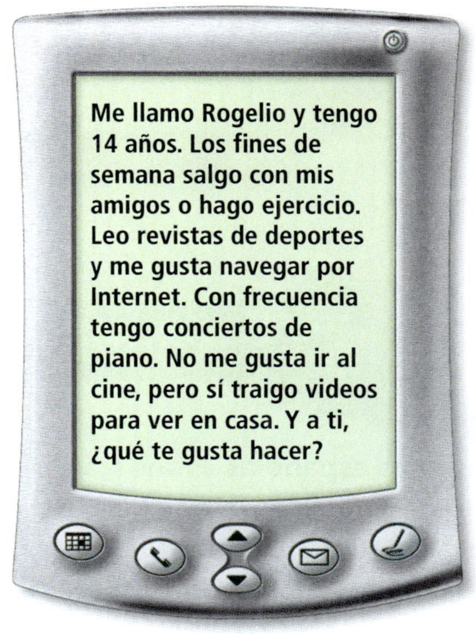


## 45 Las fiestas FL.A.3.1.1

**Hablemos/Escribamos** Answer these questions about what you do with your friends on weekends.

1. ¿Sales con amigos los fines de semana?
2. ¿Vas a la casa de tus amigos?
3. ¿Qué hacen ustedes? ¿Escuchan música o ven videos?
4. ¿Traen comida? ¿Salen a comer? ¿Qué les gusta comer?
5. ¿Les gusta ir al cine? Cuando van al cine, ¿a qué hora salen?
6. ¿Qué más haces con ellos?

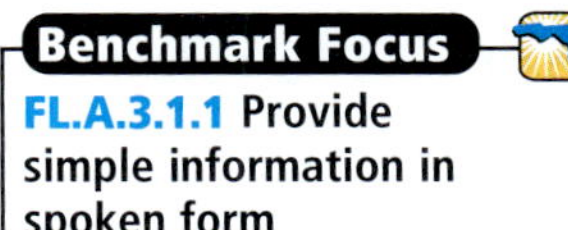


**FL.A.3.1.1** Provide simple information in spoken form

## 46 Después de clases FL.A.3.1.1

**Hablemos/Escribamos** With a partner, take turns describing this student's day after school. Include as many details as possible.

Gramática 2

# Conexiones culturales

**FCAT Mathematics Focus** 

**MA.D.1.3.1.7.4**
Predict outcomes based on a generalization of a pattern or relationship

**Misiones españolas** Franciscan friars founded missions in northern New Spain between the 1500s and 1700s in what are today the states of California, Arizona, Texas, New Mexico, and Florida. These missions were founded in order to claim land for Spain and to convert the native people to Catholicism.

**Misión San José** was built in 1720 in what is now San Antonio, Texas. At one time, the compound housed up to 350 people. The mission had fields and a farm nearby, and a large cattle and sheep ranch 25 miles to the southwest.

1. Church
2. Friar Housing
3. Convent Garden
4. Garden Well
5. Well
6. East Gate
7. Housing
8. Bastion
9. Southeast Gate
10. Southwest Gate
11. Ovens
12. West Gate
13. Granary
14. Carpentry Shop
15. Kilns
16. Mill
17. Vat
18. Aqueduct

## 1 ¿Producir o comprar? FL.B.1.1.3

According to the paragraph above and the drawing, what food and supplies could the people who lived in the mission compound produce for themselves? What other supplies might they have needed to buy? Use the list below.

| | |
|---|---|
| chicken | vegetables |
| beef | water |
| coffee | wool blankets |
| salt | horseshoes |
| corn | clothes |

## 2 El trabajo FL.B.1.1.2, FL.B.1.1.3

From the drawing above, what work would most interest you if you had lived in the San José mission? Building furniture? sewing clothes? shearing sheep? Explain your reasons.

Visit Holt Online
**go.hrw.com**
KEYWORD: EXP1A CH4
Online Edition

**Las misiones de Alta California** San Diego de Alcalá Mission was founded in 1769 in what is now San Diego, California. In 1770, San Carlos Borromeo de Carmelo was founded, 650 miles to the north in what is now the town of Carmel. In the beginning, mules were used to deliver food and supplies between San Diego and Carmel. Since the trip was both difficult and dangerous, a chain of missions was founded along **El Camino Real** to provide rest, shelter, and protection for travelers. Each mission was about one day's journey from another by mule.

## 3 Cincuenta millas en mula FL.B.1.1.3

1. San Carlos Borromeo de Carmelo is 650 miles to the north of San Diego de Alcalá. If a mule travels about fifty miles in one day, how many missions should the friars establish between San Diego de Alcalá and San Carlos Borromeo de Carmelo?
2. Count the missions from San Diego de Alcalá to San Carlos Borromeo de Carmelo on the map. How many missions were constructed? Is the number of missions the same as the number in your answer for item 1?

## 4 Las primeras misiones FL.B.1.1.3

1. Which missions were built first, the missions in Texas or in California?
2. Why do you think they built missions in that region first?

San Francisco Solano
San Rafael Arcángel
SAN FRANCISCO
San Francisco de Asís
Santa Clara de Asís
San José
Santa Cruz
San Juan Bautista
San Carlos Borromeo de Carmelo
Nuestra Señora de la Soledad
San Antonio de Padua
San Miguel Arcángel
San Luis Obispo de Tolosa
La Purísima Concepción
Santa Inés
Santa Bárbara
San Buenaventura
San Fernando Rey de España
LOS ANGELES
San Gabriel Arcángel
San Juan Capistrano
San Luis Rey de Francia
San Diego de Alcalá
SAN DIEGO
Océano Pacífico
California
Área de las misiones
N

Novela en video

# ¿Quién será?

## Episodio 4

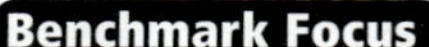

**FL.C.2.1.1** Use the target language to gain access to information that is only available through the target language or within the target culture

**ESTRATEGIA**

**Comparing and contrasting** When you compare and contrast two or more things, you look for similarities and differences. For example, you can look for similarities or differences in how the students in Mexico and those in Puerto Rico dress and behave. You can also compare and contrast the Puerto Rican and Mexican students with yourself and students in your school. What are some similarities and differences you notice as you read the **Novela** or watch the video? **FL.C.2.1.1**

### En Puerto Rico

*Marcos is trying to gather information on Nicolás. Nicolás is completely unaware.*

1

2

**Mateo** Oye, Nicolás, ¿a qué hora es tu clase de matemáticas?

**Nicolás** Tengo matemáticas a la una de la tarde. ¿Por qué?

**Mateo** Porque yo tengo matemáticas ahora y necesito muchas cosas.

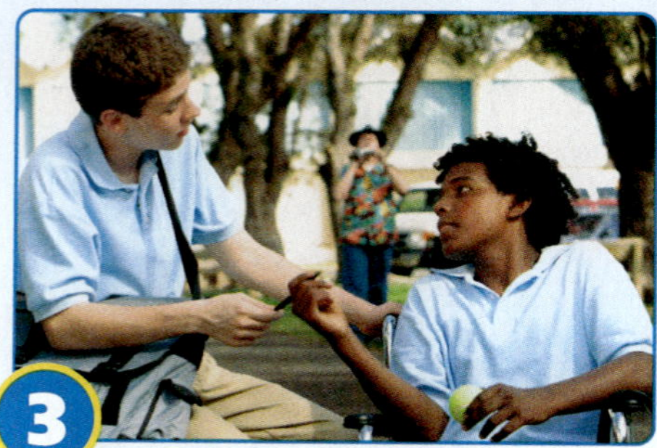
3

**Nicolás** ¿Qué necesitas?

**Mateo** Necesito un lápiz... una goma... una regla... y papel.

4

**Mateo** ¿Qué tal si vamos al partido de béisbol después de clases?

**Julia** Claro que sí.

**Nicolás** No, no tengo ganas.

**Mateo** ¿No tienes ganas? ¿Qué vas a hacer?

**Nicolás** Voy a... voy a... voy a...

**5**

**Julia** ¿Vas a qué? ¿Vas a hacer ejercicio?

**Nicolás** No, nunca hago ejercicio los lunes, ¿sabes? Los lunes son para...

**Mateo** ¿Para qué? ¿Qué vas a hacer?

**Nicolás** Voy a ver televisión. Mi programa favorito... esta noche...

**Julia** ¿Cuál es tu programa preferido?

**6**

**Mateo** ¿Y mañana? ¿Vas al concierto en el gimnasio?

**Julia** ¿Y pasado mañana?

*After school, Mateo and Julia decide to follow Nicolás to see where he's going.*

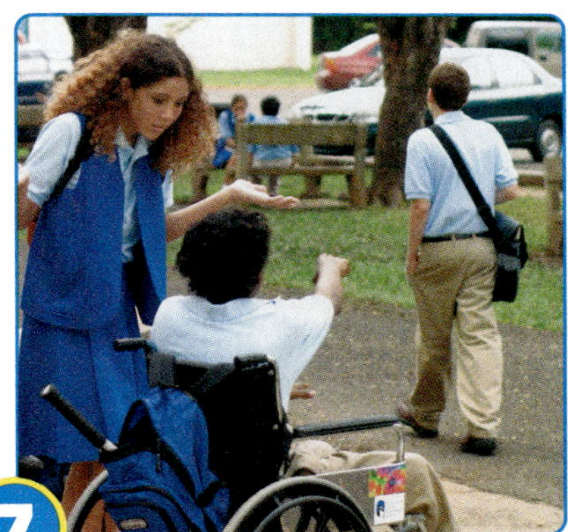

**7**

**Mateo** ¿Quieres ver adónde va Nicolás?

**Julia** Sí, pero, ¿el partido de béisbol?

**Mateo** No importa, vamos.

**8**

**Mateo** ¿Qué hace Nicolás?

**Julia** No sé. Pero...

**9**

**Julia** ¿Qué hace ese señor?

## A. Contesta

Answer the questions about the **Novela**. If you are not sure, make an educated guess! FL.A.2.1.2

1. Where are Nicolás and Mateo as the story begins?
2. Who has all his school supplies with him? Which student does not have any of the supplies that he needs?
3. Why does Nicolás try to get away from his friends after school?

## En España

*La profesora tells Marcos about her next candidate and his next trip.*

Francia
Portugal
Madrid
ESPAÑA
Mar Mediterráneo
Marruecos
Argelia

10

**La profesora** Ahora tengo un candidato de Costa Rica, Marcos. Sí, sí, después de Puerto Rico vas a El Paso y después de El Paso, a San José.

## En Puerto Rico

11

Nuevo México
Oklahoma
El Paso
TEXAS
México
Golfo de México

Nicaragua
Mar Caribe
COSTA RICA
San José
Panamá
Océano Pacífico

Océano Atlántico
San Juan
PUERTO RICO
Mar Caribe

### B. Contesta

1. What is **la profesora's** assistant doing at the end of the story?
2. What does she tell him on the phone this time?

**FL.A.2.1.2**

# Actividades

## 1 ¿Quién es? FL.A.2.1.2

Match the name of the person with the sentence that best describes him or her.

| | |
|---|---|
| **1.** Nicolás | **a.** Tiene cámara y teléfono. |
| **2.** Mateo | **b.** Tiene ganas de ir al partido de béisbol. |
| **3.** Julia | **c.** Necesita muchas cosas para la clase de matemáticas. |
| **4.** Marcos | **d.** Tiene matemáticas a la una. |

## 2 ¿Qué dice...? FL.A.2.1.2

Based on information in the **Novela**, complete each of the following questions or statements.

| | |
|---|---|
| **1.** ¿Qué necesitas... | **a.** tu programa preferido? |
| **2.** ¿Qué vas a hacer? | **b.** para la clase de matemáticas? |
| **3.** Y mañana, ¿vas al... | **c.** un candidato de Costa Rica. |
| **4.** ¿Cuál es... | **d.** concierto en el gimnasio? |
| **5.** Ahora tengo... | **e.** Voy a ver televisión. |

## 3 ¿Comprendes la Novela? FL.A.2.1.2

Check your understanding of the events in the story by answering these questions.

1. Contrast Nicolás's preparation for math class with Mateo's.
2. Does Nicolás answer his friends truthfully about his after-school plans? How can you tell?
3. Can Mateo and Julia tell what Nicolás is doing? Who else is there? What is he doing?
4. Compare and contrast the actions of Sofía in **Episodio 3** and of Nicolás in this episode. What about the actions of their friends?

**Próximo episodio**
*Can you predict what Marcos will do in Costa Rica?*
PÁGINAS 214–217

**FCAT Reading Focus**
**LA.A.2.3.1**
Identify relevant details and facts

**ESTRATEGIA**

**para leer** To improve your comprehension as you read a story, stop after each paragraph or section and ask yourself the ***who, what, where, when,*** and ***why*** of the story. Focusing on these questions as you read will not only help you check your comprehension, but also make reading in Spanish more fun.

**A Antes de leer** FL.C.2.1.1
Read the title and the first paragraph of the story. Can you answer at least one of each of the questions in the **Estrategia para leer?**

## Pepito, el niño precoz

Pepito es un niño gracioso, inteligente y precoz[1]. Tiene siete años y hoy es su primer día de colegio. Cuando viene a casa por la tarde, los padres de Pepito tienen muchas preguntas: ¿Te gusta el colegio?, ¿Cómo es tu profesora?, ¿Cuál es tu materia preferida? Pepito dice[2] que le gusta mucho el colegio: sus compañeros de clase son divertidos, la profesora es simpática y no es muy estricta y su materia preferida es matemáticas.

Por la noche, a la hora de comer, su mamá pone un plato con dos huevos[3] en la mesa. Pepito, siempre precoz, esconde[4] uno de los dos huevos y después de un minuto pregunta:

—Papá, ¿cuántos huevos ves en el plato?

—Pues, uno—contesta[5] el padre.

Pepito pone entonces el otro huevo en el plato y pregunta:

—Y ahora, papá, ¿cuántos huevos ves?

—Dos—contesta el padre.

—¡Magnífico! —exclama Pepito—los dos huevos que ves ahora y el otro huevo de antes,[6] son tres huevos, ¿verdad?

Su papá está un poco confundido.[7] Sólo ve dos huevos en el plato y no tres. Pero la mamá de Pepito, que escucha todo esto y que también es muy inteligente y graciosa dice:

—¡Claro que sí, Pepito! Hay tres huevos. El primero es para mí, el segundo[8] es para tu papá, y el tercero[9] es para ti.

**1** precocious **2** says **3** eggs **4** hides **5** answers **6** from before
**7** confused **8** second **9** third

Visit Holt Online
go.hrw.com
KEYWORD: EXP1A CH4
Online Edition

**B Comprensión** FL.C.2.1.1

Contesta las siguientes preguntas.

1. ¿Cuántos años tiene Pepito y cómo es?
2. ¿Cuál es la materia preferida de Pepito?
3. ¿Cómo es la profesora de Pepito? ¿Y los compañeros de clase?
4. ¿Qué pone la mamá en la mesa y qué hace el niño?
5. ¿Qué le pregunta Pepito a su papá? ¿Qué dice él?
6. ¿Qué dice la mamá de Pepito?

**C Después de leer** FL.A.3.1.1, FL.C.2.1.1

How would you describe Pepito? Which sentences in the story give you clues about his personality? What about his parents? What are they like? Do they have a sense of humor? Explain.

**FCAT Writing Focus**
**LA.B.1.3.2**
Draft and revise writing that has an organizational pattern that provides for a logical progression of ideas

Interactive TUTOR

## Taller del escritor

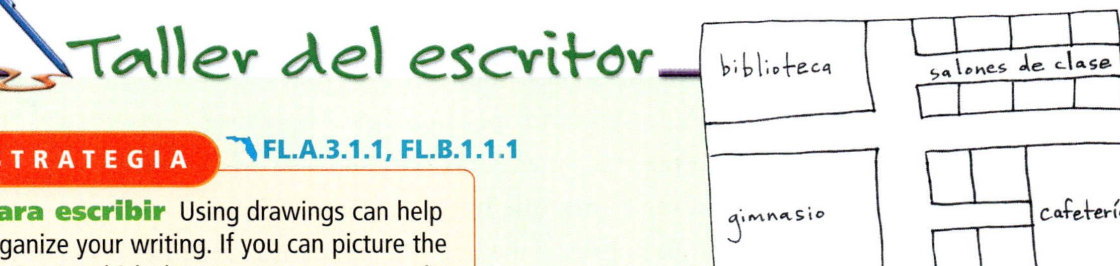


**ESTRATEGIA** FL.A.3.1.1, FL.B.1.1.1

**para escribir** Using drawings can help organize your writing. If you can picture the setting in which the events occur, your writing may be clearer to your readers.

### Un recorrido con nuevos estudiantes

Imagine you're helping with orientation at your school and you're taking two new students on a tour. Create a conversation based on your first meeting with them.

- Explain what classes they will take and when.
- Include questions new students might ask.
- Invite them to attend a club meeting, play, or another school activity.

**1 Antes de escribir**

Sketch the layout of your school. Label the places you would show new students. Draw arrows to show the route you plan to take.

**2 Escribir y revisar**

Begin your conversation based on the route you drew. The places you go should be based on the new students' questions and your explanations. End the conversation with an invitation and the students' responses.

Read over the questions, explanations, and answers. Check for correct use of grammar, spelling, and punctuation.

**3 Publicar**

Display your conversation and sketch on the bulletin board. You may wish to act out your conversations in groups of three classmates.

# Prepárate para el examen

Interactive TUTOR

**1 Vocabulario 1**
- talking about what you and others have or need
- talking about school supplies
- talking about classes

**pp. 140–145**

**2 Gramática 1**
- indefinite articles, **¿cuánto?, mucho,** and **poco**
- **tener** and **tener** idioms
- **venir** and **a** with time

**pp. 146–151**

**3 Vocabulario 2**
- talking about plans
- inviting someone to do something

**pp. 154–159**

**1** Completa la conversación de manera lógica. **FL.A.2.1.2**

—¿Qué clases tienes esta tarde?

—Tengo __1__, __2__ y __3__.

—¿Cuál es tu materia preferida?

—Bueno, me gusta __4__ porque es __5__. Y tú, ¿cuál es tu materia preferida?

—Es __6__. Bueno, ¿qué necesitas para la clase de inglés?

—Necesito __7__ y __8__.

**2** Answer the following questions about you and your friends. **FL.A.2.1.2, FL.A.3.1.1**

1. ¿A qué hora vienen ustedes al colegio por las mañanas?
2. ¿Generalmente tienen prisa ustedes cuando vienen al colegio?
3. ¿Cuántas clases tienes en un día?
4. ¿Necesitas muchas cosas para las clases?
5. ¿Qué cosas necesitas para la clase de español?
6. ¿Qué tienes que hacer después de clases?
7. ¿Qué tienes ganas de hacer este fin de semana? ¿y tu mejor amigo(a)?

**3** Invite your partner to each of the events pictured. Your partner will accept or turn down each invitation. **FL.A.1.2.2**

A

B

C

D

Visit Holt Online
**go.hrw.com**
KEYWORD: EXP1A CH4
Chapter Self-test

**4** Answer these questions about your weekend plans. FL.A.2.1.2, FL.A.3.1.1

1. ¿Vas a ir a un concierto este fin de semana?
2. ¿Ves televisión los sábados?
3. ¿Va un amigo a tu casa el domingo?
4. ¿Van a hacer la tarea en casa tu amigo y tú?
5. ¿Vas a ir a un partido de béisbol el sábado?
6. ¿Sales mucho con amigos los viernes?
7. ¿Sales a comer comida china los domingos?

**4 Gramática 2**
- **ir a** with infinitives
- **-er** and **-ir** verbs and tag questions
- **-er** and **-ir** verbs with irregular **yo** forms

**5** Answer the following questions. FL.D.2.1.1

1. How are programs of study in Latin America similar to or different from those in the United States?
2. What advantages or disadvantages are there in students repeating a semester if they fail two classes and the final exam?
3. What are the three class sessions in Costa Rican public schools called? When do they begin?

**5 Cultura**
- **Comparaciones** pp. 152–153
- **Notas culturales** pp. 142, 144, 156
- **Geocultura** pp. 134–137

**6** Escucha las preguntas y escribe las respuestas en tu papel. FL.A.2.1.3

**Benchmark Focus**

**FL.D.2.1.1** Know the similarities and differences between the patterns of behavior of the target culture and the local culture

**7** Use the drawings to describe what happens to this student who is always running late. FL.A.3.1.1

**a.**

**b.**

**c.**

**d.**

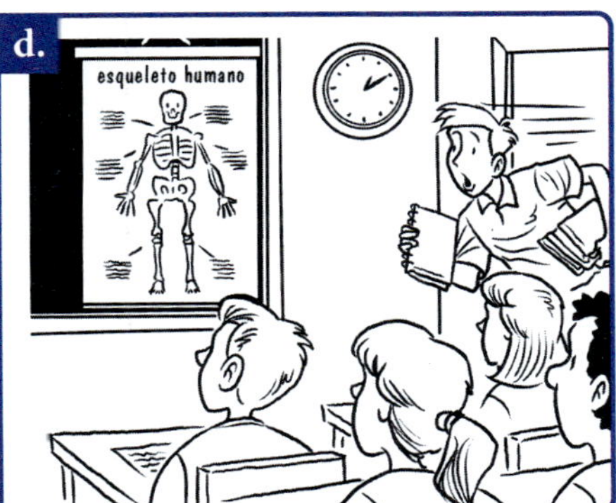

**Gramática 1**
- indefinite articles; **¿cuánto?, mucho, poco**
  **pp. 146–147**
- present tense of **tener** and some **tener** idioms
  **pp. 148–149**
- **venir** and **a** + time
  **pp. 150–151**

# Repaso de Gramática 1

| | **Masculine** | | **Feminine** | |
|---|---|---|---|---|
| **SINGULAR** | un | mucho | una | mucha |
| | cuánto | poco | cuánta | poca |
| **PLURAL** | unos | muchos | unas | muchas |
| | cuántos | pocos | cuántas | pocas |

| | |
|---|---|
| ten**go** | tenemos |
| t**ie**nes | tenéis |
| t**ie**ne | t**ie**nen |

| | |
|---|---|
| ven**go** | venimos |
| v**ie**nes | venís |
| v**ie**ne | v**ie**nen |

The preposition **a** followed by the **time** tells at what time something happens.
—¿Vienes a mi casa **a las 8:15**? —Sí. Tenemos clase **a las 9 en punto**.

**Gramática 2**
- **ir a** + infinitive
  **pp. 160–161**
- present tense of **-er** and **-ir** verbs and tag questions
  **pp. 162–163**
- **-er** and **-ir** verbs with irregular **yo** forms
  **pp. 164–165**

# Repaso de Gramática 2

The verb **ir** followed by **a** and an **infinitive** tells what is going to happen in the near future. Tag questions such as **¿no?** and **¿verdad?** ask the person listening to agree with the person speaking.

**Vas a bailar** en la fiesta, **¿no?**
Sí, también **voy a cantar.**

| **comer** | | **escribir** | |
|---|---|---|---|
| com**o** | com**emos** | escrib**o** | escrib**imos** |
| com**es** | com**éis** | escrib**es** | escrib**ís** |
| com**e** | com**en** | escrib**e** | escrib**en** |

Some irregular **yo** forms are **tengo, traigo, hago, sé, veo, salgo,** and **pongo.**

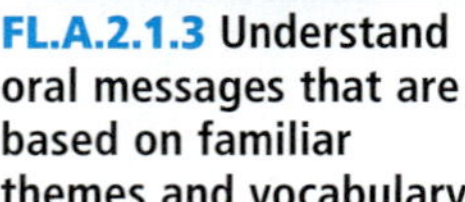
**Benchmark Focus**
**FL.A.2.1.3** Understand oral messages that are based on familiar themes and vocabulary

## Letra y sonido s z c qu

### Las letras s, z, c y qu

- In Spanish, the letter **s** sounds like the English *s* in *sun*: **s**alsa, **s**e**s**o, **s**illa, **s**olo, **s**u**s**.
- The letters **z** (before **a, o, u**), and **c** (before **e, i**) sound like the English *c* in the word *center:* **za**patos, **zo**na, a**zu**l, **ce**ntro, **ci**en**ci**as.
- In most of Spain, **z** and **c** in these combinations sound much like the English *th* in *think.*
- The letters **c** (before **a, o, u**) and **qu** (before **e** and **i**) sound like the English *k*: **ca**rpeta, **co**ro, **cu**aderno, **que**rer, **qui**én.

### Trabalenguas

Cuca Seco cose en casa de Coco Suca.
Cuando cuentes cuentos,
cuenta cuántos cuentos
cuentas.

### Dictado FL.A.2.1.3

Escribe las oraciones de la grabación.

# Repaso de Vocabulario 1

### Saying what you have and need

| | |
|---|---|
| el bolígrafo | *pen* |
| la calculadora | *calculator* |
| la carpeta | *folder* |
| la computadora | *computer* |
| el cuaderno | *notebook* |
| el diccionario | *dictionary* |
| el lápiz/los lápices | *pencil/pencils* |
| la mochila | *backpack* |
| mucho(a) | *a lot of, much* |
| muchos(as) | *a lot of, many* |
| ¿Necesitas algo para el colegio/la clase de arte? | *Do you need anything for school/art class?* |
| No, no necesito nada. | *No, I don't need anything.* |
| el papel | *paper* |
| poco(a) | *little, not much* |
| pocos(as) | *few, not many* |
| la regla | *ruler* |
| el reloj/los relojes | *clock, watch/clocks, watches* |
| la ropa | *clothes* |
| Sí, necesito muchas cosas. | *Yes, I need a lot of things.* |
| Sí, tengo un montón. | *Yes, I have a ton of them.* |
| ¿Tienes...? | *Do you have . . . ?* |
| un/una | *a, an* |
| unos/unas | *some* |
| los útiles escolares | *school supplies* |
| los zapatos | *shoes* |

### Talking about classes

| | |
|---|---|
| el alemán | *German* |
| el almuerzo | *lunch* |
| el arte, las artes | *art, the arts* |
| la biología | *biology* |
| las ciencias | *science* |
| la computación | *computer science* |
| ¿Cuál es tu materia preferida? | *What's your favorite subject?* |
| la educación física | *physical education* |
| Es fácil/difícil. | *It's easy/hard.* |
| el español | *Spanish* |
| el francés | *French* |
| la historia | *history* |
| el inglés | *English* |
| las matemáticas | *mathematics* |
| las materias | *school subjects* |
| Mi materia preferida es... | *My favorite subject is . . .* |
| Primero tengo..., y después tengo... | *First I have . . ., and afterwards I have . . .* |
| por la mañana/tarde | *in the morning/afternoon* |
| ¿Qué clases tienes esta tarde? | *What classes do you have this afternoon?* |
| la química | *chemistry* |
| el taller | *shop, workshop* |
| tener | *to have* |
| venir | *to come* |

# Repaso de Vocabulario 2

### Talking about plans . . . . . . . . . . . . . . . . . *See p. 155.*

| | |
|---|---|
| el auditorio | *auditorium* |
| la biblioteca | *library* |
| la cafetería | *cafeteria* |
| la clase de baile | *dance class* |
| el concierto | *concert* |
| el estadio | *stadium* |
| esta semana | *this week* |
| este fin de semana | *this weekend* |
| hacer | *to do, to make* |
| hay | *there is, there are* |
| llegar | *to get there, to arrive* |
| mañana | *tomorrow* |
| el partido de... | *. . . game* |
| pasado mañana | *day after tomorrow* |
| poner | *to put* |
| la próxima semana | *next week* |
| saber (de) | *to know information, to know about* |
| salir (de) | *to go out, to leave* |
| el salón de clase | *classroom* |
| traer | *to bring* |
| ver | *to watch, to see* |
| el viernes próximo | *next Friday* |

### Inviting someone to do something . . . . *See p. 158.*

# Integración
## capítulos 1-4

**1** Match each picture to the statements that best describe Lorenzo's busy day. FL.A.2.1.3

a. b. c. d.

**2** Manuel has been accepted as an exchange student in the United States. Read his e-mail to his host parents and then tell whether each statement is **cierto** or **falso.** Correct the false statements. FL.A.2.1.2

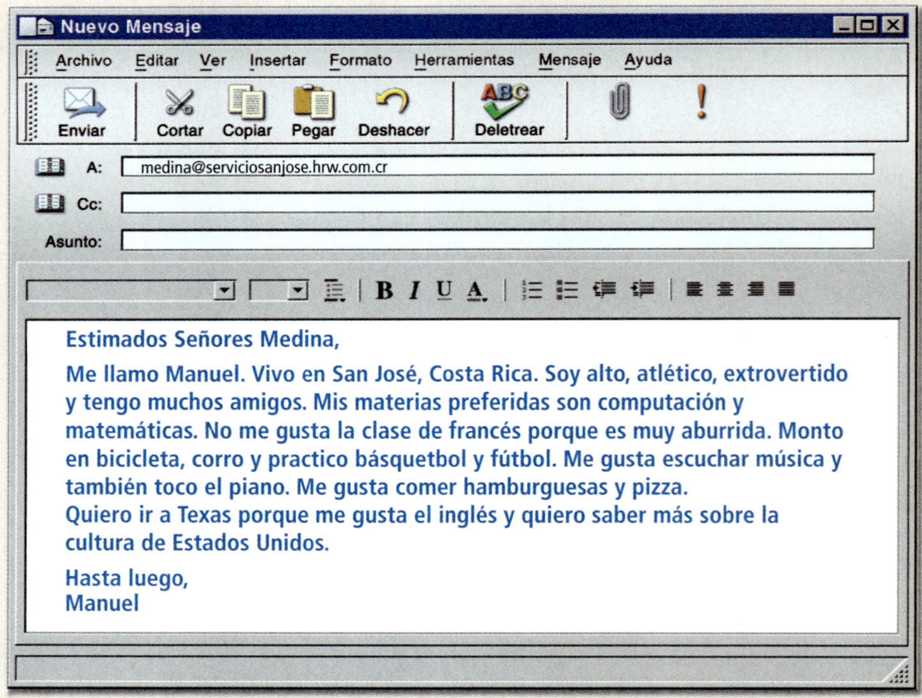


Estimados Señores Medina,

Me llamo Manuel. Vivo en San José, Costa Rica. Soy alto, atlético, extrovertido y tengo muchos amigos. Mis materias preferidas son computación y matemáticas. No me gusta la clase de francés porque es muy aburrida. Monto en bicicleta, corro y practico básquetbol y fútbol. Me gusta escuchar música y también toco el piano. Me gusta comer hamburguesas y pizza.
Quiero ir a Texas porque me gusta el inglés y quiero saber más sobre la cultura de Estados Unidos.

Hasta luego,
Manuel

1. Manuel es alto, atlético y tiene pocos amigos.
2. A Manuel le gustan más las clases de computación y matemáticas.
3. A Manuel no le gusta la clase de francés porque es difícil.
4. Manuel quiere ir a Costa Rica.
5. Manuel tiene ganas de visitar Estados Unidos.

**3**  Imagine that you lived at the time of this painting, were traveling along this path, and met these people. Write a description of the scene, answering the following questions. FL.A.2.1.2

1. ¿Qué colores ves?
2. ¿Qué tiempo hace?
3. ¿Qué día de la semana es?
4. ¿Cuántas personas hay?
5. ¿Adónde van?
6. ¿Tienen prisa?

Victor Hugo Fernández, Gráficos del Globo, S.A., Costa Rica

***Domingueando,*** **de Tomás Povedano de Arcos (1847–1943)**

**Benchmark Focus** 

**FL.A.1.2.2** Exchange information necessary to plan events or activities

**4** Situación

With a partner, role-play a scene in a school supplies store. One of you is a student shopping for supplies on the first day of school, the other is the storekeeper. Through questions and answers, say:

- what classes the student has
- what supplies the student already has
- what supplies the student needs
- when the student's first class is
- what the student's favorite class is

FL.A.1.2.2

Repaso cumulativo

GeoVisión

Capítulo 5

# Geocultura

# Chile

▲ **La costa del Pacífico** Chile's Pacific coastline is 6,000 kilometers long, but the country is less than 185 kilometers wide. The city of **Viña del Mar** is a destination for sunbathers.

▲ **Moais** More than 600 stone statues called **moais** are located on Easter Island in the Pacific Ocean. Easter Island is also known as **Rapa Nui.**

▼ **Santiago** Chile's capital was founded in 1541 by the Spanish explorer Pedro de Valdivia. This city of 5.5 million people lies at the foot of the Andes Mountains.

## Almanac

**Population**
15,498,930

**Capital**
Santiago

**Government**
republic

**Currency**
Chilean peso

**Official Language**
Spanish

**Internet Code**
www.[ ].cl

▼ **Volantines**
Flying these small kites is popular in the springtime.

## ¿Sabías que...?

**Chile and Florida are both major fruit producers and exporters. Chile's production of grapes, pears, and apples make it the largest fruit exporter in South America. Florida's biggest fruit crops are oranges and grapefruit.**

► **El desierto de Atacama** The Atacama Desert in northern Chile is the driest desert in the world.

◄ **El altiplano de los Andes en Chile** The Chilean highlands, part of a large plateau in the Andes Mountains, lie more than 4,500 meters high. **Llamas, vicuñas, guanacos,** and **alpacas** are well adapted to this extreme altitude.

▼ **El Parque Nacional Laguna San Rafael** Laguna San Rafael National Park in southern Chile has a spectacular aqua-blue glacier.

▼ **Las Torres y los Cuernos del Paine** These sharp peaks rise almost vertically from the plains below. They are more than 2,000 kilometers south of Santiago.

**¿Qué tanto sabes?**
Which three countries share a border with Chile?
FL.C.1.1.1

# A conocer Chile

## La arquitectura

▲ **La Isla Chiloé** Houses on the southern island of **Chiloé** are often painted in vivid colors. Some houses called **palafitos** are built on stilts.

▲ **Lo moderno y lo antiguo** Colonial architecture from the past contrasts with modern architecture in the capital city of Santiago, giving it a European feel.

## La comida

▼ **Los mariscos** Chileans eat a great variety of seafood from the Pacific Ocean. This dish is called **curanto.**

▲ **El pastel de choclo** This Chilean meat pie is topped with mashed corn. The word **choclo** means *corn* in the Mapuche language.

Visit Holt Online

**go.hrw.com**

KEYWORD: EXP1A CH5

Photo Tour

# Las celebraciones

▲ **La Fiesta de La Tirana** The town of La Tirana near Iquique holds this major festival each July. The festival has its roots in Incan ceremonies, Chinese carnivals, and Spanish fiestas.

▶ **Los mapuches** The culture of the Mapuche people can be seen in their customs, handicrafts, traditional dress, and festivals.

**Benchmark Focus**

FL.B.1.1.2 Recognize patterns of social behavior or interaction

FL.B.1.1.3

## ¿Sabías que...?

Mapuche defenders halted Spanish armies at the **Río Bío Bío** for over 300 years. How can you see the effects of the Mapuche and Spanish cultures on architecture, food, and celebrations in Chile today?

# Las bellas artes

▲ **Pablo Neruda (1904–1973) y Gabriela Mistral (1889–1957)** These two famous Chilean poets each won a Nobel Prize in Literature.

▶ **Pedro Lira (1845–1912)** Chilean artist Pedro Lira gained international fame for this painting, *The Founding of Santiago*.

Capítulo 5

# En casa con la familia

## Objetivos

**In Part 1 you will learn to:**

- describe people and family relationships
- use possessive adjectives
- form **o** to **ue** stem changing verbs
- use verbs with an **e** to **ie** stem change

**In Part 2 you will learn to:**

- talk about where you and others live
- talk about responsibilities
- form **estar** and use it with prepositions
- say where people and things are using prepositions
- make sentences negative using **nunca, tampoco, no, nadie,** and **nada**
- form and use the verbs **tocar** and **parecer**

## ¿Qué ves en la foto?

- **¿Qué colores ves en la foto?**
- **¿Qué les toca hacer a los muchachos?**
- **¿Qué te parece tener que ayudar en casa?**

Look for the next to each activity and the **Benchmark Focus** to help you achieve the goals of the **Florida Sunshine State Standards,** found on pages FL14–FL16.

Una familia de Santiago, Chile

**Objetivos**
- Describing people and family relationships

# Vocabulario en acción 1

Video/DVD
ExpresaVisión

▶ Vocabulario adicional — La familia, p. R9

## Tiene los ojos...

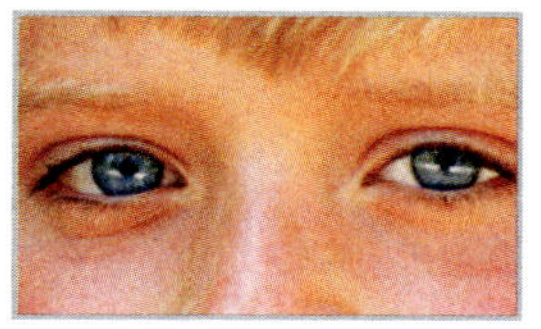
azules

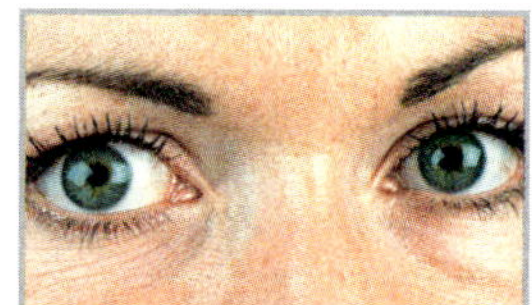
verdes

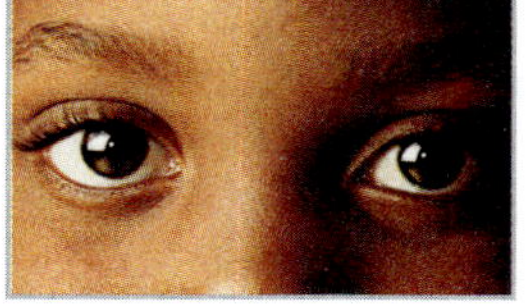
negros

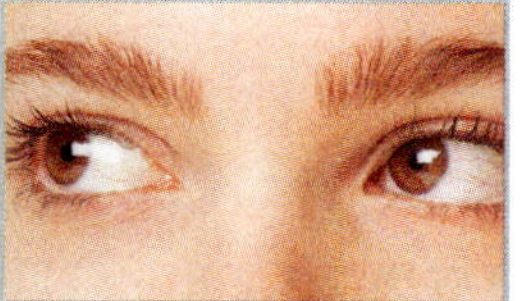
de color café

## Tiene el pelo...

castaño

canoso

negro

largo

corto

### Más vocabulario...

**¿Cómo es?**

| | | | |
|---|---|---|---|
| ciego(a) | *blind* | sordo(a) | *deaf* |
| gordo(a) | *fat* | travieso(a) | *mischievous* |
| joven | *young* | viejo(a) | *old* |

### También se puede decir...

In Florida, people from the Dominican Republic may refer to brown or hazel eyes as **ojos marrones** or **ojos galanos.** Cubans may call hazel eyes **ojos carmelitas,** and Colombians may use **ojos color miel** or **ojos castaños.**

## ¡Exprésate!

| To ask about people and family relationships | To respond |
|---|---|
| **¿Cuántas personas hay en tu familia?**<br>*How many people are in your family?* | **En mi familia somos cuatro personas.**<br>*There are four people in my family.* |
| **¿Cómo es tu familia?**<br>*What is your family like?* | **Somos delgados y tenemos el pelo rubio. Todos usamos lentes. Mi hermana María está en una silla de ruedas.**<br>*We are thin and have blond hair. We all wear glasses. My sister María is in a wheelchair.* |
| **¿Cómo es tu tía?**<br>*What is your aunt like?* | **Es profesora. Es una persona callada. Ella y mi tío tienen dos hijos pero no tienen nietos.**<br>*She's a teacher. She's a quiet person. She and my uncle have two children, but don't have any grandchildren.* |

Interactive TUTOR

Vocabulario y gramática, pp. 49–51 Online workbooks

▶ Vocabulario adicional — Profesiones, p. R10

## Nota cultural

The system of Hispanic surnames **(apellidos)** gives information about both parents' families. In most Latin American countries, people use both their parents' names, as in the name Josefa Fernández Prieto, in which Fernández is the father's last name and Prieto is the mother's maiden name. Notice that in this case, Josefa uses her father's name as her first surname. In the United States, the custom is to use only the father's last name, and Hispanics in the U.S. sometimes use their mother's maiden name as their middle name.

Compare Josefa's name to yours. **FL.D.2.1.1**

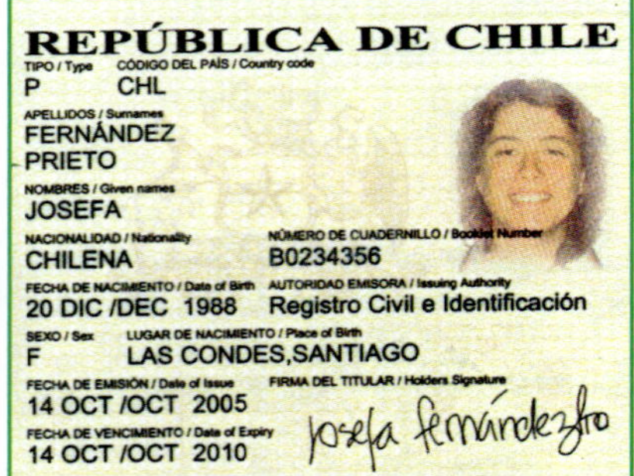
REPÚBLICA DE CHILE
TIPO / Type CÓDIGO DEL PAÍS / Country code
P CHL
APELLIDOS / Surnames
FERNÁNDEZ
PRIETO
NOMBRES / Given names
JOSEFA
NACIONALIDAD / Nationality NÚMERO DE CUADERNILLO / Booklet Number
CHILENA B0234356
FECHA DE NACIMIENTO / Date of Birth AUTORIDAD EMISORA / Issuing Authority
20 DIC /DEC 1988 Registro Civil e Identificación
SEXO / Sex LUGAR DE NACIMIENTO / Place of Birth
F LAS CONDES,SANTIAGO
FECHA DE EMISIÓN / Date of Issue FIRMA DEL TITULAR / Holders Signature
14 OCT /OCT 2005
FECHA DE VENCIMIENTO / Date of Expiry
14 OCT /OCT 2010

Carnet de identidad chileno

### 1 ¿Cierto o falso? FL.A.2.1.3

**Escuchemos** Mira el árbol genealógico *(family tree)* y escucha las oraciones. Indica si cada oración es **cierta** o **falsa.**

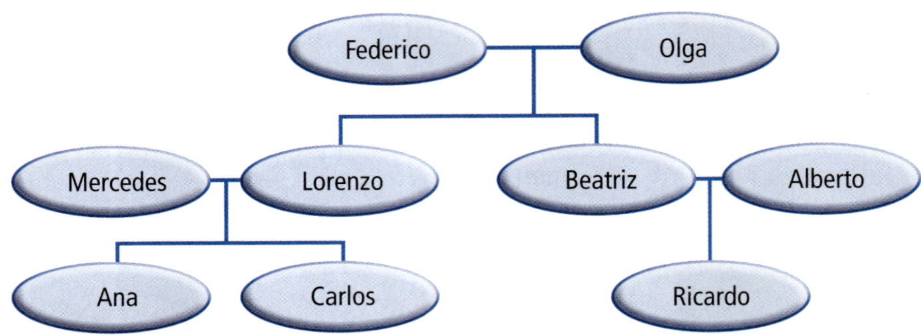


### 2 ¿Quién es quién? FL.A.2.1.2

**Leamos** Answer the questions based on the family tree in Activity 1.

1. ¿Quién es la hermana de Lorenzo?
2. ¿Cómo se llama el tío de Ricardo?
3. ¿Cómo se llama la abuela de Ana?
4. ¿Quién es la madre de Carlos?
5. ¿Cuántos nietos tienen Federico y Olga?
6. ¿Cómo se llama el padre de Ricardo?
7. ¿Cuántos hijos tienen Mercedes y Lorenzo?
8. ¿Quién es el primo de Carlos?

### 3 Descripciones FL.A.2.1.2

**Leamos/Escribamos** Completa la descripción de cada foto con una respuesta lógica.

1. Mi abuelo es ____. Tiene el pelo ____ y ____.
2. Mi tío es ____. Tiene un ____ inteligente.
3. Mi papá es ____. Usa ____.
4. Mi ____ se llama Barrigón. Es muy ____, ¿no?

1. mi abuelo

2. mi tío

3. mi papá

4. Barrigón

## 4 La familia Herrera FL.A.2.1.2

**Leamos** Imagine that your friend is an exchange student in Chile. He has sent you this photo of his host family, the Herreras. Finish the description of the Herrera family.

En la familia Herrera hay __1__ personas. La abuela está en una __2__. El abuelo es __3__ y __4__ y tiene el pelo __5__. Hay __6__ hijas y __7__ hijo. El hijo tiene un __8__. La hija mayor y la mamá tienen el pelo __9__. Me gusta esta familia, ellos son muy __10__.

**Benchmark Focus**

**FL.A.2.1.2** Restate and rephrase simple information from materials presented orally, visually, and graphically in class

La familia Herrera de Valparaíso, Chile

HOLT SoundBooth ONLINE RECORDING

## 5 ¿Quién es cómico? FL.A.1.1.2

**Hablemos** Work in pairs. Ask your partner questions using **¿Quién en tu familia es...?** and the adjectives below. Then switch roles. Remember to use the correct form of adjectives in your answers!

**MODELO** **cómico —¿Quién en tu familia es cómico?**
**—Mi hermana Anita es cómica.**

1. serio(a)
2. viejo(a)
3. joven
4. delgado(a)
5. travieso(a)
6. alto(a)
7. atlético(a)
8. callado(a)

Vocabulario 1

Grandparents and elderly aunts often live with younger members of families in Spanish-speaking countries. In general, elderly members of the family hold a place of honor and are given great respect by everyone.

Compare this situation with families you know.

FL.D.2.1.1

## 6 Retrato de familia FL.A.2.1.2

**Leamos** Read the sentences below. For each sentence, write the name of the family described.

**MODELO** **Mi hermano se llama Alberto. (Canales)**

1. Somos ocho en casa.
2. Somos seis personas en mi familia: mis padres, mi tía, mis dos hermanos y yo.
3. Somos tres hermanas, dos hermanos, mis padres y mi abuelo.
4. Mi hermana menor tiene tres años y es rubia.
5. La hermana de mi papá se llama Rosa.
6. Mi papá es rubio y tiene los ojos azules.
7. Tengo cinco nietos.
8. Tengo tres sobrinos.
9. El padre de mi papá usa lentes.
10. Mi hermana menor se llama Zenaida.

## 7 ¿Quién eres? FL.A.2.1.2

**Escribamos** Pretend you are a member of either the Canales or the Andrade family. Write five sentences that give clues to your identity.

**MODELO** **Tengo dos hermanos y dos hermanas.**

## 8 ¿Cómo son? FL.A.2.1.2

**Escribamos** Use words from each list to write at least three sentences about yourself and your family members.

**MODELO** **Mi hermano tiene doce años. Es bajo y tiene el pelo rubio. Es travieso.**

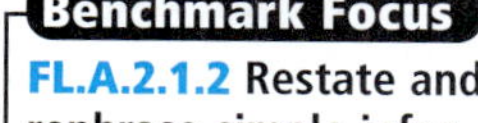

**FL.A.2.1.2** Restate and rephrase simple information from materials presented orally, visually, and graphically in class

| | | | |
|---|---|---|---|
| yo | tener | ___ años | delgado(a) |
| mi hermano(a) | (no) usar | los ojos | gordo(a) |
| mi abuelo(a) | ser | el pelo | travieso(a) |
| mi padre | | lentes | serio(a) |
| mi madre | | alto(a) | joven |
| mi perro | | bajo(a) | viejo(a) |
| mi gato | | ciego(a) | trabajador(a) |
| | | sordo(a) | perezoso(a) |

## 9 Adivina... ¿quiénes son? FL.A.3.1.1

**Escribamos/Hablemos** With a partner, write three sentences about each family below. Talk about how the people look, their family relationships to each other, and activities they do together. Then get together with another pair of classmates and exchange papers. See if you can guess correctly which of their sentences match each photo.

1. la familia Howard

2. la familia Ruiz

3. la familia Takeda

4. la familia Dean

## 10 Entrevista FL.A.1.1.2, FL.A.3.1.1

**Hablemos** Ask three classmates the following questions. Based on their answers, who is most like you? Report your findings to the class.

*¿Se te olvidó?* The preposition de, p. 72

1. ¿Cuántas personas hay en tu familia?
2. ¿Con quién de tu familia te gusta más pasar el rato? ¿Cómo es?
3. ¿Cuántos hermanos mayores tienes? ¿Cuántos menores? ¿Cómo son?
4. ¿Tienes perro o gato? ¿Cómo se llama(n)?

## Objetivos

- Possessive adjectives
- o → ue stem-changing verbs
- e → ie stem-changing verbs

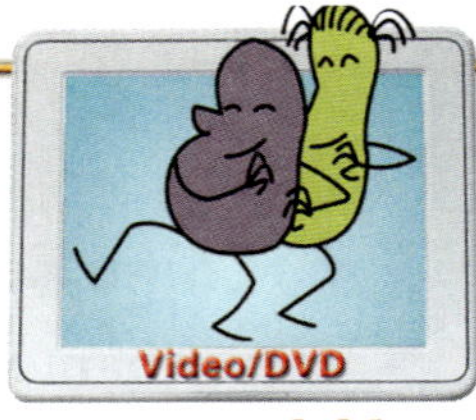


GramaVisión

## Possessive adjectives

**1** **Possessive adjectives** show ownership or relationships between people. They are placed before the noun.

| Owner | | Owner | |
|---|---|---|---|
| yo | **mi** libro<br>**mis** libros | nosotros(as) | **nuestro** libro/**nuestra** casa<br>**nuestros** libros/**nuestras** casas |
| tú | **tu** libro<br>**tus** libros | vosotros(as) | **vuestro** libro/**vuestra** casa<br>**vuestros** libros/**vuestras** casas |
| usted<br>él<br>ella | **su** libro<br>**sus** libros | ustedes<br>ellos<br>ellas | **su** libro<br>**sus** libros |

**2** While **possessive adjectives** refer to the **owner,** their form agrees in gender and number with the noun that comes after them.

*refers to* *agrees grammatically*

**Martín** vive con **sus** abuelo**s**.

*refers to* *agrees grammatically*

**Carlos y yo** vivimos con **nuestra** abuel**a**.

**3** **Su** and **sus** can take the place of a phrase with **de + a person**.

¿De dónde es la madre **de Juan**? **Su** madre es de Puebla.

### En inglés

**In English,** the possessive adjectives *his, her,* and *their* tell whether something belongs to a male, a female, or more than one person.

Which possessive adjective in English can stand for one person or more than one person?

**In Spanish,** the possessive adjective **su** has many possible meanings *(his, her, its, your, their)*, but context usually makes the meaning clear.
FL.D.1.1.2

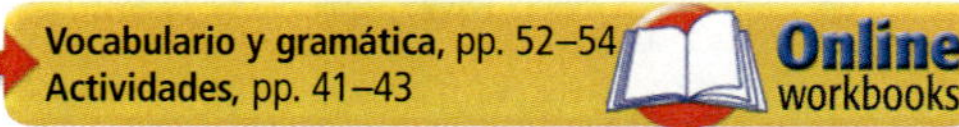


### 11 Nuestras cosas FL.A.2.1.2

**Leamos** Complete the sentences to say that each person is looking for his or her own belongings.

1. Busco (mi/su) libro de español.
2. Buscamos (sus/nuestros) cuadernos.
3. Ellos buscan (tus/sus) mochilas.
4. Mi hermana menor busca (mis/sus) lentes.
5. Buscas (tus/vuestros) lápices.
6. Mamá busca (su/tu) reloj.
7. Mis amigos y yo buscamos (vuestra/nuestra) tarea.

Visit Holt Online
go.hrw.com
KEYWORD: EXP1A CH5
Gramática 1 practice

Gramática 1

## 12 ¿De Carolina o de Marta? FL.A.2.1.3

**Escuchemos** Listen to the following sentences. Then, based on the photos, decide whether each sentence refers to Carolina's family or Marta's family.

la familia de Carolina

la familia de Marta

## 13 En mi familia FL.A.2.1.2

**Leamos/Escribamos** Juan is talking about his family with a friend. Fill in the blanks in the conversation with the correct possessive adjective and then tell the class about Juan's family.

—Juan, ¿cuántas personas hay en ___1___ familia?

—Somos cinco en mi familia: ___2___ padres, ___3___ hermana mayor, ___4___ hermano menor y yo.

—¿Dónde trabajan ___5___ padres?

—___6___ madre es profesora. ___7___ trabajo es muy interesante. ___8___ padre trabaja con ___9___ padre, mi abuelo. A mis padres les gusta mucho ___10___ trabajo.

—Ustedes tienen una casa verde, ¿verdad?

—No, ___11___ casa no es verde pero ___12___ carro es verde.

## Comunicación

## 14 La familia de mi amigo FL.A.1.1.2

**Hablemos** Interview a classmate about someone from his or her extended family. Find out the family member's name, what he or she is like, and what your classmate and he or she like to do together.

**MODELO** **—¿Cómo se llama tu abuelo?**
**—Se llama Robert Miller.**
**—¿Y cómo es?**
**—Es alto, delgado y muy simpático.**

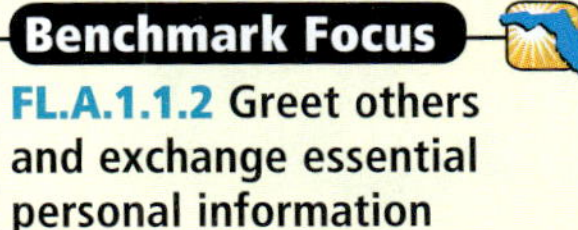

## Stem-changing verbs: o → ue

**1** Verbs with vowel variations in their stems are called **stem-changing verbs**. You have already learned **jugar** where the **u** changes to **ue**. In the verb **dormir** *(to sleep)*, the **o** of the stem changes to **ue** in all forms except **nosotros(as)** and **vosotros(as).**

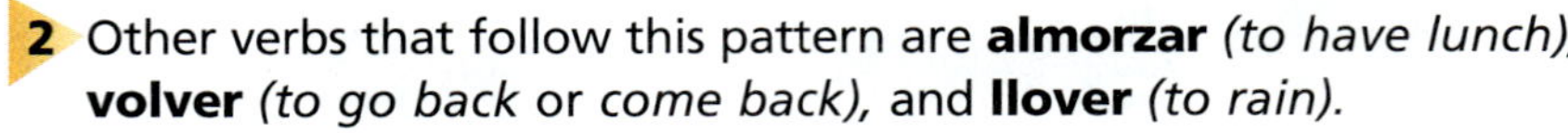

| | | | |
|---|---|---|---|
| yo | d**ue**rmo | nosotros(as) | dormimos |
| tú | d**ue**rmes | vosotros(as) | dormís |
| Ud., él, ella | d**ue**rme | Uds., ellos, ellas | d**ue**rmen |

El perro **duerme** mucho. *The dog sleeps a lot.*

**2** Other verbs that follow this pattern are **almorzar** *(to have lunch)*, **volver** *(to go back* or *come back)*, and **llover** *(to rain)*.

Cuando **llueve**, **vuelvo** a casa en el autobús.
*When it rains, I come home on the bus.*

**3** Use **dormir hasta** to say you *sleep until* a certain time.

Los domingos **dormimos hasta** las once.

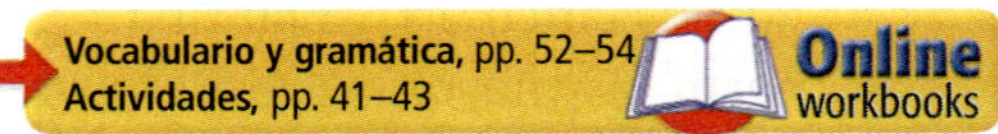


### ¿Te acuerdas?

In Spanish, regular -ar, -er, and -ir verbs have **regular stems** and regular endings.

**habl**ar

| | |
|---|---|
| **habl**o | **habl**amos |
| **habl**as | **habl**áis |
| **habl**a | **habl**an |

**com**er

| | |
|---|---|
| **com**o | **com**emos |
| **com**es | **com**éis |
| **com**e | **com**en |

**escrib**ir

| | |
|---|---|
| **escrib**o | **escrib**imos |
| **escrib**es | **escrib**ís |
| **escrib**e | **escrib**en |

### 15 Su rutina diaria FL.A.2.1.2

**Leamos** Complete the e-mail with the missing verbs. Each word is used once.

| | | | | |
|---|---|---|---|---|
| duermo | almuerzo | vuelvo | jugamos | almorzamos |
| duerme | almuerza | vuelve | dormimos | volvemos |

Nuevo Mensaje
Archivo Editar Ver Insertar Formato Herramientas Mensaje Ayuda
Enviar Cortar Copiar Pegar Deshacer Deletrear Adjuntar Prioridad

Nosotros casi siempre ___1___ en la cafetería. Mi hermano ___2___ a las once y media y yo ___3___ a la una. Siempre tengo mucha hambre. Mi hermano ___4___ a casa en su bicicleta a las dos y media y yo ___5___ a las tres. A veces nosotros ___6___ a videojuegos después de volver y a veces yo ___7___ un poco en el sofá. A las cuatro y media vamos al parque por una hora. Nosotros ___8___ del parque a las cinco y media. Después de cenar hacemos nuestra tarea. Los sábados nosotros ___9___ hasta tarde. El perro siempre ___10___ conmigo.

## 16 Un fin de semana típico FL.A.2.1.2

**Leamos/Escribamos** Complete each sentence with the correct form of the underlined verb. Sometimes the sentence requires a conjugated form and sometimes an infinitive.

1. Cuando llueve no tengo ganas de salir, pero no va a ____ mañana.
2. Voy a almorzar en el centro comercial. Yo siempre ____ con mis primos en el centro comercial los sábados.
3. Luego mi prima Juana viene a mi casa y jugamos al tenis. A ella le gusta ____ conmigo.
4. Después Juana y yo ____ al centro comercial. Nos gusta ir de compras. Pero nuestros amigos no vuelven.
5. Luego yo ____ a mi casa y Juana vuelve a su casa.
6. Cuando vuelvo a casa por la tarde siempre quiero dormir un poco. Yo ____ mucho por la tarde los sábados.
7. Los sábados duermo hasta las diez. A mi hermano no le gusta ____ hasta las diez.
8. Quiero jugar al fútbol hoy. No voy a ____ porque va a llover.
9. Mi hermana y yo vamos a almorzar después de jugar al tenis. Ella y yo siempre ____ a la una y media.

### Nota cultural

In Florida, when people speak of their **familia** they often also include their **abuelos, tíos,** and **primos**. Extended families typically live together or nearby. The relatives frequently help each other with childcare, taking care of elderly relatives, or transportation. Daily phone calls are common; getting together for dinner is more than a weekly occurrence for many.

What do families in your part of Florida do to stay in touch? FL.D.2.1.1

## Comunicación

## 17 ¿Quién de tu familia...? FL.A.1.1.2

**Hablemos** Interview your partner using the photos and question words as a guide. Your partner should talk about what he or she and at least two other family members do. Then switch roles.

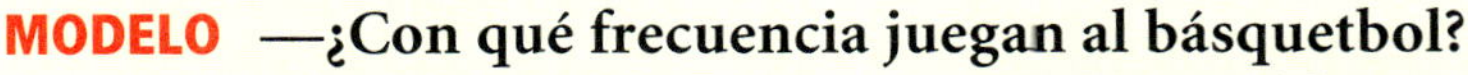

**MODELO** **—¿Con qué frecuencia juegan al básquetbol?**
**—Mi hermano y yo a veces jugamos al básquetbol. Mi madre nunca juega al básquetbol.**

¿con qué frecuencia?

a. ¿dónde?

b. ¿con qué frecuencia?

c. ¿mucho? ¿poco?

d. ¿a qué hora?

Gramática 1

## Stem-changing verbs: e → ie

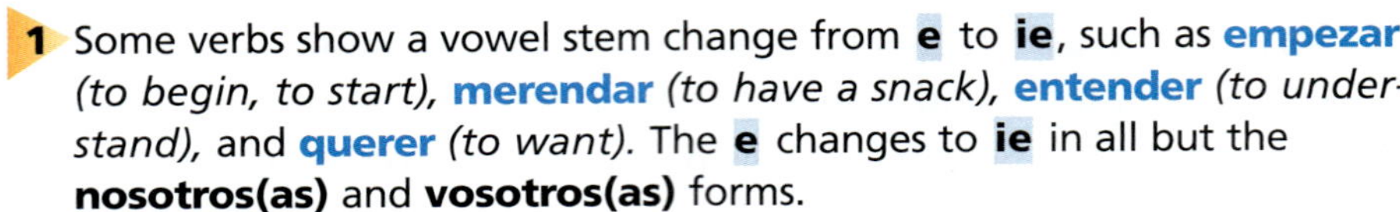

**1** Some verbs show a vowel stem change from **e** to **ie**, such as **empezar** *(to begin, to start)*, **merendar** *(to have a snack)*, **entender** *(to understand)*, and **querer** *(to want)*. The **e** changes to **ie** in all but the **nosotros(as)** and **vosotros(as)** forms.

| | | | |
|---|---|---|---|
| yo | emp**ie**zo | nosotros(as) | empezamos |
| tú | emp**ie**zas | vosotros(as) | empezáis |
| Ud., él, ella | emp**ie**za | Uds., ellos, ellas | emp**ie**zan |

—¿A qué hora **empieza** la película?
*What time does the movie start?*

—**Empieza** a las siete.
*It starts at seven o'clock.*

Tengo que estudiar más. No **entiendo** nada en la clase de matemáticas.
*I have to study more. I don't understand anything in math class.*

**2** You can also use **empezar a** followed by an **infinitive** to say what you or others start to do.

—¿A qué hora **empiezan a trabajar** tus padres?

—**Empiezan a trabajar** a las ocho de la mañana.

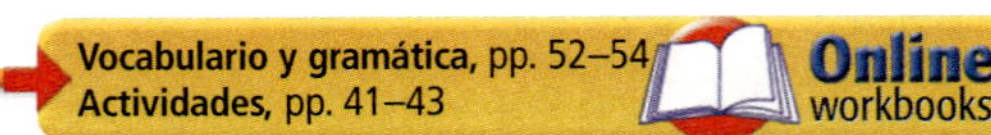
Vocabulario y gramática, pp. 52–54
Actividades, pp. 41–43
Online workbooks

### ¿Te acuerdas?

The verb t**e**ner is also an **e → ie** stem-changing verb. It is irregular in the **yo form**.

| | |
|---|---|
| **tengo** | tenemos |
| t**ie**nes | tenéis |
| t**ie**ne | t**ie**nen |

### 18 Después de clases FL.A.2.1.2

**Leamos/Hablemos** Complete the conversation using the correct verbs from the box. One verb will be used twice.

| jugamos | quieres | merendamos | tengo | tienes | empieza | entiendo |
|---|---|---|---|---|---|---|

—Hola, Guillermo.
—Hola, Fernando. ¿Cómo estás?
—Más o menos. Esta tarde __1__ mucha hambre.
—Sí, yo también. ¿Qué tal si __2__ algo? Hay fruta en la mesa.
—Sí, buena idea. Y después de comer, ¿(tú) __3__ ir al cine conmigo? La película "El perro invisible" __4__ a las cinco.
—No, no __5__ ganas de ver una película.
—Si no __6__ ganas de ir al cine, ¿quieres jugar al básquetbol? Tengo un partido mañana y necesito practicar.
—Sí, está bien. ¿Qué tal si __7__ una hora? Luego tengo que estudiar.
—¿Por qué tienes que estudiar esta tarde?
—Porque mañana hay un examen en la clase de historia y yo no __8__ nada. Es una clase difícil.

## 19 ¿A qué hora? FL.A.2.1.2

6:30 A.M.

**Leamos/Hablemos** Look at the pictures and answer the following questions. *¿Se te olvidó?* A + time, p. 150

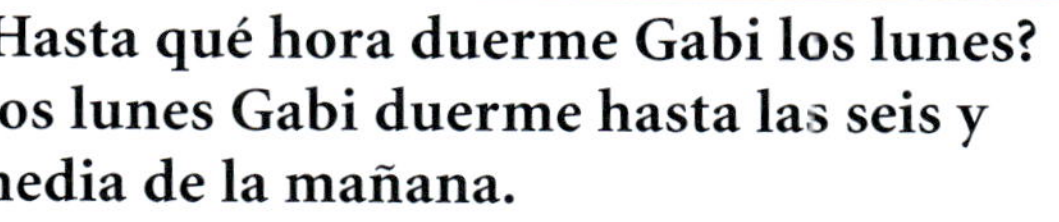

**MODELO** **¿Hasta qué hora duerme Gabi los lunes?**
**Los lunes Gabi duerme hasta las seis y media de la mañana.**

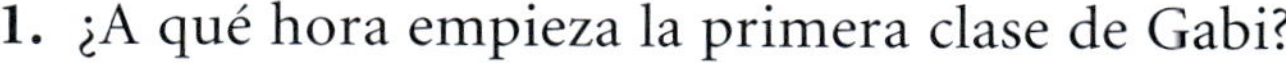

1. ¿A qué hora empieza la primera clase de Gabi?
2. ¿A qué hora almuerza?
3. ¿A qué hora tiene su ensayo de banda?
4. ¿A qué hora merienda?
5. ¿A qué hora empieza a hacer su tarea?
6. ¿Qué quiere hacer Gabi después de hacer su tarea?

8:10 A.M.

11:45 A.M.

3:00 P.M.

4:20 P.M.

7:00 P.M.

8:30 P.M.

# Comunicación

## 20 Entrevista FL.A.1.1.2, FL.A.3.1.1

**Hablemos** Use the questions from Activity 19 to ask your partner about his or her daily routine. Then report to the class what you found out.

**MODELO** **—¿Hasta qué hora duermes los lunes?**
**—Los lunes duermo hasta las seis y media.**

**Benchmark Focus**
FL.A.1.1.2 Greet others and exchange essential personal information

# Cultura

VideoCultura

**Benchmark Focus**

**FL.E.1.2.1** Know that many people in the United States use languages other than English on a daily basis

## Comparaciones

Una familia unida de Santiago

### ¿Quiénes son los miembros de tu familia y cómo son? FL.B.1.1.2

In Spain and in Latin America, it is not uncommon to see extended families sharing a house or an apartment. Young adults often continue to live at home with their parents even after graduating from college. One reason for this is the cost of housing relative to income in Spain and Latin America. Many young people simply don't make enough money to live in their own homes or apartments. What advantages and disadvantages do you see to having a large extended family living together? Think about this question as you listen to several Spanish speakers talk about their families.

### Amaru
**Santiago, Chile**

Amaru describes members of her family. How would you describe your family?

***¿Quiénes son los miembros de tu familia?***

Bueno, está mi papá, mi mamá y tengo dos hermanos y una hermana.

***¿Cómo son ellos?***

Bueno, mi mamá es muy trabajadora. Ella es pequeña y es muy linda. Mi hermano pequeño es muy grande, muy simpático, pero un poco travieso.

***¿Tienes mascotas?***

Tengo dos gatos y dos perros.

***¿Con qué frecuencia ves a tus tíos y a tus primos?***

Bueno, los veo más o menos un domingo al mes.

***¿Se llevan bien ustedes?***

Bueno, no nos vemos mucho pero nos llevamos bien.

Visit Holt Online
**go.hrw.com**
KEYWORD: EXP1A CH5
Online Edition

## Cristian

### Buenos Aires, Argentina

Christian talks about how often he sees his extended family. Do you visit relatives often?

***¿Quiénes son los miembros de tu familia?***

Bueno, los miembros de mi familia son mi papá, mi mamá, y mi hermana mayor. Después estoy yo. Me llamo Cristian. Y después está mi hermanito más chiquito.

***¿Cómo son ellos?***

Mi papá es un hombre alto como yo. Tiene el pelo negro, los ojos marrones y es un poco gordo. Mi hermana es una chica linda. Tiene los ojitos claros, pecas, el pelo castaño, y es un poquito más baja que yo.

***¿Tienes mascotas?***

Sí. Dos perros.

***¿Con qué frecuencia ves a tus tíos y a tus primos?***

A mis tíos y a mis primos, los veo en las fiestas una vez por mes, dos veces.

### Para comprender FL.C.2.1.1

1. ¿Quién es travieso de la familia de Amaru?
2. ¿Cuántas mascotas tiene Amaru?
3. ¿Cómo es el papá de Cristian?
4. ¿Cómo es la hermana de Cristian?
5. ¿Quién tiene la familia más grande? ¿Amaru o Cristian?
6. ¿Quién ve más a sus tíos y a sus primos? ¿Amaru o Cristian?

### Para pensar y hablar FL.D.2.1.1

Do you think Amaru's and Cristian's families are large or small? Are families in your community typically larger or smaller than theirs? Name two advantages to having a large family (six or more) and two advantages to having a small family (three or four).

# Comunidad en la Florida

### Los apellidos y la genealogía FL.C.2.1.1, FL.E.1.2.1

One way to learn about Spanish-speaking cultures is genealogy, the study of family histories. Research the background of a Hispanic family. It may be your own, or that of a famous Hispanic Floridian, such as Pedro Menéndez de Avilés, the founder of St. Augustine.

- Use English and Spanish resources on the Internet.
- Look for Hispanic family names on the Florida Pioneers List, published by the Florida State Genealogical Society.
- Report the results of your research to the class.

The Granger Collection, New York

**Pedro Menéndez de Avilés, fundador de San Agustín**

Cultura

**Objetivos**

- Talking about where you and others live
- Talking about responsibilities

# Vocabulario en acción 2

**ExpresaVisión**

## Una casa en Santiago

Visit Holt Online
**go.hrw.com**
KEYWORD: EXP1A CH5
Vocabulario 2 practice

## ¿Dónde vives?

en la ciudad

en el pueblo

en las afueras

en el campo

### También se puede decir...

In Florida, Dominicans may use the word **patio** to mean *yard;* for Cubans, **patio** can be *garden.* Colombians, Puerto Ricans, and Cubans may use **grama, pasto,** or **hierba** instead of **césped** *(grass).*

The word for *bedroom* has many regional variations: **la alcoba, la recámara, el dormitorio, la pieza.** Many Colombians, Puerto Ricans, and Dominicans in Florida use **el cuarto** for *bedroom.*

## ¡Exprésate!

| To ask about where someone lives | To respond |
|---|---|
| **¿Dónde viven ustedes?**<br>*Where do you live?* | **Vivimos en un apartamento pequeño. Está en un edificio de diez pisos.**<br>*We live in a small apartment. It's in a ten-story building.* |
| **¿Cuál es tu dirección?**<br>*What's your address?* | **Es calle Valdivia, número 56.**<br>*It's 56 Valdivia Street.* |
| **¿Cómo es tu casa?**<br>*What's your house like?* | **Es bastante grande. Tiene cuatro habitaciones, y un patio y jardín muy bonitos.**<br>*It's quite large. It has four bedrooms and a very pretty patio and garden.* |

Interactive TUTOR

Vocabulario y gramática, pp. 55–57 Online workbooks

Vocabulario 2

## Más vocabulario...

**los quehaceres**

**cocinar**
*to cook*

**cortar el césped**
*to cut the grass*

**hacer la cama**
*to make the bed*

**hacer los quehaceres**
*to do the chores*

**limpiar**
*to clean*

**sacar la basura**
*to take out the trash*

**Benchmark Focus** 

**FL.A.2.1.2** Restate and rephrase simple information from materials presented orally, visually, and graphically in class

## 21 ¿Dónde? FL.A.2.1.2

**Leamos/Hablemos** Complete each sentence with a logical place.

1. El carro y las bicicletas están en...
   **a.** el garaje. **b.** la sala.
2. Almorzamos en...
   **a.** el baño. **b.** el comedor.
3. Hay muchas plantas en las ventanas...
   **a.** de la sala. **b.** del jardín.
4. Descanso y veo películas en...
   **a.** la sala. **b.** el garaje.
5. Preparamos el desayuno en...
   **a.** la cocina. **b.** la habitación.
6. Hay dos habitaciones en...
   **a.** la sala. **b.** la casa.
7. Hay un escritorio y una cama en...
   **a.** el jardín. **b.** la habitación.

## 22 La casa de Mónica FL.A.2.1.2

**Leamos/Escribamos** Read Mónica's letter to Raquel, an exchange student from Spain who is coming to live at her house next year. Mónica is telling Raquel about her house. Answer the questions that follow.

Querida Raquel,

Nuestra casa es bastante grande. La dirección es Calle Hidalgo, número 365. Está en las afueras de la ciudad. La casa tiene dos pisos, con garaje, patio y jardín. Tiene una cocina, un comedor, cuatro habitaciones y tres baños. Vas a dormir en mi habitación. Tengo dos camas. Mi familia y yo pasamos las noches en la sala, donde nos gusta ver televisión o escuchar música.

¡Hasta luego!
Mónica

Casa en las afueras de Viña del Mar, Chile

1. ¿Dónde está la casa?
2. ¿Cuántas habitaciones hay? ¿baños?
3. ¿Hay más cuartos? ¿Cuáles son?
4. ¿Qué hace la familia en la sala?
5. ¿Dónde va a dormir Raquel?

# Comunicación

## 23 Cuestionario sobre la familia FL.A.2.1.2

**Leamos/Hablemos** Based on what you read in the questionnaire below, work with your partner to describe the family. Then take turns answering the questionnaire for yourselves and comparing answers.

1. En la familia Young hay tres ______.
2. La ______ es Calle Ortega, número 75.
3. El hermano ______ tiene 16 años.
4. La hermana ______ tiene 12 años.
5. Kelly ______ la cama todos los días.
6. Mike a veces corta el ______.
7. La madre siempre ______.
8. Lynn saca la ______ los sábados.

### Información Personal

**1 Datos personales**

a. Nombre completo:
Apellido: Young
Nombre(s): Kelly

b. Edad: 14 años

c. Dirección: Calle Ortega, número 75

**2 Vivo...**

a. en una casa ☐
b. en un apartamento ☒
c. en la ciudad ☒
d. en las afueras ☐

**3 Datos familiares**

a. ¿Tienes hermanos? sí
¿Cuántos? 2

b. ¿Cuántos años tiene cada uno?
Mi hermano mayor Mike tiene 16 años.
Mi hermana menor Lynn tiene 12 años.

**4 Los quehaceres**

a. hacer la cama: yo, todos los días
b. arreglar el cuarto:
c. cocinar: mi madre, siempre
d. limpiar el garaje:
e. cortar el césped: mi hermano, a veces
f. sacar la basura: mi hermana, los sábados

Vocabulario 2

## ¡Exprésate!

| To ask about responsibilities | To respond |
| --- | --- |
| **¿Qué te parece tener que ayudar en casa?**<br>*What do you think about having to help out at home?* | **A veces tengo que cuidar a mis hermanos, pero me parece bien. No es gran cosa.**<br>*Sometimes I have to take care of my brothers and sisters, but it's all right with me. It's no big deal.*<br>**A mí siempre me toca pasar la aspiradora en la sala. ¡Qué lata!**<br>*I always have to vacuum the living room. What a pain!* |
| **¿Qué te toca hacer a ti?**<br>*What do you have to do?* | **A menudo tengo que arreglar mi cuarto.**<br>*I often have to pick up my room.* |
| **¿Y a Juan?**<br>*And Juan?* | **A Juan nunca le toca lavar los platos. Me parece injusto.**<br>*Juan never has to do the dishes. It seems unfair to me.* |

Interactive TUTOR

Vocabulario y gramática, pp. 55–57 Online workbooks

### 24 En la casa FL.A.2.1.3

**Escuchemos** Match each sentence you hear with the picture to which it corresponds. Not every sentence will have a matching picture.

a.

b.

c.

d.

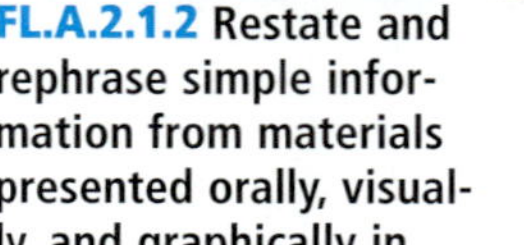

**Benchmark Focus**

**FL.A.2.1.2** Restate and rephrase simple information from materials presented orally, visually, and graphically in class

### 25 Los quehaceres FL.A.2.1.2

**Escribamos** Write complete sentences telling who does these chores in your home. Use the words **casi siempre, a veces, casi nunca,** or **nunca.** Be sure to conjugate the verb in each sentence.

**MODELO** **Mi padre casi siempre corta el césped.**

1. cortar el césped
2. pasar la aspiradora
3. limpiar el baño
4. lavar los platos
5. cocinar
6. hacer la cama
7. arreglar la sala
8. sacar la basura
9. cuidar a los hermanos
10. limpiar la cocina

## 26 Mi mascota *(pet)* increíble FL.A.2.1.2

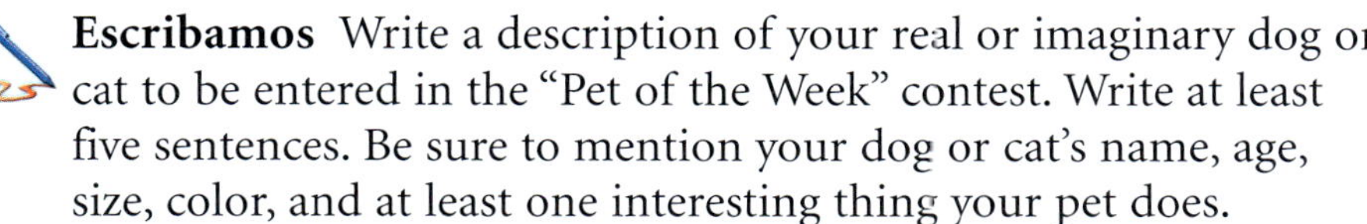

**Escribamos** Write a description of your real or imaginary dog or cat to be entered in the "Pet of the Week" contest. Write at least five sentences. Be sure to mention your dog or cat's name, age, size, color, and at least one interesting thing your pet does.

## 27 ¡A Adela le toca hacer mucho! FL.A.2.1.2

**Leamos/Escribamos** Adela's friends are coming over tomorrow for a birthday party and sleepover. Based on what you see below, rewrite her list of chores to do before they arrive.

**MODELO** **el cuarto**
**Tengo que arreglar el cuarto.**

Los quehaceres
- el cuarto
- la cama
- la cocina
- el baño
- la basura
- la pizza
- la aspiradora
- la sala
- el césped

## Comunicación

## 28 ¿Qué haces tú? FL.A.1.1.2

**Hablemos** Work with a partner. Ask each other what you do to help out at home. Tell how often and when you do various chores. Mention at least two things you do, and one thing you do not do.

**MODELO** **—¿Qué haces para ayudar en casa?**
**—A veces paso la aspiradora. Limpio la cocina todos los días. Nunca saco la basura.**

**Objetivos**
- Using **estar** with prepositions
- Negation with **nunca, tampoco, nadie,** and **nada**
- **Tocar** and **parecer**

# Gramática en acción 2

GramaVisión

Interactive TUTOR

## Estar with prepositions

**1** You've already used some forms of the verb **estar** to talk about how someone is feeling. **Estar** is irregular in the present tense.

| | | | |
|---|---|---|---|
| yo | **estoy** | nosotros(as) | **estamos** |
| tú | **estás** | vosotros(as) | **estáis** |
| Ud., él, ella | **está** | Uds., ellos, ellas | **están** |

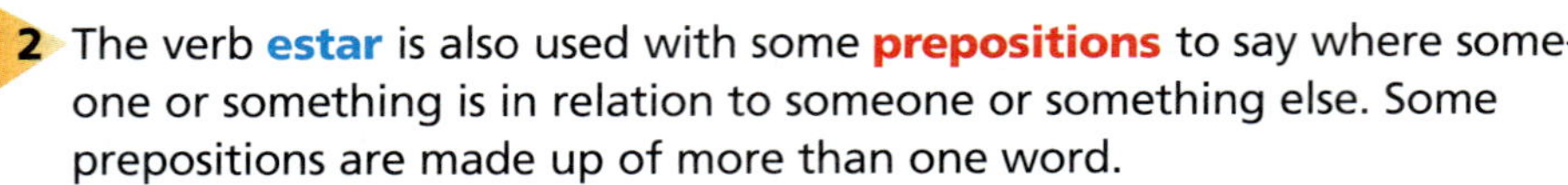

**2** The verb **estar** is also used with some **prepositions** to say where someone or something is in relation to someone or something else. Some prepositions are made up of more than one word.

—¿Dónde **está** tu apartamento?
—**Está detrás de** un edificio grande.

**Some prepositions**

| | | | |
|---|---|---|---|
| **al lado de** | *next to* | **detrás de** | *behind* |
| **cerca de** | *close to, near* | **encima de** | *on top of, above* |
| **debajo de** | *underneath* | **lejos de** | *far from* |
| **delante de** | *in front of* | | |

**Vocabulario y gramática,** pp. 58–60
**Actividades,** pp. 45–47
Online workbooks

## Nota cultural

Climate and ethnic traditions influence housing styles throughout the world. For instance, a home in southern Chile may show the influence of German or British immigrants, as well as the need for protection against the cold winters. Homes in the Amazon basin, on the other hand, may be built high off the ground and have good ventilation, providing comfort and safety from high water and hot weather.

How do the homes in your area reflect its history and climate?
**FL.B.1.1.3, FL.D.2.1.1**

Una casa del sur de Chile

### 29 Un día escolar FL.A.2.1.2

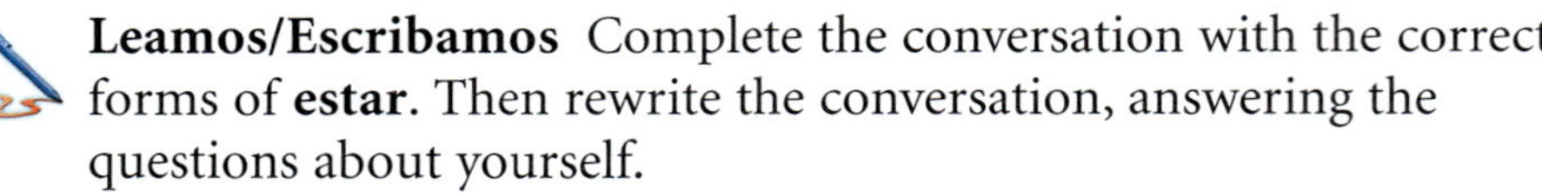

**Leamos/Escribamos** Complete the conversation with the correct forms of **estar**. Then rewrite the conversation, answering the questions about yourself.

—¿Con quiénes almuerzas en el colegio?
—Almuerzo con mis amigos Raquel y Joel.
—¿A qué hora ___1___ ustedes en la cafetería?
—___2___ en la cafetería a las doce y media.
—¿Dónde ___3___ (tú) a las dos de la tarde?
—___4___ en mi clase de matemáticas.
—¿Y después de clases? ¿___5___ (tú) en casa o en el colegio?
—___6___ en el entrenamiento de volibol. Vuelvo a la casa a las cinco.
—¿Tu casa ___7___ cerca del colegio?
—No, ___8___ bastante lejos.

Visit Holt Online
**go.hrw.com**
KEYWORD: EXP1A CH5
Gramática 2 practice

## 30 ¿Dónde están? FL.A.2.1.2

**Escribamos** Look at the drawing. Write complete sentences telling where the first thing is in relation to the second.

**MODELO** **la mochila/el bolígrafo**
**La mochila está lejos del bolígrafo.**

1. la computadora/el escritorio
2. la mochila/el perro
3. la silla/el escritorio
4. la planta/la ventana
5. el gato/la planta
6. los lentes/las revistas
7. la computadora/el bolígrafo
8. el perro/la silla
9. el diccionario/las revistas
10. las revistas/los lentes

## 31 En nuestra familia FL.A.2.1.2, FL.A.3.1.1

**Hablemos/Escribamos** Tell where you and your family members are at the following times.

**MODELO** **Los lunes a las diez de la mañana, mi padre está en su trabajo.**

1. Los viernes a las ocho de la noche, yo…
2. Los sábados a la seis de la mañana, mi madre…
3. Los miércoles a la una de la tarde, yo…
4. Los lunes a las diez de la mañana, mis hermanos…
5. Los martes a las dos de la mañana, mi familia y yo…
6. Los domingos a las tres de la tarde, mi padre…
7. Los jueves a las seis de la tarde, mis padres…
8. Los fines de semana a las diez de la noche, yo…

# Comunicación

## 32 ¿Qué es? FL.A.2.1.1

**Hablemos** Pick five things in the classroom. Tell your partner where they are, using prepositions. Your partner guesses what you're talking about. Switch roles.

**MODELO** **—Está cerca de la ventana.**
**—¿Es la computadora?**
**—Sí, es la computadora.**

**Benchmark Focus**
**FL.A.2.1.1** Follow and give simple instructions

Gramática 2

## Negation with nunca, tampoco, nadie, and nada

**1** **Nunca** *(never)* and **tampoco** *(neither, not either)* can take the place of **no**, or they can be added toward the end of a sentence that already has **no**.

| | |
|---|---|
| **No** voy a la playa. | *I don't go to the beach.* |
| **Nunca** voy a la playa. | *I never go to the beach.* |
| **No** voy a la playa **nunca**. | *I never go to the beach.* |
| **Tampoco** voy a la piscina. | *I don't go to the pool either.* |
| **No** voy a la piscina **tampoco**. | *I don't go to the pool either.* |

**2** The word **nada** means *nothing* when it is the subject of a sentence and *not anything* or *nothing* when it goes after the verb. When **nada** is after the verb, **no** must be placed before the verb.

**Nada** es fácil.
*Nothing is easy.*

**No** quiero **nada** hoy.
*I don't want anything today.*

**3** Use **nadie** to say *nobody* or *not anybody.* When **nadie** is after the verb, **no** must be placed before the verb.

**Nadie** quiere ir al cine.
*Nobody wants to go to the movies.*

**No** hay **nadie** aquí.
*There isn't anybody here.*

### ¿Te acuerdas?

The word **no** means *not, do not,* or *don't.* Place it before the verb or the pronouns that go with **gustar**.

**No** soy de Madrid.

A mí **no** me gusta la pizza.

**Vocabulario y gramática,** pp. 58–60
**Actividades,** pp. 45–47

### 33 Después de cenar FL.A.2.1.3

**Escuchemos** Escucha las oraciones y decide si son **ciertas** o **falsas** según *(according to)* las fotos.

la hija

el hijo

la madre

## 34 No queremos hacer nada FL.A.2.1.2

**Leamos** Choose the best word to complete each sentence.

1. Mis primos no van a la playa. No voy a la playa (también/tampoco).
2. No quiero hacer (nada/nunca) hoy.
3. Mis padres, mis hermanos y yo tenemos el pelo castaño. (Siempre/Nadie) en mi familia tiene el pelo rubio.
4. Cuando llueve y hace frío, mi perro no quiere salir. A mí (tampoco/nada) me gusta salir cuando hace mal tiempo.
5. Siempre preparamos la cena en la cocina. (Nunca/Tampoco) cocinamos en el patio.
6. Después de cenar, me toca lavar los platos. (Tampoco/Nadie) me ayuda.

Un cine en Viña del Mar, Chile

## 35 ¿Vas a hacer algo hoy? FL.A.2.1.2

**Leamos** Complete the conversation with your friend about this weekend using words from the box.

| tampoco | siempre | también |
|---|---|---|
| nada | nunca | algo |

—¿Vas a hacer __1__ el sábado?
—No, no voy a hacer __2__. ¿Y tú?
—Casi __3__ voy al cine los sábados. ¿Quieres ir conmigo?
—Sí, yo __4__ quiero ir al cine. ¿Sales mucho los sábados?
—Sí. Casi __5__ paso los fines de semana en casa.
—Yo __6__ paso los fines de semana en casa. Siempre salgo con mis amigos y mis primos.

## Comunicación

## 36 ¿Y tú? FL.A.1.1.2

**Hablemos** Interview a classmate using the following questions.

1. ¿Qué días siempre tienes mucho que hacer?
2. ¿Qué quehaceres casi siempre te toca hacer en casa?
3. ¿Quién te ayuda con los quehaceres?
4. ¿Qué haces cuando no tienes tarea?
5. ¿Qué haces cuando no tienes nada que hacer?

**Benchmark Focus**
**FL.A.1.1.2** Greet others and exchange essential personal information

Gramática 2

## Tocar and parecer

**¿Te acuerdas?**

The verb **gustar** uses these **pronouns** for the person who likes something. The verb agrees with what is liked.

| | |
|---|---|
| **me** gusta(n) | **nos** gusta(n) |
| **te** gusta(n) | **os** gusta(n) |
| **le** gusta(n) | **les** gusta(n) |

**1** To say what you have to do, what your duties are, or whose turn it is to do something, use the verb **tocar** followed by an **infinitive**. **Tocar** may be used like **gustar.**

| | | | |
|---|---|---|---|
| **me** | toca(n) | **nos** | toca(n) |
| **te** | toca(n) | **os** | toca(n) |
| **le** | toca(n) | **les** | toca(n) |

—A ti **te toca sacar** la basura hoy.
*It's your turn to take out the trash today.*

—¿A mí? No. Hoy **le toca** a Fernando.
*My turn? No. It's Fernando's turn today.*

**2** The verb **parecer** means *to seem* and may also be used like **gustar.** It's very common to use this verb when asking for and giving opinions.

| | | | |
|---|---|---|---|
| **me** | parece(n) | **nos** | parece(n) |
| **te** | parece(n) | **os** | parece(n) |
| **le** | parece(n) | **les** | parece(n) |

Siempre me toca a mí lavar los platos. **Me parece** injusto.
*I always have to wash the dishes. It seems unfair to me.*

A mi papá **le** parece una lata **cortar** el césped.
*My dad thinks cutting the grass is a pain.*

### 37 ¡Qué lata! FL.A.2.1.3

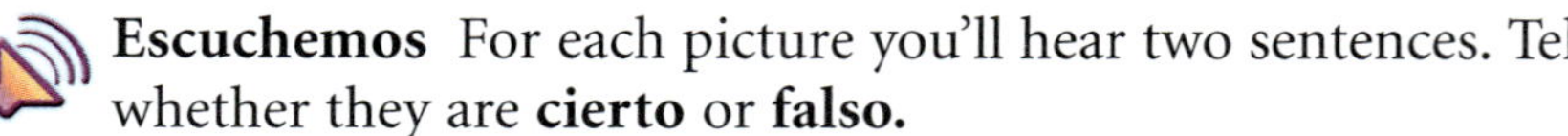

**Escuchemos** For each picture you'll hear two sentences. Tell whether they are **cierto** or **falso.**

mi hermana

mi hermano

mi papá y mi hermano menor

mi mamá y yo

## 38 ¿A quién le toca? FL.A.2.1.2

**Hablemos/Escribamos** Tell your sister it's her turn to do the chores and your turn to have fun.

**MODELO** **A ti te toca limpiar el baño. A mí me toca jugar.**

1. descansar/cortar el césped
2. lavar los platos/ir de compras
3. cocinar/ver televisión
4. jugar/hacer la cama
5. leer/limpiar la casa
6. limpiar el baño/cantar

## 39 ¿Qué les parece? FL.A.3.1.1

**Hablemos/Escribamos** Say how the following activities seem to you. Then name someone you know who has a different opinion.

**MODELO** **A mí me parece divertido ir de compras. Pero a mi padre le parece aburrido.**

| | | | |
|---|---|---|---|
| divertido | fácil | muy bien | interesante |
| difícil | aburrido | fenomenal | pésimo |

1. trabajar en el jardín
2. vivir en el campo
3. jugar con los perros
4. ir al centro comercial
5. jugar a videojuegos
6. hablar por teléfono
7. bailar
8. hacer ejercicio

### Nota cultural

Recently, there has been a boom in housing construction in south Florida. Many new homes reflect a Spanish-inspired style, consisting of clay-tiled roofs, decorative towers, and arches. These homes were originally painted in pastel shades. Inside, the homes feature high ceilings and tall windows.

How would you describe the style of homes in your community? FL.B.1.1.3

## Comunicación

## 40 Mi familia FL.A.3.1.1

**Hablemos** Take turns with a partner. Imagine that one of you is the teenage girl in the drawings below. Ask and answer questions about the girl's family, her house, and her family's activities.

**Benchmark Focus**

**FL.A.3.1.1** Provide simple information in spoken form

a.

b.

c.

Gramática 2

# Conexiones culturales

FCAT Reading Focus 

**LA.A.2.3.5**
Locate, organize, and interpret written information for a variety of purposes

**La familia** The word "family" has different meanings for different people. **La familia extendida** *(extended family)* includes relatives such as grandparents, aunts and uncles, and cousins. When Spanish speakers talk about **mi familia,** they often include their extended family.

Look at the two portraits of families, one by Miguel Cabrera and the other by Joan Miró. Miguel Cabrera lived in Mexico in the 1700s. He is famous for his paintings of families. Joan Miró, born near Barcelona, Spain, in 1893, is famous for his playful drawings and paintings.

**Miguel Cabrera, from *Español y mestiza, castiza,* 1763**

## 1 La familia y el arte FL.B.1.1.3

Work with a partner to answer these questions about the family portraits.

1. How many people are in each family?
2. Identify the family members.
3. What perspectives on families and family life are presented in each painting?

## 2 Un dibujo FL.D.2.1.1

Draw a picture of your idea of family. Show your drawing to a classmate and explain it. How does your drawing compare to your classmate's? How does your drawing compare with the paintings on this page?

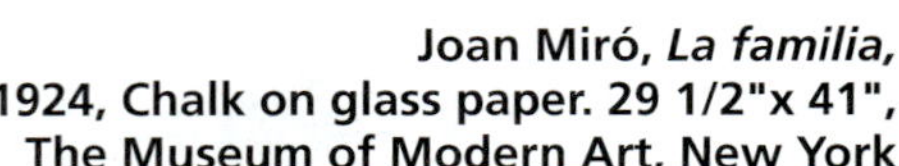

**Joan Miró, *La familia,* 1924, Chalk on glass paper. 29 1/2"x 41", The Museum of Modern Art, New York**

**Un árbol genealógico** Have you ever seen your own family tree? How many relatives can you think of in your family? Family trees can be drawn in many different ways. Gabriela's family tree goes from the top (the past) down the page to the present.

**La familia de Gabriela**

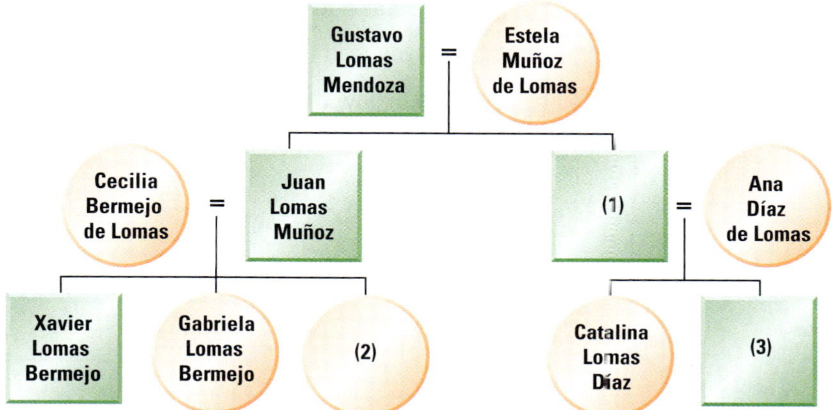


## 3 ¿Cómo se llaman? FL.A.2.1.2

1. ¿Cómo se llama el hermano de Gabriela?
2. ¿Cómo se llaman sus abuelos paternos (los padres de su padre)?
3. ¿Cómo se llama la tía de Gabriela?

## 4 La familia de Gabriela FL.A.2.1.2

Copy the family tree above on your own paper. Then, using the information in the following sentences, write the complete names of the missing relatives on the family tree.

1. El hermano de Juan es Antonio.
2. La sobrina de Ana es Leticia.
3. El primo de Gabriela es Pablo.

## 5 ¡Te toca a ti! FL.D.2.1.1

Work with a partner to draw your own real or imaginary family trees. Use your own symbols for marriages, divorces, deaths, and other important events. Compare the last names in your family tree with the last names in the family tree on this page.

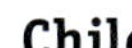

Novela en video

# ¿Quién será?

**Benchmark Focus**

**FL.C.2.1.1** Use the target language to gain access to information that is only available through the target language or within the target culture

## ESTRATEGIA

**Understanding humor** Understanding humor is an important part of enjoying a story on video. Sometimes humor can be created by contrasting what a character is actually experiencing with what a character *feels* like he or she is experiencing. As you read the **Novela** or watch the video, compare Sofía's and Nicolás's real household chores with how they see those chores. Does the comparison make you laugh? Do you feel the same way about household chores? **FL.C.2.1.1**

## En México

***Es sábado, un día que a veces no le gusta mucho a Sofía...***

1 **Sofía** Hoy es sábado. Los sábados mi familia y yo hacemos el quehacer.

2 **Sofía** ¿Ves a esa señora de pelo negro y ojos de color café? Ella es mi madre. Le gusta tener la casa muy, pero muy limpia.

## A. Contesta

Check your understanding of the **Novela** by answering the questions. **FL.A.2.1.2**

1. What does Sofía's family do on Saturdays?
2. What does Sofía's mother want Sofía to do?

3

**Sofía** ¿Ves a ese señor canoso con los lentes y la sonrisa graciosa? Es mi padre. No le gusta lavar los platos.

4

**Sofía** ¿Ves a ese niño travieso? Es Quique, mi hermano. A Quique no le toca hacer los quehaceres. ¡Me parece injusto!

5

**Sofía** ¡Qué lata! No puedo descansar nunca.

## B. Contesta

1. What does Sofía's father want Sofía to do?
2. Does Sofía's brother also have to do chores? If not, why not?
3. What is Sofía thinking about when she says, **"No puedo descansar nunca."**? FL.A.2.1.2

## En Puerto Rico

*Es sábado en la casa de Nicolás, en San Juan...*

6 **Nicolás** Hoy es sábado. Quiero salir de casa antes de que...

7 **Nicolás** ¡El césped! ¡Ay, no! Mi abuela es muy exigente. ¡Quiere todo perfecto!

8 **Nicolás** Mi papá es mecánico. ¡Está loco por los carros! Le gusta tener el garaje muy organizado.

9 **Nicolás** Un sábado bonito ¡arruinado! Y, ¿para qué? ¡Para hacer labores! ¡Me parece injusto!

## En Chile

*As Marcos learns more about the Chilean candidate, he gets a call from la profesora telling him to go to Mexico next.*

10

### C. Contesta

1. What does Nicolás's grandmother want him to do?
2. What does his father want him to do?
3. Why does he look so frustrated? FL.A.2.1.2

# Actividades

## 1 ¿Cómo son ellos? FL.A.2.1.2

Match each name with a description that fits based on information in the **Novela.**

| | |
|---|---|
| **1.** El Sr. Corona | **a.** es muy travieso. |
| **2.** La Sra. Corona | **b.** tiene el pelo negro. |
| **3.** Quique | **c.** tiene muchos quehaceres. |
| **4.** Sofía | **d.** es canoso. |

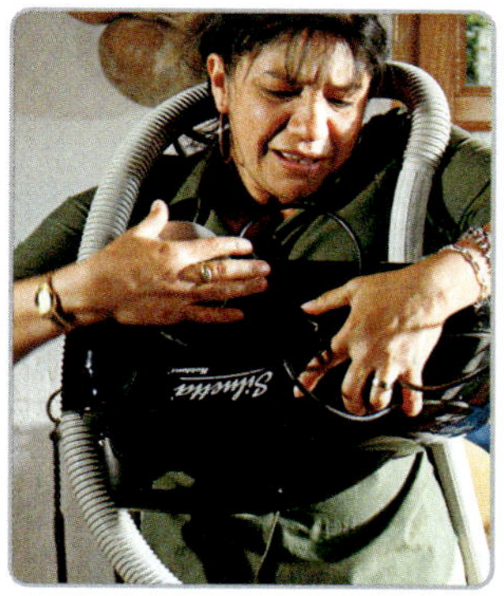

## 2 En casa de Nicolás FL.A.2.1.2

Find the information in the **Novela** to complete the paragraph.

La ___1___ de Nicolás quiere todo perfecto. Nicolás tiene que ___2___ el césped y ___3___ el garaje. Su padre quiere el ___4___ muy organizado. A Nicolás le parece ___5___ tener que hacer los quehaceres los sábados.

## 3 ¿Comprendes la Novela? FL.A.2.1.2

Check your understanding of the events in the story by answering these questions.

1. Which statement by Sofía tells you something about her mother's personality?
2. Why does Sofía think her father doesn't like to wash dishes?
3. Why does Sofía call her little brother **"ese niño travieso"**?
4. Is Sofía right when she feels that she is being treated unjustly?
5. How does Nicolás end up spending his Saturday?
6. Why are the attitudes of Sofía and Nicolás amusing?

FCAT Reading Focus 

LA.A.2.3.1
Identify relevant details and facts

**ESTRATEGIA**

**para leer** Scanning for specific information means reading to find a particular fact—a price, a feature, or a location, for example. When that is your purpose, you don't have to read or understand every word. Simply scan the text until you find what you are looking for.

**A Antes de leer** FL.C.2.1.1

Scan the following ads. What can you find out about the prices and the locations of the properties?

# CASAS Y APARTAMENTOS

## AGENCIA INMOBILIARIA[1]

**Zamora + Asociados**
**Calle Loma Linda 546**
**Tel: 5-55-69-32**
**www.vivienda[2]enlínea.hrw.com**

**A.** Se vende[3] casa, estilo chalet, en pueblo tranquilo. 5 dormitorios, 3 baños, gran sala/comedor, sala de juegos, oficina, cocina moderna, garaje doble y piscina. ¡Precio incomparable!

**B.** Se alquila[4] apartamento remodelado. Av. Providencia 3192. 2 dormitorios, 2 baños, sala, cocina/comedor y garaje. A sólo tres cuadras[5] de la universidad. ¡Un sitio ideal!

**C.** Se vende casa en las afueras de la ciudad. El Rosal, calle Margarita 89. Aire y calefacción[6] central. 2 dormitorios, 1 baño, sala, comedor, cocina, garaje y magnífico jardín. Precio negociable.

**D.** Se alquila apartamento amueblado[7]. Nuevo edificio en el centro de la ciudad. Perfecto para hombre o mujer profesional. 1 habitación, 1 baño, sala, cocina y balcón con magnífica vista[8] de la ciudad. ¡Gran oportunidad!

**E.** Se vende pequeño condominio en zona residencial. Enfrente de un parque y cerca de la Escuela Primaria Salazar. 3 dormitorios, 2 baños, sala con chimenea, comedor, cocina y garaje. ¡Gran precio!

1 real estate company 2 properties 3 for sale 4 for rent 5 blocks 6 heating 7 furnished 8 view

## B Comprensión FL.C.2.1.1

Based on each person's profile, match these prospective home buyers or tenants with the properties in the previous ads.

1. Una abuela que vive con su nieto de cuatro años y un gato.
2. Dos hermanos que empiezan sus estudios en la universidad.
3. Una mujer de negocios joven.
4. Una familia con tres hijos y dos perros grandes.
5. Una familia pequeña con dos hijos de siete y nueve años.

## C Después de leer FL.A.3.1.1

What kinds of things, other than size and cost, do people take into consideration when looking for a home to rent or buy? Describe the ideal home for your real family or an imaginary one. Explain why the features of your prospective home make it ideal.

**FCAT Writing Focus** 

**LA.B.1.3.2** Draft and revise writing that conveys a sense of completeness and wholeness with adherence to the main idea

Interactive TUTOR

# Taller del escritor

**ESTRATEGIA** FL.A.2.1.4

**para escribir** Draw bubbles and list in them the characteristics of the things you describe. Then connect the bubbles to each other to help you see your writing plan.

A mi mamá le gusta trabajar en el jardín.

A mi mamá le toca cortar el césped.

Mamá

### ¿Qué les toca hacer?

Think of your dream home. Write a paragraph describing it. Explain:

- where it is and what it's like
- who lives there with you
- what each person likes and dislikes doing
- each person's chores.

### 1 Antes de escribir

Draw a bubble and inside of it write the name of a person living with you in the dream home. Link that bubble to another in which you write that person's likes and dislikes. **(A mi papá le gusta cocinar.)** Draw another line linking the person to a bubble that lists her or his chores. **(A mi papá le toca limpiar la cocina.)** Do this for each person. Also draw linked bubbles describing your home. **(En mi casa ideal hay...)**

### 2 Escribir y revisar

Begin with a detailed description of your dream home. Explain why the location is ideal. Then write about the people who live there, their likes and dislikes, and each person's chores.

Read your draft at least twice. Check for spelling, punctuation, and correct grammar.

### 3 Publicar

You may want to include a drawing of your dream home with your paragraph. How does it compare to your classmates' dream homes?

Capítulo 5
Repaso

# Prepárate para el examen

Interactive TUTOR

**1** Imagine that these photos come from your family album. Describe the family members and tell how old they are. Write at least three sentences for each picture. **FL.A.2.1.2**

1. mis hermanos

2. mi abuelo

3. mis padres

4. mi gato

**1 Vocabulario 1**
- describing people and family relationships

**pp. 186–191**

**2 Gramática 1**
- possessive adjectives
- stem-changing verbs

**pp. 192–197**

**2** Pablo is describing his and his family's activities. Complete his description with the correct form of the verb or possessive adjective. **FL.A.2.1.2**

Los domingos, ___1___ (mis/tus) hermanos y yo ___2___ (empezar/volver) el día muy temprano. Mi hermano corre por el parque y después ___3___ (empezar/volver) a casa y ayuda a ___4___ (tus/mis) padres en el jardín. Vamos a la iglesia y ___5___ (volver/dormir) a la una. A la una y media mi familia y yo ___6___ (almorzar/merendar). Después de almorzar, los abuelos ___7___ (volver/jugar) a juegos de mesa. Yo nunca ___8___ (volver/jugar) con ellos. Me gusta más salir con ___9___ (nuestro/mis) amigos. A mis amigos y a mí nos gusta ___10___ (arreglar/merendar) a las tres y media.

**3 Vocabulario 2**
- talking about where you and others live
- talking about your responsibilities

**pp. 200–205**

**3** Tell how often you have to do the following chores. If you never do them, say who does. **FL.A.2.1.2, FL.A.3.1.1**

1. hacer las camas
2. lavar los platos
3. sacar la basura
4. limpiar el baño
5. cuidar a mis hermanos
6. cocinar
7. cortar el césped
8. pasar la aspiradora

Visit Holt Online
**go.hrw.com**
KEYWORD: EXP1A CH5
Chapter Self-test

**4** Complete the following sentences. FL.A.2.1.2

1. A mí me ______ (tocar/parecer) hacer todo en casa.
2. Los libros de mi papá ______ (hacer/estar) encima del sofá.
3. A mi hermano le ______ (tocar/parecer) fenomenal salir con sus amigos.
4. El perro no quiere jugar ______ (siempre/nunca).
5. Mis amigos nunca hacen nada. Yo no hago nada ______ (también/tampoco).

**4 Gramática 2**
- using **estar** with prepositions
- negation
- **tocar** and **parecer**
**pp. 206–211**

**5** Answer the following questions. FL.B.1.1.2, FL.B.1.1.3

1. What information do Latin American last names provide? How is that different from names in the U.S.?
2. How do culture and climate influence home architecture?
3. When Spanish speakers talk about their **familia,** are they referring to an immediate or an extended family?

**5 Cultura**
- **Comparaciones**
**pp. 198–199**
- **Notas culturales**
**pp. 188, 190, 206**
- **Geocultura**
**pp. 180–183**

**6** Complete the paragraph based on what you hear. FL.A.2.1.3

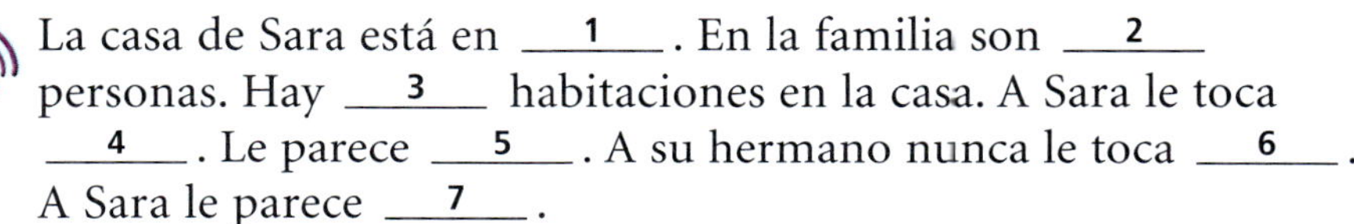
La casa de Sara está en __1__. En la familia son __2__ personas. Hay __3__ habitaciones en la casa. A Sara le toca __4__. Le parece __5__. A su hermano nunca le toca __6__. A Sara le parece __7__.

**Benchmark Focus** 
**FL.B.1.1.2** Recognize patterns of social behavior or social interaction in various settings

**7** Tell what José says about himself and his sister based on the drawings. FL.A.3.1.1

a.

b.

c.

d.

**Gramática 1**

- possessive adjectives **pp. 192–193**
- **o → ue** stem-changing verbs **pp. 194–195**
- **e → ie** stem-changing verbs **pp. 196–197**

# Repaso de Gramática 1

**Possessive adjectives** show ownership or relationship between people.

| | |
|---|---|
| **mi/s** | **nuestro/a/os/as** |
| **tu/s** | **vuestro/a/os/as** |
| **su/s** | **su/s** |

**Almorzar, dormir, llover,** and **volver** are **o → ue** stem-changing verbs. **Empezar, entender, querer,** and **merendar** are **e → ie** stem-changing verbs.

| | |
|---|---|
| alm**ue**rzo | almorzamos |
| alm**ue**rzas | almorzáis |
| alm**ue**rza | alm**ue**rzan |

| | |
|---|---|
| emp**ie**zo | empezamos |
| emp**ie**zas | empezáis |
| emp**ie**za | emp**ie**zan |

**Gramática 2**

- **estar** with prepositions **pp. 206–207**
- negation with **nunca, tampoco, nadie,** and **nada** **pp. 208–209**
- **tocar** and **parecer** **pp. 210–211**

# Repaso de Gramática 2

Use **estar** with **prepositions** to say where someone or something is located.

| estar | |
|---|---|
| **estoy** | **estamos** |
| **estás** | **estáis** |
| **está** | **están** |

| prepositions of location | | |
|---|---|---|
| **al lado de** | **delante de** | **encima de** |
| **cerca de** | **detrás de** | **lejos de** |
| **debajo de** | | |

**Negation**

| | | | | |
|---|---|---|---|---|
| nada | nunca | nadie | no | tampoco |

| tocar | | | | parecer | | | |
|---|---|---|---|---|---|---|---|
| **me** | toca(n) | **nos** | toca(n) | **me** | parece(n) | **nos** | parece(n) |
| **te** | toca(n) | **os** | toca(n) | **te** | parece(n) | **os** | parece(n) |
| **le** | toca(n) | **les** | toca(n) | **le** | parece(n) | **les** | parece(n) |

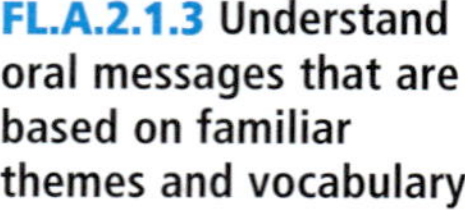


**FL.A.2.1.3** Understand oral messages that are based on familiar themes and vocabulary

## Letra y sonido b v

### Las letras b y v

- The letters **b** and **v** follow these rules: At the beginning of a sentence, and after **m** or **n**, both are pronounced as *b* in the English word *boy.* **V**oy a casa., ¿**B**ailas mucho?, diciem**b**re, un **b**aile
- Everywhere else, their pronunciation is softer with the lips barely touching: vi**v**ir, a**b**uelo, re**v**ista, a**b**urrido

### Trabalenguas

El buen abuelo Vicente vende bonitas boinas baratas, baberos babosos, bolillos verdes, botas bellas y revistas aburridas.

### Dictado FL.A.2.1.3

Escribe las oraciones de la grabación.

# Repaso de Vocabulario 1

### Describing people and family relationships

| | |
|---|---|
| los abuelos | *grandparents* |
| el/la abuelo(a) | *grandfather, grandmother* |
| almorzar (ue) | *to have lunch* |
| callado(a) | *quiet* |
| canoso(a) | *gray-haired* |
| castaño(a) | *dark brown* |
| corto(a) | *short* |
| ciego(a) | *blind* |
| de color café | *brown* |
| delgado(a) | *thin* |
| dormir (ue) | *to sleep* |
| empezar (ie) | *to begin, to start* |
| En mi familia somos cuatro personas. | *There are four people in my family.* |
| entender (ie) | *to understand* |
| estar en una silla de ruedas | *to be in a wheelchair* |
| el/la gato(a) | *cat* |
| gordo(a) | *fat* |
| hasta | *until* |
| los hermanos | *siblings* |
| el/la hermano(a) | *brother, sister* |
| los hijos | *children, sons* |
| el/la hijo(a) | *son, daughter* |
| joven | *young* |
| largo(a) | *long* |
| la madre | *mother* |
| mayor | *older* |
| menor | *younger* |
| merendar (ie) | *to have a snack* |
| negro(a) | *black* |
| los nietos | *grandsons, grandchildren* |
| los padres | *parents* |
| el padre | *father* |
| el pelo | *hair* |
| el/la perro(a) | *dog* |
| la persona | *person* |
| el/la primo(a) | *cousin* |
| los primos | *cousins* |
| el/la sobrino(a) | *nephew, niece* |
| los sobrinos | *nephews, nieces and nephews* |
| sordo(a) | *deaf* |
| tener (ie) los ojos azules | *to have blue eyes* |
| los tíos | *aunts and uncles* |
| el/la tío(a) | *uncle, aunt* |
| todos(as) | *everyone, all of us* |
| travieso(a) | *mischievous* |
| usar lentes | *to wear glasses* |
| verde | *green* |
| viejo(a) | *old* |
| volver (ue) | *to go back or come back* |

# Repaso de Vocabulario 2

### Talking about where you and others live

| | |
|---|---|
| las afueras | *outskirts* |
| el apartamento | *apartment* |
| el baño | *bathroom* |
| el campo | *countryside* |
| la casa | *house* |
| la ciudad | *city* |
| la cocina | *kitchen* |
| cocinar | *to cook* |
| el comedor | *dining room* |
| cortar el césped | *to cut the grass* |
| la dirección | *address* |
| el edificio (de diez pisos) | *(ten-story) building* |
| el escritorio | *desk* |
| el garaje | *garage* |
| grande | *big, large* |
| hacer la cama | *to make the bed* |
| hacer los quehaceres | *to do the chores* |
| la habitación | *bedroom* |
| el jardín | *garden* |
| limpiar | *to clean* |
| la mesa | *table* |
| nadie | *nobody, not anybody* |
| el patio | *patio, yard* |
| pequeño(a) | *small* |
| las plantas | *plants* |
| el pueblo | *town, village* |
| la puerta | *door* |
| sacar la basura | *to take out the trash* |
| la sala | *living room* |
| la silla | *chair* |
| el sofá | *couch* |
| tampoco | *neither, not either* |
| la ventana | *window* |
| vivir | *to live* |

**Talking about your responsibilities** . . . . . . *See p. 204.*

Prepárate para el examen

Repaso cumulativo

# Integración

## capítulos 1-5

**1** Listen to Josefina talk about her family and then match her descriptions with the correct photo. **FL.A.2.1.3**

A

B

C

D

**Benchmark Focus**
**FL.A.2.1.3** Understand oral messages based on familiar themes and vocabulary

**2** Esteban is writing to "Metida," an advice columnist. Read his letter and then answer the questions that follow. **FL.A.2.1.2**

### Querida Metida,

**"Quiero salir más con mis amigos los fines de semana, pero no tengo tiempo. Los viernes por la tarde practico fútbol en el estadio. No llego a casa hasta las 8:00. Los sábados tengo un montón que hacer en casa. Arreglo mi cuarto y corto el césped. Ayudo a lavar los platos después de comer. Los domingos cuido a mi hermano menor porque mis padres juegan al tenis. Por la noche tengo que hacer la tarea. Me parece injusto pero, ¿qué puedo hacer?"**

–Esteban

1. ¿Qué problema tiene Esteban?
2. ¿Por qué no sale los viernes?
3. ¿Qué le toca hacer a Esteban los sábados?
4. ¿Cuándo salen los padres de Esteban? ¿Qué hacen?
5. ¿Qué le toca hacer a Esteban cuando salen sus padres?
6. ¿Qué necesita hacer Esteban? En tu opinión, ¿qué consejos *(advice)* le va a escribir "Metida" a él para resolver *(solve)* su problema?

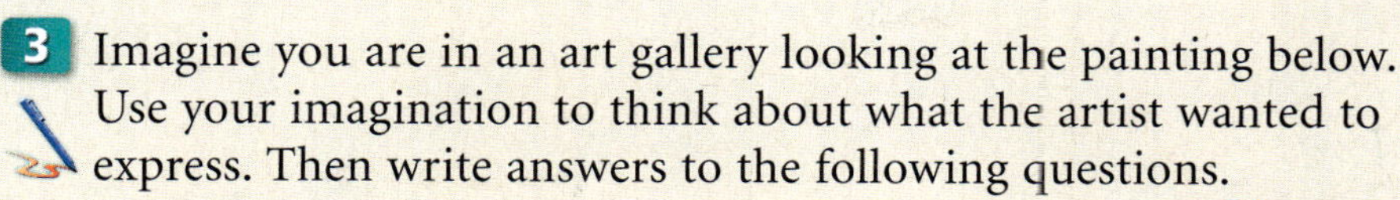

**3** Imagine you are in an art gallery looking at the painting below. Use your imagination to think about what the artist wanted to express. Then write answers to the following questions.

FL.A.2.1.2, FL.B.1.1.3

1. ¿Qué colores ves?
2. ¿Qué tiempo hace?
3. ¿Dónde están las personas?
4. ¿Son una familia? ¿Quiénes son?
5. ¿Cuántos años tiene cada *(each)* persona?
6. ¿Cómo son ellos?

Isidoro Molleda, Chilean painter. MarPau Art Gallery, Viña del Mar, Chile

***Esperando a los pescadores,*** **de Isidoro Molleda (n. 1930)**

**4** Situación

In small groups, create an imaginary family. Decide on roles; each person takes on the identity of a family member. Take turns introducing a member of your "family" to the class by giving the following information:

FL.A.3.1.1

- name and age
- role in the family (father, son, aunt, and so on)
- physical description of the imaginary family member
- what chores he or she does and when the chores are done

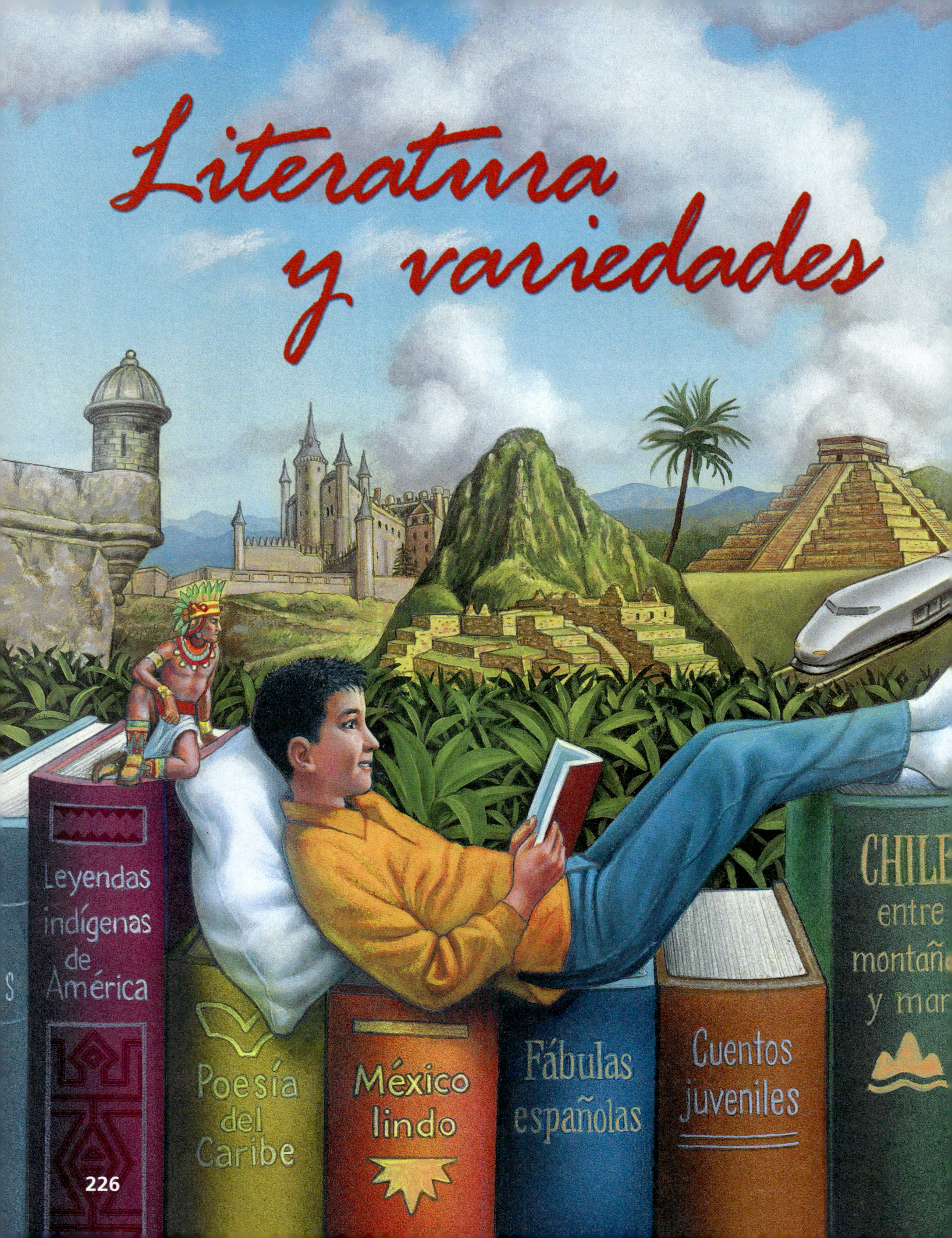

Literatura y variedades
Leyendas indígenas de América
Poesía del Caribe
México lindo
Fábulas españolas
Cuentos juveniles
CHILE entre montañ y mar

**Capítulo 1 • España** .................................... 228–229
El Museo del Prado (folleto)

**Capítulo 2 • Puerto Rico** ............................. 230–231
El coquí (artículo)

**Capítulo 3 • Texas** ...................................... 232–233
Obras de Carmen Lomas Garza (comentarios)

**Capítulo 4 • Costa Rica** ............................... 234–235
La artesanía chorotega (entrevista)

**Capítulo 5 • Chile** ...................................... 236–237
Las novelas de Isabel Allende (comentario y fragmento)

# España

FCAT Reading Focus 

**LA.A.1.3.2**
Use a variety of strategies to analyze words and text; use context and word structure clues

## El Museo del Prado

The Prado Museum, in downtown Madrid, Spain, is one of the largest and best-known art museums in the world. It houses over 9,000 works of art. The collection is so vast that only a tenth of it can be displayed at any one time. Although most of its paintings and sculptures are by European artists, it holds works by artists from around the world and reveals centuries of history through art. Read the following information in the visitor brochure and the descriptions of the paintings by three famous Spanish artists to learn more about the Prado and its collection.

**ESTRATEGIA**

Look for cognates (words with similar meanings and spellings in English and Spanish) to help you understand some of the words you do not know.
**FL.D.1.2.1**

MUSEO NACIONAL DEL PRADO

ESPAÑOL

Plano del Museo
Localización de colecciones

MUSEO NACIONAL DEL PRADO

Ruiz de Alarcón, 23. 28014 Madrid
http://museoprado.mcu.es

**Información General:**
**Dirección:**
Ruiz de Alarcón, 23, 28014 Madrid
**Teléfono:**
34 913 30 28 00
**Correo electrónico:**
museo.nacional@prado.mcu.es
**Internet:**
http://museoprado.mcu.es

**Horario:**
**martes a domingo:**
9.00-19.00 h
**24 y 31 de diciembre:**
9.00-14.00 h
**Cerrado[1]:**
los lunes; 1 de enero; Viernes Santo, 1 de mayo y 25 de diciembre

**Precio de Entrada:[2]**
**Público general:**
3,01 Euros
**Menores[3] de 18 años:**
gratuito[4]

1 closed 2 admission 3 younger 4 free

## Cesto Con Flores[1]

Juan de Arellano, famoso pintor español, se especializó en la pintura[2] de flores. Esta obra es una de muchas obras que pintó con ese tema[3]. Como puedes ver, es una composición magnífica. Las flores están iluminadas en el centro para acentuar[4] los colores y la belleza[5].

1 basket with flowers  2 painting  3 theme  4 to highlight
5 beauty

## La Familia de Carlos IV

Esta obra es de Francisco de Goya y Lucientes, uno de los artistas más famosos y el artista oficial de la Corte[1] de España. Es de la Familia Real y se llama *La Familia del Rey Carlos IV*. Los colores en esta pintura son extraordinarios. Hay muchas obras de Goya en el Prado.

1 Court

## El Caballero[1]

Esta pintura es de El Greco, uno de los más famosos pintores[2] españoles. En realidad, el verdadero nombre de El Greco es Doménikos Theotokópoulos. La mayoría de los temas de sus pinturas son religiosos y los colores en estas pinturas son vívidos y vibrantes. También son importantes sus retratos[3], como éste de un caballero.

1 knight  2 painters  3 portraits

## Después de leer

FL.C.1.1.2, FL.C.2.1.1

1. What time does the Prado generally close?
2. How much is admission to the museum?
3. What is the subject of many of Arellano's paintings?
4. Who are the people in Goya's painting?
5. What is El Greco's real name?

# Puerto Rico

## El coquí

Puerto Rico's Yunque rainforest covers 28,000 acres and is one of the oldest reserves in the Western Hemisphere. It is the only rainforest in the U.S. National Forest System. The rainforest averages 240 inches of rain a year. The Yunque is home to 13 species of a tiny frog called the **coquí**. These frogs are considered a national symbol for the island. Read the following article to learn more about this unique amphibian.

**ESTRATEGIA**

Background knowledge is the information you already know about a subject. Before you read, take a minute to recall what you know about the topic.

**FCAT Reading Focus** 

**LA.A.1.3.2**

Use a variety of strategies to analyze words and text

### Estruendo[1] musical

La voz[2] más famosa de Puerto Rico es la de una pequeña especie de rana que se llama coquí. Hay dieciséis especies de coquíes en Puerto Rico y trece de ellas viven en el Parque Nacional del Yunque. Se llama coquí porque por la noche miles de estas ranas salen y emiten un coro de cantos[3], "co-quí". El estruendo es muy fuerte porque una sola rana puede emitir hasta 100 decibeles, igual que una guitarra eléctrica. ¡Imagina un concierto de miles de guitarras eléctricas en tu vecindario[4] cada noche! El canto del coquí se oye por toda la isla de Puerto Rico.

1 racket 2 voice 3 calls, songs 4 neighborhood

## No soy renacuajo[1]

El coquí es una especie de rana muy interesante porque nunca pasa por una etapa[2] de renacuajo. La madre, o hembra[3], pone aproximadamente 28 huevos[4]. El padre, o macho[5], cuida de[6] los huevos. Después salen los coquíes bebés, ¡ya en forma de rana!

## De muchos colores

Algunas personas, aun los puertorriqueños, piensan que el coquí es solamente[7] verde. La verdad[8] es que hay coquíes de muchos colores: marrones, grises, amarillos, azules, verdes o anaranjados, como el coquí dorado en esta foto. El coquí es muy importante en Puerto Rico porque come gran cantidad de insectos como mosquitos. Es un símbolo nacional y su música resuena[9] por toda la isla.

**1** tadpole **2** stage **3** female **4** eggs **5** male
**6** takes care of **7** only **8** the truth **9** resonates

## Después de leer

FL.C.1.1.1, FL.C.2.1.1

1. What is **El Yunque**?
2. How did the **coquí** get its name?
3. Given the tiny size of the **coquí,** what is surprising about its call?
4. In what way are **coquíes** different from other frogs?
5. What color is the **coquí**?
6. Why is the **coquí** important in Puerto Rico?

**FCAT Reading Focus**

**LA.A.1.3.2**

Use a variety of strategies to analyze words and text; use context clues

# Obras de Carmen Lomas Garza

Carmen Lomas Garza is one of the best-known Mexican American painters. In 1990 she published her first children's book, ***Cuadros de familia***, in which she combines her paintings with her own warm writing style. She uses the book to explain her work and describe her childhood in Kingsville, Texas, near the border with Mexico. In her second book, ***En mi familia***, 1996, Lomas Garza once again shares her memories of growing up in a traditional Mexican American community and family. Read the following excerpts from these two books to experience a slice of life on the Texas border.

**ESTRATEGIA**

Actively picture in your mind what you are reading—the setting, the way the characters look and are dressed, their actions and speech. Visualization helps you create a context for what you are reading.

## *Tamalada* de *Cuadros de familia*

Ésta es una escena de la cocina de mis padres. Todos están haciendo tamales. Mi abuelo tiene puesto rancheros[1] azules y camisa azul. Yo estoy al lado de él, con mi hermana Margie. Estamos ayudando a remojar[2] las hojas secas[3] del maíz[4]. Mi mamá está esparciendo la masa[5] de maíz sobre las hojas, y mis tíos están esparciendo la carne[6] sobre la masa. Mi abuelita está ordenando los tamales que ya están enrollados, cubiertos y listos[7] para cocer[8]. En algunas familias sólo las mujeres preparan tamales, pero en mi familia todos ayudan.

▲ ***Tamalada*** (1990)

**1** overalls **2** soak **3** dry leaves **4** corn **5** spreading the dough **6** meat **7** rolled, covered, and ready **8** to cook

▲ ***Baile en el Jardín*** (1995)

## *Baile en el Jardín* de *En mi familia*

Ésta es una noche de sábado en El Jardín, un restaurante familiar de mi pueblo natal[1]. Es verano y hace tanto calor que la gente baila afuera[2]. Un conjunto[3] toca con tambora[4], acordeón, guitarra y bajo[5]. Ésta es la música con la que crecí[6]. Todos bailan formando un gran círculo: las parejas[7] jóvenes, las parejas más grandes[8], y los viejitos bailan con adolescentes o criaturas[9]. Hasta los bebés se ponen a bailar.

Para mí, el baile representa fiesta, celebración. Aquí está la música, los hermosos vestidos, y todos los miembros de la familia bailan juntos. Es como el cielo. Es la gloria.

**1** hometown
**2** outside
**3** band
**4** drum
**5** bass
**6** I grew up with
**7** couples
**8** older
**9** little ones

## Después de leer

**FL.B.1.1.2, FL.C.2.1.1**

1. Name the four steps to making tamales that the author mentions.
2. In Lomas Garza's family, who makes the tamales?
3. In ***Baile en el Jardín***, what is the weather like?
4. What instruments are in the band?
5. Who is dancing in ***El jardín***?
6. Why does Lomas Garza like the dance?

# La artesanía chorotega

The small village of Guaitil is one of the centers of Costa Rican folk art. Nearly the entire town is dedicated to making pottery using the methods, tools, and designs that their ancestors, the Chorotegas, used hundreds of years ago. The craftsmen of Guaitil use natural paints and basic colors like red, black, white, and brown to decorate their pottery with traditional symbols of nature and daily life. Learn more about Chorotega artistry in the following interview with Gustavo, who is one of the youngest and most famous potters in the village.

**ESTRATEGIA**

Many words can be understood based on how they are used in the sentence or paragraph. When you come to an unknown word, try to guess its meaning based on context (the other words around it).

**FCAT Reading Focus**

**LA.A.1.3.2**

Use a variety of strategies to analyze words and text; use context and word structure clues

## Gustavo

**¿Desde cuándo ayudas a tus padres en el taller[1] de cerámica?**

Siempre me ha gustado ayudar a mi madre, Luz Marina; pero cuando era[2] pequeño lo que más me gustaba era modelar, hacer figuritas.

**¿Y ahora?**

Ahora pintar y decorar las piezas.

**¿De dónde sacas estas ideas?**

Bueno, los dibujos[3] que yo hago son aquellos que están en los libros antiguos[4] pero hay veces que invento otros dibujos para cambiar[5] y esos los saco de la mente[6], sólo de la mente.

**¿Se te ocurren cuando estás pintándolas, o las pintas antes en un papel?**

No, las pinto directamente sobre la tinaja[7].

1 workshop 2 I was 3 drawings 4 old 5 to change 6 mind 7 ceramic jar

**¿Hay algún sitio donde enseñan esta artesanía[1]?**

Sí, la cooperativa de artesanos[2] del pueblo tiene una escuela y ahí se enseñan los diseños[3] que hacían nuestros antepasados[4] chorotegas.

**¿Tienes en casa libros de dibujos precolombinos?**

No, yo los diseños los tengo grabados[5] en la mente.

**¿Cuánto tardas en pintar una tinaja grande?**

Normalmente media hora, o tal vez un poco más.

**¿Cuántas horas dedicas a esto?**

Bueno, a veces mis padres tienen mucho trabajo y todos tenemos que colaborar[6]. Entonces puedo hacer hasta 20 vasijas medianas en un día. Pero cuando hay menos trabajo, pinto en mis ratos libres.

**¿Te quieres dedicar exclusivamente a esto?**

Ahora estoy empezando y me gusta mucho. Es posible que siga[7] con el taller de mis padres.

---

**1** folk art
**2** craftmen's cooperative
**3** designs
**4** ancestors
**5** etched
**6** to help out
**7** that I may continue

## Después de leer

FL.B.1.1.3, FL.C.2.1.1

1. What did Gustavo like to do when he was a small child?
2. What does he do now?
3. Does Gustavo draw his designs on paper first?
4. Where does Gustavo get his ideas for his designs?
5. How long does it take him to paint a piece of pottery?

**FCAT Reading Focus** 

**LA.A.2.3.1**

Determine the main idea or essential message in a text

# Las novelas de Isabel Allende

Isabel Allende is from Peru, but she was raised in Chile. She is one of the most famous modern Latin American writers. Her novels and stories are read throughout the world. Her family is the theme of many of her stories and often her relatives are the inspiration for the characters in her novels. Today, Isabel Allende lives with her husband and family in California. Read the following commentary and the excerpt from one of her novels to learn more about her work and life in Chile.

**ESTRATEGIA**

Look at the title, the photos, and the important words in the text. Then read the first sentence of each paragraph. Skimming helps you understand the main ideas.



En 1981, Isabel Allende empezó[1] a escribir una carta a su abuelo en Chile. Un año más tarde esta carta de 500 páginas se convirtió[2] en su primera novela, ***La casa de los espíritus** (The House of the Spirits, 1982)*.

Su novela ***Paula*** (1994) es la historia de su vida. Es dedicada a su hija, Paula, quien murió[3] a la edad[4] de 24 años, después de estar en el hospital por un año.

Vas a leer un fragmento de su libro ***Mi país inventado***, en el que escribe sobre su familia y la historia de Chile. A través de[5] sus propios parientes[6] ilustra el carácter de los chilenos.

**1** began **2** became **3** died **4** age
**5** by means of **6** her own relatives

Por encima de[1] los clanes está la familia, inviolable y sagrada,[2] nadie escapa a sus deberes[3] con ella. Por ejemplo, el tío Ramón suele llamarme por teléfono a California, donde vivo, para comunicarme que murió un tío en tercer grado,[4] a quien no conocí,[5] y dejó[6] una hija en mala situación. La joven quiere estudiar enfermería,[7] pero no tiene medios[8] para hacerlo. Al tío Ramón, como el miembro de más edad del clan, le corresponde ponerse en contacto con cualquiera que tenga lazos de sangre con el difunto,[9] desde los parientes cercanos hasta los más remotos, para financiar los estudios de la futura enfermera. Negarse sería un acto vil,[10] que sería recordado[11] por varias generaciones.

1 at the top of 2 sacred 3 obligations 4 distant 5 hadn't met 6 left 7 nursing 8 means 9 whomever is related to the deceased 10 would be despicable 11 would be remembered

## Después de leer

FL.B.1.1.2, FL.C.2.1.1

1. What is the theme of Isabel Allende's novels?
2. How did her first novel begin?
3. Who is Paula?
4. To whom do Chileans have obligations?
5. What does the daughter of Allende's uncle want to study?
6. Who helps her?

# La Península Ibérica

# México

ESTADOS UNIDOS DE AMÉRICA
MÉXICO
Golfo de México
OCÉANO PACÍFICO
Golfo de Tehuantepec
Trópico de Cáncer
BELICE
GUATEMALA
HONDURAS
Sierra Madre Occidental
Sierra Madre Oriental
Río Grande
Río Bravo del Norte
Río Conchos
Río Lerma
Río Balsas
Río Usumacinta
BAJA CALIFORNIA
BAJA CALIFORNIA SUR
SONORA
CHIHUAHUA
COAHUILA
SINALOA
DURANGO
ZACATECAS
TAMAULIPAS
JALISCO
MICHOACÁN
GUERRERO
OAXACA
VERACRUZ
CHIAPAS
CAMPECHE
YUCATÁN
QUINTANA ROO
San Diego
Tijuana
Mexicali
Tucson
Nogales
Nogales
Hermosillo
La Paz
Ciudad Juárez
El Paso
Chihuahua
Culiacán
Mazatlán
Del Río
San Antonio
Houston
Galveston
Puerto Arturo
Baton Rouge
Nueva Orleáns
Laredo
Nuevo Laredo
McAllen
Reynosa
Brownsville
Matamoros
Monterrey
Ciudad Victoria
Torreón
Durango
Zacatecas
Aguascalientes
San Luis Potosí
Guanajuato
Querétaro
Tepic
Puerto Vallarta
Guadalajara
Morelia
Colima
Toluca
México, D.F.
Pachuca
Tlaxcala
Puebla
Taxco
Acapulco
Veracruz
Oaxaca
Villahermosa
San Cristóbal de Las Casas
Campeche
Mérida
Chetumal
Cozumel
N
0 125 250 Kilómetros
0 125 250 Millas
CLAVE DE ESTADOS
1 NAYARIT
2 COLIMA
3 AGUASCALIENTES
4 GUANAJUATO
5 QUERÉTARO
6 HIDALGO
7 MÉXICO
8 DISTRITO FEDERAL
9 MORELOS
10 PUEBLA
11 TLAXCALA
12 NUEVO LEÓN
13 SAN LUIS POTOSÍ
14 TABASCO

# Estados Unidos de América

# América Central y las Antillas

# América del Sur

# Vocabulario adicional

This list includes additional vocabulary that you may want to use to personalize activities. If you can't find a word you need here, try the Spanish-English and English-Spanish vocabulary sections, beginning on page R23.

## Materias *(School Subjects)*

| | |
|---|---|
| **el álgebra** | *algebra* |
| **el cálculo** | *calculus* |
| **la contabilidad** | *accounting* |
| **la física** | *physics* |
| **la geometría** | *geometry* |
| **el italiano** | *Italian* |
| **el japonés** | *Japanese* |
| **el latín** | *Latin* |
| **la literatura** | *literature* |
| **el ruso** | *Russian* |

## Celebraciones *(Celebrations)*

| | |
|---|---|
| **el bautizo** | *baptism* |
| **la canción** | *song* |
| **El Día de los Reyes** | *Three Kings Day* |
| **la Pascua Florida** | *Easter* |
| **las Pascuas** | *Christmas* |
| **el Ramadán** | *Ramadan* |
| **Rosh Hashaná** | *Rosh Hashanah* |

## Comida *(Food)*

| | |
|---|---|
| **el ají picante (el chile)** | *hot pepper* |
| **el aguacate** | *avocado* |
| **las arvejas** | *peas* |
| **el azúcar** | *sugar* |
| **la banana (el guineo)** | *banana* |
| **la batida, el batido** | *milkshake* |
| **la cereza** | *cherry* |
| **la coliflor** | *cauliflower* |
| **el champiñón (el hongo)** | *mushroom* |
| **los condimentos** | *seasonings* |
| **los fideos** | *noodles* |
| **el filete de pescado** | *fish fillet* |
| **la lechuga** | *lettuce* |
| **la mayonesa** | *mayonnaise* |
| **el melón** | *cantaloupe* |
| **la mostaza** | *mustard* |
| **la pimienta** | *pepper* |
| **la piña** | *pineapple* |
| **el plátano** | *plantain* |
| **la sal** | *salt* |
| **el yogur** | *yogurt* |

## Computadoras *(Computers)*

| | |
|---|---|
| **arrastrar** | *to drag* |
| **la búsqueda** | *search* |
| **buscar** | *to search* |
| **comenzar la sesión** | *to log on* |
| **la contraseña, el código** | *password* |
| **el disco duro** | *hard drive* |
| **en línea** | *online* |
| **grabar** | *to save* |
| **hacer clic** | *to click* |
| **la impresora** | *printer* |
| **imprimir** | *to print* |
| **el marcapáginas, el separador** | *bookmark* |
| **el ordenador** | *computer* |
| **la página Web inicial** | *homepage* |
| **el ratón** | *mouse* |
| **la Red** | *the Net* |
| **la tecla de aceptación** | *return key* |
| **la tecla de borrar, la tecla correctora** | *delete key* |
| **el teclado** | *keyboard* |
| **terminar la sesión** | *to log off* |
| **la unidad de CD-ROM** | *CD-ROM drive* |
| **el Web, la Telaraña Mundial** | *World Wide Web* |

## De compras *(Shopping)*

| | |
|---|---|
| **cobrar** | *to charge* |
| **el dinero en efectivo** | *cash* |
| **el descuento** | *discount* |
| **en venta** | *for sale* |
| **la rebaja** | *sale, sale price* |
| **regatear** | *to bargain* |
| **la tarjeta de crédito** | *credit card* |
| **el (la) vendedor, -ora** | *salesperson* |

Vocabulario adicional

## Deportes y pasatiempos (Sports and Hobbies)

| | |
|---|---|
| **el anuario** | *yearbook* |
| **las artes marciales** | *martial arts* |
| **la astronomía** | *astronomy* |
| **el ballet** | *ballet* |
| **el boxeo** | *boxing* |
| **coleccionar sellos (monedas, muñecas)** | *to collect stamps (coins, dolls)* |
| **coser** | *to sew* |
| **el drama** | *drama* |
| **la fotografía** | *photography* |
| **la gimnasia** | *gymnastics* |
| **jugar a las cartas** | *to play cards* |
| **jugar a las damas** | *to play checkers* |
| **la orquesta** | *orchestra* |
| **el patinaje en línea, (sobre hielo)** | *inline (ice) skating* |

## En el cine o el teatro (At the Movies or Theater)

| | |
|---|---|
| **el actor** | *actor* |
| **actuar** | *to act* |
| **la actriz** | *actress* |
| **aplaudir** | *to applaud* |
| **la butaca** | *box seat* |
| **la escena** | *scene* |
| **el escenario** | *stage* |
| **el espectáculo** | *performance, show* |
| **la estrella** | *star* |
| **la pantalla** | *screen* |
| **el telón** | *curtain* |

## En el consultorio (At the Clinic)

| | |
|---|---|
| **la alergia** | *allergy* |
| **el antibiótico** | *antibiotic* |
| **ponerle a uno una inyección** | *to give someone a shot* |
| **el dolor** | *pain* |
| **los escalofríos** | *chills* |
| **estornudar** | *to sneeze* |
| **la gripe** | *flu* |
| **la medicina** | *medicine* |
| **las pastillas, las píldoras** | *pills, tablets* |
| **el síntoma** | *symptom* |
| **la tos** | *cough* |
| **toser** | *to cough* |

## En el zoológico (At the Zoo)

| | |
|---|---|
| **el ave, las aves** | *bird, birds* |
| **el canguro** | *kangaroo* |
| **la cebra** | *zebra* |
| **el cocodrilo** | *crocodile* |
| **el delfín** | *dolphin* |
| **el elefante** | *elephant* |
| **el gorila** | *gorilla* |
| **el hipopótamo** | *hippopotamus* |
| **la jirafa** | *giraffe* |
| **el león** | *lion* |
| **la foca** | *seal* |
| **el mono, el chango** | *monkey* |
| **el oso** | *bear* |
| **el oso polar** | *polar bear* |
| **el pingüino** | *penguin* |
| **la serpiente** | *snake* |
| **el tigre** | *tiger* |

## En la casa (Around the House)

| | |
|---|---|
| **la alfombra** | *rug, carpet* |
| **el ático** | *attic* |
| **el balcón** | *balcony* |
| **las cortinas** | *curtains* |
| **el despertador** | *alarm clock* |
| **las escaleras** | *stairs* |
| **el espejo** | *mirror* |
| **el estante** | *bookcase* |
| **el fregadero** | *kitchen sink* |
| **la galería** | *porch* |
| **la lámpara** | *lamp* |
| **el lavamanos** | *bathroom sink* |
| **la lavadora** | *washing machine* |
| **la mesita de noche** | *nightstand* |
| **los muebles** | *furniture* |
| **la secadora** | *dryer* |

| | |
|---|---|
| **el sillón** | *easy chair* |
| **el sótano** | *basement* |
| **el timbre** | *doorbell* |
| **el tocador** | *dresser* |

## En las afueras y en la ciudad *(Places around Town)*

| | |
|---|---|
| **la autopista** | *highway* |
| **el banco** | *bank* |
| **la esquina** | *street corner* |
| **la estación de autobuses (trenes)** | *bus (train) station* |
| **la fábrica** | *factory* |
| **la ferretería** | *hardware store* |
| **la farmacia** | *drugstore* |
| **la gasolinera** | *gas station* |
| **el hospital** | *hospital* |
| **la mezquita** | *mosque* |
| **el mercado** | *market* |
| **la oficina** | *office* |
| **la parada de autobuses** | *bus stop* |
| **la peluquería** | *barbershop* |
| **el puente** | *bridge* |
| **el rascacielos** | *skyscraper* |
| **el salón de belleza** | *beauty salon* |
| **el semáforo** | *traffic light* |
| **el supermercado** | *supermarket* |

## Instrumentos musicales *(Musical Instruments)*

| | |
|---|---|
| **el acordeón** | *accordion* |
| **el arpa, las arpas** | *harp* |
| **la armónica** | *harmonica* |
| **el bajo** | *bass* |
| **la batería** | *drum set* |
| **el clarinete** | *clarinet* |
| **la flauta dulce** | *recorder* |
| **la flauta** | *flute* |
| **la guitarra** | *guitar* |
| **la mandolina** | *mandolin* |
| **las maracas** | *maracas* |
| **el oboe** | *oboe* |
| **el saxofón** | *saxophone* |
| **el sintetizador** | *synthesizer* |
| **el tambor** | *drum* |
| **el trombón** | *trombone* |
| **la trompeta** | *trumpet* |
| **la tuba** | *tuba* |
| **la tumbadora** | *conga drum* |
| **la viola** | *viola* |
| **el violín** | *violin* |

## La familia *(Family)*

| | |
|---|---|
| **el (la) ahijado(a)** | *godson, goddaughter* |
| **el (la) bisabuelo(a)** | *great-grandfather, great-grandmother* |
| **el (la) biznieto(a)** | *great-grandson, great-granddaughter* |
| **el (la) cuñado(a)** | *brother-in-law, sister-in-law* |
| **el (la) hijastro(a)** | *stepson, stepdaughter* |
| **la madrina** | *godmother* |
| **la madrastra** | *stepmother* |
| **la nuera** | *daughter-in-law* |
| **el padrino** | *godfather* |
| **el padrastro** | *stepfather* |
| **el (la) suegro(a)** | *father-in-law, mother-in-law* |
| **el yerno** | *son-in-law* |

## Palabras descriptivas *(Descriptive Words)*

**amistoso(a)** *friendly*
**la barba** *beard*
**bien educado(a)** *well-mannered*
**el bigote** *mustache*
**calvo(a)** *bald*
**la estatura** *height*
**flaco(a)** *skinny*
**lindo(a)** *pretty*
**las pecas** *freckles*
**las patillas** *sideburns*
**el pelo lacio** *straight hair*
**el pelo rizado** *curly hair*
**pesar** *to weigh*
**tranquilo(a)** *quiet*

## Partes del cuerpo *(Parts of the Body)*

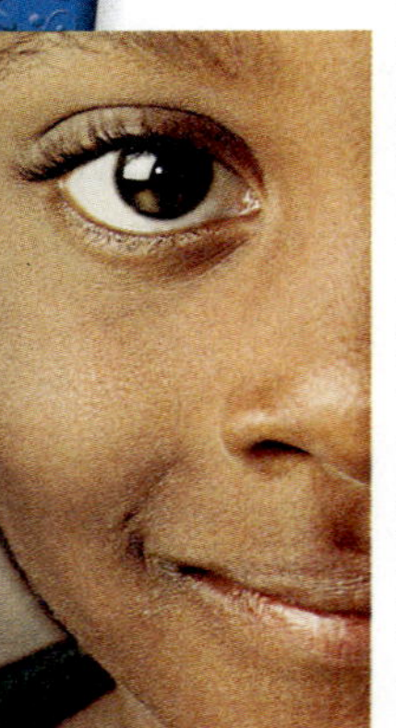

**la barbilla** *chin*
**las cejas** *eyebrows*
**la cintura** *waist*
**el codo** *elbow*
**la frente** *forehead*
**los labios** *lips*
**la muñeca** *wrist*
**el muslo** *thigh*
**las pestañas** *eyelashes*
**la rodilla** *knee*
**la sien** *temple*
**el tobillo** *ankle*
**la uña** *nail*

## Profesiones *(Professions)*

**el (la) abogado(a)** *lawyer*
**el (la) arquitecto(a)** *architect*
**el (la) bombero(a)** *firefighter*
**el (la) cartero(a)** *mail carrier*
**el (la) cocinero(a)** *cook*
**el (la) conductor, -ora** *driver*
**el (la) constructor, -ora** *builder*
**el (la) decorador, -ora** *interior decorator*
**el (la) dentista** *dentist*
**el (la) detective** *detective*
**el (la) enfermero(a)** *nurse*
**el (la) escritor, -ora** *writer*
**el hombre (la mujer) de negocios** *businessman, businesswoman*
**el (la) ingeniero(a)** *engineer*
**el (la) médico(a)** *doctor*
**el (la) piloto(a)** *pilot*
**el (la) (mujer) policía** *police officer*
**el (la) secretario(a)** *secretary*

## Regalos *(Gifts)*

**la agenda** *agenda, daily planner*
**el álbum** *album*
**el animal de peluche** *stuffed animal*
**los bombones** *chocolates*
**el calendario** *calendar*
**los claveles** *carnations*
**la colonia** *cologne*
**las flores** *flowers*
**el llavero** *key chain*
**el perfume** *perfume*
**el rompecabezas** *puzzle*
**las rosas** *roses*

## Ropa *(Clothes)*

**la bata** *robe*
**la bufanda** *scarf*
**el chaleco** *vest*
**las chancletas** *flip-flops*
**la corbata** *tie*
**los guantes** *gloves*
**las medias** *socks, stockings, hose*
**las pantuflas, las zapatillas** *slippers*
**el pañuelo** *handkerchief*
**el paraguas** *umbrella*
**la ropa interior** *underwear*
**los tacones, los zapatos de tacón** *high heels*

## Temas de actualidad *(Current Issues)*

**el bosque tropical** *rain forest*
**la contaminación** *pollution*
**el crimen** *crime*
**los derechos humanos** *human rights*
**la economía** *economy*
**la educación** *education*
**la guerra** *war*

**el medio ambiente** *environment*
**el mundo** *world*
**las noticias** *news*
**la paz** *peace*
**la política** *politics*
**la tecnología** *technology*
**la violencia** *violence*

## Vacaciones *(Vacation)*

**la agencia de viajes** *travel agency*
**el andén** *train platform*
**el asiento** *seat*
**los cheques de viajero** *traveler's checks*
**hacer una reservación** *to make a reservation*
**el horario** *schedule, timetable*
**el mar** *sea*

**la parada** *stop*
**el pasillo** *aisle*
**reservado(a)** *reserved*
**la ventanilla** *window*
**la visa** *visa*
**visitar los lugares de interés** *to sightsee*
**volar** *to fly*

## Refranes *(Proverbs)*

**Más vale pájaro en mano que cien volando.**
*A bird in the hand is worth two in the bush.*

**Hijo no tenemos y nombre le ponemos.**
*Don't count your chickens before they're hatched.*

**Quien primero viene, primero tiene.**
*The early bird catches the worm.*

**Más vale tarde que nunca.**
*Better late than never.*

**El hábito no hace al monje.**
*Clothes don't make the man.*

**Más ven cuatro ojos que dos.**
*Two heads are better than one.*

**Querer es poder.**
*Where there's a will, there's a way.*

**Ojos que no ven, corazón que no siente.**
*Out of sight, out of mind.*

**No todo lo que brilla es oro.**
*All that glitters is not gold.*

**Caras vemos, corazones no sabemos.**
*You can't judge a book by its cover.*

**Donde una puerta se cierra, otra se abre.**
*Every cloud has a silver lining.*

**En boca cerrada no entran moscas.**
*Silence is golden.*

**Dime con quién andas y te diré quién eres.**
*Birds of a feather flock together.*

**Al mal tiempo buena cara.**
*When life gives you lemons, make lemonade.*

**Antes que te cases mira lo que haces.**
*Look before you leap.*

# Expresiones de ¡Exprésate!

*Functions* are the ways in which you use a language for particular purposes. In specific situations, such as in a restaurant, in a grocery store, or at school, you will want to communicate with those around you. In order to do that, you have to "function" in Spanish: you place an order, make a purchase, or talk about your class schedule.

Here is a list of the functions presented in ***¡Exprésate! 1A*** for Chapters 1–5 along with the Spanish expressions you'll need to communicate in a wide range of situations. Following each function is the chapter and page number from the book where it is introduced.

## Socializing

***Greetings***
**Ch. 1, p. 8**
Buenos días, señor.
Buenas noches, señora.
Buenas tardes, señorita.

***Saying Goodbye***
**Ch. 1, p. 8**
Adiós.
Tengo que irme.
Hasta luego.
Buenas noches.
Hasta mañana.
Nos vemos.
Hasta pronto.

***Asking how someone is and saying how you are***
**Ch. 1, p. 8**
Hola, ¿cómo estás?
¿Cómo está usted?
¿Qué tal?
Estoy bien/regular/mal.
¿Y usted?
Más o menos. ¿Y tú?

***Introducing people***
**Ch. 1, p. 10**
Éste(a) es... Es un(a) compañero(a) de clase.
Encantado(a).
Mucho gusto.
Igualmente.
Ésta es... (Ella) es mi profesora de...
Éste es... (Él) es mi profesor de...

***Inviting others to do something***
**Ch. 4, p. 158**
¿Qué tal si vamos a...?
No sé. ¿Sabes qué? No tengo ganas.
Vienes conmigo a..., ¿no?
¡Claro que sí! Tengo mucha hambre.
Hay un concierto.
Vas a ir, ¿verdad?
No, no voy a ir. Tengo que...

## Exchanging Information

***Asking and giving names***
**Ch. 1, p. 6**
¿Cómo te llamas?
¿Cómo se llama usted?
Me llamo... ¿Y tú?
Soy...
¿Quién es...?
Él (Ella) es...
¿Cómo se llama (él/ella)?
(Él/Ella) se llama...

***Saying where you and others are from***
**Ch. 1, p. 11**
¿De dónde eres?
¿De dónde es usted?
Soy de...
¿De dónde es...?
Es de...

***Asking and giving phone numbers***
**Ch. 1, p. 19**
¿Cuál es tu teléfono?
Es tres-dos-cinco-uno-dos-tres-uno.
¿Cuál es el teléfono de...?
Es...

***Saying what time it is***
**Ch. 1, p. 20**
¿Qué hora es?
Son las seis y cuarto de la mañana.
Es la una en punto.
Son las... y trece de la tarde.
Son las... y media de la tarde.
Son las... menos cuarto.

Son las... menos diez de la noche.
Es mediodía.
Es medianoche.

***Asking and giving the date and the day***
**Ch. 1, p. 21**
¿Qué fecha es hoy?
Es el primero (dos, tres...) de enero.
¿Qué día es hoy?
Hoy es...

***Asking how words are spelled and giving e-mail addresses***
**Ch. 1, p. 23**
¿Cómo se escribe...?
Se escribe...
¿Cuál es tu correo electrónico?
Es...
¿Cuál es el correo electrónico de...?
Es eme punto ge-o-ene-zeta-a-ele-o arroba ere-e-de punto hache-ere-uve doble punto a-ere.

***Describing people***
**Ch. 2, p. 49**
¿Cómo es...?
... es moreno(a). También es... y un poco...
¿Cómo eres? ¿Eres cómico(a)?
Sí, soy bastante cómico(a).

***Asking and saying how old someone is***
**Ch. 2, p. 52**
¿Cuántos años tienes?
Tengo ... años.
¿Cuántos años tiene...?
... tiene ... años.
¿Cuándo es tu cumpleaños?
Es el 6 de mayo.
¿Cuándo es el cumpleaños de...?
Es el...

***Describing things***
**Ch. 2, p. 66**
¿Cómo es...?
Es...
Es (muy)...
Es bastante...
Es algo...

***Talking about what you and others want to do***
**Ch. 3, p. 98**
¿Qué quieres hacer hoy?
Ni idea.
¿Quieres ir a... conmigo?
Está bien.
No, gracias. No quiero ir a... hoy.

***Talking about everyday activities***
**Ch. 3, p. 109**
¿Qué haces los fines de semana?
Los sábados, cuando hace buen tiempo, voy...
¿Qué hace... cuando hace mal tiempo?
Le gusta...
No va a ninguna parte.

***Asking and saying how often***
**Ch. 3, p. 112**
¿Con qué frecuencia vas a...?
Casi nunca. No me gusta...
¿Te gusta...?
Sí. Después de clases, casi siempre vamos a...
A veces vamos también a...

***Talking about what you and others have or need***
**Ch. 4, p. 141**
¿Necesitas algo para el colegio?
Sí, necesito muchas cosas.
No, no necesito nada.
¿Necesitas algo para la clase de...?
Sí, necesito...
¿Tienes...?
Sí, tengo un montón.
No, no tengo.

***Talking about classes***
**Ch. 4, p. 144**
¿Qué clases tienes...?
Primero tengo... y después tengo...
¿Cuál es tu materia preferida?
Mi materia preferida es... Es fácil.
No me gusta la clase de... porque es difícil.

***Talking about plans***
**Ch. 4, p. 155**
¿Vas a ir a... el... por la...?
No. Tengo...
¿Qué vas a hacer el... próximo?
Voy a... y después... Luego regreso...
¿A qué hora vas a llegar a...?
Voy a llegar temprano (a tiempo). No me gusta llegar tarde.

***Describing people and family relationships***
**Ch. 5, p. 187**
¿Cuántas personas hay en tu familia?
En mi familia somos... personas.
¿Cómo es tu familia?
Somos delgados y tenemos el pelo rubio. Todos usamos lentes. Mi... está en una silla de ruedas.

¿Cómo es tu...?
Es... Es una persona... (Él/Ella) y mi... tienen... hijos pero no tienen...

***Describing where someone lives***
**Ch. 5, p. 201**
¿Dónde viven ustedes?
Vivimos en un apartamento. Está en un edificio de... pisos.
¿Cuál es tu dirección?
Es calle..., número...
¿Cómo es tu casa?
Es bastante... Tiene... habitaciones y un... y... muy bonitos.

***Talking about your responsibilities***
**Ch. 5, p. 204**
¿Qué te parece tener que ayudar en casa?
A veces tengo que..., pero me parece bien. No es gran cosa.
¿Qué te toca hacer a ti?
A mí siempre me toca... ¡Qué lata!
A menudo tengo que...
A... nunca le toca... Me parece injusto.

## Expressing Attitudes and Opinions

***Talking about what you and others like***
**Ch. 2, p. 63**
¿Te gusta(n)...?
Sí, me gusta(n) mucho.
No, no me gusta(n).
¿Te gusta(n) más... o...?
Me gusta(n) más...
Me da igual.

***Talking about what you and others like to do***
**Ch. 3, pp. 94–95**
¿Qué te gusta hacer?
A mí me gusta...
¿A... les gusta...?
Sí, porque les gusta...

# Síntesis gramatical

## NOUNS AND ARTICLES

### Gender of Nouns

In Spanish, nouns (words that name a person, place, or thing) are grouped into two classes or genders: masculine and feminine. All nouns, both persons and objects, fall into one of these groups. Most nouns that end in **-o** are masculine, and most nouns that end in **-a, -ción, -tad,** and **-dad** are feminine. Some nouns, such as **estudiante** and **cliente,** can be either masculine or feminine.

| Masculine Nouns | Feminine Nouns |
|---|---|
| libro | casa |
| chico | universidad |
| cuaderno | situación |
| bolígrafo | mesa |
| vestido | libertad |

FORMATION OF PLURAL NOUNS

| | Add **-s** to nouns that end in a vowel. | | Add **-es** to nouns that end in a consonant. | | With nouns that end in **-z**, the **-z** changes to a **-c**. | |
|---|---|---|---|---|---|---|
| **SINGULAR** | libro | casa | profesor | papel | vez | lápiz |
| **PLURAL** | libro**s** | casa**s** | profesor**es** | papel**es** | ve**ces** | lápi**ces** |

### Definite Articles

There are words that signal the gender of the noun. One of these is the *definite article.* In English, there is one definite article: *the.* In Spanish, there are four: **el, la, los, las.**

SUMMARY OF DEFINITE ARTICLES

| | Masculine | Feminine |
|---|---|---|
| **SINGULAR** | **el** chico | **la** chica |
| **PLURAL** | **los** chicos | **las** chicas |

CONTRACTIONS

a + el → **al**
de + el → **del**

### Indefinite Articles

Another group of words that are used with nouns are the *indefinite articles:* **un, una,** (*a* or *an*) and **unos, unas** (*some* or *a few*).

| | Masculine | Feminine |
|---|---|---|
| **SINGULAR** | **un** chico | **una** chica |
| **PLURAL** | **unos** chicos | **unas** chicas |

## Pronouns

| Subject Pronouns | Direct Object Pronouns | Indirect Object Pronouns | Objects of Prepositions | Reflexive Pronouns |
|---|---|---|---|---|
| **yo** | **me** | **me** | **mí** | **me** |
| **tú** | **te** | **te** | **ti** | **te** |
| **él, ella, usted** | **lo, la** | **le** | **él, ella, usted** | **se** |
| **nosotros, nosotras** | **nos** | **nos** | **nosotros, nosotras** | **nos** |
| **vosotros, vosotras** | **os** | **os** | **vosotros, vosotras** | **os** |
| **ellos, ellas, ustedes** | **los, las** | **les** | **ellos, ellas, ustedes** | **se** |

# ADJECTIVES

Adjectives are words that describe nouns. The adjective must agree in gender (masculine or feminine) and number (singular or plural) with the noun it modifies. Adjectives that end in **-e** or a consonant only agree in number.

| | | Masculine | Feminine |
|---|---|---|---|
| Adjectives that end in **-o** or **-a** | SINGULAR<br>PLURAL | chico alt**o**<br>chicos alt**os** | chica alt**a**<br>chicas alt**as** |
| Adjectives that end in **-e** | SINGULAR<br>PLURAL | chico inteligent**e**<br>chicos inteligent**es** | chica inteligent**e**<br>chicas inteligent**es** |
| Adjectives that end in a consonant | SINGULAR<br>PLURAL | examen difícil<br>exámenes difícil**es** | clase difícil<br>clases difícil**es** |

## Demonstrative Adjectives

| | Masculine | Feminine | | Masculine | Feminine |
|---|---|---|---|---|---|
| SINGULAR | **este** chico | **esta** chica | SINGULAR | **ese** chico | **esa** chica |
| PLURAL | **estos** chicos | **estas** chicas | PLURAL | **esos** chicos | **esas** chicas |

When demonstratives are used as pronouns, they match the gender and number of the noun they replace and are written with an accent mark: **éste, éstos, ésta, éstas, ése, ésos, ésa, ésas.**

## Possessive Adjectives

These words also modify nouns and show ownership or relationships between people (*my* car, *his* book, *her* mother).

| SINGULAR | | PLURAL | |
|---|---|---|---|
| **Masculine** | **Feminine** | **Masculine** | **Feminine** |
| **mi** libro | **mi** casa | **mis** libros | **mis** casas |
| **tu** libro | **tu** casa | **tus** libros | **tus** casas |
| **su** libro | **su** casa | **sus** libros | **sus** casas |
| **nuestro** libro | **nuestra** casa | **nuestros** libros | **nuestras** casas |
| **vuestro** libro | **vuestra** casa | **vuestros** libros | **vuestras** casas |

## Comparatives

Comparatives are used to compare people or things. With comparisons of inequality, the same structure is used with adjectives, adverbs, or nouns. With comparisons of equality, **tan** is used with adjectives and adverbs, and **tanto/a/os/as** with nouns.

COMPARISONS OF INEQUALITY

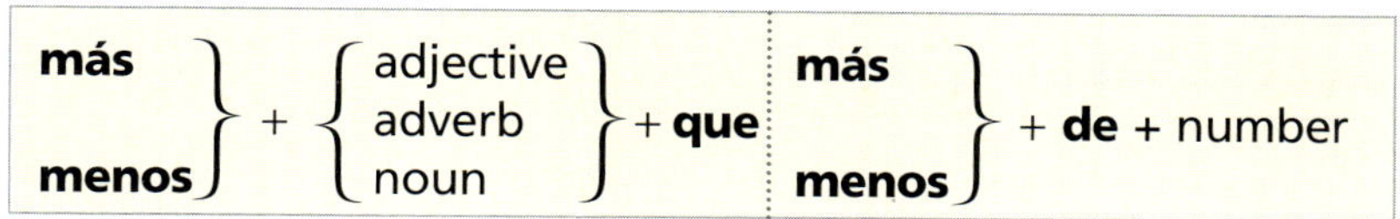


COMPARISONS OF EQUALITY

**tan** + adjective or adverb + **como**
**tanto/a/os/as** + noun + **como**

These adjectives have irregular comparative forms.

| | | | |
|---|---|---|---|
| bueno(a) *good* | malo(a) *bad* | joven *young* | viejo(a) *old* |
| **mejor(es)** *better* | **peor(es)** *worse* | **menor(es)** *younger* | **mayor(es)** *older* |

## Ordinal Numbers

Ordinal numbers are used to express ordered sequences. They agree in number and gender with the noun they modify. The ordinal numbers **primero** and **tercero** drop the final **o** before a singular, masculine noun. Ordinal numbers are seldom used after 10. Cardinal numbers are used instead: **Alfonso XIII, Alfonso Trece.**

| | | | | | |
|---|---|---|---|---|---|
| **1st** | **primero/a** | **5th** | **quinto/a** | **9th** | **noveno/a** |
| **2nd** | **segundo/a** | **6th** | **sexto/a** | **10th** | **décimo/a** |
| **3rd** | **tercero/a** | **7th** | **séptimo/a** | | |
| **4th** | **cuarto/a** | **8th** | **octavo/a** | | |

## Affirmative and Negative Expressions

| Affirmative | Negative |
|---|---|
| **algo** | **nada** |
| **alguien** | **nadie** |
| **alguno (algún), -a** | **ninguno (ningún), -a** |
| **o ... o** | **ni ... ni** |
| **siempre** | **nunca** |

## Interrogative words

| | | | |
|---|---|---|---|
| **¿Adónde?** | **¿Cuándo?** | **¿De dónde?** | **¿Qué?** |
| **¿Cómo?** | **¿Cuánto(a)?** | **¿Dónde?** | **¿Quién(es)?** |
| **¿Cuál(es)?** | **¿Cuántos(as)?** | **¿Por qué?** | |

## Adverbs

Adverbs make the meaning of a verb, an adjective, or another adverb more definite. These are some common adverbs of frequency.

| | | | |
|---|---|---|---|
| **siempre** | *always* | **casi nunca** | *almost never* |
| **nunca** | *never* | **a veces** | *sometimes* |
| **todos los días** | *every day* | | |

## Prepositions

Prepositions are words that show the relationship of a noun or pronoun to another word. These are common prepositions in Spanish.

| | | | | | |
|---|---|---|---|---|---|
| **a** | *to* | **delante** | *before* | **hacia** | *toward* |
| **al lado** | *next to* | **desde** | *from* | **hasta** | *until* |
| **antes de** | *before* | **detrás** | *behind* | **para** | *for, in order to* |
| **con** | *with* | **en** | *in, on* | **por** | *for, by* |
| **de** | *of, from* | **encima** | *over, on top of* | **sin** | *without* |
| **debajo de** | *under* | | | | |

# VERBS

## Present Tense of Regular Verbs

In Spanish, we use a formula to conjugate regular verbs. The endings change in each person, but the stem of the verb remains the same.

| **Infinitive** | habl**ar** | | com**er** | | escrib**ir** | |
|---|---|---|---|---|---|---|
| **Present** | habl**o** | habl**amos** | com**o** | com**emos** | escrib**o** | escrib**imos** |
| | habl**as** | habl**áis** | com**es** | com**éis** | escrib**es** | escrib**ís** |
| | habl**a** | habl**an** | com**e** | com**en** | escrib**e** | escrib**en** |

## Verbs with Irregular *yo* Forms

| **hacer** | | **poner** | | **saber** | | **salir** | | **traer** | |
|---|---|---|---|---|---|---|---|---|---|
| **hago** | hacemos | **pongo** | ponemos | **sé** | sabemos | **salgo** | salimos | **traigo** | traemos |
| haces | hacéis | pones | ponéis | sabes | sabéis | sales | salís | traes | traéis |
| hace | hacen | pone | ponen | sabe | saben | sale | salen | trae | traen |

| **tener** | | **venir** | | **ver** | | **conocer** | |
|---|---|---|---|---|---|---|---|
| **tengo** | tenemos | **vengo** | venimos | **veo** | vemos | **conozco** | conocemos |
| tienes | tenéis | vienes | venís | ves | veis | conoces | conocéis |
| tiene | tienen | viene | vienen | ve | ven | conoce | conocen |

## Verbs with Irregular Forms

| ser | | estar | | ir | |
|---|---|---|---|---|---|
| soy | somos | estoy | estamos | voy | vamos |
| eres | sois | estás | estáis | vas | vais |
| es | son | está | están | va | van |

## Present Progressive

The present progressive in English is formed by using the verb *to be* plus the *-ing* form of another verb. In Spanish, the present progressive is formed by using the verb **estar** plus the -**ndo** form of another verb.

| **-ar** verbs | **-er** and **-ir** verbs |
|---|---|
| hablar → estoy habl**ando** | comer → está com**iendo** |
| trabajar → estás trabaj**ando** | escribir → estamos escrib**iendo** |

| For **-er** and **-ir** verbs with a stem that ends in a vowel, the **-iendo** changes to **-yendo:** |
|---|
| leer → están le**yendo** |

## Stem-Changing Verbs

In Spanish, some verbs have an irregular stem in the present tense. The final vowel of the stem changes from **e → ie, o → ue, u → ue,** and **e → i** in all forms except **nosotros** and **vosotros**.

| e → ie | | o → ue | | u → ue | | e → i | |
|---|---|---|---|---|---|---|---|
| **preferir** | | **poder** | | **jugar** | | **pedir** | |
| pref**ie**ro | preferimos | p**ue**do | podemos | j**ue**go | jugamos | p**i**do | pedimos |
| pref**ie**res | preferís | p**ue**des | podéis | j**ue**gas | jugáis | p**i**des | pedís |
| pref**ie**re | pref**ie**ren | p**ue**de | p**ue**den | j**ue**ga | j**ue**gan | p**i**de | p**i**den |

| Some **e → ie** stem-changing verbs are: | | Some **o → ue** stem-changing verbs are: | | Some **e → i** stem-changing verbs are: |
|---|---|---|---|---|
| **empezar** | **venir** | **almorzar** | **dormir** | **vestirse** |
| **pensar** | **merendar** | **llover** | **probar** | **servir** |
| **querer** | **calentar** | **encontrar** | **acostarse** | |
| **nevar** | **tener** | **volver** | **costar** | |

## The Verbs *gustar* and *encantar*

The verb endings for **gustar** and **encantar** always agree with what is liked or loved. The indirect object pronouns always precede the verb forms.

| gustar (to like) | | encantar (to really like or love) | |
|---|---|---|---|
| one thing: | more than one: | one thing: | more than one: |
| **me**<br>**te**<br>**le**<br>**nos** } **gusta**<br>**os**<br>**les** | **me**<br>**te**<br>**le**<br>**nos** } **gustan**<br>**os**<br>**les** | **me**<br>**te**<br>**le**<br>**nos** } **encanta**<br>**os**<br>**les** | **me**<br>**te**<br>**le**<br>**nos** } **encantan**<br>**os**<br>**les** |

## Verbs with Reflexive Pronouns

If the subject and object of a verb are the same, include the reflexive pronoun with the verb.

| lavarse | | ponerse | | vestirse | |
|---|---|---|---|---|---|
| **me** lavo | **nos** lavamos | **me** pongo | **nos** ponemos | **me** visto | **nos** vestimos |
| **te** lavas | **os** laváis | **te** pones | **os** ponéis | **te** vistes | **os** vestís |
| **se** lava | **se** lavan | **se** pone | **se** ponen | **se** viste | **se** visten |

Here are other verbs with reflexive pronouns.

| | | | |
|---|---|---|---|
| **acostarse** | **bañarse** | **maquillarse** | **secarse** |
| **afeitarse** | **levantarse** | **peinarse** | **sentirse** |

## Preterite of Regular and Irregular Verbs

The preterite is used to talk about what happened at a specific point in time.

| Infinitive | Preterite of Regular Verbs | |
|---|---|---|
| habl**ar** | habl**é** | habl**amos** |
| | habl**aste** | habl**asteis** |
| | habl**ó** | habl**aron** |
| com**er** | com**í** | com**imos** |
| | com**iste** | com**isteis** |
| | com**ió** | com**ieron** |
| escrib**ir** | escrib**í** | escrib**imos** |
| | escrib**iste** | escrib**isteis** |
| | escrib**ió** | escrib**ieron** |

| hacer | ir | ser | ver |
|---|---|---|---|
| hice | fui | fui | vi |
| hiciste | fuiste | fuiste | viste |
| hizo | fue | fue | vio |
| hicimos | fuimos | fuimos | vimos |
| hicisteis | fuisteis | fuisteis | visteis |
| hicieron | fueron | fueron | vieron |

| sacar | llegar | comenzar |
|---|---|---|
| saqué | llegué | comencé |
| sacaste | llegaste | comenzaste |
| sacó | llegó | comenzó |
| sacamos | llegamos | comenzamos |
| sacasteis | llegasteis | comenzasteis |
| sacaron | llegaron | comenzaron |

## Imperative Mood

The imperative is used to tell people to do things. Its forms are sometimes referred to as *commands*. Regular affirmative commands are formed by dropping the **s** from the end of the **tú** form of the verb. For negative commands, switch the **-as** ending to **-es** and the **-es** ending to **-as.**

| | |
|---|---|
| (tú) hablas → habla (no hables) | you speak → speak (don't speak) |
| (tú) escribes → escribe (no escribas) | you write → write (don't write) |
| (tú) pides → pide (no pidas) | you ask for → ask for (don't ask for) |

Some verbs have irregular **tú** imperative forms.

| | |
|---|---|
| tener → ten (no tengas) | ser → sé (no seas) |
| venir → ven (no vengas) | hacer → haz (no hagas) |
| poner → pon (no pongas) | salir → sal (no salgas) |
| ir → ve (no vayas) | decir → di (no digas) |

## The Verbs *ser* and *estar*

Both **ser** and **estar** mean *to be*, but they differ in their uses.

Use **ser:**

1. with nouns to identify and define the subject
   **La mejor estudiante de la clase es Katia.**
2. with **de** to indicate place of origin, ownership, or material
   **Carmen es de Venezuela.**
   **Este libro es de mi abuela.**
   **La blusa es de algodón.**
3. to describe identifying characteristics, such as physical and personality traits, nationality, religion, and profession
   **Mi tío es profesor. Es simpático e inteligente.**
4. to express the time, date, season, or where an event is taking place
   **Hoy es sábado y la fiesta es a las ocho.**

Use **estar:**

1. to indicate location or position of the subject
   **Lima está en Perú.**
2. to describe a condition that is subject to change
   **Maricarmen está triste.**
3. with the present participle (**-ndo** form) to describe an action in progress
   **Mario está escribiendo un poema.**
4. to convey the idea of *to look, to feel, to seem, to taste*
   **Tu hermano está muy guapo hoy.**
   **La sopa está deliciosa.**

## Common Expressions

### EXPRESSIONS WITH *TENER*

| | | | |
|---|---|---|---|
| **tener ... años** | *to be . . . years old* | **tener (mucha) prisa** | *to be in a (big) hurry* |
| **tener mucho calor** | *to be very hot* | **tener que** | *to have to* |
| **tener ganas de...** | *to feel like . . .* | **tener (la) razón** | *to be right* |
| **tener mucho frío** | *to be very cold* | **tener mucha sed** | *to be very thirsty* |
| **tener mucha hambre** | *to be very hungry* | **tener mucho sueño** | *to be very sleepy* |
| **tener mucho miedo** | *to be very afraid* | **tener mucha suerte** | *to be very lucky* |

### EXPRESSIONS OF TIME

To ask how long someone has been doing something, use:
**¿Cuánto tiempo hace que** + present tense?

To say how long someone has been doing something, use:
**Hace** + quantity of time + **que** + present tense.
Hace **seis meses** que **vivo en Los Ángeles.**

You can also use:
present tense + **desde hace** + quantity of time
**Vivo en Los Ángeles** desde hace **seis meses.**

### WEATHER EXPRESSIONS

| | |
|---|---|
| **Hace muy buen tiempo.** | *The weather is very nice.* |
| **Hace mucho calor.** | *It's very hot.* |
| **Hace fresco.** | *It's cool.* |
| **Hace mucho frío.** | *It's very cold.* |
| **Hace muy mal tiempo.** | *The weather is very bad.* |
| **Hace mucho sol.** | *It's very sunny.* |
| **Hace mucho viento.** | *It's very windy.* |
| But: | |
| **Está lloviendo mucho.** | *It's raining a lot.* |
| **Hay mucha neblina.** | *It's very foggy.* |
| **Está nevando.** | *It's snowing.* |
| **Está nublado.** | *It's overcast.* |

# Vocabulario español-inglés

This vocabulary includes almost all words in the textbook, both active (for production) and passive (for recognition only). An entry in **boldface** type indicates that the word or phrase is active. Active words and phrases are practiced in the chapter and are listed on the **Repaso de gramática** and **Repaso de vocabulario** pages at the end of each chapter. You are expected to know and be able to use active vocabulary.

All other words are for recognition only. These words are found in exercises, in optional and visual material, in **Instrucciones** on pages xviii–xix, in **Geocultura,** which is referenced by chapter (1G), **Comparaciones, Leamos y escribamos, También se puede decir,** and **Literatura y variedades.** You can usually understand the meaning of these words and phrases from the context or you can look them up in this vocabulary index. Many words have more than one definition; the definitions given here correspond to the way the words are used in ***¡Exprésate!.***

Nouns are listed with definite articles and plural forms when the plural forms aren't formed according to general rules. The number after each entry refers to the chapter where the word or phrase first appears or where it becomes an active vocabulary word. This vocabulary index follows the rules of the **Real Academia,** with **ch** and **ll** in the same sequence as in the English alphabet.

Stem changes are indicated in parentheses after the verb: **poder (ue).**

**a** *to,* 3; *on,* 4; *at,* 8; a base de *based on,* 6; a continuación *that follows,* 7; a finales *at the end,* 10G; **a la (última) moda** *in the (latest) style,* 8; a la vez *at the same time,* 8; **a la vuelta** *around the corner,* 10; **A ...les gusta...** *They like to . . .,* 3; **a menudo** *often,* 5; **¿A qué hora vas a...?** *What time are you going to . . .?,* 4; **a tiempo** *on time,* 4; **a todo dar** *great,* 9; **Estuvo a todo dar.** *It was great.,* 9; a través de *through,* 5G; **a veces** *sometimes,* 3
**abordar** *to board,* 10
abrazar *to hug,* 9
el abrazo *hug,* 9
**el abrigo** *(over)coat,* 8
**abril** *April,* 1
**abrir** *to open,* 4; **abrir regalos** *to open gifts,* 9
**la abuela** *grandmother,* 5
**el abuelo** *grandfather,* 5
**los abuelos** *grandparents,* 5
**aburrido(a)** *boring,* 2; **estar aburrido(a)** *to be bored,* 7
**acabar de** *to just (have done something),* 7
**acampar** *to camp,* 3
acariciar *to caress,* 7
la acción *action,* 2
el aceite de oliva *olive oil,* 1G
el acento *accent,* 1; el acento ortográfico *written accent,* 8
acerca de *about,* 8
acompañar *to go with,* 6; *to accompany,* 1G; estar acompañada *to be accompanied,* 3
acordarse (ue) *to remember,* 9
**acostarse (ue)** *to go to bed,* 7
la actividad *activity,* 3
**activo(a)** *active,* 2
la actualidad *present time,* 6
el acuerdo *agreement;* **Estoy de acuerdo.** *I agree.,* 6; **No estoy de acuerdo.** *I disagree.,* 6
adaptado(a) *adapted,* 5G
**además** *besides,* 8
**Adiós.** *Good-bye.,* 1
adivinar *to guess,* 2
el adjetivo *adjective,* 5
la admiración *admiration,* 1
admirar *to admire,* 10
el adolescente *adolescent,* 3
**¿adónde?** *where?,* 8; **¿Adónde fuiste?** *Where did you go?,* 8; **¿Adónde vas...?** *Where do you go . . .?,* 3
**la aduana** *customs,* 10
el adulto *adult,* 7
los aeróbicos *aerobics,* 7; hacer aeróbicos *to do aerobics,* 7
**el aeropuerto** *airport,* 10
**afeitarse** *to shave,* 7
afuera *outside,* 3
**las afueras** *suburbs,* 5
la agencia inmobiliaria *real estate agency,* 5
**el agente, la agente** *agent,* 10
agitar *to shake,* 3
**agosto** *August,* 1
**el agua** (f.) *water,* 6
el águila (f.) *eagle,* 7
ahí *there,* 4
**ahora** *now,* 9
**ahorrar** *to save money,* 8
el aire *air,* 3; el aire central *central air conditioning,* 5; el aire libre *open air,* 8
**el ajedrez** *chess,* 1
el ají *hot pepper,* 10G
el ajo *garlic,* 6
ajustado(a) *tight-fitting,* 8
**al (a + el)** *to, to the,* 3; *upon,* 6; al fin *finally,* 10; **al lado de** *next to,* 5
la alberca *swimming pool,* 3
alcanzar *to reach,* 7G
la alcoba *bedroom,* 5
alegre *happy,* 2
**el alemán** *German,* 4
**el alfabeto** *alphabet,* 1
**algo** *something, anything,* 4; **algo** + adjective *kind of* + adjective, 2
**el algodón** *cotton,* 8; **de algodón** *made of cotton,* 8
**algún día** *some day,* 10
algunas *some,* 2
el alimento *food,* 6
alistarse *to get ready,* 7
allá *there,* 8
**allí** *there,* 10

**el almacén** *department store,* 8
el almanaque *almanac,* 1G
**almorzar** *to have lunch,* 5
**el almuerzo** *lunch,* 4
**Aló** *Hello. (telephone greeting),* 8
el alpinismo *mountain climbing,* 7
**alquilar** *to rent,* 3; **alquilar videos** *to rent videos,* 3
alrededor *around,* 6
el altiplano *high plateau,* 10G
**alto(a)** *tall,* 2
la altura *height,* 6G
amanecer *to dawn,* 9
el amarillo *yellow,* 1G
**amarillo(a)** *yellow,* 8
el ambiente *atmosphere,* 5G
ambos *both,* 5G
amigable *friendly,* 2
**el amigo(a)** *friend,* 1; **mi mejor amigo(a)** *my best friend,* 1
el amor *love,* 8; **de amor** *romance,* 2
amueblado(a) *furnished,* 5
analítico(a) *analytical,* 2
**anaranjado(a)** *orange,* 8
ancho *width,* 5G; *wide,* 8
andar *to walk, to go,* 2; andar en bicicleta *to ride a bike,* 3; dime con quien andas y te diré quien eres *a person is known by the company he/she keeps,* 2
andino(a) *of the Andes,* 7G
el anfibio *amphibian,* 2G
la anguila *eel,* 7
el ángulo *angle,* 7
**el anillo** *ring,* 8
**el animal** *animal,* 2
**el aniversario** *anniversary,* 9
el año year, 2; **el Año Nuevo** *New Year,* 9; **el año pasado** *last year,* 9; **¿Cuántos años tiene...?** *How old is . . .?,* 2; **¿Cuántos años tienes?** *How old are you?,* 2
**anoche** *last night,* 9
**anteayer** *day before yesterday,* 8
anterior *previous,* 9
antes *before,* 1; **antes de** *before,* 7; de antes *from before,* 4
antiguo(a) *old,* 6G
**antipático(a)** *unfriendly,* 2
**añadir** *to add,* 6
aparecer *to appear,* 6
**el apartamento** *apartment,* 5
apasionado(a) *passionate,* 2
apellido *last name,* 2
apetecer *to appeal,* 6
aplicar *to apply,* 2
aportar *to contribute,* 8G
aprender *to learn,* 1
apropiado(a) *appropriate,* 7
aproximadamente *approximately,* 2
los apuntes *notes,* 8
aquella *that,* 6
aquello *that,* 4
aquí *here,* 6
árabe *Arab,* 5G
el árbol *tree,* 1; la copa del árbol *top of the tree,* 4G
**los aretes** *earrings,* 8
la argamasa *mortar,* 10G
argentino(a) *Argentine,* 7
árido(a) *dry,* 10G
la armonía *harmony,* 2
armonizar *to harmonize,* 7G
el arquitecto *architect,* 3G
arquitectónico(a) *architectural,* 10G
la arquitectura *architecture,* 2G
**arreglar** *to pick up,* 5; **arreglar el cuarto** *to pick up the room,* 5
el arrendamiento *rental,* 10
**la arroba** *@,* 1
**el arroz** *rice,* 6
**el arte** *art,* 4; las artes plásticas *sculpture,* 2
la artesanía *crafts,* 4
el artista, la artista *artist,* 1
artístico(a) *artistic,* 2
asegurar *to reassure,* 6
el asentamiento *colony, settlement,* 8G
el aseo *restroom,* 10
así *like this;* así que *so,* 8; Así es., *That's how it is.,* 2
asistente *assistant,* 10
**asistir (a)** *to attend,* 4
asomar *to peek out,* 9
el asterisco *asterisk,* 7
**atlético(a)** *athletic,* 2
el atole *Mexican drink made of cornmeal, milk or water, and flavoring,* 6
atraer *to attract,* 1G
atravesar *to cross,* 10G
atreverse *to dare,* 9
**el atún** *tuna,* 6
**los audífonos** *headphones,* 8
**el auditorio** *auditorium,* 4
aun *even,* 2
aún *still,* 10
aunque *even though,* 6
**el autobús** *bus,* 10
el autor *author,* 7
el autorretrato *self-portrait,* 6G
avanzado(a) *advanced,* 10G
el ave (pl. las aves) *bird,* 4G
**la aventura** *adventure,* 2
averiguar *to find out,* 10
**el avión** *airplane,* 10; por avión *by plane,* 10
**¡Ay no!** *Oh, no!,* 6
¡ay! *ouch!,* 8
**ayer** *yesterday,* 8
el aymara indigenous *language in Peru,* 10G
**la ayuda** *help,* 6
**ayudar** *to help,* 5; **ayudar en casa** *to help out at home,* 5; Estamos ayudando. *We are helping.,* 3
el azúcar *sugar,* 6
el azul *blue,* 1G
**azul** *blue,* 5

la bahía *bay,* 8G
**bailar** *to dance,* 3; bailando *dancing,* 1; ponerse a bailar *to start dancing,* 3
la bailarina *dancer (fem.),* 3
**el baile** *dance,* 3
bajar *to descend,* 7; **bajar de peso** *to lose weight,* 7
**bajo(a)** *short,* 2
balanceado(a) *balanced,* 6
el balcón *balcony,* 5
balear *to shoot,* 5
el ballet *ballet,* 1
el baloncesto *basketball,* 3
**bañarse** *to bathe,* 7
la bandeja *platter,* 7G
la bandera *banner,* 9
el bandido *bandit,* 5
**el baño** *bathroom,* 5; *restroom,* 10
**barato(a)** *inexpensive,* 8
la barbacoa *barbecue,* 3G
**el barco** *boat,* 10; el barquito *little boat,* 5
la barranca *cliff,* 6G
el barrio *neighborhood,* 7G
básico(a) *basic,* 6
**el básquetbol** *basketball,* 3
basta *it's enough,* 5
**bastante** + adjective *quite, pretty* + adjective, 2
**la basura** *trash,* 5; **sacar la basura** *to take out the trash,* 5
la batalla *battle,* 3G
**el batido** *milkshake,* 8
el bebé, la bebé *baby,* 1
**beber (algo)** *to drink (something),* 4; **beber ponche** *to drink punch,* 9
la bebida *drink,* 6
la beca *scholarship,* 10
**el béisbol** *baseball,* 3
bello(a) *beautiful,* 2G
**la biblioteca** *library,* 4
**la bicicleta** *bike,* 3; **montar en bicicleta** *to ride a bike,* 3
**bien** *all right, fine,* 1; *really,* 2; bien dicho *well said,* 6; **Está bien.** *It's okay.,* 3; **Estoy bien.** *I'm fine.,* 1; **Me parece bien.** *It's all right/ seems fine to me.,* 5; **quedar bien** *to fit well,* 8; **Que te vaya bien.** *Hope things go well for you.,* 9
bienvenido *welcome,* 10
el billete *ticket,* 10
**la billetera** *wallet,* 10

**la biología** *biology,* 4
**blanco(a)** *white,* 8; **en blanco** *blank,* 8
el blanquillo *egg,* 6
**la blusa** *blouse,* 8
**la boca** *mouth,* 7
el bocadillo *sandwich (Spain),* 6; *finger food (Dom. Rep.),* 9
el bocadito *small servings of food,* 7G
las bocas *finger food (Costa Rica),* 9
**la boda** *wedding,* 9
la boleta *ticket,* 10
**el boleto de avión** *plane ticket,* 10
**el bolígrafo** *pen,* 4
**la bolsa** *purse,* 8; *bag,* 8; *travel bag,* 10
la bomba *music and dance style,* 2G
la bombilla *straw used for sipping* ***mate,*** 7
**bonito(a)** *pretty,* 2
el borde *edge,* 7G
el borrador *rough draft,* 1
el bosque *forest,* 2G; el bosque húmedo *rain forest,* 4G
la botana *finger food (Mex.),* 9
botar *to throw out,* 5
**las botas** *boots,* 8
el bote *boat,* 9G; **el bote de vela** *sailboat,* 10; **pasear en bote de vela** *to go out in a sailboat,* 10
**el brazo** *arm,* 7
brillar *to shine,* 7
brindar *to offer,* 5
**el bróculi** *broccoli,* 6
**bueno(a)** *good,* 2; **Buenas noches.** *Good evening., Good night.,* 1; **Buenas tardes.** *Good afternoon.,* 1; **Buenos días.** *Good morning.,* 1
**Bueno.** *Hello. (telephone greeting),* 8
burlarse de *to make fun of,* 8
el burro *donkey,* 1
**buscar** *to look for,* 7; **buscar un pasatiempo** *to find a hobby,* 7; búsquenme *look for me,* 3

el caballo de paso *horse with high-stepping gait,* 10G
caber *to fit,* 10G
**la cabeza** *head,* 7
el cacao *cocoa,* 6G
cada *each,* xxii; cada uno(a) *each one,* 6; cada vez *each time,* 8
**el café** *coffee,* 6; **el café con leche** *coffee with milk,* 6; *brown,* 1G; **de color café** *brown,* 5
**la cafetería** *cafeteria,* 4; *coffee shop,* 6
la caída de agua *waterfall,* 7G
el caimán *caiman (reptile),* 7G
la caja *box,* 9
**el cajero automático** *automatic teller machine,* 10
la calabaza *squash, pumpkin,* 6G; la calabacita *gourd used for* ***mate*** *tea,* 7G
**los calcetines** *socks,* 8; **un par de calcetines** *a pair of socks,* 8
**la calculadora** *calculator,* 4
la calefacción *heating,* 5; la calefacción central *central heating,* 5
el calendario *calendar,* 1
**calentar (ie)** *to heat up,* 6
**caliente** *hot,* 6
**callado(a)** *quiet,* 5
la calle *street,* 2G
el calor *heat,* 3; **Hace calor.** *It's hot.,* 3; **tener calor** *to be hot,* 7
la caloría *calorie,* 6
**la cama** *bed,* 5; **hacer la cama** *to make the bed,* 5
**la cámara** *camera,* 10; **la cámara desechable** *disposable camera,* 10
el camarero *waiter,* 6
cambiar *to change,* 4
**cambiar dinero** *to change money,* 10
el cambio *change,* 9
**caminar** *to walk,* 7
el camino *path,* 10G
el camión *bus (Mex.),* 10
**la camisa** *shirt,* 8
**la camiseta** *T-shirt,* 8; la camiseta deportiva *sport shirt,* 8
el camote *sweet potato,* 4G
**el campo** *countryside,* 5
la canción *song,* 8
candidato(a) *candidate,* 4
**la canoa** *canoe,* 10
el cañón *canyon,* 6G
**canoso(a)** *graying,* 5
**cansado(a)** *tired,* 7; **estar cansado(a)** *to be tired,* 7
**cantar** *to sing,* 3; cantaba *he sang,* 9
el cantar *singing,* 2
la cantidad *amount,* 2; *quantity,* 6; las cantidades *large numbers,* 6
el canto *song,* 1G
la capilla *chapel,* 3G
la capital *capital,* 1G
el capítulo *chapter,* 1
**la cara** *face,* 7; cara de tortilla *tortilla face,* 1
el carácter *character,* 5
la característica *characteristic,* 6
caracterizar *to characterize,* 5G
la cárcel *jail,* 8
caribeño(a) *Caribbean,* 4G
el cariño *affection; (addressing someone) dear, 3;* con cariño *affectionately,* 10
**la carne** *meat, beef,* 6; la carne de res *beef,* 6; la carne molida *ground beef,* 6
**el carnet de identidad** *ID,* 10
**caro(a)** *expensive,* 8
**la carpeta** *folder,* 4
la carreta *cart,* 4G
**el carro** *car,* 2
la carroza *float,* 9G
**la carta** *letter,* 3
**la casa** *house,* 5; **ayudar en casa** *to help out at home,* 5; **la casa de...** *...'s house,* 3; **decorar la casa** *to decorate the house,* 9
el casabe *flat, dry bread made from manioc,* 9G
casarse *to get married,* 10
la cascada *waterfall,* 2G
la cáscara *shell,* 2G
**casi** *almost,* 3, **casi nunca** *almost never,* 3, **casi siempre** *almost always,* 3
el caso *case,* 2
**castaño(a)** *dark brown,* 5
las castañuelas *castanets,* 1G
el castellano *Spanish,* 1G
el castillo *castle,* 2G
el catalán *language from Catalonia, Spain,* 1G
el catálogo *catalog,* 8
la catarata *cataract, waterfall,* 7G
la catedral *cathedral,* 1G
**catorce** *fourteen,* 1
el cayo *key (island),* 8G
el cazador *hunter,* 7G
la cebolla *onion,* 10G
celebérrimo(a) *most famous,* 8
la celebración *celebration,* 1
**celebrar** *to celebrate,* 9; celebrará *will celebrate,* 8; se celebra *is celebrated,* 2G
célebre *famous,* 8
celeridad *speed,* 8
celta *Celtic,* 1G
**la cena** *dinner,* 6
**cenar** *to eat dinner,* 6
**el centro** *downtown,* 10; *center,* 3G
**el centro comercial** *mall,* 3
**el cepillo de dientes** *toothbrush,* 7
la cerámica *pottery,* 4
**cerca de** *close to, near,* 5
cercano(a) *close,* 5
**los cereales** *cereal,* 6
el cerebelo *cerebellum,* 8
el cerebro *brain,* 8
la ceremonia *ceremony,* 6
**cero** *zero,* 1
cerrado(a) *closed,* 1
**cerrar (ie)** *to close,* 8
el césped *grass,* 5
la cesta de paja *straw basket,* 8G
el ceviche *dish made with seafood, lemon, and seasonings,* 10G
**chao** *Bye,* 9
**la chaqueta** *jacket,* 8
**charlar** *to talk, chat,* 9
el chayote *type of squash,* 4G

la chica *girl,* 8
chicano(a) *Mexican that has emigrated to the United States,* 3G
el chile *hot pepper, 6G;* chile en nogada *hot peppers in walnut and spice sauce,* 6G
el chileno *Chilean,* 5
la chimenea *fireplace,* 5
el chiste *joke,* 9
el choclo *corn on the cob,* 5G
**el chocolate** *chocolate,* 6; *hot chocolate,* 6
el churro *sugar-coated fritter,* 6
el ciclismo *cycling,* 1
**ciego(a)** *blind,* 5
el cielo *heaven,* 3
**cien** *one hundred,* 2
**la ciencia ficción** *science fiction,* 2
**las ciencias** *science,* 4; **...de ciencias** *science . . .,*1
el científico *scientist,* 6
**ciento un(o)** *one hundred one,* 8
cierto(a) *true,* xxii
la cifra *number,* 8
la cima *mountain top,* 7G
**cinco** *five,* 1
**cincuenta** *fifty,* 2
**el cine** *movie theater,* 3
el cinturón *belt,* 8
el círculo *circle,* 3
el citrón *lemon,* 6
**la ciudad** *city,* 5
**¡Claro que sí!** *Of course!,* 4
claro(a) *clear,* 6G
la clase *class,* 3; **después de clases** *after class,* 3; **la clase de baile** *dance class,* 4
clasificar *to classify,* 6
clavar *to nail,* 10
el clavo *nail,* 10
**el cliente, la cliente** *client,* 8
**el club de...** *the . . . club,* 4
el cobre *copper,* 6G
cocer *to cook,* 3
el coche *car,* 10
**la cocina** *kitchen,* 5; *cooking,* 3G
**cocinar** *to cook,* 5
el coco *coconut,* 2G
el cocodrilo *crocodile,* 8G
el código *code,* 2G
cohabitar *to live together,* 8G
**la cola** *line,* 10
el colectivo *bus (Bol., Perú, Ecuador),* 10
**el colegio** *school,* 3
**colgar** *to hang,* 9
la colina *hill,* 9G
la colonia *colony,* 7G
el colonizador *colonist,* 6G
el color *color,* 5
el colorido *coloring,* 7G
colorido(a) *colorful,* 4G
la columna *column,* xxii
los combates *battles,* 10
la combinación *combination,* 1
combinar *to combine,* 5G
**el comedor** *dining room,* 5
**comenzar(ie)** *to start,* 10; **comenzar un viaje** *to begin a trip,* 10; comiencen *begin,* 8
**comer** *to eat,* 3; se comen *are eaten,* 2G
el comercio *commerce,* 3G
el comestible *food,* 3
**cómico(a)** *funny,* 2
**la comida** *food,* 2; *lunch,* 6; **la comida china (italiana, mexicana)** *Chinese (Italian, Mexican) food,* 2; la comida típica *traditional food,* 6
como *like,* 2; as, 9; **como siempre** *as always,* 9
**cómo** *how?, what?,* 1; **¿Cómo eres?** *What are you like?,* 2; **¿Cómo es...?** *What is . . . like?,* 2; **¿Cómo está(s)?** *How are you?,* 1; **¿Cómo me quedan...?** *How does . . . look?,* 8; **¿Cómo se escribe...?** *How do you spell . . .?,* 1; **¿Cómo se llama?** *What's his (her/your) name?,* 1; **¿Cómo te llamas?** *What's your name? (fam.),* 1
**la compañera de clase** *classmate (female),* 1; **una compañera de clase** *a (female) classmate,* 1
**el compañero de clase** *classmate (male),* 1; **un compañero de clase** *a (male) classmate,* 1
la comparación *comparison,* 1
comparar *to compare,* 8
compasivo(a) *compassionate,* 6
el complemento directo *direct object,* 6
completar *to complete,* xxii
completo *complete,* 6; por completo *completely,* 6
**comprar** *to buy,* 8; comprarías *you would buy,* 8
las compras *shopping,* 2; estar de compras *to be on a shopping trip,* 8; **ir de compras** *to go shopping,* 3
la comprensión *comprehension,* 10
comprender *to understand,* 2; nos comprendemos *we understand each other,* 2
**la computación** *computer science,* 4
**la computadora** *computer,* 4
común *common,* 9
comunicar *to communicate,* 5
la comunidad *community,* 1
**con** *with,* 3; con base en *based on,* xxii; **con mis amigos** *with my friends,* 3; **con mi familia** *with my family,* 3; con motivo de *on the occasion of,* 9; **¿Con qué frecuencia vas...?** *How often do you go . . .?,* 3; con relación a *in relation to,* 5
**el concierto** *concert,* 4
el concurso *competition,* 9G
el condominio *condominium,* 5
conectar *to connect,* 8G
confundido(a) *confused,* 4
confundir *to confuse,* 10
el conjunto *musical group,* 3G
conmemorar *commemorate,* 3G
**conmigo** *with me,* 3
**conocer** *to know, to meet, be familiar with,* 9; **conocimos...** *we visited . . .,* 10; **quiero conocer...** *I want to see . . .,* 10; se conoce *is known,* 2G
conocido(a) *known,* 2G
el conocimiento *knowledge,* 7
conquistar *to conquer,* 10
**conseguir (i, i)** *to get,* 10
el consejo *advice,* 7
conservar *to preserve,* 2G
considerar *to consider,* 2; *to regard,* 9
constituir *to make up,* 6
construir *to build,* 3G; construye *construct,* 10; fue construido *was built,* 3G
el consultorio médico *doctor's office,* 7
consumir *to consume,* 6; se consumen *are consumed,* 6
el consumo *consumption,* 6
contar *to count,* 1; *to tell,* 4; contando *counting,* 1; **contar chistes** *to tell jokes,* 9; contar con *to count on,* 10; cuenta *tells,* 6; cuentan *it is told,* 6
contemplar *to contemplate,* 9
contemporáneo *contemporary,* 1G
contener (ie) *to contain,* 10G; que contengan *that contain,* 10
**contento(a)** *happy,* 7; **estar contento(a)** *to be happy,* 7
contestar *to answer,* xxii
**contigo** *with you,* 3
el continente *continent,* 6
continuo *continual,* 8
contra *against,* 10
al contrario *to the contrary,* 6
la contribución *contribution,* 2G
contribuir *to contribute,* 8G
**el control de seguridad** *security checkpoint,* 10
controlar *to control,* 3G
el convento *convent,* 3G
la conversación *conversation,* xxii
convertirse *to become,* 10
la copa *treetop,* 4
el coquí *small tree frog,* 2G
el corazón *heart,* 7G
la cordillera *mountain range,* 2G
el coro *chorus,* 2
correcto(a) *right, correct,* xxii
corregir *to correct,* xxii
**el correo electrónico** *e-mail address,* 1; **¿Cuál es el correo electrónico de...?** *What is . . .'s e-mail address?,* 1; **¿Cuál es tu correo electrónico?**

*What's your e-mail address?*, 1
**correr** *to run*, 3
la correspondencia *correspondence*, 1
corresponder *to correspond*, xxii; Le corresponde. *It falls to him.*, 5; que le correspondan *that correspond to it*, 9
correspondiente *corresponding*, 8
la corriente *current*, 8
**cortar** *to cut*, 6; **cortar el césped** *to cut the grass*, 5
la Corte Suprema *Supreme Court*, 6
**corto(a)** *short*, 5
**la cosa** *thing*, 4; **Necesito muchas cosas.** *I need lots of things*, 4; **No es gran cosa.** *It's not a big deal.*, 5
coser *to sew*, 4
la costa *coast*, 3G
**costar (ue)** *to cost*, 8; costará *will cost*, 9
costeño(a) *coastal*, 10G
la costumbre *custom*, 5G
la creación *creation*, 3
crear *to create*, 7; creado por *created by*, 7G; fue creado *was created*, 3G
la creatividad *creativity*, 6G
creativo(a) *creative*, 2
crecer *to grow*, 9G; Crecí. *I grew up.*, 3
creer *to believe*, 6; *to think*, 9
la crema *cream*, 6
la criatura *child*, 3
crudo(a) *raw*, 10G
**el cuaderno** *notebook*, 4
la cuadra *block*, 5
cual: los cuales *which*, 10
el cuadro *box, chart*, xxii; *painting*, 1
**¿cuál?** *what?, which?*, 4; **¿Cuál es el correo electrónico de...?** *What is . . .'s e-mail address?*, 1; **¿Cuál es el teléfono de...?** *What's . . . telephone number?*, 1; **¿Cuál es tu correo electrónico?** *What's your e-mail address?*, 1; **¿Cuál es tu materia preferida?** *What's your favorite subject?*, 4; **¿Cuál es tu teléfono?** *What's your telephone number?*, 1
**cualquier** *any*, 10
cualquiera *whichever*, 6G
**cuando** *when*, 3
**¿cuándo?** *when?*, 2; **¿Cuándo es el cumpleaños de...?** *When is . . .'s birthday?*, 2; **¿Cuándo es tu cumpleaños?** *When is your birthday?*, 2
**¿cuánto(a)?** *how much?*, 4
¡cuántos! *so many!*, 4
**¿cuántos(as)?** *How many . . .?*, 2; **¿Cuántos años tiene… ?** *How old is . . .?*, 2; **¿Cuántos años tienes?** *How old are you?*, 2
**cuarenta** *forty*, 2
**cuarto** *quarter*, 4; **menos cuarto** *a quarter to (the hour)*, 4; **y cuarto** *quarter past*, 1
**el cuarto** *room*, 5; **arreglar el cuarto** *to pick up the room*, 5
**cuatro** *four*, 1
**cuatrocientos** *four hundred*, 8
cubierto(a) *covered*, 3
**la cuchara** *spoon*, 6
**el cuchillo** *knife*, 6
**el cuello** *neck*, 7
**la cuenta** *bill*, 6
el cuento *story*, 4
el cuerno *horn*, 2G
el cuerpo *body*, 7
el cuerpo de bomberos *fire department*, 2G
**cuesta(n)...** *cost(s) . . .*, 8
la cueva *cave*, 1G
el cuidado *care*, 1; Ten cuidado. *Take care.*, 6
cuidadosamente *carefully*, 9
**cuidar** *to take care of*, 5; **cuidar a mis hermanos** *take care of my brothers and sisters*, 5
**cuidarse** *to take care of oneself*, 7; **cuidarse la salud** *to take care of one's health*, 7; **Para cuidarte la salud debes...** *To take care of your health, you should . . .*, 7; **Para cuidarte mejor, debes...** *To take better care of yourself, you should . . .*, 7; **Cuídate.** *Take care.*, 9
culinario(a) *culinary*, 6
cultivar *to cultivate*, 6
el cultivo *crop*, 4G
la cultura *culture*, 1
**el cumpleaños** *birthday*, 9; **¿Cuándo es el cumpleaños de...?** *When is . . .'s birthday?*, 2; **¿Cuándo es tu cumpleaños?** *When is your birthday?*, 2; **el cumpleaños de...** *birthday of . . .*, 2; **la tarjeta de cumpleaños** *birthday card*, 8
curioso(a) *odd, unusual*, 1
la curva *curve*, 3G

dado(a) *given*, 7
la danza *dance*, 1G
**dar** *to give*, 7; le dan *they give*, 7; **no des** *don't give*, 7; se da *is held*, 8G
darse cuenta *to realize*, 8
el dato *fact*, 10
**de** *of, from, in, by*, 1; *made of*, 8; **...de ciencias** *science . . .*, 1; **de color café** *brown*, 5; **¿De dónde eres?** *Where are you from? (fam.)*, 1; **¿De dónde es usted?** *Where are you from? (formal)*, 1; **¿De dónde es...?** *Where is . . . from?*, 1; de...en... *from . . . to . . .*, 8; **. . . de español** *Spanish . . .*, 1; **de la mañana** *in the morning*, A.M., 1; **de la noche** *at night*, P.M., 1; **de la tarde** *in the afternoon, evening*, P.M., 1; de nuevo *again*, 7; de nada *you're welcome*, xxii; **¿De parte de quién?** *Who's calling?*, 8; ¿de quién? *about whom?*, 1; de todo *everything*, 8; de todo tipo *all kinds*, 8; de todos modos *in any event*, 8; de veras *really*, 8
debajo *underneath*, 8; **debajo de** *underneath*, 5
deber *should*, 6; ¿Debo...? *Should I . . .?*, 8; **No debes...** *You shouldn't . . .*, 7; se debe hacer *should be done*, 6
los deberes *chores*, 5; *responsibilities*, 5
debido a *due to*, 7G
el decibel *decibel*, 2
decidir *to decide*, xxii
decir *to say*, 3; bien dicho *well said*, 6; di *say*, 4; dice *says*, 3; diciéndome *telling me*, 9; Me han dicho. *They have told me.*, 6; Se dicen adiós. *They say goodbye.*, 3; si lo hubiera dicho *if I had said it*, 6; Te diré. *I'll tell you.*, 2; yo he dicho *I have said*, 6
declarar *to declare*, 6
**la decoración** *decoration*, 9
**decorar** *to decorate*, 9; **decorar la casa** *to decorate the house*, 9
dedicado(a) a *dedicated to*, 2G
dedicar *to dedicate*, 4; es dedicada *is dedicated*, 5; dedicación dedication, 10; se dedica is dedicated, 2G
**el dedo** *finger*, 7; *toe*, 4G
deducir *to deduce*, 7
la definición *definition*, 10
definido(a) *defined*, 8
definitivamente *definitely*, 8; *permanently*, 9
**dejar** *to allow*, 3; *to leave*, 10; **dejar un recado** *to leave a message*, 8
**dejar de** + infinitive *to stop doing something*, 7; **dejar de fumar** *to stop smoking*, 7
**del (de + el)** *of the*, 2
**delante de** *in front of*, 5
**delgado(a)** *thin*, 5
**delicioso(a)** *delicious*, 2
**demasiado(a)** *too much*, 7
demostrar (ue) *to show*, 10G
dentro *inside*, 9
el departamento *apartment (México)*, 5; *district (Perú)*, 10
**el dependiente, la dependiente** *salesclerk*, 8

**los deportes** *sports,* 2
deportivo(a) (adj.) *sports,* 8
la derecha *right,* 1
el desarrollo *development,* 7G
desarrollar *to develop,* 4
el desastre *disaster,* 9
**desayunar** *to eat breakfast,* 6
**el desayuno** *breakfast,* 6
**descansar** *to rest,* 3
el descendiente *descendant,* 10
describir *to describe,* 5
descubrir *to discover,* 8; fue descubierto *was discovered,* 7G
desde *since,* 4; *from,* 10; ¿desde cuándo? *since when?,* 4; desde hace *since,* 6; desde joven *since her youth,* 8; desde luego *of course,* 7
**desear** *to want, to wish for, to desire,* 6; deseando *wanting to,* 8
**desechable** *disposable,* 10
**desembarcar** *to disembark, to deplane,* 10
desembocar *to flow,* 10G
el deseo *desire,* 9
desesperado(a) *desperate,* 6
el desfile *parade, procession,* 4G
el desierto *desert,* 5G
la despedida *farewell,* 9; la fiesta de despedida *goodbye party,* 10
**despertarse (ie)** *to wake up,* 7
despierto(a) *awake,* 7
**después** *after,* 3; *afterwards,* 4; **después de** *after,* 7; **después de clases** *after class,* 3
destinado(a) *destined,* 6
el destino *destination,* 10
el detalle *detail,* 7
determinar *to determine,* 7
**detrás de** *behind,* 5
**devolver (ue)** *to return something,* 8
di *say,* 8
**el día** *day,* 1; **algún día** *some day,* 10; **el Día de Acción de Gracias** *Thanksgiving Day,* 9; **el Día de la Independencia** *Independence Day,* 9; **el Día de la Madre** *Mother's Day,* 9; **el día de la semana** *day of the week,* 1; **el Día de los Enamorados** *Valentine's Day,* 9; **el Día del Padre** *Father's Day,* 9; **el día de tu santo** *your saint's day,* 9; **el día festivo** *holiday,* 9; **¿Qué día es hoy?** *What day is today?,* 1
diablado(a) *devilish,* 5G
el diablo *devil,* 7G
el diálogo *dialogue,* xxii
diario(a) *daily,* 3G
**dibujar** *to draw,* 3
el dibujo *drawing,* xxii
**el diccionario** *dictionary,* 4
dice (inf. decir) *(he/she) says,* 4
la dicha *happiness,* 9
**diciembre** *December,* 1
el dictado *dictation,* 1
**diecinueve** *nineteen,* 1
**dieciocho** *eighteen,* 1
**dieciséis** sixteen, 1
**diecisiete** *seventeen,* 1
**los dientes** *teeth,* 7
**la dieta** *diet,* 7; **seguir una dieta sana** *to eat a balanced diet,* 7
**diez** *ten,* 1
diferente *different,* 2
**difícil** *difficult,* 4; **Es difícil.** *It's difficult.,* 4
**Diga.** Hello. *(telephone greeting),* 8
**el dinero** *money,* 8
el dinosaurio *dinosaur,* 1
el dios *god,* 6; gracias a Dios *thank goodness,* 6
**la dirección** *address,* 5; **Mi dirección es...** *My address is . . .,* 5
directamente *directly,* 4
director (-a) *director,* 10
el directorio de teléfono *phone book,* 1
disciplinado(a) *disciplined,* 2
el disco *record,* 8
**el disco compacto** *compact disc,* 8; **el disco compacto en blanco** *blank compact disc,* 8
diseñar *to design,* 3G; fue diseñado(a) *was designed,* 3G
el diseño *design,* 5G
el disfraz *costume,* 9G
disfrazar *to wear a costume,* 4G
disfrutar *to enjoy,* 2G
disponible *available,* 7
dispuesto(a) *willing,* 6G
la distancia *distance,* 10
distinguirse *to distinguish oneself,* 10
distinto(a) *different,* 6G
la diversión *fun,* 2
diverso(a) *diverse,* 6
**divertido(a)** *fun,* 2; **¡Qué divertido!** *What fun!,* 10
divertirse *to have fun,* 1; diviértanse *have a good time* (pl.), 1; que me divierta *to have fun,* 9
doblado(a) *folded,* 9
doble *double,* 5
**doce** *twelve,* 1
el documento *document,* 1
el dólar *dollar,* 8
**doler (ue)** *to hurt,* 7; **Me duele(n)...** *My . . . hurt(s).,* 7; **¿Te duele algo?** *Does something hurt?,* 7
**el domingo** *Sunday,* 1; **los domingos** *on Sundays,* 3
dominicano(a) *Dominican,* 9
donde *where,* 8
**¿dónde?** *where?,* 5; **¿Dónde se puede...?** *Where can I . . .?,* 10
dorado(a) *golden,* 2
dormido(a) *asleep,* 7
**dormir (ue)** *to sleep,* 5; **dormir lo suficiente** *to get enough sleep,* 7
el dormitorio *bedroom,* 5
**dos** *two,* 1
**dos mil** *two thousand,* 8
**dos millones (de)** *two million,* 8
**doscientos** *two hundred,* 8
dramatizar *to dramatize, to role-play,* xxii
la duda *doubt,* 6; sin duda *without a doubt,* 6
**dulce** *sweet,* 7
**el dulce** *candy,* 9
la duración *duration,* 7
**durante** *during,* 10; *throughout,* 6G
durar *to last,* 10G
**el durazno** *peach,* 6
**el DVD** *DVD,* 8

e *and,* 5
la economía *economy,* 3G; la economía doméstica *home economics,* 6G
la edad *age,* 2G; de más edad *the oldest,* 5
**el edificio** *building,* 5; **el edificio de... pisos** *. . . story building,* 5
**la educación física** *physical education,* 4
eficaz *efficient,* 10G
eficiente *efficient,* 2
el ejemplo *example,* 3G
el ejercicio *exercise,* 3; **hacer ejercicio** *to exercise,* 3
**el** *the* (masc.), 2
**él** he, 1; **Él es...** *He is . . .,* 1; **Él se llama...** *His name is . . .,* 1
el elefante *elephant,* 1
la elegancia *elegance,* 5G
elegante *elegant,* 2
el elemento *element,* 1
elevar *to raise,* 5G
la elite *elite,* 6
**ella** *she,* 1; A ella le gusta + infinitive *She likes to . . .,* 3; **Ella es...** *She is . . .,* 1; ella misma *herself,* 6; **Ella se llama...** *Her name is . . .,* 1
**ellas** *they (f.),* 1
**ellos** *they (m.),* 1
el elote *corn on the cob (Mexico),* 6
emitir *to emit,* 2
emocionado(a) *excited,* 9
**la empanada** *turnover-like pastry,* 9
el emparedado *sandwich,* 6

**empezar (ie)** *to start,* 5
el empleado, la empleada *employee,* 7
el empleo *job,* 9
emplumado(a) *feathered,* 6
**en** *on, in, at,* 1; en frente *in front,* 3G; **en blanco** *blank,* 8; en las cuales *about which,* 8; en negrilla *bold,* 9; **en punto** *on the dot,* 1; en que *in which,* 8; **¿En que le puedo servir?** *Can I help you?,* 8
enamorado(a) *in love,* 10
**Encantado(a).** *Pleased to meet you., Nice to meet you.,* 1
**encantar (me encanta(n))** *to really like, to love,* 6
encerrar *to lock up,* 10
**encima de** *on top of, above,* 5
**encontrar (ue)** *to find,* 7; encontrará *will find,* 10; se encuentra *is/it's located* 1G; se encuentran *they can be found,* 6
**encontrarse con alguien** *to meet up with someone,* 10
energético(a) *energetic,* 2
la energía *energy,* 2
**enero** *January,* 1
la enfermera *nurse,* 5
enfermo(a) *sick,* 7
en frente *in front,* 10
enhorabuena *congratulations,* 10
**enojado(a)** *angry,* 7
**enojarse** *to get angry,* 7
enrollado(a) *rolled up,* 3
**la ensalada** *salad,* 6
**el ensayo** *rehearsal,* 3
enseñar *to show, to teach,* 4; **enseñar fotos** *to show photos,* 9
**entender** *to understand,* 5
**enterarse** *to find out,* 10
entonces *then,* 4
entrar *to enter,* 4
entre *between,* 2; *in, within,* 6; *among,* 7
entregar *to hand over,* 9
**los entremeses** *appetizers,* 9
la entrenadora *trainer,* 7
**el entrenamiento** *practice,* 3
**entrenarse** *to work out,* 7
la entrevista *interview,* 2
entrevistar *to interview,* 2
enviar *to send,* 1
la envoltura *wrapping,* 9
la época *era,* 6; la época colonial *Spanish colonial era,* 2G
**el equipaje** *luggage,* 10
el equipo *equipment,* 3G; *team,* 9G; el equipo de transporte *transportation equipment,* 3G
**¿Eres...?** *Are you . . .?,* 2
la erupción *eruption,* 6G
**Es...** *He (She, It) is . . .,* 2; **Es algo divertido.** *It's kind of fun.,* 2; **Es bastante bueno.** *It's pretty good.,* 2; **Es de...** *He (She) is from . . .,* 1; **Es delicioso.** *It's delicious.,* 2; **Es el... de...** *It's the . . . of . . .,* 2; **Es facíl/difícil** *It's easy/hard,* 4; **Es el primero (dos, tres) de...** *It's the first (second, third) of . . .,* 1; **Es la una.** *It is one o'clock.,* 1; **Es pésimo.** *It's awful.,* 2; **Es que...** *It's because; It's just that . . .,* 7; **¡Es un robo!** *It's a rip-off!,* 8
ese(a) *that,* 5
escapar *to escape,* 5
la escena *scene,* 3
escoger *to pick,* 9; *to choose,* 6
escolar *school (adj.),* 4
esconder *to hide,* 4
**escribir** *to write,* 1; **¿Cómo se escribe...?** *How do you spell . . .?,* 1; escribamos *let's write,* 1; **escribir cartas** *to write letters,* 3; **Se escribe...** *It's spelled . . .,* 1
el escritor, la escritora *writer,* 1
**el escritorio** *desk,* 5
**escuchar** *to listen,* 3; **escuchar música** *to listen to music,* 3; escuchemos *let's listen,* 1; has escuchado *you have heard,* 2; he escuchado *I have heard,* 2
la escuela *school,* 2; la escuela primaria *elementary school,* 5; la escuela secundaria *high school,* 9
el escultor *sculptor,* 4G
la escultura *sculpture,* 2G
**ese(a)** *that,* 8
eso *that,* 2
esos(as) *those,* 8
espacial *space,* 8G
**la espalda** *back,* 7
**el español** *Spanish,* 1
el español *Spaniard,* 6
esparcir *to spread,* 3; está esparciendo *is spreading,* 3
la especia *spice,* 8G
la especialidad *specialty,* 6
la especie *species,* 2G
específico(a) *specific,* 10
los espejuelos *glasses,* 5
la esperanza *hope,* 9
**esperar** *to wait,* 8; *to hope,* 10; *to expect,* 10; **Espera un momento.** *Hold on a moment.,* 8; **Espero ver...** *I hope to see . . .,* 10
**las espinacas** *spinach,* 6
el espino *thorn,* 8
espiritual *spiritual,* 9
espontáneo(a) *spontaneous,* 2
la esposa *wife,* 9
el esposo *husband,* 5
**esquiar** *to ski,* 10; **esquiar en el agua** *to water-ski,* 10
**Está a la vuelta.** *It's around the corner.,* 10
**ésta, éste** *this (pron.),*1; **Ésta es.../la señora...** *This is . . . /Mrs. . . .,* 1; **Éste es.../el señor...** *This is . . . /Mr. . . .,* 1
establecer *to establish,* 8G, fue establecido *was established,* 8G
el establecimiento *colony,* 8G
estacionar *to park,* 10
**el estadio** *stadium,* 4
el estado *state,* 2G
los Estados Unidos *United States,* 1
estadounidense *pertaining to the United States,* 7
**estar** *to be,* 1; **¿Cómo está(s)?** *How are you?,* 1; **¿Está...?** *Is . . . there?,* 8; **Está bien.** *All right.,* 3; **Está nublado.** *It's cloudy.,* 3; **Está (un poco) salado(a)** *It's (a little) salty,* 6; **estar aburrido(a)** *to be bored,* 7; **estar bien** *to be (doing) fine,* 7; **estar cansado(a)** *to be tired,* 7; **estar contento(a)** *to be happy,* 7; **estar mal** *to be (doing) badly,* 7; **estar enfermo(a)** *to be sick,* 7; **estar enojado(a)** *to be angry,* 7; **estar en una silla de ruedas** *to be in a wheelchair,* 5; **estar listo(a)** *to be ready,* 7; **estar nervioso(a)** *to be nervous,* 7; **estar triste** *to be sad,* 7; **¿Está todo listo?** *Is everything ready?,* 9; **Estoy bien, gracias.** *I'm fine, thanks.,*1; **Estoy de acuerdo.** *I agree.,* 6; **Estoy mal.** *I'm not so good.,* 1; **Estoy regular.** *I'm all right.,* 1; **No está.** *He/She is not here.,* 8; **no estés** *don't be,* 7; **Estuvo a todo dar.** *It was great.,* 9; **No estoy de acuerdo.** *I disagree.,* 6
**estas, estos** *these (adj.),* 6
la estatua *statue,* 5G
éste *this (pron.),* 6
**este(a)** *this,* 8; **este fin de semana** *this weekend,* 4
el estilo *style,* 3G
**estirarse** *to stretch,* 7
**el estómago** *stomach,* 7
el Estrecho de la Florida *Strait of Florida,* 8
la estrella *star,* 5
el estrés *stress,* 7
estricto(a) *strict,* 4
el estruendo *noise,* 10
**el estudiante, la estudiante** *student,* 1; el estudiante de intercambio *exchange student,* 10
**estudiar** *to study,* 3
los estudios *studies,* 5; los estudios sociales *social studies,* 4
**estupendo(a)** *great,* 10; **Fue estupendo.** *It was great.,* 10
la etapa *stage,* 2
el europeo *European,* 6G
el evento deportivo *sporting event,* 1

**el examen** *test,* 4; **presentar el examen de...** *to take a . . . test,* 4
exclamar *to exclaim,* 9
exclusivamente *exclusively,* 4
**la excursión** *hike,* 10; **ir de excursión** *to go on a hike,* 10
la excursión turística *to go on a trip,* 1
exigente *strict,* 5
existir *to exist,* 7
el éxito *success,* 10
la experiencia *experience,* 6
el explorador *explorer,* 5G
exponer *to display,* 4G
el exportador *exporter,* 8G
exportar *to export,* 1G
la exposición *exposition,* 5G; *exhibition,* 10G
expresar *to express,* 6G
la expresión *expression,* xxii; *saying,* 2
extender *to cover,* 3G; se extiende *it extends,* 5G
la extensión *length,* 10G
extranjero(a) *foreign,* 10
el extranjero *abroad,* 10
extraño(a) *strange,* 7G
extremo(a) *far,* 7G
**extrovertido(a)** *outgoing,* 2

## F

fabuloso(a) *fabulous,* 6
**fácil** *easy,* 4; **Es fácil.** *It's easy.,* 4
**facturar** *to check,* 10; **facturar el equipaje** *to check luggage,* 10
**la falda** *skirt,* 8
falso(a) *false,* xxii
faltar *to be missing,* 1; nos faltan *we're missing,* 3
la fama *fame,* 5G
**la familia** *family,* 3; **En mi familia somos...** *There are . . . people in my family.,* 5; la Familia Real *Royal Family,* 1
familiar *pertaining to the family,* 7
famoso(a) *famous,* 2
fascinar *to love, to like very much,* 2
fastidiar *to annoy,* 9
favorito(a) *favorite,* 1
**febrero** *February,* 1
**la fecha** *date,* 1
la felicidad *happiness,* 9
felicitar *to congratulate,* 9
el felino *cat,* 10G
feliz (pl. felices) *happy,* 8; **¡Feliz...!** *Happy (Merry) . . .,* 9
**fenomenal** *awesome,* 2
**feo(a)** *ugly,* 8
**festejar** to celebrate, 9
festivo *holiday* (adj), 9
la fibra de vidrio *fiberglass,* 3G
**la fiesta** *party,* 2; la fiesta patria *national holiday,* 5G; la fiesta patronal *feast celebrating the patron saint,* 4G; **la fiesta sorpresa** *surprise party,* 9; **hacer una fiesta** *to have a party,* 9
la figurita *shape, figurine,* 4
fijarse *to notice,* 7
el fin *end,* 9; al fin *finally,* 10
**el fin de semana** *weekend,* 3; **este fin de semana** *this weekend,* 4; **los fines de semana** *weekends,* 3
finales: a finales *at the end,* 10G
finalmente *finally,* 8
financiar *to finance,* 5
fino(a) *fine,* 2G
**el flan** *flan, custard,* 6
las flautas *rolled tortillas that are stuffed and fried,* 9
la flor *flower,* 1
**las flores** *flowers,* 9
las fogatas *campfires,* 3
el folleto *pamphlet,* 7
la forma *form,* xxii
formaba *formed*
la formación geológica *geological formation,* 7G
formar *to form,* 3
**formidable** *formidable,* 2
la fortaleza *fortress,* 10
**la fortuna** *fortune,* 8
**la foto** *photo,* xxii; **enseñar fotos** *to show photos,* 9; **sacar fotos** *to take photos,* 10
la fotografía *photograph,* 8
el fragmento *excerpt,* 5
**el francés** *French,* 4
la frase *phrase,* 8; *sentence,* 9
la frecuencia *frequency,* 8; con frecuencia *often,* 8; **¿Con qué frecuencia vas...?** *How often do you go . . .?,* 3
frecuentado(a) *visited,* 1G
frente *front;* al frente *to the front,* xxii; en frente *in front,* 3G
el fresco cool, 3; **Hace fresco.** *It's cool.,* 3
el frijol *bean,* 2G
**frío(a)** *cold,* 6; **Hace frío.** *It's cold.,* 3; **tener frío** *to be cold,* 7
la frontera *border,* 7G
**la fruta** *fruit,* 2; la fruta cítrica *citrus fruit,* 8G
el fuego *fire,* 3
**¡Fue estupendo!** *It was great!,* 10
**los fuegos artificiales** *fireworks,* 9; **ver los fuegos artificiales** *to see fireworks,* 9
fuera *outside,* 7G
fuera (inf. ser) *was,* 6G
fuerte *loud,* 2; *strong,* 3G
**fumar** *to smoke,* 7; **dejar de fumar** *to stop smoking,* 7
el funcionalismo *functional architectural style,* 6G
funcionar *to work,* 10
fundado(a) *founded,* 2G
**el fútbol** *soccer,* 3
**el fútbol americano** *football,* 3
el futuro *future,* 3
futuro(a) *future,* 5

## G

el gabinete *cabinet,* 9
las gafas *glasses,* 5
el gallego *romance language from Galicia, Spain,* 1G
**la galleta** *cookie,* 9
la gana *desire;* **tener ganas de** + infinitive *to feel like doing something,* 4
la ganadería *cattle raising,* 7G
el ganado *cattle,* 3G
ganar *to win,* 5G
**la ganga** *bargain,* 8
**el garaje** *garage,* 5
**la garganta** *throat,* 7
la garita *sentry box,* 2G
**gastar** *to spend,* 8
**el gato, la gata** *cat,* 5
el gazpacho *cold tomato soup*
la generación *generation,* 5
generalmente *generally,* 8
el género *genre,* 8G
generoso(a) *generous,* 6
la gente *people,* 3
la geografía *geography,* 1
geográfico(a) *geographical,* 10
geometría *geometry,* 4
gigante *giant,* 6
**el gimnasio** *gym,* 3
el glaciar *glacier,* 5G
la gloria *heaven,* 3
glorioso *glorious,* 9
el gobierno *government,* 1G
el Golfo de México *Gulf of Mexico,* 8G
**gordo(a)** *fat,* 5
la gorra *cap,* 7
gótico(a) *gothic,* 3G
la grabación *recording,* 1
**gracias** *thank you,* 1, **Estoy bien, gracias.** *I'm fine, thanks,* 1; **no, gracias** *no thank you,* 8
**gracioso(a)** *witty,* 2
**la graduación** *graduation,* 9
gran *big,* 5; *great,* 5; *large,* 3
la granada *pomegranate,* 6
**grande** *big, large,* 5
el grano *grain,* 6
**la grasa** *fat,* 7
gratuito *free,* 1
**gris** *gray,* 8

gritar *to yell,* 7
la grúa *tow truck,* 9
el grupo *group,* 6
la guagua *bus (P.R., Dom. Rep.),* 10
los guandules *pigeon peas,* 6
**guapo(a)** *good-looking,* 2
guardar *to store,* 10
la guayabera *man's short-sleeved shirt,* 8
la guerra *war,* 7
la guía telefónica *telephone directory,* 10
guiar *to guide,* 10; *to drive,* 10
el güiro *percussive instrument played by scratching with a stick across a rough surface,* 3
el guiso *stew,* 6
**la guitarra** *guitar,* 2; la guitarra eléctrica *electric guitar,* 2
**gustar** *to like,* 2; **A ellos/ellas les gusta...** *They like . . .,* 3; **A mis amigos y a mí nos gusta...** *My friend and I like . . .,* 3; **Le gusta...** *He/She likes . . .,* 3; **Me gusta(n)...** *I like . . .,* 2; **Me gusta(n)... mucho.** *I like . . . a lot.,* 2; me gustaba *I liked,* 4; **Me gusta(n) más...** *I like . . . more.,* 2; **Me gustaría...** *I would like . . .,* 8; **Me gustaría más...** *I would prefer . . .,* 10; Me ha gustado... *I have liked . . .,* 4; **No, no me gusta(n)...** *No, I don't like . . .,* 2; **¿Te gusta(n)...?** *Do you like . . .?,* 2; **¿Te gusta(n) más... o...?** *Do you like . . . or . . . more?,* 2
el gusto *pleasure,* 9
los gustos *likes,* 2

haber *to have;* hubo *there was,* 10
las habichuelas *beans,* 2G
**la habitación** *bedroom,* 5
habitar *to inhabit,* 7G
el habla *speech,* 8
**hablar** *to talk, to speak,* 3; **Habla...** *. . . speaking (on the telephone),* 8; **hablar por teléfono** *to talk on the phone,* 3; Hablemos. *Let's talk.,* 1
**hacer (-go)** *to make, to do,* 4; **estamos haciendo** *we are making/doing,* 9; están haciendo *are making,* 3; **Hace buen (mal) tiempo.** *The weather is nice (bad).,* 3; **Hace calor.** *It's hot.,* 3; **Hace fresco.** *It's cool.,* 3; **Hace frío.** *It's cold.,* 3; Hace más de... años. *It's more than . . . years ago.,* 7G; **Hace sol.** *It's sunny.,* 3; Hace tanto... que... *It's so . . . that . . .,* 3; Hace tiempo. *It's been a long time.,* 9; **Hace viento.** *It's windy.,* 3; **hacer cola** *to wait in line,* 10; **hacer ejercicio** *to exercise,* 3; **hacer la cama** *to make the bed,* 5; **hacer la maleta** *to pack your suitcase,* 10; **hacer la tarea** *to do homework,* 3; **hacer los quehaceres** *to do the chores,* 5; **hacer una fiesta** *to have a party,* 9; **hacer un viaje** *to take a trip,* 10; **hacer yoga** *to do yoga,* 7; hacían *they made,* 4; **haz** *make, do,* 6; hizo *he/she did,* 9; **no hagas** *don't do,* 10; **¿Qué están haciendo?** *What are they doing?,* 9; qué hicieron *what they did,* 9; **¿Qué hiciste?** *What did you do?,* 8; se hace *is made,* 6
hallar *to find,* 7G
**el hambre** *hunger,* 4; **tener hambre** *to be hungry,* 4
**la hamburguesa** *hamburger,* 2
**el Hanukah** *Hanukkah,* 9
**hasta** *until,* 5; *up to,* 5; **Hasta luego.** *See you later.,* 1; **Hasta mañana.** *See you tomorrow.,* 1; **Hasta pronto.** *See you soon.,* 1
**hay** (inf. **haber**) *there is, there are,* 4; **Hay un(a)...** *There's a . . .,* 4
**haz** *make, do,* 6; Hazme caso. *Pay attention to me.,* 8
hecho(a) *made,* 2G
**la heladería** *ice cream shop,* 8
**el helado** *ice cream,* 2
la hembra *female,* 2
el hemisferio *hemisphere,* 7G
la herencia inheritance; la herencia alemana *German cultural tradition,* 7G; la herencia española *Spanish cultural tradition,* 10G
**la hermana** *sister,* 5
**el hermano** *brother,* 5
**los hermanos** *brothers, brothers and sisters,* 5
el héroe *hero,* 4G
la hierba *grass,* 8G; la hierba fina *herb,* 8G
**la hija** *daughter,* 5
**el hijo** *son,* 5
**los hijos** *sons, children,* 5
el hipo *hiccup,* 3; estar con hipo *to have hiccups,* 3
el hipopótamo *hippopotamus,* 1
hispano(a) *Hispanic,* 1
hispanohablante *Spanish-speaking,* 6
**la historia** *history,* 4
el hogar *home,* 3G
las hojas de maíz *cornhusks,* 3
**hola** *hi, hello,* 1
**el hombre** *man,* 8; el hombre de negocios *businessman,* 5, los hombres *men, humans,* 6; **para hombres** *for men,* 8
**el hombro** *shoulder,* 7
el homenaje *tribute,* 1G
hondo(a) *deep,* 8G
el honor *honor,* 3
la hora *hour,* 1; **¿A qué hora vas a...?** *What time are you going to . . .?,* 4; **¿Qué hora es?** *What time is it?,* 1
el horario *schedule,* 3
la horchata mexicana *sweet rice drink,* 6
la hormiga *ant,* 6
**el horno** *oven,* 6; el horno microondas *microwave oven,* 6
**horrible** *horrible,* 2; **¡Fue horrible!** *It was horrible!,* 10
**el hotel** *hotel,* 10; **quedarse en un hotel** *to stay in a hotel,* 10
**hoy** *today,* 1; hoy en día *nowadays,* 6G; **Hoy es...** *Today is . . .,* 1; **¿Qué día es hoy?** *What day is today?,* 1
**el huevo** *egg,* 6
húmedo(a) *damp;* el bosque húmedo *rainforest,* 4G
el huracán *hurricane,* 3

la idea *idea,* 6; la idea principal *main idea,* 6
el idioma *language,* 1G; idioma oficial *official language,* 1G
identificar *to identify,* 10
**la iglesia** *church,* 3
igual que *same as,* 2
igualmente *equally,* 8
**Igualmente.** *Likewise.,* 1
la iguana *iguana,* 1
ilustrar *to illustrate,* 5
imaginar *to imagine,* 2
el imperativo *imperative,* 9
el imperio *empire,* 10G
imponente *imposing,* 6
importado(a) *imported,* 5G
la importancia *importance,* 6
impresionante *impressive,* 7G
incaico(a) *Incan,* 10G
incesante *without stopping,* 8
inclusive *including,* 8
incluso *including,* 8G
incomparable *incomparable,* 5
la independencia *independence,* 6G
independiente *independent,* 2
indicar *to indicate,* xxii
indígena *indigenous,* 6G
la Infanta *princess,* 10
la influencia *influence,* 1G
Inglaterra *England,* 7G
**el inglés** *English,* 4
**injusto** *unfair,* 5; **Me parece injusto.** *It seems unfair to me,* 5

inmediato(a) *immediate,* 10G
inmenso(a) *immense,* 6
el inmigrante *immigrant,* 7G
inmigrar *to immigrate,* 7G
el insecto *insect,* 2
inseparable *inseparable,* 3
inspirar *to inspire,* 1G
el instrumento *instrument,* 8G
intacto(a) *intact,* 10
**intelectual** *intellectual,* 2
**inteligente** *intelligent,* 2
la intensidad *intensity,* 7
el interés *of interest,* 10
**interesante** *interesting,* 2
internacional *international,* 6
**interrumpir** *to interrupt,* 4
el invasor *invader,* 4G
inventar *to invent,* 4
el inventario *inventory,* 8
inventivo(a) *inventive,* 2
la investigación *research,* 4G
el invierno *winter,* 3
inviolable *inviolable,* 5
**la invitación** *invitation,* 9; **mandar invitaciones** *to send invitations,* 9
**el invitado** *guest,* 9; el invitado de honor *guest of honor,* 9
**invitar** *to invite,* 9
**ir** *to go,* 2; **¿Adónde fuiste?** *Where did you go?,* 8; fue *went,* 8; fuimos *we went,* 8; **ir+ a +** infinitive *to be going to (do something),* 4; **ir de compras** *to go shopping,* 3; **ir de excursión** *to go hiking,* 10; **ir de pesca,** *to go fishing,* 10; **ir al cine** *to go to the movies,* 3; **No vayas.** *Don't go.,* 7; **Quiero ir...** *I want to go . . .,* 2; se va *leaves,* 6; **¿Vas a...?** *Are you going to . . .?,* 4; **Vas a ir, ¿verdad?** *You're going to go, aren't you?,* 4; **ve** go, 6
**irse** *to leave,* 10
**la isla** *island,* 10
italiano(a) *Italian,* 6
la izquierda *left*

**el jabón** *soap,* 7
**el jamón** *ham,* 6
**el jardín** *garden,* 5
el jefe *chief,* 10
el jersey *sweater,* 8
la jirafa *giraffe,* 1
**joven** *young,* 5
el joven, la joven *young person,* 9; **los jóvenes** *young people,* 9
**la joyería** *jewelry store,* 8
**el juego** *game, 3;* **el juego de mesa** *board game,* 3; el juego de palabras *word game,* 7
**el jueves** *Thursday,* 1; **los jueves** *on Thursdays,* 3
el jugador *player,* 2G
**jugar (ue)** *to play,* 3
**el jugo** *juice,* 6; **el jugo de** . . . *juice,* 6
**el juguete** *toy,* 8
**la juguetería** *toy store,* 8
el juicio *judgment,* 6
**julio** *July,* 1
**junio** *June,* 1
juntos(as) *together,* 1
justo(a) *fair, just,* 10

K

el karate *karate,* 1
el kilómetro *kilometer,* 3
el kiosko *stand or stall,* 9G

**la** *the* (fem. article), 2
**la** *you, it,* (pronoun), 6; *you,* 9
las labores *chores,* 5
el lado: por todos lados *everywhere,* 8G
**el lago** *lake,* 10
la lágrima *tear,* 9
**la lana** *wool,* 8; **de lana** *made of wool,* 8
**la lancha** *motorboat,* 10; **pasear en lancha** *to go out in a motorboat,* 10
**el lápiz** (pl. **los lápices**) *pencil,* 4
**largo(a)** *long,* 5
**las** *the* (pl. fem. article), 2
**las** *you, them* (pronoun), 6
la lástima *pity,* 8; ¡Qué lástima! *What a shame!,* 8
la lata *can,* 9
latinoamericano(a) *Latin American,* 1
**lavar** *to wash,* 5; **lavar los platos** *to do the dishes,* 5
**lavarse** *to wash,* 7
**le** *to/for him, her, you,* 2
**la leche** *milk,* 6
**leer** *to read,* 3; al leer *upon reading,* 6; antes de leer *before reading,* 1; leamos *let's read,* 1; leer en voz alta *to read aloud,* 6; se leen *are read,* 5; **leer revistas y novelas** *to read magazines and novels,* 3
el legado *legacy,* 8G
lejano(a) *distant,* 10
lejos *far,* 9; **lejos de** *far from,* 5
la lengua *language,* 9
**los lentes** *glasses,* 5; **usar lentes** *to wear glasses,* 5
lento(a) *slow,* 4G
el león *lion,* 1
**les** *to/for you* (pl.), *them,* 2
**levantar** *to lift,* 7; **levantar pesas** *to lift weights,* 7
**levantarse** *to get up,* 7
la leyenda *legend,* 10
libre *free,* 6G
**la librería** *bookstore,* 8
**el libro** *book,* 2; **el libro de amor** *romance book,* 2; **el libro de aventuras** *adventure book,* 2
el líder, la líder *leader,* 2
el limón *lemon,* 6
**limpiar** *to clean,* 5; limpio(a) *clean,* 5
lindo(a) *beautiful, pretty,* 6
**listo(a)** *ready,* 7; **estar listo(a)** *to be ready,* 7; **¿Está todo listo?** *Is everything ready?,* 9
llamado(a) *called,* 9G
**llamar** *to call,* 9; **llamar por teléfono** *to make a phone call,* 8; **Llamo más tarde.** *I'll call back later.,* 8; **Te llamo más tarde.** *I'll call you later.,* 9
**la llegada** *arrival,* 10
**llegar** *to arrive, to get there,* 4; al llegar *upon arriving,* 6; ha llegado *she has come,* 9
llenar *to fill up,* 3
lleno(a) *full,* 9
**llevar** *to wear,* 8; *to take,* 6; lo llevó *took it,* 6G; lleva años trabajando *he has been working for years,* 9
llevarse *to get along,* 2
**llover (ue)** *to rain,* 3; **llueve (mucho)** *it rains (a lot),* 3
la lluvia *rain,* 4G
**lo** *him, it,* 6; *you,* 9; **Lo siento.** *I'm sorry.,* 8
**lo: lo de siempre** *same as usual,* 9; lo que *what,* 6; lo que pasa *what is happening,* xxii
loco *crazy,* 5
lógico(a) *logical,* 2
el lonche *lunch (Southwest U.S.),* 6
**los** *the* (pl. masc.), 2
**los** *you, them* (pronoun), 6
luchar *to struggle,* 8; *to fight,* 4G
**luego** *then, later,* 4
el lugar *place,* 1G
**los lugares de interés** *places of interest,* 10
la luna *moon,* 9
**lunes** *Monday,* 3; **los lunes** *on Mondays,* 3
la luz *light,* 7G

el macho *male*, 2
la madera *wood*, 5G
**la madre** *mother*, 5
madrina *godmother*, 1
el maestro *master*, 7G
magnífico(a) *magnificent*, 4
**el maíz** *corn*, 6
majestuoso(a) *majestic*, 9G
**mal** *bad*; **Estoy mal.** *I'm not so good.*, 1; **Te veo mal.** *You don't look well.*, 7
**la maleta** *suitcase*, 10
**malo(a)** *bad*, 2
malvado(a) *evil*, 10
**la mamá** *mom*, 5
el mamífero *mammal*, 4G
**la mañana** *morning*, 4; **de la mañana** *in the morning*, A.M., 1; **por la mañana** *in the morning*, 4
**mañana** *tomorrow*, 4; **Hasta mañana.** *See you tomorrow.*, 1
**mandar** *to send*, 9; **mandar invitaciones** *to send invitations*, 9; **mandar tarjetas** *to send cards*, 9
el mandato *command*, 6
manejar *to manage*, 7
la manera *way*, 9
**la mano** *hand*, 7
el manojo *bunch*, 8
mantener *to preserve, to keep*, 6
**mantenerse (ie)** *to maintain*, 7; **mantenerse (ie) en forma** *to stay in shape*, 7
**la manzana** *apple*, 6
**el mapa** *map*, 10
**el maquillaje** *makeup*, 7
**maquillarse** *to put on makeup*, 7
marcado(a) *marked*, 7
marcar *to set, to dial*, 1
marcharse *to leave*, 9
el marisco *shellfish*, 5G
marítimo(a) *maritime*, 3G
marrón *brown*, 2; los ojos marrones *brown eyes*, 5
**el martes** *Tuesday*, 1; **los martes** *on Tuesdays*, 3
**marzo** *March*, 1
**más** *more*, 2; **Más o menos.** *So-so.*, 1; **más que** *more than*, 8; **más... que** more *. . . than*, 8
la masa *dough*, 3
la máscara *mask*, 2G
la mascarada *masquerade*, 4G
la mascota *pet*, 5
el mate *Argentinean and Paraguayan tea*, 7
**las matemáticas** *mathematics*, 4
**la materia** *subject*, 4; las materias obligatorias *required subjects*, 4; las materias opcionales *electives*, 4
matutino(a) *(in the) morning*, 4
**mayo** *May*, 1
**mayor(es)** *older*, 5; *greater*, 3G
la mayoría *majority*, 4G
la mazorca *corn on the cob*, 6
**me** *to/for me*, 2; **Me da igual.** *It's all the same to me.*, 2; **Me duele(n)...** *My . . . hurt(s).*, 7; **Me gusta(n)...** *I like . . .*, 2; **Me gusta(n) más...** *I like . . . more.*, 2; **Me gusta(n)... mucho.** *I like . . . a lot.*, 2; **Me llamo...** *My name is . . .*, 1; **No, no me gusta(n)...** *No, I don't like . . .*, 2; **Me parece bien.** *It seems fine to me.*, 5; **Me parece injusto.** *It's not fair.*, 5
**me** *me*, 9
mecánico *mechanic*, 5
la medalla *medal*, 5G
mediano(a) *medium*, 4
**la medianoche** *midnight*, 1
médico(a) *medical*, 7
medio(a) *half*, 4; **y media** *half past*, 1
**los medios de transporte** *means of transportation*, 10
**el mediodía** *midday, noon*, 1
medir (i) *to measure*, 5G
**mejor(es)** *better, best*, 7
el melocotón *peach*, 6
**menor(es)** *younger*, 5
**menos** *less*, 8; **menos cuarto** *a quarter to . . .*, 1; **menos que** *less than*, 8; **menos... que** *less . . . than*, 8
el mensaje *message*, 7G
la mente *mind*, 4
el mercado *market*, 6; el mercado al aire libre *open-air market*, 8
**merendar (ie)** *to have a snack*, 5
el merengue *music and dance style*, 9G
la merienda *snack*, 6
**la mesa** *table*, 5; **poner la mesa** *to set the table*, 6
**los meses del año** *months of the year*, 1
meter *to put in*, 8
meterse *to set*, 9
metódico(a) *methodical*, 2
el metro *meter*, 1G
**el metro** *subway*, 10
**mezclar** *to mix*, 6; mezcla *mixture*, 6
la mezquita *mosque*, 1G
**mí** *me*, 5; **A mí me gusta** + infinitive *I like to . . .*, 3; **A mí me toca...** *I have to . . .*, 5
**mi(s)** *my*, 1; **Mi materia preferida es...** *My favorite subject is . . .*, 4 **mi mejor amigo(a)** *my best friend*, 1, **mi profesor(-a)** *my teacher*, 1
la miel *honey*, 6
el miembro *member*, 3
mientras *while*, 6
**el miércoles** *Wednesday*, 1; **los miércoles** *on Wednesdays*, 3
**mil** *one thousand*, 8; miles *thousands*, 2
la milla cuadrada *square mile*, 3
**un millón (de)** *one million*, 8; **dos millones (de)** *two million*, 8
mío *mine*, 8
mirar *to look*, 9; **Nada más estoy mirando.** *I'm just looking.*, 8; **mirar las vitrinas** *to window-shop*, 8
**la misa** *Mass*, 9
la misión *mission*, 3G
mismo(a) *same*, 6
**el misterio** *mystery*, 2
misterioso(a) *mysterious*, 2
la mitad *half*, 6G
**la mochila** *backpack*, 4
**la moda** *style, fashion*, 8; **a la última moda** *in the latest fashion*, 8; muy de moda *very fashionable*, 8; **pasado(a) de moda** *out of style*, 8
modelar *to shape*, 4
moderno(a) *modern*, 7
el módulo *module*, 10
el mogote *knoll*, 9G
el mole *sauce made with chiles and flavored with chocolate*, 6
el molino *windmill*, 1G
el momento *moment*, 6; **Espera un momento.** *Hold on a moment.*, 8
la monarquía parlamentaria *constitutional monarchy*, 1G
la moneda *currency*, 2; *coin*, 8
el mono *monkey*, 4G
**la montaña** *mountain*, 10; **subir a la montaña** *to go up a mountain*, 10
montañoso(a) *mountainous*, 7G
montar a caballo *to ride a horse*, 3G; **montar en bicicleta** *to ride a bike*, 3
**un montón** *a ton*, 4
el monumento *monument*, 1G
el morado *purple*, 1G
**morado(a)** *purple*, 8
**moreno(a)** *dark-haired; dark-skinned*, 2
morir (ue) *to die*, 5; murió *died*, 5
el moro *rice and beans*, 9G
el mosaico *mosaic*, 6G
el mosquito *mosquito*, 2
**el mostrador** *counter*, 10
mostrar (ue) *to show*, 1G
el movimiento *movement*, 4G
**la muchacha** *girl*, 1
**el muchacho** *boy*, 1
**mucho** *a lot (of)*, 2; *much*, 4; **Mucho gusto.** *Pleased/Nice to meet you.*, 1
**muchos(as)** *a lot of, many*, 4
mudarse *to move*, 8G
mudéjar *Moslem*, 5G
la muerte *death*, 4G

**la mujer** *woman,* 8; **la mujer de negocios** *business woman,* 5; **para mujeres** *for women,* 8
mundialmente *worldwide,* 6
el mundo *world,* 1G; todo el mundo *everybody,* 9
el mural *mural painting,* 6G
la muralla *wall, rampart,* 1G
**el museo** *museum,* 10
**la música** *music,* 2; **la música de...** *music of/by . . .,* 2; la música clásica *classical music,* 2G
el músico *musician,* 2
**muy** *very,* 2

nacer *to be born,* 7G; había nacido *had been born,* 7G; nacido(a) *born,* 8G
nacional *national,* 1
**nada** *nothing,* 4; *not anything,* 5
**Nada más estoy mirando.** *I'm just looking.,* 8
**nadar** *to swim,* 3
**nadie** *nobody, not anybody,* 5
**la naranja** *orange,* 6
el naranjo *orange tree,* 8G
**la nariz** *nose,* 7
la natación *swimming,* 7
nativo(a) *native,* 6
la naturaleza *nature,* 2
**la navaja** *razor,* 7
navegar *to sail,* 5; *to navigate,* 10; **navegar por Internet** *to surf the Internet,* 3
**la Navidad** *Christmas,* 9
la necesidad *necessity,* 7
**necesitar** *to need,* 4; **¿Necesitas algo?** *Do you need anything?,* 4; **Necesito muchas cosas.** *I need a lot of things.,* 4; **No, no necesito nada.** *No, I don't need anything.,* 4
negarse *to refuse,* 5
negociable *negotiable,* 5
el negocio *business,* 9
**negro(a)** *black,* 5
**nervioso(a)** *nervous,* 7
**nevar (ie)** *to snow,* 3
**ni** *neither, nor,* 7; **Ni idea.** *I have no idea.,* 3
el nido *nest,* 1
**la nieta** *granddaughter,* 5
**el nieto** *grandson,* 5
**los nietos** *grandsons, grandchildren,* 5
**nieva** *it snows,* 3
la niña *girl,* 1
ninguno(a) *no, none,* 10G; **ninguna parte** *nowhere,* 3; **no va a ninguna parte** *he/she doesn't go anywhere,* 3
el niño *male child,* 8
**los niños** *children,* 8
el nivel del mar *sea level,* 9G
**no** no, 3; *not, do not,* 5; **No debes...** *You shouldn't . . .,* 7; **No es gran cosa.** *It's not a big deal.,* 5; **No está.** *He/She is not here.,* 8; **No estoy de acuerdo.** *I disagree.,* 6; **no, gracias** *no thank you,* 8; **no más** *just, only,* 8; **No sé.** *I don't know.,* 4; **No, no me gusta(n)...** *No, I don't like . . .,* 2; **No, no necesito nada.** *No, I do not need anything.,* 4; **No, no voy a ir.** *No, I'm not going to go.,* 4; **No seas...** *Don't be . . .,* 7; **No va a ninguna parte.** *He/She doesn't go anywhere.,* 3; **No vayas.** *Don't go.,* 7
**¿no?** *right?,* 4
**la noche** *night,* 1; **de la noche** *at night,* P.M., 1; **por la noche** *at night,* 4
**la Nochebuena** *Christmas Eve,* 9
**la Nochevieja** *New Year's Eve,* 9
nocturno(a) *(in the) evening,* 4
nombrado(a) *named,* 9G
el nombre *name,* 10
el noreste *northeast,* 2G
normalmente *normally,* 4
el noroeste *northwest,* 7G
el norte *north,* 5G
norteamericano(a) *North American,* 8
norteño(a) *northern,* 5G
Noruega *Norway,* 7G
**nos** *(to/for) us,* 2; **Nos vemos.** *See you.,* 1
**nosotros(as)** *we,* 1
la nota *grade,* 6
la noticia *news,* 9
**novecientos** *nine hundred,* 8
**la novela** *novel,* 3
**noventa** *ninety,* 2
**noviembre** *November,* 1
la nube *cloud,* 7
**nuestro(a)** *our,* 5
**nuestros(as)** *our,* 5
nuevamente *again,* 9
**nueve** *nine,* 1
nuevo(a) *new,* 2
las nueces *nuts,* 6
**el número** *number,* 1; *shoe size,* 8
numeroso(a) *numerous,* 2G
**nunca** *never,* 5; **casi nunca** *almost never,* 3; nunca más *never again,* 6
la nutricionista *nutritionist,* 7

**o** *or,* 2
oaxaqueño *from the Mexican state of Oaxaca,* 6
el objetivo *objective,* 1
el objeto *object,* 1
la obra *work,* 7G; la obra de teatro *play,* 6G; la obra maestra *masterpiece,* 6G
observar *to observe,* 1
la ocasión *occasion,* 9
occidental *western,* 7G
**ochenta** *eighty,* 2
**ocho** *eight,* 1
**ochocientos** *eight hundred,* 8
el ocio *leisure time,* 8
**octubre** *October,* 1
el ocupante *occupant,* 10
ocupar *to occupy,* 7G
ocurrir *to occur;* ¿Se te ocurren? *Do they occur to you?,* 4
la oficina *office,* 5
**la oficina de cambio** *money exchange,* 10
**la oficina de correos** *post office,* 10
ofrecer *to offer,* 6
**el oído** *ear,* 7
oír *to hear,* 2; oyes *(you) hear,* 2; se oye *is heard,* 2
**los ojos** *eyes,* 5; los ojos borrados *hazel eyes,* 5; los ojos cafés *brown eyes,* 5; **tener los ojos azules** *to have blue eyes,* 5
la ola *wave,* 2G
la olla *pot,* 4G
olor *smell,* 7
olvidar *to forget,* 9; No te olvides. *Don't forget.,* 8
**once** *eleven,* 1
la oportunidad *opportunity,* 5
la oración *sentence,* xxii
el orden *order,* 1; el orden cronológico *chronological order,* 8
ordenar *to organize,* 3; está ordenando *is organizing,* 3
organizado(a) *organized,* 2
**organizar** *to organize,* 10
orgulloso(a) *proud,* 6
oriental *eastern,* 10G
el origen *origin,* 6G
originalmente *originally,* 3G
**os** *(to/for) you* (pl.), 2
el oso *bear,* 1
el otoño *fall,* 3
**otro(a)** *other, another,* 8
**otros(as)** *other, others,* 8

el paciente *patient,* 7
**el padre** *father,* 5
**los padres** *parents,* 5; los padres peregrinos *pilgrims,* 8G
**pagar** *to pay,* 8; **pagar una fortuna** *to pay a fortune,* 8
la página *page,* xxii; la página Web *Web page,* 1
**el país** *country,* 6; el país de origen *native country,* 6
el paisaje *landscape,* 4G
el pájaro *bird,* 9
la palabra *word,* xxii; la palabra clave *key word,* 1
el palacio *palace,* 1
**el pan** *bread,* 6; **el pan dulce** *pastries,* 6; **el pan tostado** *toast,* 6
**la pantalla** *monitor, screen,* 10
**los pantalones (vaqueros)** *pants (jeans),* 8
**los pantalones cortos** *shorts,* 8
la pantomima *pantomime,* 9
**la pantorrilla** *calf,* 7
**el papá** *dad,* 5
el Papá Noel *Santa Claus,* 9
**la papa** *potato,* 6; **las papas fritas** *french fries,* 6
**el papel** *paper,* 4
**las papitas** *potato chips,* 9
el paquete *package,* 9
**el par** *pair,* 8
**para** *for,* 4; *to, in order to,* 7
el paraíso *paradise,* 8G
**parecer** *to seem,* 5; *to think,* 8; me parece *it seems to me,* 9; **Me parece bien.** *It's all right/seems fine to me.,* 5; **Me parece injusto.** *It seems unfair to me.,* 5; No parezco. *I don't seem to be.,* 9; **¿Qué te parece...?** *What do you think of . . .?,* 8
parecido(a) similar, 2
la pared *wall,* 10G
la pareja *pair;* en parejas *in pairs,* xxii, *couple,* 3
el paréntesis *parenthesis,* 8
el pareo *matching,* 1
el pariente *relative,* 5
**el parque** *park,* 3; **el parque de diversiones** *amusement park,* 10
el párrafo *paragraph,* xxii
la parrilla *barbecue,* 7
la parrillada *Argentine barbecue,* 7G
la parte *part,* 6
participar *to participate,* 1
particular *particular,* 6
**el partido de…** *the . . . game,* 4
la pasa *raisin,* 6
el pasado *past,* 8
**pasado mañana** *day after tomorrow,* 4
**pasado(a)** *last,* 8; **el año pasado** *last year,* 9
**pasado(a) de moda** *out of style,* 8
el pasaje *ticket,* 10
**el pasajero, la pasajera** *passenger,* 10
el pasapalo *finger food (Ven.),* 9
**el pasaporte** *passport,* 10
**pasar** *to spend (time, occasion),* 9; con quien tú te pasas *who you spend time with,* 2; **La pasamos en casa de...** *We spent it at . . .'s house,* 9; lo que pasa *what is happening,* 9; **pasar el rato solo(a)** *to spend time alone,* 3; **pasar la aspiradora** *to vacuum,* 5; **pasar por** *to stop at/by,* 10; *to go through,* 2; qué pasa *what's happening,* 6
**pasartelo(la)** *to get someone for a telephone call,* 8
**el pasatiempo** *hobby,* 7; **buscar un pasatiempo** *to find a hobby,* 7
**pasear** *to go for a walk,* 3; *to go out in,* 10; **pasear en bote de vela** *to go out in a sailboat,* 10; **pasear en lancha** *to go out in a motorboat,* 10
el pasillo *corridor,* 10
**la pasta de dientes** *toothpaste,* 7
**el pastel** *cake,* 6
el pastel en hojas *mashed plantain dough filled with meat and wrapped in plantain leaves,* 9
la patata *potato,* 1G; *sweet potato,* 6
el patinaje en hielo *ice skating,* 7
**patinar** *to skate,* 3
**el patio** *patio, yard,* 5
la patrona *patron,* 9G
la pava *kettle used to make* ***mate,*** 7
el pavo *turkey,* 6G
el payaso *clown,* 4G
**las pecas** *freckles,* 5
**el pecho** *chest,* 7
**pedir (i)** *to order,* 6
**peinarse** *to comb your hair,* 7
**el peine** *comb,* 7
**la película** *film, movie,* 2; **(de ciencia ficción, de terror, de misterio)** *(science fiction, horror, mystery),* 2
el peligro de extinción *danger of extinction,* 8G
**pelirrojo(a)** *red-headed,* 2
**el pelo** *hair,* 5
la pelota *ball,* 9G
**pensar (ie)** *to think,* 8; **pensar** + inf. *to plan,* 9; **Pensamos...** *We plan to . . .,* 9
**peor(es)** *worse,* 8
**pequeño(a)** *small,* 5; **bastante pequeño(a)** *pretty small,* 5
la pera *pear,* 1
**perder (ie)** *to lose,* 10; *to miss,* 10; **perder el vuelo** *miss the flight,* 10; si me pierden *if you lose me*
perdido(a) *lost,* 10G
perdone *I'm sorry,* 1
el perezoso *sloth,* 4G
**perezoso(a)** *lazy,* 2
perfecto *perfect,* 8
el periódico *newspaper,* 8G
la perla *pearl,* 2G
permiso *excuse me,* 9
permitir *to allow,* 6
**pero** *but,* 5
**el perro, la perra** *dog,* 5
**la persona** *person,* 2
el personaje *character,* 1G; el personaje ficticio *fictional character,* 1G
la personalidad *personality,* 2
**las pesas** *weights,* 7; **levantar pesas** *to lift weights,* 7
**la pesca** *fishing,* 10; **ir de pesca** *to go fishing,* 10; la pesca comercial *commercial fishing,* 8G
**el pescado** *fish,* 6
**pescar** *to fish,* 10
**pésimo(a)** *very bad,* 2
**el peso** *weight,* 7
el pez *fish,* 1
la picadera *finger food (Dom. Rep.),* 9
el picante *spice,* 6
**picante** *spicy,* 6
**el picnic** *picnic,* 9; **tener un picnic** *to have a picnic,* 9
el pico *peak,* 1G
el pico de gallo *spicy relish made with tomatoes, hot peppers, and onions,* 3G
**el pie** *foot,* 7
la piedra *stone,* 5G
**la pierna** *leg,* 7
la pieza *bedroom,* 5; *piece,* 4
la pileta *swimming pool (Arg.),* 3
**la piñata** *piñata,* 9
el pingüino *penguin,* 7G
pintado(a) *painted,* 2G
pintar *to paint;* fue pintado *was painted,* 1
el pintor *painter,* 2G
pintoresco(a) *picturesque,* 7G
la pintura *painting,* 1; la pintura al óleo *oil painting,* 3G
**la pirámide** *pyramid,* 10; la pirámide alimenticia *food pyramid,* 7
**la piscina** *swimming pool,* 3
**el piso** *floor,* 5; **de... pisos** *. . . story,* 5
**el piyama** *pajamas,* 7
**la pizza** *pizza,* 2
el placer *pleasure,* 9
**planes** *plans,* 9; **¿Qué planes tienen para...?** *What plans do you have for . . .?,* 9
plano(a) *flat,* 7G
**las plantas** *plants,* 5
el plátano *plantain,* 8G
platicar *to chat,* 3

**el plato** *dish, plate,* 6; **lavar los platos** *to do the dishes,* 5; **el plato hondo** *bowl,* 6; el plato típico *traditional dish,* 2
**la playa** *beach,* 3
la playera *T-shirt,* 8
**la plaza de comida** *food court in a mall,* 8
la plena *music and dance style,* 2
la población *population,* 1G
poblado(a) *populated,* 4G
pobre *poor,* 8
**poco(a)** *few, little, not much,* 4; poco a poco *little by little,* 4; **un poco** *a little,* 2
**pocos(as)** *not many,* 4
**poder (ue)** *to be able to, can,* 6
el poema *poem,* 8
la poesía *poetry,* 8
el poeta, la poeta *poet,* 5G
**el pollo** *chicken,* 6; el pollo frito *fried chicken,* 2G
**el ponche** *punch,* 9
**poner (-go)** *to put,* 4; **no pongas** *don't put,* 10; **pon** *put,* 6; poner en orden *to put in order,* xxii; poner huevos *to lay eggs,* 2; poner la comida *to set out the food,* 9; **poner la mesa** *to set the table,* 6; tener puesto(a) *to have on,* 8
**ponerse (-go)** *to put on,* 7, *to get,* 6; ponerse *to start,* 7; ponerse a bailar *to start dancing,* 3; ponerse en contacto *to get in contact,* 5; ponerse rojo *to flush, to turn red,* 10
**por** in, by, 4; por ejemplo *for example,* 6G; por eso *that's why,* 6; por el estilo *of that sort,* 7; **por favor** *please,* 6; por fin *at last,* 8; **por la mañana** *in the morning,* 4; por la noche *at night,* 2; **por la tarde** *in the afternoon,* 4; por lo general *generally,* 8; por lo menos *at least,* 9; por más que *no matter how much,* 7; por medio de *by means of,* 10
**¿por qué?** *why?,* 2
la porción *portion, serving,* 7
**porque** *because,* 2
posible *possible,* 4
**el postre** *dessert,* 6
el pozole *soup made with hominy, meat, and chile,* 6
practicando *practicing,* 7
**practicar deportes** *to play sports,* 3
el precio *price,* 1; el precio de entrada *entry fee,* 1
precolombino(a) *of the New World era before the arrival of Europeans,* 2G
precoz *precocious,* 4
la preferencia *preference,* 3
**preferido(a)** *favorite,* 4
**preferir (ie)** *to prefer,* 6
la pregunta *question,* xxii
preguntar *to ask,* xxii
prehistórico(a) *prehistoric,* 7G
preocuparse *to worry,* 9
**preocuparse** *to worry,* 10; **No te preocupes.** *Don't worry.,* 10
**preparar** *to prepare,* 6
prepararse *to get ready,* 7
**los preparativos** *preparations,* 9
la preposición *preposition,* 2
la presentación *introduction,* 9
presentar *to present,* 6; *to introduce,* 9; **presentar el examen** *to take an exam,* 4; se presentó *was performed,* 10; **Te presento a...** *I'd like you to meet . . .,* 9
presentarse *to present oneself,* 6
el presente *present,* 9
prestar: prestar atención *to pay attention,* 7
el pretérito *preterite,* 8
**la primavera** *spring,* 3
**el primero** *first,* 1
**primero(a)** *first,* 4
**el primo, la prima** *cousin,* 5; el primo hermano, la prima hermana *first cousin,* 5
**los primos** *cousins,* 5
la princesa *princess,* 10
principal *main,* 4G; *primary,* 9G
el prisionero *prisoner,* 10
**probar (ue)** *to try, to taste,* 6
producir *to produce,* 1
el producto *product,* 3G; los productos petroleros *petroleum products,* 3G; los productos químicos *chemicals,* 3G
**el profesor** *teacher (male),* 1; **mi profesor** *my teacher,* 1
**la profesora** *teacher (female),* 1; **mi profesora** *my teacher,* 1
prometer *to promise,* 8
el pronombre *pronoun,* 6; el pronombre de complemento directo *direct object pronoun,* 9; el pronombre reflexivo *reflexive pronoun,* 7
pronto *soon,* 1; **Hasta pronto.** *See you soon.,* 1; tan pronto *as soon,* 9
la propiedad *property,* 5
propio(a) *own,* 4
el propósito *purpose,* 6
el provecho *benefit;* Buen provecho. *Enjoy your meal.,* 6
la provincia *province,* 10
**próximo(a)** *next,* 4; **la próxima semana** *next week,* 4; **el** *(day of the week)* **próximo** *next (day of the week),* 4
el proyecto *project,* 1
publicar *to publish,* 1
el pueblo *town, village,* 5; el pueblo natal *hometown,* 3
**¿Puedo...?** *Can I . . .?,* 6
el puente *bridge,* 8G
**la puerta** *door,* 5; *gate,* 10
el puerto *port,* 3G
el puesto *stall,* 9G
**la pulsera** *bracelet,* 8
**el punto** *dot,* 1
el punto de vista *point of view,* 9
puntual *punctual, on time,* 2
el puré de papas *mashed potatoes,* 6

**que** *that;* **que me llame después** *tell him/her to call me later,* 8; **Que te vaya bien.** *Hope things go well for you.,* 9
**¡Qué...!** *How . . .!;* **¡Qué bien!** *How great!,* 10; **¡Qué fantástico!** *How fantastic!,* 10; **¡Qué gusto verte!** *It's great to see you!,* 9; **¡Qué lástima!** *What a shame!,* 10; **¡Qué lata!** *What a pain!,* 5; **¡Qué mala suerte!** *What bad luck!,* 10
**¿qué?** *what?,* 1; **¿Qué clases tienes ...?** *What classes do you have . . . ?,* 4; **¿Qué día es hoy?** *What day is today?,* 1; **¿Qué están haciendo?** *What are they doing?,* 9; **¿Qué fecha es hoy?** *What's today's date?,* 1; **¿Qué hace...?** *What does . . . do?,* 3; **¿Qué haces para ayudar en casa?** *What do you do to help out at home?,* 5; **¿Qué haces...?** *What do you do . . .?,* 3; **¿Qué haces para relajarte?** *What do you do to relax?,* 7; **¿Qué hay de nuevo?** *What's new?,* 9; **¿Qué hiciste?** *What did you do?,* 8; **¿Qué hora es?** *What time is it?,* 1; **¿Qué planes tienen para...?** *What plans do you have for . . .?,* 9; **¿Qué quieres hacer?** *What do you want to do?,* 3; **¿Qué tal?** *How's it going?,* 1; **¿Qué tal...?** *How is . . .?,* 6; **¿Qué tal estuvo?** *How was it?,* 9; **¿Qué tal si...?** *How about if. . .?,* 6; **¿Qué tal si vamos a...?** *How about if we go to . . .?,* 4; **¿Qué te falta hacer?** *What do you still have to do?,* 7; **¿Qué te gusta hacer?** *What do you like to do?,* 3; **¿Qué te pasa?** *What's wrong with you?,* 7; **¿Qué te toca hacer a ti?** *What do you have to do?,* 5; **¿Qué tiempo hace?** *What's the weather like?,* 3; **¿Qué tiene...?** *What's the matter with . . .?,* 7; **¿Qué tienes que hacer?**

*What do you have to do?*, 7; **¿Qué vas a hacer?** *What are you going to do?*, 4
el quechua *indigenous language in Peru*, 10G
**quedar** *to fit, to look*, 8; *to remain*, 3G; **¿Cómo me queda...?** *How does it fit?*, 8; **quedar bien/mal** *to fit well/poorly*, 8
quedarse *to stay*, 9; **quedarse en...** *to stay in . . .*, 10
**los quehaceres** *household chores*, 5; **hacer los quehaceres** *to do the chores*, 5
**querer (ie)** *to want to*, 3; *to love*, 9; **Quiero conocer...** *I want to see . . .*, 10; queriendo *wanting to*, 8; **Quiero ir...** *I want to go . . .*, 3
querido(a) *dear*, 9
la quesadilla *tortillas with melted cheese*, 3G
**el queso** *cheese*, 6
**¿quién?** *who?*, 1; **¿De parte de quién?** *Who's calling?*, 8; **Quién es...?** *Who is . . .?*, 1; ¿de quién? *about whom?*, 1
**¿quiénes?** *who?* (pl.), 2
**la química** *chemistry*, 4
**quince** *fifteen*, 1
**la quinceañera** *girl's fifteenth birthday*, 9
**quinientos** *five hundred*, 8
el quiosco *stand*, 10
**Quisiera...** *I would like . . .*, 6
**quitarse** *to take off*, 7

# R

las raciones *servings*, 6
la raíz (pl. las raíces) *root*, 1G
rallado(a) *grated*, 6
la rana *frog*, 2
los rancheros *overalls*, 3
rápidamente *quickly*, 6
rápido(a) *fast*, 8
raro *odd, strange*, 3
**el rato** *time*, 3; el rato libre *free time*, 4
reaccionar *to react*, 10
el realismo *realism*, 1
realizar *to carry out*, 10, ha realizado *has carried out*, 10G
**el recado** *message*, 8
la recámara *bedroom*, 5
**recibir** *to receive*, 9; **recibir regalos** *to receive gifts*, 9
reclamar *to reclaim*, 6G
**el reclamo de equipaje** *baggage claim*, 10
**recoger** *to pick up*, 10
la recomendación *recommendation*, 7
reconocido(a) *well-known*, 1G
recordar *to remember*, 6
**recorrer** *to tour*, 10
el recorrido *tour*, 4
el recreo *recreation time*, 4
la red *network*, 10G
redondo(a) *round*, 7
reducir *to reduce*, 7
referir *to refer*, 3; se refiere *refers*, 3G
reflejar *to reflect*, 1G
el refrán *proverb, saying*, 6
**el refresco** *soft drink*, 6
**el refrigerador** *refrigerator*, 6
el refugio de fauna *wildlife refuge*, 8G
**el regalo** *gift*, 9; **abrir regalos** *to open gifts*, 9; **recibir regalos** *to receive gifts*, 9
regatear *to bargain*, 8
la región *region*, 3
regional *regional*, 6
**la regla** *ruler*, 4
**regresar** *to return, to go back*, 4
**regular** *all right*, 1; **Estoy regular.** *I'm all right.*, 1
regularidad: con regularidad *regularly*, 6
reírse *to laugh*, 8; ríe *he/she laughs*, 9; se ríen *they laugh*, 8
**relajarse** *to relax*, 7
religioso(a) *religious*, 1
**el reloj** *clock, watch*, 4
remodelado(a) *remodeled*, 5
remojar *to soak*, 3
remoto(a) *distant*, 5
el renacuajo *tadpole*, 2
el repaso *review*, 1
representar *to represent*, 3
representativo(a) *representative*, 6
la respuesta *answer*, xxii
**el restaurante** *restaurant*, 6
la república *republic*, 5G
el res *beef*, 6
la reservación *reservation*, 6
requerir (ie) *to require*, 7
la resolución de Año Nuevo *New Year's resolution*, 9
resolver (ue) *to solve*, 7
respectivo(a) *respective*, 8
responder *to answer*, 9
la respuesta *answer*, 3
**el restaurante** *restaurant*, 6
el restaurante familiar *family restaurant*, 3
el retrato *portrait*, 1G
**la reunión** *meeting*, 3; *reunion*, 9
reunir *to bring together*, 1G
**reunirse** *to get together*, 9; **reunirse con (toda) la familia** *to get together with the (whole) family*, 9
revisar *to check, to revise, to correct*, 1
**la revista** *magazine*, 3; **la revista de tiras cómicas** *comic book*, 8
el revolucionario *revolutionary*, 9G
el rey *king*, 1
rico(a) *magnificent*, 9
ridículo(a) *ridiculous*, 8
riguroso(a) *harsh*, 5G
el río *river*, 3G
las riquezas *riches*, 10
**riquísimo(a)** *delicious*, 6
el ritmo *rhythm*, 5G; el ritmo del momento *the latest rhythm*, 1
el rito *ritual*, 6
**el robo** *rip-off*, 8; **¡Es un robo!** *It's a rip-off!*, 8
rodeado(a) *surrounded*, 1G
rodear *to surround*, 7G
el rodeo *rodeo*, 3G
**rojo(a)** *red*, 8
**romántico(a)** *romantic*, 2
el rompecabezas *puzzle*, 4
**la ropa** *clothes*, 4
**rubio(a)** *blond*, 2
**las ruinas** *ruins*, 10
la rutina *routine*, 2

# S

**el sábado** *Saturday*, 1; **los sábados** *on Saturdays*, 3
**saber** *to know information*, 4; **saber de** *to know about*, 4; no sabe cómo *doesn't know how*, 9; **No sé.** *I don't know.*, 4; **¿Sabes qué?** *You know what?*, 4; Sé. *I know.*, 9
el sabor *flavor*, 8G
**sacar** *to take out*, 6; **sacar el dinero** *to get money*, 10; **sacar fotos** *to take photos*, 10; **sacar la basura** *to take out the trash*, 5; sacar una idea *to get an idea*, 4
**el saco** *sportscoat*, 8
**sal** *go out, leave*, 6
la sal *salt*, 6
**la sala** *living room*, 5; **la sala de espera** *waiting room*, 10; la sala de juegos *game room*, 5
**salado(a)** *salty*, 6; **Está (un poco) salado(a)** *It's (a little) salty.*, 6
**la salida** *departure*, 10; *exit*, 10
**salir (-go)** *to go out*, 3; *to leave*, 4; **No salgas.** *Don't leave.*, 10; que salga *go out*, 9; **sal** *go out, leave*, 6; salir bien *to work out well*, 7; **salir con amigos** *to go out with friends*, 3

el salón *room*, 1; **el salón de clase** *classroom*, 4
**la salsa** *sauce, gravy*, 6; **la salsa picante** *hot sauce*, 6
el salto *waterfall*, 2G
el salto en el tiempo *time warp*, 7
**la salud** *health*, 7
saludable *healthy*, 6
saludar *to greet*, 1
el saludo *greeting*, 9
salvarse *to save oneself*, 10
el salvavidas *lifeguard*, 1
el sancocho *stew made with meat, root vegetables, and plantains*, 9G
**las sandalias** *sandals*, 8
**el sándwich de...** *. . . sandwich*, 6
los sanitarios *restrooms*, 10
sano(a) *healthy*, 7; **seguir (i) una dieta sana** *to eat a balanced diet*, 7
el santo, la santa *saint*, 2G
la sartén *frying pan*, 6
**sé** *be*, 6
**la secadora de pelo** *hair dryer*, 7
**secarse** *to dry*, 7
la sección rítmica *rhythm section*, 8G
seco(a) *dry*, 2G
secreto(a) *secret*, 1
**la sed** *thirst*, 4; **tener (-go, ie) sed** *to be thirsty*, 4
**la seda** silk, 8; **de seda** made of silk, 8
**seguir (i)** *to follow*, 10; **seguir (i) una dieta sana** *to eat a balanced diet*, 7; sigue el modelo *follow the model*, xxii; siguiéndote *following you*, 8
según *according to*, 2
el segundo *second*, 4
segundo(a) *second*, 6
**seis** *six*, 1
**seiscientos** *six hundred*, 8
la selección *selection*, 6
la selva *jungle*, 10
**la semana** *week*, 4; **el día de la semana** *day of the week*, 1; **esta semana** *this week*, 4; **la próxima semana** *next week*, 4
**la Semana Santa** *Holy Week*, 9
**el señor** *sir, Mr.*, 1; *gentleman*, 8
el Señor *the Lord*, 9
**la señora** *ma'am; Mrs.*, 1
**la señorita** *Miss*, 1
la sensación *feeling*, 1
**sentarse (ie)** *to sit down*, 10
sentir (ie) *to feel*, 9
**sentirse (ie)** *to feel*, 7
separados *separately*, 8
separar *to separate*, 1G
**septiembre** *September*, 1
**ser** *to be*, 1; **¿Cómo eres?** *What are you like?*, 2; **¿Cómo es...?** *What is . . . like?*, 2; No puede ser. *It can't be true.*, 9; **no seas** *don't be*, 7; **sé** *be*, 6; **será** *will be*, 10; **Soy...** *I'm . . .*, 2; **Soy de...** *I'm from . . .*, 1
el ser *being*, 8
la serenata *serenade*, 9
la serenidad *serenity*, 1
la serie *series*, 6G
**serio(a)** *serious*, 2
la serpiente *serpent*, 6
**el servicio** *restroom*, 10
**la servilleta** *napkin*, 6
**servir (i)** *to serve*, 6; **¿En qué le puedo servir?** *Can I help you?*, 8
**sesenta** *sixty*, 2
el seso *brain*, 4
**setecientos** *seven hundred*, 8
**setenta** *seventy*, 2
si *if*, 3; si no *otherwise*, 3
**sí** *yes*, 4; **Sí, necesito muchas cosas.** *Yes, I need a lot of things.*, 4; **Sí, tengo un montón.** *Yes, I have a ton of them.*, 4
**siempre** *always*, 5; **casi siempre** *almost always*, 3; **como siempre** *as always*, 9; **lo de siempre** *same as always*, 9
la sierra *mountain range*, 10G
**siete** *seven*, 1
el siglo *century*, 3G
el significado *meaning*, 7
significar *to mean*, 2
siguiente *following*, 5; **lo siguiente** *the following*, 6
la sílaba *syllable*, 2
**la silla** *chair*, 5; **la silla de ruedas** *wheelchair*, 5
el símbolo *symbol*, 2
**simpático(a)** *friendly*, 2
simplemente *simply*, 6
sin *without*, 6; sin embargo *however*, 6
**la sinagoga** *synagogue*, 9
sincero(a) *sincere*, 2
sino *but also*, 6
los sirvientes *servants*, 8
el sistema *system*, 10G
el sitio *place*, 3; *site*, 7
la situación *situation*, 5
sobre *over*, 3; *on*, 4; *about*, 2
**la sobrina** *niece*, 5
**el sobrino** *nephew*, 5
**los sobrinos** *nephews, nieces and nephews*, 5
sociable *social*, 2
**el sofá** *sofa*, 5
el sol *sun*, 3; **Hace sol.** *It's sunny.*, 3
solamente *only*, 3G
el soldado *soldier*, 6G
soler *to usually do*, 5; suele *usually*, 5
sólido(a) *solid*, 6
**solo(a)** *alone*, 3; **pasar el rato solo(a)** *to spend time alone*, 3
**sólo** *only*, 7
**el sombrero** *hat*, 8
**somos** (inf. **ser**) *we are*, 5; **Somos... personas.** *There are . . . people.*, 5
**Son las...** *It's . . . o'clock.*, 1
el sonido *sound*, 2G
**la sopa** *soup*, 6; **la sopa de verduras** *vegetable soup*, 6
**sordo(a)** *deaf*, 5
sorprendido(a) *surprised*, 8
**Soy...** (inf. **ser**) *I'm . . .*, 2; **Soy de...** *I'm from . . .*, 1
**su(s)** *his, her, its, their*, 5
suave *soft*, 7
subir *to rise*, 7
**subir a la montaña** *to go up a mountain*, 10; **subir de peso** *to gain weight*, 7
el subtítulo *subtitle*, 10
sucio(a) *dirty*, 6
el sudeste *southeast*, 10G
Suele + inf. *He (She) usually +* verb, 10
el sueño *dream*, 1G
**la suerte** *luck*, 10; **Si tengo suerte...** *If I'm lucky . . .*, 10; **Tuviste suerte.** *You were lucky.*, 10
**el suéter** *sweater*, 8
**suficiente** *enough*, 7; **dormir (ue) lo suficiente** *to get enough sleep*, 7
la sugerencia *suggestion*, 7
sugerir *to suggest*, 6
Suiza *Switzerland*, 7G
la superficie *surface*, 8
el sur *south*, 2G
sureño(a) *southern*, 7G
el surf a vela *windsurfing*, 9G
sus *his/her*, 4; *their, your*, 5
la sustancia *substance*, 6
suyo(a) *his*, 4G

Tailandia *Thailand*, 6
taíno(a) *belonging to the Tainos, Native Americans dominant in early Puerto Rico*, 2G
tal *such*, 7; tal vez *perhaps*, 4
**la talla** *(clothing) size*, 8
tallado(a) *carved, cut*, 10G
los tallarines *noodles*, 7
**el taller** *shop, workshop*, 4
la tamalada *gathering to make tamales*, 3G
**los tamales** *tamales*, 9
el tamaño *size*
**también** *also*, 2
la tambora *drum*, 9G
**tampoco** *neither, not either*, 5
tan *so*, 10G

tan sólo *only,* 9
**tan... como** *as . . .as,* 8
**tanto** *so much,* 7; *as much,* 1G; tanto... *como... both . . . and . . .,* 3G; **Tanto gusto.** *So nice to meet you.,* 9; **Tanto tiempo.** *It's been a long time.,* 1; **¡Tanto tiempo sin verte!** *Long time, no see!,* 9
la tapa *small servings of food,* 7G
tardar *to take;* ¿Cuánto tardas? *How long do you take?,* 4
**la tarde** *afternoon, evening,* 1; **de la tarde** *in the afternoon, evening,* P.M., 1; **esta tarde** *this afternoon,* 4; **por la tarde** *in the afternoon,* 4
**tarde** *late,* 4; **más tarde** *later,* 8
la tarea *homework,* 1; **hacer la tarea** *to do homework,* 3
**la tarjeta** *greeting card,* 8; *card,* 9; **mandar tarjetas** *to send cards,* 9; **la tarjeta de cumpleaños** *birthday card,* 8; la tarjeta de crédito *credit card,* 10; **la tarjeta de embarque** *boarding pass,* 10; la tarjeta postal *postcard,* 10
el tataranieto *great-great-grandson,* 10
**el taxi** *taxi,* 10
la taza *cup,* 6
**te** *(to/for) you,* 2; **¿Te duele algo?** *Does something hurt?,* 7; **¿Te gusta(n)...?** *Do you like . . .?,* 2; **¿Te gusta(n) más... o...?** *Do you like . . . or . . . more?,* 2; **Te llamo más tarde.** *I'll call you later.,* 9; **Te presento a...** *I'd like you to meet . . .,* 9; **Te veo mal.** *You don't look well.,* 7
el teatro *theater,* 8
el techo de zinc *sheet-metal roof,* 9G
la tecnología *technology,* 4
tejano(a) *Texan,* 3G
el tejido *weaving,* 10G
la tele *TV,* 4
**el teléfono** *telephone number,* 1; *telephone,* 8; **¿Cuál es el teléfono de...?** *What's . . . 's telephone number?,* 1; **¿Cuál es tu teléfono?** *What's your telephone number?,* 1; **hablar por teléfono** *to talk on the phone,* 3; llamar por teléfono *to make a phone call,* 8; el teléfono público *pay phone,* 10
**la televisión** *television (TV),* 3; **ver televisión** *to watch TV,* 3
el tema *theme,* 6
temblar *to shake,* 9
tembloroso(a) *trembling,* 9
la temperatura *temperature,* 2G
templado(a) *temperate,* 2G
**el templo** *temple,* 9
**temprano** *early,* 4
**ten** *have,* 6
**el tenedor** *fork,* 6
**tener (-go, ie)** *to have,* 4; **Cuántos años tiene... ?** *How old is . . .?,* 2; **¿Cuántos años tienes?** *How old are you?,* 2; **Él (Ella) tiene... años.** *He's (She's) . . . years old.,* 2; **no tengas** *don't have,* 10; **ten** *have,* 6; tendrán que separarse *will have to separate,* 3; **tener calor** *to be hot,* 7; **tener catarro** *to have a cold,* 7; **tener frío** *to be cold,* 7; **tener ganas** *to feel like (doing something),* 4; **tener ganas de** + infinitive *to feel like doing something,* 4; **tener hambre** *to be hungry,* 4; **tener los ojos azules** *to have blue eyes,* 5; **tener miedo** *to be afraid,* 7; **tener prisa** *to be in a hurry,* 4; tener puesto *to have on,* 3; **tener que** + infinitive *to have to do something,* 4; **tener razón** *to be right,* 8; **tener sed** *to be thirsty,* 4; **tener sueño** *to be sleepy,* 7; **tener suerte** *to be lucky,* 10; **tener un picnic** *to have a picnic,* 9; **Tengo que irme.** *I have got to go.,* 1; **Tengo... años.** *I am . . . years old.,* 2; **Tiene... años.** *He (She) is . . . years old.,* 2; tuvo *had,* 7G
**el tenis** *tennis,* 3
el tentempié *snack,* 3G
el tercero *third,* 4
**terminar** *to finish,* 9
**la terraza de comidas** *food court in a mall,* 8
el territorio *territory,* 6G
**el terror** *horror,* 2
el testimonio *testimony,* 6G
el texto *text,* 6
**ti** *you* (emphatic), 3; a ti *to you,* 6; A ti te gusta + infinitive *You like . . .,* 3; para ti *for you,* 2
**la tía** *aunt,* 5
el tico *nickname for Costa Rican,* 4G
**el tiempo** *weather,* 3; *time,* 1G; **a tiempo** *on time,* 4; **cuando hace buen/mal tiempo** *when the weather's good/bad,* 3
**la tienda de...** *. . . store,* 8
**tiene** *he/she/it has,* 2; **Cuántos años tiene... ?** *How old is . . .?,* 2; **Él (Ella) tiene... años.** *He's (She's) . . . years old.,* 2; **Tiene... años.** *He's (She's) . . . years old.,* 2
**tienes** *you have,* 4; **¿Cuántos años tienes?** *How old are you?,* 2; **¿Tienes...?** *Do you have . . .?,* 4
la tierra *earth,* 6; *land,* 6G
el tigre *tiger,* 2
la tilde *wavy line above the ñ,* 1
**tímido(a)** *shy,* 2
la tinta *ink,* 10
**el tío** *uncle,* 5
**los tíos** *uncles, uncles and aunts,* 5
típico(a) *typical,* 2G
el tipo *type;* de todo tipo *all kinds,* 8;
el título *title,* 5
**la toalla** *towel,* 7
**tocar** *to play,* 3; *to touch,* 8; **A mí siempre me toca...** *I always have to . . .,* 5; **A... nunca le toca...** *It's never . . .'s turn.; . . . never has to . . .,* 5; Le toca a él. *It's his turn.,* 9; **¿Qué te toca hacer a ti?** *What do you have to do?,* 5, Te toca a ti. *It's your turn.,* 6; **tocar el piano** *to play the piano,* 3; tocar la puerta *to knock on the door,* 3
**el tocino** *bacon,* 6
**todavía** *yet,* 10; *still,* 1G; **todavía no** *not yet,* 10
**todo(a)** *all, every,* 2; *whole,* 9; todo el mundo *everybody,* 9; de todo *everything,* 8; de todo tipo *all kinds,* 8; **todos(as)** *everyone,* 5; **todos los días** *every day,* 3
**tomar** *to drink,* 6; *to eat,* 8; *to take,* 9; siguen tomándolo *keep drinking it,* 6; *to take,* 7; **tomar el sol** *to sunbathe,* 10; tomar las cosas con calma *to take things calmly,* 7; tomar una decisión *to make a decision,* 9; **tomar un batido** *to have a milkshake,* 8
**el tomate** *tomato,* 6
la tonelada *ton,* 10
**tonto(a)** *dumb,* 2
el tornado *tornado,* 3
la toronja *grapefruit,* 3G
la torre *tower,* 9G
la torta *sandwich (Mexico),* 6
la tortilla *Spanish omelet,* 1G; *pancake-like bread made from corn,* 6
la tortuga *turtle,* 1
el tostón *fried green plantain,* 2G
**trabajador(a)** *hard-working,* 2
**trabajar** *to work,* 3
**el trabajo** *job,* 3; *work,* 4
el trabalenguas *tongue twister,* 1
la tradición *tradition,* 2
tradicional *traditional,* 1G
**traer (-igo)** *to bring,* 4; me trajo *he/she brought me,* 4; quiero que me traigas *I want you to bring me,* 9
el tráfico *traffic,* 3G
tragar *to swallow,* 2
el traje *suit,* 3; *dress,* 1G
**el traje de baño** *swimsuit,* 8
tranquilo(a) *quiet,* 5; *calm,* 9
la transpiración *perspiration,* 8
transportar *to transport,* 10; fueron transportadas *were transported,* 10
el transporte *transportation,* 10
el trasto *utensil, piece of junk,* 2
tratar *to try,* 10
**travieso(a)** *mischievous,* 5
**trece** *thirteen,* 1
**treinta** *thirty,* 1

**treinta y cinco** *thirty-five,* 2
**treinta y dos** *thirty-two,* 2
**treinta y uno** *thirty-one,* 1
**el tren** *train,* 10
**tres** *three,* 1
**trescientos** *three hundred,* 8
el trigal *wheat field,* 2
el trigo *wheat,* 2
**triste** *sad,* 7; **estar triste** *to be sad,* 7
el trozo *piece,* 6
**tú** *you,* 1
**tu(s)** *your,* 5
el turismo *tourism,* 8G
el turista *tourist,* 1G
turnarse *to take turns,* xxii
el turno *shift,* 4
tutear *to speak to someone informally,* 10
los tuyos, las tuyas *yours,* 9

**último(a)** *latest,* 8; la última vez *last time,* 8
el último, la última *last one,* 3
**un(a)** *a, an,* 4; **un poco** *a little,* 2; **un montón** *a ton,* 4
únicamente *only,* 9
único(a) *only,* 4G
la unidad *unity,* 3G
la universidad *university,* 5
**uno** *one,* 1
**unos(as)** *some,* 4
urgente *urgent,* 1
**usar** *to use, to wear,* 8; **usar el/la...** *to wear size . . .,* 8; **usar lentes** *to wear glasses,* 5; **usando** *using,* xxii
el uso *use,* 6
**usted** *you* (formal), 1
**ustedes** *you* (pl.), 1
**los útiles escolares** *school supplies,* 4
utilizar *to use,* 7
la uva *grape,* 1
**¡Uy!** *Oh!,* 1

**Vale.** *Okay.,* 9
valeroso(a) *brave,* 4G
valiente *brave,* 5
la valija *suitcase,* 10
el valle *valley,* 3G
vamos *let's go, we go,* 3
el vaquero *cowboy,* 3G
vaquero(a) *referring to cowboys,* 3G
**los vaqueros** *jeans,* 8
variado(a) *varied,* 7
varias *various,* 6G
la variedad *variety,* 6
**vas** *you are going,* 4; **¿Vas a (a la)...?** *Are you going to the. . .?,* 4; **Vas a ir, ¿verdad?** *You're going to go, aren't you?,* 4
el vasco *language from Basque Provinces, Spain,* 1G
la vasija *pot,* 4
**el vaso** *glass,* 6
**ve** *go,* 6
veces *times,* 7; **a veces** *sometimes,* 3; **hay veces** *there are times,* 4
**veinte** *twenty,* 1
**veintiún** *twenty-one,* 1
**ven** *come,* 6
vencido(a) *defeated,* 6; no se da por vencido *doesn't give up,* 6
el vendedor *vendor,* 8
**vender** *to sell,* 8; se vende *for sale,* 5; se venden *are sold,* 8; **vender de todo** *to sell everything,* 8
**venir** *to come,* 4; ha venido *has come,* 9; **No vengas.** *Don't come.,* 10; **ven** *come,* 6; venga *will come,* 9; **Vienes conmigo a...** *You're coming with me to . . .,* 4
**la ventana** *window,* 5
el ventanal *large window,* 6G
la ventura *happiness,* 5
**ver** *to watch, to see,* 4; nunca ha visto *never has seen,* 6; **Te veo mal.** *You don't look well.,* 7; **ver televisión** *to watch television,* 3; vi *I saw,* 8
**el verano** *summer,* 3
el verbo *verb,* xxii
la verdad *truth,* 2
**¿verdad?** *right?,* 4
**verde** *green,* 5; verde mar *sea green,* 5G
**las verduras** *vegetables,* 2
vespertino(a) *(in the) afternoon,* 4
**el vestido** *dress,* 8
**vestirse (i)** *to get dressed,* 7
vete *go,* 7
vez *time,* 4; cada vez *each time,* 8; hay veces *there are times,* 4; la última vez *last time,* 8
**viajar** *to travel,* 10
**el viaje** *trip,* 10
el viajero *traveler,* 10
la vida *life,* 3G
**el video** *video,* 3; **alquilar videos** *to rent videos,* 3
**los videojuegos** *videogames,* 2
los viejitos *older folks,* 3
**viejo(a)** *old,* 5
el viento *wind,* 3; **Hace viento.** *It's windy.,* 3
**el viernes** *Friday,* 1; **los viernes** *on Fridays,* 3; **el viernes próximo** *next Friday,* 4
el Viernes Santo *Good Friday,* 1
el violín *violin,* 1
visitar *to visit,* 6
la vista *view,* 5
**la vitrina** *shop window,* 8; **mirar las vitrinas** *to window-shop,* 8
**vivir** *to live,* 5
vivo(a) *bright,* 5G
el vocabulario *vocabulary,* xxii
volar *to fly,* 7
el volcán *volcano,* 4G
**el volibol** *volleyball,* 3
**volver (ue)** *to go or come back,* 5; nunca más volverá *never will do it again,* 9; se vuelve *it becomes,* 6
**vosotros(as)** *you* (plural; informal), 1
**el vuelo** *flight,* 10
**vuestra(s)** *your,* 5
**vuestro(s)** *your,* 5

el wáter *restroom,* 10
el windsurfing *windsurfing,* 7

**y** *and,* 1; **y cuarto** *a quarter past,* 1; **y media** *half past,* 1
**ya** *already,* 10
**Ya te lo (la) paso.** *I'll get him (her).,* 8
la yerba mate *herb used to make Argentinean and Paraguayan tea,* 7
**yo** *I,* 1
el yogur *yogurt,* 7
la yuca *yucca,* 8G

**la zanahoria** *carrot,* 6
**la zapatería** *shoe store,* 8
las zapatillas de tenis *tennis shoes,* 8
**los zapatos** *shoes,* 4; **los zapatos de tenis** *tennis shoes,* 8
la zona *area,* 4; la zona residencial *residential area,* 5
**el zoológico** *zoo,* 10
el zumo *juice (Spain),* 6

# Vocabulario inglés-español

This vocabulary includes all of the words presented in the **Vocabulario** sections of the chapters. These words are considered active—you are expected to know them and be able to use them. Expressions are listed under the English word you would be most likely to look up.

Spanish nouns are listed with the definite article and plural forms, when applicable. If a Spanish verb is stem-changing, the change is indicated in parentheses after the verb: **dormir (ue)**. The number after each entry refers to the chapter in which the word or phrase is introduced.

To be sure you are using Spanish words and phrases in their correct context, refer to the chapters listed. You may also want to look up Spanish phrases in **Expresiones de ¡Exprésate!,** pp. R12–R14.

**a little** *un poco,* 2
**a lot** *mucho,* 2
**a lot of, many** *muchos(as),* 4
**a ton** *un montón,* 4
**a, an** *un(a),* 4
**active** *activo(a),* 2
**to add** *añadir,* 6
**address** *la dirección,* 5; **My address is...** *Mi dirección es...,* 5; e-mail address *correo electrónico,* 1
**adventure** *la aventura,* 2; **adventure book** *el libro de aventuras,* 2
**after** *después,* 3; *después de,* 7; **after class** *después de clases,* 3
**afternoon** *la tarde,* 1; **this afternoon** *esta tarde,* 4; **in the afternoon** *de la tarde,* P.M., 1; *por la tarde,* 4
**afterwards** *después,* 4
**agent** *el agente, la agente,* 10
**agree: I don't agree.** *No estoy de acuerdo.,* 6; **I agree.** *Estoy de acuerdo.,* 6
**airplane** *el avión,* 10; **by plane** *por avión,* 10
**airport** *el aeropuerto,* 10
**all** *todas,* 1; *todo(a),* 2
**all right** *regular,* 1
**to allow** *dejar,* 3
**almost** *casi,* 3; **almost never** *casi nunca,* 3; **almost always** *casi siempre,* 3
**alone** *solo(a),* 3
**alphabet** *el alfabeto,* 1
**already** *ya,* 10
**also** *también,* 2
**always** *siempre,* 5; **almost always** *casi siempre,* 3; **as always** *como siempre,* 9
**amusement park** *el parque de diversiones,* 10
**an** *un, una,* 4
**and** *y,* 1
**animal** *el animal,* 2
**anniversary** *el aniversario,* 9
**another** *otro,* 8
**any** *cualquier,* 10
**anything** *algo,* 4; *nada,* 4
**apartment** *el apartamento,* 5
**apple** *la manzana,* 6
**April** *abril,* 1
**Are you...?** *¿Eres...?,* 2
**arm** *el brazo,* 7
**around the corner** *a la vuelta,* 10
**arrival** *la llegada,* 10
**to arrive** *llegar,* 4
**art** *el arte,* 4
**as...as** *tan...como,* 8
**as always** *como siempre,* 9
**at** *a(l),* 8; **@** *la arroba,* 1; *en,* 3
**athletic** *atlético(a),* 2
**to attend** *asistir (a),* 4
**auditorium** *el auditorio,* 4
**August** *agosto,* 1
**aunt** *la tía,* 5
**automatic teller machine** *el cajero automático,* 10
**awesome** *fenomenal,* 2

**back** *la espalda,* 7, **I'll call back later** *Llamo más tarde,* 8; **to go (come) back** *volver (ue),* 5
**backpack** *la mochila,* 4
**bacon** *el tocino,* 6
**bad** *malo(a),* 2
**bag** *bolsa,* 8
**baggage** *el equipaje,* 10; **baggage claim** *el reclamo de equipaje,* 10
**bargain** *la ganga,* 8
**baseball** *el béisbol,* 3
**basketball** *el básquetbol,* 3
**to bathe** *bañarse,* 7
**bathroom** *el baño,* 5
**be** *sé,* 6
**to be able to** *poder,* 6
**to be** *estar,* 1; **How are you?** *¿Cómo está(s)?,* 1; **to be all right** *estar regular,* 1; **to be angry** *estar enojado,* 7; **to be bored** *estar aburrido(a)* 7; **to be familiar with** *conocer,* 9; **to be fine** *estar bien,* 1; **to be hungry** *tener hambre,* 4; **to be tired** *estar cansado(a),* 7; **to be happy** *estar contento(a)* 7; **to be sick** *estar enfermo(a)* 7; **to be in a hurry** *tener prisa,* 7; **to be in a wheelchair** *estar en una silla de ruedas,* 5; **to be ready** *estar listo(a),* 7; **to be nervous** *estar nervioso(a)* 7; **to be right** *tener razón,* 7; **to be sad** *estar triste,* 7; **to be scared** *tener miedo,* 7; **to be sleepy** *tener sueño,* 7; **to be lucky** *tener suerte,* 7; **to be thirsty** *tener sed,* 7; **don't be** *no estés,* 7
**to be** *ser,* 1; **don't be** *no seas,* 7
**beach** *la playa,* 3
**because** *porque,* 2
**bed** *la cama,* 5; **to make the bed** *hacer la cama,* 5; **to go to bed** *acostarse (ue),* 7
**bedroom** *la habitación,* 5
**beef** *la carne,* 6
**before** *antes de,* 7
**behind** *detrás de,* 5
**besides** *además,* 8
**best** *el/la/los/las mejor(es),* 1
**better** *mejor(es),* 7
**big** *grande,* 5
**bike** *la bicicleta,* 3; **to ride a bike** *montar en bicicleta,* 3
**bill** *la cuenta,* 6
**biology** *la biología,* 4

**birthday** *el cumpleaños,* 9; **When is . . .'s birthday?** *¿Cuándo es el cumpleaños de...?,* 2; **When is your birthday?** *¿Cuándo es tu cumpleaños?,* 2; **. . .'s birthday** *el cumpleaños de...,* 2; **birthday card** *la tarjeta de cumpleaños,* 8; **girl's fifteenth birthday** *la quinceañera,* 9
**black** *negro(a),* 5
**blank** *en blanco,* 8
**blind** *ciego(a),* 5
**blond** *rubio(a),* 2
**blouse** *la blusa,* 8
**blue** *azul,* 5; **to have blue eyes** *tener los ojos azules,* 5
**board game** *el juego de mesa,* 3
**to board** *abordar,* 10
**boarding pass** *la tarjeta de embarque,* 10
**boat** *el barco,* 10
**book** *el libro,* 2; **adventure book** *el libro de aventuras,* 2; **comic book** *la revista de tiras cómicas,* 8; **romance book** *el libro de amor,* 2
**bookstore** *la librería,* 8
**boots** *las botas,* 8
**boring** *aburrido(a),* 2; **to be bored** *estar aburrido,* 7
**bowl** *el plato hondo,* 6
**boy** *el muchacho,* 1
**bracelet** *la pulsera,* 8
**bread** *el pan,* 6
**breakfast** *el desayuno,* 6
**to bring** *traer (-igo),* 4
**broccoli** *el bróculi,* 6
**brother** *el hermano,* 5
**brothers, brothers and sisters** *los hermanos,* 5
**brown** *castaño(a),* 5; *de color café,* 5
**building** *el edificio,* 5; **. . . story building** *el edificio de... pisos,* 5
**bus** *el autobús,* 10
**but** *pero,* 5
**to buy** *comprar,* 8; **you would buy** *comprarías,* 8
**by plane** *por avion,* 10
**Bye** *chao,* 9

**cafeteria** *la cafetería,* 4
**cake** *el pastel,* 6
**calculator** *la calculadora,* 4
**calf** *la pantorrilla,* 7
**to call** *llamar,* 9; **I'll call back later.** *Llamo más tarde.,* 8
**camera** *la cámara,* 10; **disposable camera** *la cámara desechable,* 10
**to camp** *acampar,* 10
**can** *poder,* 6
**Can I . . .?** *¿Puedo...?,* 6
**Can I help you?** *¿En que le puedo servir?,* 8
**candy** *el dulce,* 9
**canoe** *la canoa,* 10
**car** *el carro,* 2
**card** *la tarjeta,* 8
**carrot** *la zanahoria,* 5
**cat** *el gato, la gata,* 5
**to celebrate** *festejar,* 9
**cereal** *los cereales,* 6
**chair** *la silla,* 5; **wheelchair** *la silla de ruedas,* 5
**to change money** *cambiar dinero,* 10
**to chat** *charlar,* 9
**to check luggage** *facturar el equipaje,* 10
**checkpoint: security checkpoint** *control de seguridad,* 10
**cheese** *el queso,* 6
**chemistry** *la química,* 4
**chess** *ajedrez,* 1
**chest** *el pecho,* 7
**chicken** *el pollo,* 6
**children** *los hijos,* 5; *los niños,* 8
**chocolate** *el chocolate,* 6
**chores** *los quehaceres,* 5
**Christmas** *la Navidad,* 9; **Christmas Eve** *la Nochebuena,* 9
**church** *la iglesia,* 3
**city** *la ciudad,* 5
**class** *la clase,* 3; **after class** *después de clases,* 3
**classmate** (female) *la (una) compañera de clase,* 1
**classmate** (male) *el (un) compañero de clase,* 1
**to clean** *limpiar,* 5
**to clean the room** *arreglar el cuarto,* 5
**client** *el cliente, la cliente,* 8
**climb** *subir,* 10
**clock** *el reloj,* 4
**close to,** *cerca de,* 5
**to close** *cerrar (ie),* 8
**clothes** *la ropa,* 4
**cloudy** *nublado,* 7
**club** *el club de...,* 4
**coat** *el abrigo,* 8
**coffee** *el café,* 6; **coffee with milk** *el café con leche,* 6; **coffee shop** *la cafetería,* 6
**cold** *frío(a),* 6; **It's cold.** *Hace frío.,* 3; **to be cold** *tener frío,* 7;
**to have a cold** *tener catarro,* 7
**comb** *el peine,* 7
**to comb your hair** *peinarse,* 7
**to come** *venir,* 4; **come** *ven,* 6; **don't come** *no vengas,* 10; **to come back** *volver,* 5; **you're coming with me to . . .** *vienes conmigo a...,* 4
**comic book** *la revista de tiras cómicas,* 8
**compact disc** *el disco compacto,* 8;
**blank compact disc** *el disco compacto en blanco,* 8
**computer** *la computadora,* 4; **computer science** *la computación,* 4
**concert** *el concierto,* 4
**to cook** *cocinar,* 5
**cookie** *la galleta,* 9
**cool** *fresco,* 3; **It's cool.** *Hace fresco.,* 3
**corn** *el maíz,* 6
**to cost** *costar (ue),* 8; **costs . . .** *cuesta(n)...,* 8; **It will cost.** *Costará.,* 9
**cotton** *el algodón,* 8; **made of cotton** *de algodón,* 8
**counter** *el mostrador,* 10
**country** *el país,* 10
**countryside** *el campo,* 5
**court: food court in a mall** *la terraza de comidas,* 8
**cousin** *el primo, la prima,* 5
**custard** *el flan,* 6
**customs** *la aduana,* 10
**to cut** *cortar,* 6; **to cut the grass** *cortar el césped,* 5

**dad** *el papá,* 5
**dance** *el baile,* 3; **dance class** *la clase de baile,* 4
**to dance** *bailar,* 3; **dancing** *bailando,* 1; **to start dancing** *ponerse a bailar,* 3
**dark: dark-skinned; dark-haired** *moreno(a),* 2
**date** *la fecha,* 1
**daughter** *la hija,* 5
**day** *el día,* 1; **day after tomorrow** *pasado mañana,* 4; **day before yesterday** *anteayer,* 8; **day of the week** *el día de la semana,* 1; **Father's Day** *el Día del Padre,* 9; **holiday** *el día festivo,* 9; **Independence Day** *el Día de la Independencia,* 9; **Mother's Day** *el Día de la Madre,* 9; **some day** *algún día,* 10; **Thanksgiving Day** *el Día de Acción de Gracias,* 9; **Valentine's Day** *el Día de los Enamorados,* 9; **What day is today?** *¿Qué día es hoy?,* 1; **your saint's day** *el día de tu santo,* 9
**deaf** *sordo(a),* 5
**December** *diciembre,* 1
**to decorate** *decorar,* 9; **to decorate the house** *decorar la casa,* 9
**decoration** *la decoración,* 9
**delicious** *delicioso(a),* 2; *riquísimo(a),* 6
**to delight** *encantar,* 6

**department store** *el almacén,* 8
**departure** *la salida,* 10
**to desire** *desear,* 6
**desk** *el escritorio,* 5
**dessert** *el postre,* 6
**destination** *el destino,* 10
**destined** *destinado(a),* 6
**detail** *el detalle,* 7
**to determine** *determinar,* 7
**dictionary** *el diccionario,* 4
**diet** *la dieta,* 7; **to eat a balanced diet** *seguir una dieta sana,* 7
**difficult** *difícil,* 4; **It's difficult.** *Es difícil.,* 4
**dining room** *el comedor,* 5
**dinner** *la cena,* 6
**disc: compact disc** *el disco compacto,* 8; **blank compact disc** *el disco compacto en blanco,* 8
**to disembark** *desembarcar,* 10
**dish** *el plato,* 6
**disposable** *desechable,* 10; **disposable camera** *la cámara desechable,* 10
**Do you like . . .?** *¿Te gusta(n)...?,* 2
**to do** *hacer,* 4; **we are doing** *estamos haciendo,* 9; **to do homework** *hacer la tarea,* 3; **to do the chores** *hacer los quehaceres,* 5; **to do the dishes** *lavar los platos,* 7; **to do yoga** *hacer yoga,* 7; **do** *haz,* 6; **don't do** *no hagas,* 10; **What are they doing?** *¿Qué están haciendo?,* 9; **What did you do?** *¿Qué hiciste?* 8
**dog** *el perro, la perra,* 5
**door** *la puerta,* 5
**dot** *el punto,* 1; **on the dot** *en punto,* 1
**downtown** *el centro,* 10
**to draw** *dibujar,* 3
**dress** *el vestido,* 8
**dressed: to get dressed,** *vestirse (i),* 7
**to drink (something)** *beber (algo),* 4; *tomar,* 6; **to drink punch** *beber ponche,* 9
**to dry** *secarse,* 7
**during** *durante,* 10
**DVD** *el DVD,* 8

**ear** *el oído,* 7
**early** *temprano,* 4
**earphones** *los audífonos,* 8
**earrings** *los aretes,* 8
**easy** *fácil,* 4; **It's easy.** *Es fácil.,* 4
**to eat a balanced diet** *seguir una dieta sana,* 7; **to eat breakfast** *desayunar,* 6; **to eat dinner** *cenar,* 6; **to eat lunch** *almorzar (ue),* 6
**to eat** *comer,* 3; *tomar,* 8
**egg** *el huevo,* 6
**eight** *ocho,* 1
**eight hundred** *ochocientos,* 8
**eighteen** *dieciocho,* 1
**eighty** *ochenta,* 2
**eleven** *once,* 1
**e-mail address** *el correo electrónico,* 1; **What is . . .'s e-mail address?** *¿Cuál es el correo electrónico de...?* 1; **What's your e-mail address?** *¿Cuál es tu correo electrónico?,* 1
**English** *el inglés,* 4
**enough** *suficiente,* 7; **to get enough sleep** *dormir lo suficiente,* 7
**evening** *la tarde,* 1; **in the evening** *de la tarde,* P.M., 1
**everyone** *todos(as),* 5
**everybody** *todos (as),* 5
**everything** *todo,* 8
**to exercise** *hacer ejercicio,* 3
**to expect** *esperar,* 9
**expensive** *caro(a),* 8
**eyes** *los ojos,* 5; **to have blue eyes** *tener los ojos azules,* 5

**face** *la cara,* 7
**fall** *el otoño,* 3
**family** *la familia,* 3; **There are . . . people in my family.** *En mi familia somos...,* 5
**familiar: to be familiar** *conocer,* 9
**fantastic: How fantastic!** *¡Qué fantástico!,* 10
**fat (in food)** *la grasa,* 7
**fat (overweight)** *gordo(a),* 5
**father** *el padre,* 5; **Father's Day** *el Día del Padre,* 9
**favorite** *preferido(a),* 4
**flan** *el flan,* 6
**February** *febrero,* 1
**to feel** *sentirse (ie),* 7; **to feel like doing something** *tener ganas de + infinitive,* 4
**few** *pocos(as),* 4
**fifteen** *quince,* 1
**fifteenth: girl's fifteenth birthday** *quinceañera,* 9
**fifty** *cincuenta,* 2
**film** *la película,* 2
**to find** *encontrar (ue),* 7; *to find a hobby* **buscar un pasatiempo,** 7
**fine** *bien,* 1; **I'm fine** *Estoy bien,* 1
**finger** *el dedo,* 7
**finish** *terminar,* 9
**fireworks** *los fuegos artificiales,* 9
**first** *el primero,* 1
**first** (adj) *primero(a),* 4
**fish** *el pescado,* 6
**to fish** *pescar,* 10
**fishing** *la pesca,* 10; **to go fishing** *ir de pesca,* 10
**to fit** *quedar,* 8; **How does it fit?** *¿Cómo me queda?,* 8
**five** *cinco,* 1
**five hundred** *quinientos,* 8
**flight** *el vuelo,* 10
**floor** *el piso,* 5
**folder** *la carpeta,* 4
**to follow** *seguir (i),* 10
**food** *la comida,* 2; **Chinese (Italian, Mexican) food** *la comida china (italiana, mexicana),* 2, **food court in a mall** *la plaza (terraza) de comida,* 8
**foot** *el pie,* 7
**football** *el fútbol americano,* 3
**for** *para,* 4
**for example** *por ejemplo,* 6G
**fork** *el tenedor,* 6
**formidable** *formidable,* 2
**fortune** *la fortuna,* 8
**forty** *cuarenta,* 2
**four** *cuatro,* 1
**four hundred** *cuatrocientos,* 8
**fourteen** *catorce,* 1
**French** *el francés,* 4
**French fries** *las papas fritas,* 6
**frequency** *la frecuencia,* 8
**Friday** *el viernes,* 1; **on Fridays** *los viernes,* 3
**friend** *el amigo* (male), *la amiga* (female), 1
**from** *de,* 1
**fruit** *la fruta,* 2
**fun** *divertido(a),* 2; **What fun!** *¡Qué divertido!,* 10
**funny** *cómico(a),* 2

**to gain weight** *subir de peso,* 7
**game: board game** *el juego de mesa,* 3; **the . . . game** *el partido de...,* 4
**garage** *el garaje,* 5
**garden** *el jardín,* 5
**German** *el alemán,* 4
**to get angry** *enojarse,* 7
**to get dressed** *vestirse (i),* 7
**to get off a plane** *desembarcar,* 10
**to get someone for a telephone call,** *pasartelo(la),* 8
**to get together** *reunirse,* 9
**to get up** *levantarse,* 7
**to get** *conseguir (i, i),* 10
**gift** *el regalo,* 9
**girl** *la muchacha,* 1
**girl's fifteenth birthday** *la quinceañera,* 9

**to give** *dar*, 7; **don't give** *no des*, 7
**glass** *el vaso*, 6
**glasses** *los lentes*, 5; **to wear glasses** *usar lentes*, 5
**go** *ve*, 6
**to go** *ir*, 2; **Where did you go?** *¿Adónde fuiste?*, 8; **to go shopping** *ir de compras*, 2; **to go to the movies** *ir al cine*, 3; **to go hiking** *ir de excursión*, 10; **don't go** *no vayas*, 7; **I want to go . . .** *Quiero ir...*, 3; **Are you going to the . . .?** *¿Vas a...?*, 4; **You're going to go, aren't you?** *Vas a ir, ¿verdad?*, 4
**to go back** *regresar*, 4; *volver (ue)*, 5
**to go for a walk** *pasear*, 3
**go out** *sal*, 6
**to go out** *salir*, 3; **to go out with friends** *salir con amigos*, 3; **to go out in a sailboat (motorboat)** *pasear en bote de vela (lancha)*, 10
**to go to bed** *acostarse (ue)*, 7
**good** *bueno(a)*, 2; **Good evening., Good night.** *Buenas noches.*, 1; **Good afternoon.** *Buenas tardes.*, 1; **Good morning.** *Buenos días.*, 1
**good-looking** *guapo(a)*, 2
**Goodbye.** *Adiós.*, 1
**graduation** *la graduación*, 9
**grandchildren** *los nietos*, 5
**granddaughter** *la nieta*, 5
**grandfather** *el abuelo*, 5
**grandmother** *la abuela*, 5
**grandparents** *los abuelos*, 5
**grandson** *el nieto*, 5
**grandsons, grandchildren** *los nietos*, 5
**grass** *el césped*, 5; **to cut the grass** *cortar el césped*, 5
**gravy** *salsa*, 6
**gray** *gris*, 8
**graying** *canoso(a)*, 5
**great** *estupendo(a)*, 10; *a todo dar*, 10; **it was great** *fue estupendo*, 10
**green** *verde*, 5
**greeting card** *la tarjeta*, 8
**guest** *el (la) invitado(a)*, 9
**guitar** *la guitarra*, 2
**gym** *el gimnasio*, 3

**hair** *el pelo*, 5; **to comb your hair** *peinarse*, 7; **hair dryer** *la secadora de pelo*, 7
**half** *medio*, 1; **half past** *y media*, 1
**ham** *el jamón*, 6
**hamburger** *la hamburguesa*, 2
**hand** *la mano*, 7
**hang** *colgar (ue)*, 9
**Hanukkah** *el Hanukah*, 9
**happy** *contento(a)*, 7; **to be happy** *estar contento(a)*, 7
**Happy (Merry) . . .** *¡Feliz...!*, 9
**hard** *difícil*, 4
**hard-working** *trabajador(a)*, 2
**hat** *el sombrero*, 8
**to have** *tener (-go, ie)*, 4; **have** *ten*, 6; **don't have** *no tengas*, 10; **to have a cold** *tener catarro*, 7; **to have a milkshake** *tomar un batido*, 8; **to have a picnic** *tener un picnic*, 9; **to have blue eyes** *tener los ojos azules*, 5; **to have to do something** *tener que + infinitive*, 4; **I have to . . .** *A mí me toca...*, 5
**to have a party** *hacer una fiesta*, 9; **to have a snack** *merendar*, 5; **to have lunch** *almorzar*, 5
**he** *él*, 1; **He is . . .** *Él es...*, 1
**head** *la cabeza*, 7
**health** *la salud*, 7
**heat** *el calor*, 3
**to heat** *calentar (ie)*, 6
**Hello.** *Aló.*; *Bueno.*; *Diga.*, 8
**help** *la ayuda*, 6; **to help out at home** *ayudar en casa*, 5
**hi, hello** *hola*, 1
**hike** *la excursión*, 10; **to go on a hike** *ir de excursión*, 10
**his** *su(s)*, 5
**history** *la historia*, 4
**hobby** *el pasatiempo*, 7; **to look for a hobby** *buscar un pasatiempo*, 7
**holiday** *el día festivo*, 9
**Holy Week** *la Semana Santa*, 9
**homework** *la tarea*, 3
**Hope things go well for you.** *Que te vaya bien.*, 9
**horrible** *horrible*, 2; **It was horrible!** *¡Fue horrible!*, 10
**horror** *el terror*, 2
**hot** *caliente*, 6; **hot sauce** *la salsa picante*, 6
**hot chocolate** *el chocolate*, 6
**hotel** *el hotel*, 10; **to stay in a hotel** *quedarse en un hotel*, 10
**hour** *la hora*, 1
**house** *casa*, 5; **. . .'s house** *la casa de...*, 3; **to decorate the house** *decorar la casa*, 9
**household chores** *los quehaceres*, 5
**how** *¿cómo?*, 1; **How are you?** *¿Cómo está(s)?*, 1; **How do you spell . . .** *¿Cómo se escribe...?*, 1; **How does it fit?** *¿Cómo me queda?*, 8; **How fantastic!** *¡Qué fantástico!*, 10; **How great!** *¡Qué bien!*, 10; **How many . . .** *¿cuántos(as)?*, 2; **how much?** *¿cuánto(a)?*, 4; **How often do you go . . .?** *¿Con qué frecuencia vas...?*, 3; **How old are you?** *¿Cuántos años tienes?*, 2
**hunger** *el hambre*, 4
**hungry, to be** *tener hambre*, 4
**to hurt** *doler (ue)*, 7; **My . . . hurt(s)** *Me duele(n)...*, 7; **Does something hurt?** *¿Te duele algo?*, 7

**ID** *carnet de identidad*, 10
**I** *yo*, 1
**I agree.** *Estoy de acuerdo*, 6; **I don't agree.** *No estoy de acuerdo.*, 6
**I have no idea.** *Ni idea.*, 3
**I have to go.** *Tengo que irme.*, 1
**I want to see . . .** *Quiero conocer...*, 10
**I would like . . .** *Quisiera...*, 6
**I'd like you to meet . . .** *Te presento a...*, 9
**I'll get him (her).** *Ya te lo (la) paso.*, 8
**I'm fine.** *Estoy bien.*, 1
**I'm sorry** *lo siento*, 8
**I'm . . .** *Soy...*, 2; **I'm from** *Soy de...*, 1
**I'm just looking.** *Nada más estoy mirando.*, 8
**I'm not so good.** *Estoy mal.*, 1
**ice cream** *el helado*, 2
**ice cream shop** *la heladería*, 8
**Independence Day** *El Día de la Independencia*, 9
**in front of** *delante de*, 5
**in the (latest) fashion** *a la (última) moda*, 8
**in, by** *por*, 4
**inexpensive** *barato(a)*, 8
**intellectual** *intelectual*, 2
**intelligent** *inteligente*, 2
**interest** *el interés*, 10
**interesting** *interesante*, 2
**to interrupt** *interrumpir*, 4
**to introduce** *presentar*, 9
**invitation** *la invitación*, 9
**to invite** *invitar*, 9
**island** *la isla*, 10
**it** *lo, la*, 6
**It seems all right/fine to me.** *Me parece bien.*, 5
**it snows** *nieva*, 3
**It's (a little) salty.** *Está (un poco) salado*, 6
**It's a rip-off!** *¡Es un robo!*, 8
**It's all the same to me.** *Me da igual.*, 2
**It's awful.** *Es pésimo.*, 2
**It's cold.** *Hace frío.*, 3
**It's cool.** *Hace fresco.*, 3
**It's delicious.** *Es delicioso.*, 2
**It's hot.** *Hace calor.*, 3
**It's kind of fun.** *Es algo divertido.*, 2
**It's not a big deal.** *No es gran cosa*, 5
**It's okay.** *Está bien.*, 3

It's pretty good/bad. *Es bastante bueno(a)/malo(a).*, 2
It's sunny. *Hace sol.*, 3
It's windy. *Hace viento.*, 3

**jacket** *la chaqueta*, 8; *el saco*, 8
**January** *enero*, 1
**jeans** *los vaqueros*, 8
**jewelry store** *la joyería*, 8
**job** *el trabajo*, 3
**joke** *el chiste*, 9; **to tell jokes** *contar chistes*, 9
**juice** *el jugo*, 6
**July** *julio*, 1
**June** *junio*, 1
**to just (have done something)** *acabar de*, 7

**kitchen** *la cocina*, 5
**knife** *el cuchillo*, 6
**to know** (facts) *saber*, 4; **I don't know** *no sé*, 4; **to know people** *conocer*, 9

**lake** *el lago*, 10
**large** *grande*, 6
**last** *pasado(a)*, 8; **last night** *anoche*, 9
**late** *tarde*, 4; **later** *más tarde*, 8; **latest** *último(a)*, 8
**lazy** *perezoso(a)*, 2
**to leave** *irse*, 10; *dejar*, 10; *salir*, 3; **leave** *sal*, 6; **to leave a message** *dejar un recado*, 8; **don't leave** *no salgas*, 10
**leg** *la pierna*, 7
**letter** *la carta*, 3
**library** *la biblioteca*, 4
**lift** *levantar*, 7; **to lift weights** *levantar pesas*, 7
**to like** *gustar*, 2; **I (you, . . .) like** *Me (te,...) gusta(n)*, 2; **I would like . . .**, *me gustaría*, 10; **My friends and I like . . .** *A mis amigos y a mí nos gusta...*, 3; **They like . . .** *A ellos/ellas les gusta...*, 3
**Likewise.** *Igualmente.*, 1
**line** *la cola*, 10; **to wait in line** *hacer cola*, 10
**to listen** *escuchar*, 3; **to listen to music** *escuchar música*, 3
**little** (adv.) *poco*, 2; **a little** *un poco*, 2
**live** *vivir*, 5
**living room** *la sala*, 5
**long** *largo(a)*, 5; **Long time no see.** *¡Tanto tiempo sin verte!*, 9
**to look** *mirar*, 8
**to look for** *buscar*, 7
**to lose weight** *bajar de peso*, 7
**to lose** *perder*, 10
**luck** *la suerte*, 10
**luggage** *el equipaje*, 10
**lunch** *el almuerzo*, 4; *la comida*, 6; **to have lunch** *almorzar*, 5

**ma'am; Mrs.** *la señora*, 1
**magazine** *la revista*, 3
**mail** *el correo*, 7
**to maintain** *mantenerse(ie)*, 7; **to stay in shape** *mantenerse en forma*, 7
**to make** *hacer*, 4; **make** *haz*, 6; **to make the bed** *hacer la cama*, 5
**makeup** *el maquillaje*, 7
**mall** *el centro comercial*, 3
**man** *el hombre*, 6; **for men** *para hombres*, 8
**many** *muchos (as)*, 4
**map** *el mapa*, 10
**March** *marzo*, 1
**Mass** *la misa*, 9
**mathematics** *las matemáticas*, 4
**May** *mayo*, 1
**me** *mí*, 5; *me*, 9
**meat** *la carne*, 6
**to meet** *encontrarse (ue)*, 10
**meeting** *la reunión*, 3
**Merry . . .** *¡Feliz...!*, 9
**message** *el recado*, 8
**microwave** *el (horno) microondas*, 6
**midday, noon** *el mediodía*, 1
**midnight** *la medianoche*, 1
**milk** *la leche*, 6
**milkshake** *el batido*, 8
**million** *un millón de*, 8
**mischievous** *travieso(a)*, 5
**Miss** *la señorita*, 1
**to miss** *perder(ie)*, 10
**mix** *mezclar*, 6
**mom** *la mamá*, 5
**moment** *un momento*, 8
**Monday** *lunes*, 3; **on Mondays** *los lunes*, 3
**money** *el dinero*, 8
**money exchange** *la oficina de cambio*, 10
**monitor, screen** *la pantalla*, 10
**months of the year** *los meses del año*, 1
**month** *mes*, 1
**more** *más*, 2; **more than** *más que*, 8; **more . . . than** *más... que*, 8
**morning** *la mañana*, 1; **in the morning, A.M.** *de la mañana*, 1; *por la mañana*, 4
**mother** *la madre*, 5; **Mother's Day** *El Día de la Madre*, 9
**motorboat** *la lancha*, 10; **to go out in a motorboat** *pasear en lancha*, 10
**mountain** *la montaña*, 10
**mouth** *la boca*, 7
**movie** *la película*, 2
**movie theater** *el cine*, 3
**museum** *el museo*, 10
**music** *la música*, 2; **music by. . .** *la música de*, 2
**my** *mi(s)*, 1; **my best friend** *mi mejor amigo(a)*, 1; **my favorite subject** *mi materia preferida*, 4; **my teacher** *mi profesor(-a)*, 1
**mystery** *el misterio*, 2

**napkin** *la servilleta*, 6
**neck** *el cuello*, 7
**to need** *necesitar*, 4
**neither, not either** *tampoco*, 5; *ni*, 7
**nephew** *el sobrino*, 5
**nervous** *nervioso(a)*, 7; **to be nervous** *estar nervioso(a)*, 7
**never** *nunca*, 5; **almost never** *casi nunca*, 3
**New Year's Eve** *la Nochevieja*, 9
**next** *próximo(a)*, 4; **next to** *al lado de*, 5
**nice** *simpático(a)*, 2; **Nice to meet you.** *Encantado(a)*, 1; *Mucho gusto.*, 1
**niece** *la sobrina*, 5
**night** *la noche*, 1; **at night, P.M** *de la noche*, 1; *por la noche*, 4
**nine** *nueve*, 1
**nine hundred** *novecientos*, 8
**nineteen** *diecinueve*, 1
**ninety** *noventa*, 2
**no** *no*, 3
**nobody, not anybody** *nadie*, 5
**noon** *mediodía*, 1
**nor** *ni*, 7
**nose** *la nariz*, 7
**not yet** *todavía no*, 10
**notebook** *el cuaderno*, 4
**nothing** *nada*, 4
**novel** *la novela*, 2
**November** *noviembre*, 1
**now** *ahora*, 9
**nowhere** *ninguna parte*, 3
**number** *el número*, 1

**October** *octubre*, 1
**Of course!** *¡Claro que sí!*, 4
**of the** *del, de la, de las, de los*, 2
**of** *de*, 1
**office: post office** *oficina de correos*, 10
**often** *a menudo*, 5

**Oh, no!** *¡Ay, no!*, 6
**Okay.** *Vale.*, 9
**old** *viejo(a)*, 5
**older** *mayor(es)*, 5
**on the dot** *en punto*, 1
**on time** *a tiempo*, 4
**on top of, above** *encima de*, 5
**one** *uno*, 1
**one hundred** *cien*, 2
**one hundred one** *ciento uno*, 8
**one million** *millón (de)*, 8
**one thousand** *mil*, 8
**only** *sólo*, 7; *no más*, 8
**to open** *abrir*, 4; **to open gifts** *abrir regalos*, 9
**or** *o*, 2
**orange** *la naranja*, 6; *anaranjado(a)*, 8
**to order** *pedir (i)*, 6
**to organize** *organizar*, 10
**our** *nuestro(a)(s)*, 5
**out of style** *pasado(a) de moda*, 8
**outgoing** *extrovertido(a)*, 2
**oven** *el horno*, 6
**overcoat** *el abrigo*, 8

**to pack your suitcase** *hacer la maleta*, 10
**pain: What a pain!** *¡Que lata!*, 5
**pair** *el par*, 8
**pajamas** *el piyama*, 7
**pants (jeans)** *los pantalones*, 7
**paper** *el papel*, 4
**parents** *los padres*, 5
**park** *el parque*, 3; **amusement park** *el parque de diversiones*, 10
**party, to have a** *hacer una fiesta*, 9; **surprise party** *la fiesta de sorpresa*, 9
**pass: boarding pass** *la tarjeta de embarque*, 10
**passenger** *el pasajero, la pasajera*, 10
**passport** *el pasaporte*, 10
**pastry** *el pan dulce*, 6
**patio** *el patio*, 5
**to pay** *pagar*, 8
**peach** *el durazno*, 6
**pen** *el bolígrafo*, 4
**pencil** *el lápiz (pl. los lápices)*, 4
**person** *la persona*, 2
**photo** *la foto*, 9; **to show photos** *enseñar fotos*, 9; **to take photos** *sacar fotos*, 10
**physical education** *la educación física*, 4
**to pick up** *recoger*, 10
**picnic** *el picnic*, 9
**piñata** *la piñata*, 9
**pizza** *la pizza*, 2
**place** *el lugar*, 10
**plane ticket** *el boleto de avión*, 10
**plans** *los planes*, 9
**plants** *las plantas*, 5
**plate** *el plato*, 6
**to play an instrument** *tocar*, 3; **to play the piano** *tocar el piano*, 3
**to play a game or sport** *jugar (ue)*, 3
**to play sports** *practicar deportes*, 3
**please** *por favor*, 6
**Pleased to meet you.** *Encantado(a).*, 1; *Mucho gusto.*, 1
**pool** *la piscina*, 3
**porch** *el patio*, 5
**post office** *la oficina de correos*, 10
**potato** *la papa*, 6; **potato chips** *las papitas*, 9
**practice** *el entrenamiento*, 3
**to prefer** *preferir (ie)*, 6
**preparations** *los preparativos*, 9
**to prepare** *preparar*, 6
**pretty** *bonito(a)*, 2
**pretty** + adjective *bastante* + adjective, 2
**punch** *el ponche*, 9
**purple** *morado(a)*, 8
**purse** *la bolsa*, 8
**to put** *poner*, 4; **put** *pon*, 6; **don't put** *no pongas*, 10; **to put on makeup** *maquillarse*, 7; **to put on** *ponerse*, 7
**pyramid** *la pirámide, 10*

**quarter past (the hour)** *y cuarto*, 1
**quarter to (the hour)** *menos cuarto*, 4
**quiet** *callado(a)*, 5
**quite** + adjective *bastante* + adjective, 2

**to rain** *llover (ue)*, 3; **It rains a lot.** *Llueve mucho.*, 3
**rather** *bastante* + adjective, 2
**razor** *la navaja*, 7
**to read** *leer*, 3; **to read magazines and novels** *leer revistas y novelas*, 3
**ready** *listo(a)*, 7; **to be ready** *estar listo(a)*, 7
**to receive** *recibir*, 9; **to receive gifts** *recibir regalos*, 9
**red** *rojo(a)*, 8
**red-headed** *pelirrojo(a)*, 2
**refrigerator** *el refrigerador*, 6
**rehearsal** *el ensayo*, 3
**to relax** *relajarse*, 7
**to rent** *alquilar*, 3; **to rent videos** *alquilar videos*, 3
**to rest** *descansar*, 3
**restaurant** *el restaurante*, 6
**restroom** *el baño*, 5; *el servicio*, 10
**to return, to go back** *regresar*, 4; *volver*, 5
**rice** *el arroz*, 6
**to ride a bike** *montar en bicicleta*, 3
**right?** *¿no?*, 4; *¿verdad?*, 4; **to be right** *tener razón*, 8
**ring** *el anillo*, 8
**rip off** *el robo*, 8
**romance book** *el libro de amor*, 2
**romantic** *romántico(a)*, 2
**room** *el cuarto*, 5
**ruins** *las ruinas*, 10
**rule** *la regla*, 4
**to run** *correr*, 3

**sad** *triste*, 7; **to be sad** *estar triste*, 7
**sailboat** *el bote de vela*, 10; **to go out in a sailboat** *pasear en bote de vela*, 10
**salad** *la ensalada*, 6
**salesclerk** *el dependiente, la dependiente*, 8
**salty** *salado(a)*, 6; **It's (a little) salty.** *Está (un poco) salado(a).*, 6
**same as usual** *lo de siempre*, 9
**sandals** *las sandalias*, 8
**sandwich** *el sándwich*, 6
**Saturday** *el sábado*, 1; **on Saturdays** *los sábados*, 3
**sauce, gravy** *la salsa*. 6; **hot sauce** *la salsa picante*, 6
**to save: to save money** *ahorrar dinero*, 8
**school** *el colegio*, 3
**school supplies** *los útiles escolares*, 4
**science** *las ciencias*, 4; **science fiction** *la ciencia ficción*, 2; **computer science** *la computación*, 4
**security checkpoint** *el control de seguridad*, 10
**to see** *ver*, 4; **See you tomorrow.** *Hasta mañana.*, 1; **See you.** *Nos vemos.*, 1
**to seem** *parecer*, 5
**to sell** *vender*, 8
**to send** *mandar*, 9
**September** *septiembre*, 1
**serious** *serio(a)*, 2
**to serve** *servir (i)*, 6
**to set** *poner (-go)*, 6; **to set the table** *poner la mesa*, 6
**seven** *siete*, 1
**seven hundred** *setecientos*, 8
**seventeen** *diecisiete*, 1
**seventy** *setenta*, 2
**to shave** *afeitarse*, 7

**shirt** *la camisa,* 8
**shoe store** *la zapatería,* 8
**shoes** *los zapatos,* 4; **tennis shoes** *los zapatos de tenis,* 8
**shop window** *la vitrina,* 8; **to window-shop** *mirar las vitrinas,* 8; **to go shopping** *ir de compras,* 2
**short** (height) *bajo(a), 2;* (length) *corto(a),* 5
**shorts** *los pantalones cortos,* 8
**should** *deber,* 6
**shoulder** *el hombro,* 7
**to show** *enseñar,* 4; **to show photos** *enseñar fotos,* 9
**shy** *tímido(a),* 2
**sick: to be** *estar enfermo(a),* 7
**silk** la seda, 8
**silly** *tonto(a),* 3
**to sing** *cantar,* 3
**sir, Mr.** *el señor,* 1
**sister** *la hermana,* 5
**to sit down** *sentarse (ie),* 10
**six** *seis,* 1
**six hundred** *seiscientos,* 8
**sixteen** *dieciséis,* 1
**sixty** *sesenta,* 2
**size,** *la talla,* 8
**to skate** *patinar,* 3
**to ski** *esquiar,* 10; **to water-ski** *esquiar en el agua,* 10
**skirt** *la falda,* 8
**to sleep** *dormir (ue),* 5; **to get enough sleep** *dormir lo suficiente,* 7
**small** *pequeño(a),* 5; **pretty small** *bastante pequeño,* 5
**to smoke** *fumar,* 7; **to stop smoking** *dejar de fumar,* 7
**to snack** *merendar (ie),* 5
**to snow** *nevar (ie),* 3
**so-so** *más o menos,* 1
**so much** *tanto,* 7
**soap** *el jabón,* 7
**soccer** *el fútbol,* 3
**socks** *los calcetines,* 8; **a pair of socks** *un par de calcetines,* 8
**sofa** *el sofá,* 5
**soft drink** *el refresco,* 6
**some** *unos(as),* 4
**some day** *algún día,* 10
**something** *algo,* 4
**sometimes** *a veces,* 3
**son** *el hijo,* 5
**soup** *la sopa,* 6; **vegetable soup** *la sopa de verduras,* 6
**Spanish** *el español,* 1
**to speak** *hablar,* 3
**to spend time alone** *pasar el rato solo(a),* 3
**to spend** (money) *gastar,* 8; (time) *pasar,* 9
**spicy** *picante,* 6
**spinach** *las espinacas,* 6
**spoon** *la cuchara,* 6
**sports** *los deportes,* 2
**spring** *la primavera,* 3
**stadium** *el estadio,* 4
**to start** *empezar (ie),* 5; *comenzar (ie),* 10; **to start a trip** *comenzar un viaje,* 10
**to stay** *quedarse,* 10; **to stay in shape** *mantenerse (-go, ie) en forma,* 7
**stomach** *el estómago,* 7
**to stop doing something** *dejar de + infinitive,* 7
**store** *la tienda de...,* 8
**story** *el piso,* 5; **. . . story building** *el edificio de . . .pisos,* 5
**to stretch** *estirarse,* 7
**student** *el estudiante, la estudiante,* 1
**to study** *estudiar,* 3
**style** *la moda,* 8; **in the latest style** *a la última moda* 8; **out of style** *pasado de moda,* 8
**subject** *la materia,* 4
**suburbs** *las afueras,* 5
**subway** *el metro,* 10
**suitcase** *la maleta,* 10
**summer** *el verano,* 3
**to sunbathe** *tomar el sol,* 10
**Sunday** *el domingo,* 1; **on Sundays** *los domingos,* 3
**supplies: school supplies** *los materiales escolares,* 4
**to surf the Internet** *navegar por Internet,* 7
**surprise party** *la fiesta de sorpresa,* 9
**sweater** *el suéter,* 8
**sweet** *dulce,* 7
**to swim** *nadar,* 3
**swimsuit** *el traje de baño,* 8
**synagogue** *la sinagoga,* 9

**table** *la mesa,* 5
**to take care of** *cuidar,* 5; **to take care of oneself** *cuidarse,* 7; **Take care.** *Cuídate.,* 9
**to take off** *quitarse,* 7
**to take out** *sacar,* 6; **to take out the trash** *sacar la basura,* 5
**to take** *tomar,* 9; **to take photos** *sacar photos,* 10; **to take a test** *presentar el examen,* 4
**to talk** *hablar,* 3
**tall** *alto(a),* 2
**tamales** *los tamales,* 9
**to taste** *probar (ue),* 6
**taxi** *el taxi,* 10
**teacher** *la profesora* **(female),** *el profesor* **(male),** 1
**teeth** *los dientes,* 7
**telephone number** *el teléfono,* 1
**television** *la televisión,* 3; **to watch TV** *mirar la televisión,* 3
**to tell jokes** *contar chistes,* 9
**temple** *el templo,* 9
**ten** *diez,* 1
**tennis** *el tenis,* 3; **tennis shoes** *los zapatos de tenis,* 8
**test** *el examen,* 4; **to take a . . . test** *presentar el examen de...,* 4
**Thanksgiving Day** *el Día de Acción de Gracias,* 9
**thank you** *gracias,* 1
**that** *ese(a),* 8
**the** *el, la, los, las,* 2
**their** *su(s),* 5
**them** *los, las,* 6
**then** *luego,* 4
**there** *allí,* 10
**there is, there are** *hay,* 4
**these** *estos, estas,* 8
**they** *ellas, ellos,* 1
**They like to . . .** *A ...les gusta...,* 3
**thin** *delgado(a),* 5
**thing** *la cosa,* 4
**to think** *pensar (ie),* 8
**thirst** *la sed,* 4
**thirteen** *trece,* 1
**thirty** *treinta,* 1
**this** *ésta, éste,* 1; **this** *este(a),* 8; **this weekend** *este fin de semana,* 4
**those** *esos, esas,* 8
**three** *tres,* 1
**three hundred** *trescientos,* 8
**throat** *la garganta,* 7
**Thursday** *el jueves,* 1; **on Thursdays** *los jueves,* 3
**ticket** *el boleto,* 10; **plane ticket** *el boleto de avión,* 10
**time** *el rato,* 3
**tired** *cansado(a),* 7; **to be tired** *estar cansado,* 7
**to/for me** *me,* 2; **you** *te,* 2; **us** *nos,* 2; **him, her, you, them** *le(s),* 2
**toast** *el pan tostado,* 6
**today** *hoy,* 1
**tomato** *el tomate,* 6
**tomorrow** *mañana,* 4
**ton: a ton of** *un montón de,* 4
**too much** *demasiado(a),* 7
**toothbrush** *el cepillo de dientes,* 7
**toothpaste** *la pasta de dientes,* 7
**to tour** *recorrer,* 10
**towel** *la toalla,* 7
**town** *el pueblo,* 5
**toy** *el juguete,* 8
**toy store** *la juguetería,* 8
**train** *el tren,* 10
**trash** *la basura,* 5
**to travel** *viajar,* 10
**trip** *el viaje,* 10
**to try, taste** *probar (ue),* 6
**T-shirt** *la camiseta,* 8
**Tuesday** *el martes,* 1; **on Tuesdays** *los martes,* 3
**tuna** *el atún,* 6

**turnover-like pastry** *la empanada,* 9
**twelve** *doce,* 1
**twenty** *veinte,* 1
**two** *dos,* 1
**two hundred** *doscientos,* 8
**two thousand** *dos mil,* 8

**ugly** *feo(a),* 2
**uncle** *el tío,* 5
**under, underneath** *debajo (de),* 5
**to understand** *entender,* 5
**unfair** *injusto,* 5
**unfriendly** *antipático(a),* 2
**until** *hasta,* 5; **See you later.** *Hasta luego.,* 1; **See you tomorrow.** *Hasta mañana.,* 1; **See you soon.** *Hasta pronto.,* 1
**up to** *hasta,* 5
**us** *nos,* 2; *nosotros(as),* 3
**usual: the usual** *lo de siempre,* 9

**to vacuum** *pasar la aspiradora,* 5
**vacuum cleaner** *la aspiradora,* 4
**Valentine's Day** *el Día de los Enamorados,* 9
**vegetables** *las verduras,* 2
**very** *muy + adjective,* 2
**very bad** *pésimo(a),* 2
**video** *el video,* 3
**video games** *los videojuegos,* 2
**village** *el pueblo,* 5
**volleyball** *el volibol,* 3

**to wait** *esperar,* 8
**waiting room** *la sala de espera,* 10
**to wake** *despertarse (ie),* 7
**to walk** *caminar,* 7; **to go for a walk** *pasear,* 3
**wallet** *la billetera,* 10
**to want** *querer (ie),* 3
**to wash** *lavar,* 5; *lavarse,* 7
**watch, clock** *el reloj,* 4
**to watch** *ver,* 4; **to watch television** *ver televisión,* 3
**water** *el agua (f.),* 6; **to water ski** *esquiar en el agua,* 10
**we** *nosotros(as),* 1
**to wear** *llevar,* 8; **to wear glasses** *usar lentes,* 5
**weather** *el tiempo,* 3; **The weather is nice (bad).** *Hace buen (mal) tiempo.,* 3
**wedding** *la boda,* 9
**Wednesday** *el miércoles,* 1; **on Wednesdays** *los miércoles,* 3
**week** *la semana,* 4
**weekend** *el fin de semana,* 3; **weekends** *los fines de semana,* 3
**weight** el peso, 7; **to gain weight** *subir de peso,* 7; **to lose weight** *bajar de peso,* 7
**weights** *las pesas,* 7; **to lift weights** *levantar pesas,* 7
**What?** *¿Cómo?, ¿Qué?,* 1; **What a pain!** *¡Qué lata!,* 5; **What a shame!** *¡Qué lástima!,* 10; **What are you going to do?** *¿Qué vas a hacer?,* 7; **What bad luck!** *¡Qué mala suerte!,* 10; **What fun!** *¡Qué divertido!,* 10; **What are you like?** *¿Cómo eres?,* 2; **What day is today?** *¿Qué día es hoy?,* 1; **What did you do?** *¿Qué hiciste?,* 8; **What do you do to help out at home?** *¿Qué haces para ayudar en casa?,* 5; **What do you do to relax?** *¿Qué haces para relajarte?,* 7; **What do you have to do?** *¿Qué tienes que hacer?,* 7; **What do you like to do?** *¿Qué te gusta hacer?,* 3; **What do you still have to do?** *¿Qué te falta hacer?,* 7; **What do you want to do?** *¿Qué quieres hacer?,* 3; **What does . . . do?** *¿Qué hace...?,* 3; **What is . . . like?** *¿Cómo es...?,* 2; **What plans do you have for . . .?** *¿Qué planes tienen para...?,* 9; **What time are you going to. . .?** *¿A qué hora vas a...?,* 4; **What time is it?** *¿Qué hora es?,* 3; **What is . . .'s e-mail address?** *¿Cuál es el correo electrónico de...?,* 1; **What's . . . telephone number?** *¿Cuál es el teléfono de...?,* 1; **what?, which?** *¿cuál?,* 4; **What's his (her, your) name?** *¿Cómo se llama?,* 1; **What's new?** *¿Qué hay de nuevo?,* 9; **What's the matter with . . .?** *¿Qué tiene...?,* 7; **What's the weather like?** *¿Qué tiempo hace?,* 3; **What's today's date?** *¿Qué fecha es hoy?,* 1; **What's wrong with you?** *¿Qué te pasa?,* 7; **What's your name?** *¿Cómo te llamas?,* 1
**wheelchair** *la silla de ruedas,* 5; **to be in a wheelchair** *estar en una silla de ruedas,* 5
**when** *cuando,* 3
**when?** *¿cuándo?,* 2
**Where did you go?** *¿Adónde fuiste?,* 8
**where?** *¿dónde?,* 5; **Where can I . . .?** *¿Dónde se puede...?,* 10; **Where do you go?** *¿Adónde vas?,* 3; **Where did you go?** *¿Adónde fuiste?,* 8; **from where** *de dónde,* 1
**white** *blanco(a),* 8
**whole** *todo(a),* 9
**Who's calling?** *¿De parte de quién?,* 8
**Who is . . .?** *¿Quién es...?,* 1
**why** *¿por qué?,* 2
**window** *la ventana,* 5; **to window-shop** *mirar las vitrinas,* 8
**winter** *el invierno,* 3
**to wish for** *desear,* 6
**with** *con,* 3
**with me** *conmigo,* 3
**with you** *contigo,* 3
**witty** *gracioso(a),* 2
**woman** *la mujer,* 5
**wool** *la lana,* 8; **made of wool** *de lana,* 8
**work** *trabajar,* 3; *el trabajo,* 4
**to work out** *entrenarse,* 7
**workshop** *el taller,* 4
**to worry** *preocuparse,* 10; **Don't worry.** *No te preocupes.,* 10
**worse** *peor(es),* 8
**to write** *escribir,* 1; **How do you spell . . .?** *¿Cómo se escribe...?,* 1; **It's spelled . . .** *Se escribe,* 1

**yard** *el patio,* 5
**year** *el año,* 2; **New Year** *el Año Nuevo,* 9; **last year** *el año pasado,* 9
**yellow** *amarillo(a),* 8
**yes** *sí,* 4; **Yes, I need a lot of things.** *Sí, necesito muchas cosas.,* 4; **Yes, I have a ton of them.** *Sí, tengo un montón.,* 4
**yesterday** *ayer,* 8
**yoga: to do yoga** *hacer yoga,* 7
**you** *usted, ustedes* (formal), 1; *tú, vosotros(as)* (informal), 1; **You were lucky!** *Ah, ¡tuviste suerte!,* 10
**young** *joven,* 5
**young people** *los jóvenes,* 9
**younger** *menor(es),* 5
**your** *tu(s), su(s), vuestro(a)(s),* 5

**zero** *cero,* 1
**zoo** *el zoológico,* 10

# Índice gramatical

Page numbers in boldface type refer to the first presentation of the topic. Other page numbers refer to grammar structures presented in the **¡Exprésate!** features, subsequent references to the topic, or reviewed in **Repaso de Gramática.** Page numbers beginning with R refer to the **Síntesis gramatical** in this Reference Section (pages R15–R22).

**a:** for clarification **70,** 102; with pronouns **102,** 130; after **ir** or **jugar 116;** combined with **el** to form **al 116;** with time **150,** 176; with **empezar: 196;** with infinitives **160,** 176, 196
**abrir: 162**
accent marks: **26,** 38
adjectives: function of **54,** 84; agreement with nouns–masculine and feminine **56,** 84, R16; singular and plural **56,** 84, R16; placement **146;** possessive adjectives all forms **192,** 222, R16
**adónde: 116,** R18; see also question words
adverbs: adverbs of frequency **112,** R18; adverbs of sequence **144;** adverbs of time **20**
agreement: nouns and adjectives **56,** 84, 192, R16; nouns and definite articles **68,** 84, R16; nouns and indefinite articles **146,** R15; nouns and possessive adjectives **192,** R16; see also adjectives
**al: 116**
**almorzar: 194,** R24; all present tense forms **222**
**-ar** verbs: regular present tense **114,** 130, 194, R18; see also verbs
articles: definite **el, la, los, las 68,** 70, 160; indefinite **un, una, unos, unas 146,** 176
**asistir: 162**

**beber: 162**

calendar expressions: dates, days of the week, months **21**
**comer: 100,** 114; all present tense forms **162,** 176, 194
**cómo: 58,** 84, R17; see also question words
**con:** with pronouns **102,** 130; see also prepositions
conjunctions: **porque 70**
**conmigo, contigo: 102**
contractions: **al 116,** R15; **del 72,** 116, R15
**correr: 162**
**cuál:** 19, 23, 58, R17; see also question words
**cuándo: 58,** 84, R17; see also question words
**cuánto:** agreement with nouns **146,** 176, R17; see also question words

dates (calendar): **21**
days of the week: **21,** 160
**de:** used in showing possession or ownership **72,** 84, 192; to indicate a type of thing **72,** 143; to say where someone is from 12, **72;** with **el 72;** with pronouns **102;** used as a preposition 102, 130, **164;** with **salir** and **saber 164; de** + person **192;** see also prepositions
definite articles: **el, la, los, las 68,** 70, 84, 160
**del:** contraction of **de** + **el 72,** 116, R15
**dormir:** all present tense forms **194**

**el: 68,** 70; with weekdays **160;** see also definite articles
**empezar: 196,** 222; **empezar a** + infinitive **196;** see also verbs
**en:** with pronouns **102,** 130
**-er** verbs: regular **-er** and **-ir** all present tense forms **162,** R18; affirmative and negative command forms R21; see also verbs
**escribir:** all present tense forms **162,** 176, 194
**estar:** all present tense forms **206,** 222; to ask how someone is and say how you are 8, **58,** 206; to tell where people and things are located **206;** with prepositions **206,** 222

frequency: adverbs of frequency **siempre 112; nunca, todos los días 112; casi nunca 112; a veces 112,** R18
future plans: expressions in the present tense **ir a** + infinitive **160,** 176

gender: adjectives: **56,** 84, R16; nouns: **56,** 68, 84, R15
**gustar:** likes and dislikes **70,** 84, 208, 210, R20; all present tense forms **70;** with infinitives **100,** 130; with **a** + pronouns **102**

**hablar: 114;** all present tense forms 130, **194**
**hacer:** all present tense forms **164;** with weather **118,** 130, R22
**hasta: 194**
**hay: 158,** 187

indefinite articles: **un, una, unos, unas 146,** 176, R15
indirect object pronouns: **me, te, le, nos, os, les 102,** 210, R16; with **a** for clarification **70**
infinitives: **100,** 104, 114, 130; with **gustar 100,** 104, 130; with **querer 104,** 130; with **empezar 196;** with **tocar 210**
interrogatives (question words) R17; **cuál** 19, 23; **cómo 58; qué 58; quién(es) 58; cuándo 58; por qué 70; adónde 116**
**interrumpir: 162**
**-ir** verbs: regular present tense **162,** R18
**ir:** all present tense forms **116,** 130, R19; **ir a** + infinitive **160,** 176
irregular verbs: **116,** 164, 176, 206, R18–R21; see also verbs

**jugar:** all present tense forms **116,** 130, 194

**la:** used as a definite article **68,** 70, R15
**la, los, las: 68,** 70, R15; see also definite articles
**leer: 162;** see also verbs
**le, les:** 70, 102, 210, R16; see also pronouns, indirect object pronouns
**llamarse: 6**
**llover: 118,** 194; see also verbs

**me:** 70, 100, 210, R16; see also pronouns, indirect object pronouns
**merendar: 196**
**mucho(a), muchos(as):** agreement with nouns **146,** 176

**nada: 208,** 222, R17
**nadie: 208,** 222, R17
**necesitar:** to express needs 141, 146
negative expressions: **no 24,** 54, 58, 70, 208, R17; **nada, nadie, nunca, tampoco 208,** 222, R17
negation: with **no** 24, 54, 58, 70, 208; **nada, nunca, nadie,** and **tampoco 208,** 222
**nevar: 118**
**nos:** indirect object pronoun **70,** 102, 210, R16
nouns: as subjects **12,** 24; replaced with pronouns **12;** masculine and feminine forms **68,** 84, R15; singular and plural forms **68,** 84, R15; with definite articles **68,** 84; used with **tener 148**
number, singular and plural: 14, **56,** 68, 70, 84, 146, 192, R16
numbers 0–31 **18;** 32–100 **52,** R17
**nunca: 208,** 222, R18; see also negative expressions or negation

**o→ue** stem-changing verbs: R19 **llover 118,** 194; **almorzar, volver 194; dormir 194**
object pronouns: indirect object pronouns **me, te, le, nos, os, les 70,** 210, R16; see also pronouns
objects of prepositions: **102,** R16; **conmigo, contigo 102;** see also prepositions
**os:** indirect object pronoun 70, **102,** 210, R16

plural nouns: 56, **68,** R15
**poco(a), pocos(as):** agreement with nouns **146,** 176
**poner:** all present tense forms **164**
**porque: 70;** see also conjunctions
**por qué: 70,** R17; see also question words
possessive adjectives: **192, 222,** R16
prepositions: **a 70,** 102, 116, 150, 196; **al 116,** R15; **de** 11, **72,** 102, 144, 164, 192; **con, conmigo, contigo 102,** 130; **al lado de, cerca de, debajo de, delante de, detrás de, encima de, lejos de 206, 222; del 72,** 116, R15; **de** with **salir, saber 164; en 102; estar** with prepositions 206, 222
present tense: **114,** R18
pronouns: replacing nouns **12,** 102; indirect object pronouns **me, te, le, nos, os, les 70,** 102, 210, R16; subject pronouns 12, **14,** 38, 54, 102, 114, 150, R16; direct object pronouns R16; after prepositions **mí, ti, él, ella, usted(es), nosotros(as) 102,** 130, R16
punctuation marks: **26,** 38

**qué: 58, 70, 84,** R17; see also question words
**querer:** all present tense forms **104,** 196; with infinitives **104,** 130; see also verbs
question formation: **58,** 70, 84, 150
question words (interrogatives): R17; **adónde 116; cuál** 19, 23, 58; **cómo 58,** 84; **cuándo 58,** 84; **de dónde** 11, **qué 58,** 70, 84; **quién(es) 58,** 84; with the preposition **a 70; por qué 70; cuánto(a), cuántos(as) 146,** 176
**quién: 58,** 84, R17; with preposition **a 70;** see also question words

regular verbs: **-ar** all present tense forms **114,** R18; **-er** and **-ir** all present tense forms **162,** R18; see also verbs

**saber:** all present tense forms **164;** with **de 164**
**salir:** all present tense forms **164;** see also verbs
**ser:** to say who someone is 6, 10, 12, **24,** 38; to identify people and things **6,** 10, 12, 38; to say where people are from **11,** 12, 24, 38; for telling day, date, and time **20,** 21, 24; to give phone numbers **24;** all present tense forms **24,** 38, 54; with adjectives **54,** 58, 84; to talk about what something is like **54,** 58; contrasted with **estar** 58, R21; see also verbs
**siempre:** as an adverb of frequency **112,** R18
stem-changing (spelling-change) verbs **e→ie** verbs: **196,** 222; **querer 104,** 196; **nevar 118; tener 148,** 196; **venir 150; empezar 196,** 222; **merendar 196,** 222; **u→ue** stem-changing verbs: **jugar 116,** 194, R19; **o→ue: llover 118,** 194; **almorzar, volver, empezar 194, 222; dormir 194, 222;** see also verbs

subjects in sentences: **12,** 38
subject pronouns: 12, **14,** 38, 102, 114, 150, R16; see also pronouns

tag questions: **¿no?, ¿verdad? 158,** 162, 176
**tampoco: 208**
**te:** indirect object pronoun 63, 70, 102, 210, R16; see also pronouns
**tener:** present tense all forms **148,** 176, 196; with age 52, 148; idioms: **tener ganas de, tener prisa, tener hambre, tener sed, tener que** + infinitive **148;** see also verbs
**tilde (~): 26**
time: adverbs of, **de la mañana, de la tarde, de la noche 20;** at what time **150;** telling time **20,** R22; see also adverbs
**tocar:** all present tense forms **210,** 222
**traer:** all present tense forms **164**
**tú** and **usted** contrasted **14,** 38; see also subject pronouns

**u→ue** stem-changing verbs: **jugar 116,** 194, R19
**una, un, unos, unas:** 146, 176, R15
**ustedes** and **vosotros** contrasted **14,** 38; see also subject pronouns

**venir:** all present tense forms **150,** 176, R18; see also verbs
**ver:** all present tense forms **164,** R18; see also verbs
verbs: in sentences **12,** 38; irregular verb **ser** 6, 10, 11, 12, **24,** 38, 49, 54, 84, R21; regular **-ar** present tense forms 114, 130, 194, R18; irregular verb **ir** all present tense forms **116,** 130, R19; **ir a** + infinitive **160,** 176; regular **-er** and **-ir** all present tense forms **162,** 194, R18; irregular verb **ver** all present tense forms **164,** R18; **e→ie** stem-changing verbs: **196; querer 104,** 130, 196, R19; **nevar 118; tener 148,** 176, 196; **venir 150,** 176; **empezar 196; merendar 196; u→ue** stem-changing verbs: R19; **jugar 116,** 130, 194; **o→ue** stem-changing verbs: R19; **llover 118,** 194; **almorzar, volver 194; dormir 194; tener 148,** 176, 196; **venir 150,** 176; **hacer 164,** 176; **poner 164,** 176; **salir 164,** 176; **traer 164,** 176; **ver 164,** 176; **saber 164,** 176; irregular verb **estar** 8, 58, **206,** R21; **e→i** stem-changing verbs R19; verbs followed by infinitives; **gustar** 100, 104, 130; **querer** 104, 130; **empezar** 196; **tocar** 210

weather: with **hacer 118,** R22; see also **hacer**

# Agradecimientos

## STAFF CREDITS

**Editorial**
Priscilla Blanton, Barbara Kristof, Amber P. Nichols, Douglas Ward

**Editorial Development Team**
Marion Bermondy, Konstanze Alex Brown, Lynda Cortez, Janet Welsh Crossley, Zahydée González, Jean Miller, Beatriz Malo Pojman, Paul Provence, Jaishree Venkatesan, J. Elisabeth Wright

**Editorial Staff**
Sara Anbari, Hubert W. Bays, Yamilé Dewailly, Milagros Escamilla, Rita Ricardo, Glenna Scott, Géraldine Touzeau-Patrick

**Editorial Permissions**
Ann B. Farrar, Yuri Muñoz

**Design**

**Book Design**
Kay Selke, Marta Kimball, Robin Bouvette, José Garza, Sally Bess, Bruce Albrecht, Liann Lech, Lana Kaupp

**Image Acquisitions**
Curtis Riker, Jeannie Taylor, Cindy Verheyden, Michelle Dike, Sam Dudgeon, Victoria Smith

**Media Design**
Richard Metzger, Chris Smith

**Cover Design**
Marc Cooper, Kay Selke

**eMedia**
Edwin Blake, Kimberly Cammerata, Grant Davidson, Nina Degollado, Lydia Doty, Cathy Kuhles, Jamie Lane, Sean McCormick, Robert Moorhead, Beth Sample, Annette Saunders, Dakota Smith, Kenneth Whiteside

**Production, Manufacturing, and Inventory**
Marleis Roberts, Diana Rodriguez, Rose Degollado, Jeffrey Atkins, Jevara Jackson, Rhonda Fariss

## ACKNOWLEDGMENTS

**HOLT, ¡EXPRÉSATE!,** and **the "Owl Design"** are trademarks licensed to Holt, Rinehart and Winston, registered in the United States of America and/or other jurisdictions.

**ExpresaVisión** and **GramaVisión** are trademarks of Holt, Rinehart and Winston.

**For permission to reprint copyrighted material, grateful acknowledgment is made to the following sources:**

***Agencia Literaria Carmen Balcells:*** From "Una antigua casa encantada" from *Mi país inventado* by Isabel Allende. Copyright © 2003 by Isabel Allende.

***Children's Book Press, San Francisco, CA:*** "Baile en el jardín" from *In My Family/En mi familia* by Carmen Lomas Garza, translated into Spanish by Francisco X. Alarcón. Text copyright © 1996 by Carmen Lomas Garza. "Tamalada" from *Family Pictures/Cuadros de familia* by Carmen Lomas Garza, translated into Spanish by Rosalma Zubizarreta. Text copyright © 1990 by Carmen Lomas Garza.

***Dover Publications, Inc.:*** From "El fracaso matemático de Pepito" from First Spanish Reader: *A Beginner's Dual-Language Book,* edited by Ángel Flores. Copyright © 1988 by Ángel Flores.

***Editorial Fundación Ross:*** "Dos buenas piernas tenemos..." and "Siempre quietas,..." from *Adivinanzas para mirar en el espejo* by Carlos Silveyra. Copyright © 1985 by Editorial Fundación Ross.

***Editorial Sudamericana S.A.:*** "2" and "16" from *Los rimaqué* by Ruth Kaufman. Copyright © 2002 by Editorial Sudamericana S.A.

***Museum of New Mexico Press:*** "Los cuatro elementos" from Cuentos: *Tales from the Hispanic Southwest,* selected and adapted in Spanish by José Griego y Maestas. Copyright © 1980 by Museum of New Mexico Press.

## PHOTOGRAPHY CREDITS

COVER PHOTOGRAPHY CREDITS

FRONT COVER (from top left to bottom right): ©Royalty-free/CORBIS; ©Kelly-Mooney Photography/CORBIS; ©Frans Lanting/Minden Pictures; ©Peter Adams/Index Stock Imagery.

BACK COVER: Gary Russ/HRW.

Abbreviations used: c-center, b-bottom, t-top, l-left, r-right, bkgd-background. Others indicate image label.

AUTHORS: page iii (Smith) Courtney Baker, courtesy Stuart Smith; (McMinn) Courtney Baker, courtesy John McMinn; (Chiquito) courtesy Ana B. Chiquito; (Madrigal Velasco) courtesy Sylvia Madrigal; (Humbach) courtesy Nancy Humbach.

TABLE OF CONTENTS: page v (br) Don Couch/HRW; vi (br) Don Couch/HRW; vi (tr) ©Guido Alberto Rossi/Getty Images/The Image Bank; vii (cr) John Langford/HRW; vii (tr) ©Dennis Degnan/CORBIS; viii (cr) Gary Russ/HRW; (t) Photo Researchers, Inc.; ix (cr) Don Couch/HRW; ix (tr) ©Buddy Mays/CORBIS; x (cr, tr) Don Couch/HRW; xi (bl) ©Dennis Degnan/CORBIS; (br) ©Buddy Mays/CORBIS.

WHY STUDY SPANISH: page xii (Argentina) ©Jeremy Woodhouse/Digital Vision; (Costa Rica) ©Buddy Mays/CORBIS; (Dominican Republic) John Langford/HRW; (Mexico) Corbis Images; (Peru, Chile) Don Couch/HRW; (Spain) Corbis Images; xiii (b) Sam Dudgeon/HRW; (br, cl) Don Couch/HRW; (bl, t) Álvaro Ortiz/HRW; (cl) ©Royalty-Free/CORBIS; (cr) Edward M. Pío Roda ® ©2003 CNN, an AOL Time Warner Co., All Rights Reserved; (t) Álvaro Ortiz/HRW (tc) John Langford/HRW; xiv xv (br) ©Image 100 Ltd.; (t) Álvaro Ortiz/HRW.

IN SPANISH CLASS: page xvi (bl) HRW Photo; (tr) ©Brand X Pictures. COMMON NAMES: xvii (bkgrd) Álvaro Ortiz/HRW. DIRECTIONS: page xviii (b) Digital Image ©2006 PhotoDisc;

xix (bl) Michael Newman/PhotoEdit; (br) Digital Image ©2006 Artville; (tl) Gabe Palmer/CORBIS; (tr) Sam Dudgeon/HRW. TIPS: page xx (b) Álvaro Ortiz/HRW; (cl) ©John Burwell/ FoodPix; (tr) ©Brand X Pictures.

CHAPTER 1 All photos by Don Couch/HRW except: page xxi (bc) Steve Vidler/SuperStock; (c) ©Guido Alberto Rossi/Getty Images/The Image Bank; (tr) ©Robert Frerck/Getty Images; 1 (bc) ©Nik Wheeler/CORBIS; (cr) ©Larry Lee Photography/ CORBIS; (tr) ©Stephen Saks/Lonely Planet Images; 2 (bl) ©Brand X Pictures; (br) Álvaro Ortiz/HRW; (cr) ©Chip & Rosa María de la Cueva Peterson; (tl) ©Robert Frerck/Odyssey Productions; (tr) Digital Image ©2006 PhotoDisc; 3 (bl) ©Christie's Images/CORBIS; (br) ©James A. Sugar/CORBIS; (cl) ©Robert Frerck/Getty Images/Stone; (cr) ©Chip & Rosa María de la Cueva Peterson; (tc) Zefa Visual Media - Germany/Index Stock Imagery, Inc.; 6 (icon) HRW photo; (l) Álvaro Ortiz/HRW; 7 (all) Álvaro Ortiz/HRW; 8 (all) Álvaro Ortiz/HRW; 10 (cr) Álvaro Ortiz/HRW; 11 (1) Christine Galida/HRW; (2) ©David H. Wells/CORBIS; (3, 4, Carolina) Marty Granger/Edge Video Productions/HRW; (5) Peter Van Steen/HRW; 12 (bl) Álvaro Ortiz/HRW; 13 (1, 4) Digital Image ©2006 PhotoDisc; (2) ©Digital Vision; (3) Marty Granger/Edge Video Productions/ HRW; 14 (l) (c)Pixtal; 15 (A, F) Victoria Smith/HRW; (B) Peter Van Steen/HRW; (C) ©COMSTOCK, Inc.; (D) ©Digital Vision; (E) ©BananaStock; 17 (b) © Jeffery Allan Salter/CORBIS; 18 (all except icon) Victoria Smith/HRW; 22 (a, b, e, h, m, p, q, z ) Corbis Images; (c, ch, f, i, k, l, ll, n, o, r, rr, t, u, w) Digital Image ©2006 PhotoDisc; (g, ñ, s, v) Sam Dudgeon/HRW; (j) ©Royalty Free/CORBIS; (x, y) Victoria Smith/HRW; 25 (cl) Mark Antman/HRW; (cr, r) Marty Granger/Edge Video Productions/ HRW; (l) ©Alison Wright/CORBIS; 26 (b) Don Couch/HRW; 28 (br) ©Robert Frerck/Odyssey/Chicago; 34 (bc) Victoria Smith/HRW; (br) Corbis Images; (cr) Digital Image ©2006 PhotoDisc; 36 (tc) ©A. Parada/Alamy Photos; (tl) ©Jimmy Dorantes/Latin Focus; (tr) Sam Dudgeon/HRW; 40 (A) Peter Van Steen/HRW; (B, C - girl) Dennis Fagan/HRW; (C - boy, D) Victoria Smith/HRW.

CHAPTER 2 All photos by John Langford/HRW except: page 42 (c) ©Andrea Pistolesi/Getty Images/The Image Bank; (tr) ©Mark Bacon/Latin Focus; 43 (bl) ©Mark Bacon/Alamy Photos; (cr) ©Kevin Schafer/CORBIS; (tl) ©Steve Fitzpatrick/Latin Focus; (tr) ©Steve Bly/Getty Images/The Image Bank; 44 (bl) Victoria Smith/HRW; 45 (bc) ©Dennis Degnan/CORBIS; (bl) Ricardo Alcaras/HRW; (br) ©Michael Friang/Alamy Photos; (tl) Tony Arruza; (tr) ©Robert Fried/Robert Fried Photography; 49 (alta, atlética, baja) Victoria Smith/HRW; 50 (1, 2, 4) Victoria Smith/HRW; (3, cr ) Sam Dudgeon/HRW; (tl) Randal Alhadeff/HRW; 52 © Miami Herald/Silver Image; 55 (cl) ©John Kelly/Getty Images/The Image Bank; (cr, l, r) Victoria Smith/HRW; 56 © Fred Fox/Tampa Tribune/Silver Image. 61 (b) © Mike Boom/Regata del Sol al Sol 2005; (tl) Don Couch/HRW; 62 (ajedrez) Digital Image ©2006 PhotoDisc; (CD, mexicana, pizza) Victoria Smith/HRW; (china) Sam Dudgeon/HRW; (helado, italiana) Corbis Images; (icon) Don Couch/HRW; 63 (animales-kangaroo, lion) Digital Image ©2006 PhotoDisc; (animales-zebra) Digital Image ©2006 PhotoDisc; (carros, deportes, fiestas, frutas, hamburguesas, verduras, videojuegos) Victoria Smith/HRW; 64 (A, B) Sam Dudgeon/HRW; (C) Victoria Smith/HRW; (D) Scott Vallance/VIP Photo/HRW; 69 (1-6) Victoria Smith/HRW; (7, 8) Digital Image ©2006 PhotoDisc; (frutas) ©Brand X Pictures; 70 (bl) Mari Biasco Photography; 71 (burritos, zebras) Corbis Images; (cl, pizza, tr) Victoria Smith/HRW; (guitar) Digital Image ©2006 PhotoDisc; (marquee) Scott Vallance/VIP Photo/HRW; 72 (1) Corbis Images; (2, 3, 5) Victoria Smith/HRW; (4) ©Lisa Anne Auerbach/CORBIS; (6) Sam Dudgeon/HRW; (animales) Digital Image ©2006 PhotoDisc; 75 (all) Martha Granger/Edge Video Productions/HRW; 80 (all) Victoria Smith/HRW; 82 (1, 4, graciosa, romántica, tímida) Victoria Smith/HRW; (2) Digital Image ©2006 PhotoDisc; (3) Corbis Images; 86 (A, C) Victoria Smith/HRW.

CHAPTER 3 All photos by Gary Russ/HRW except: page 88 (c) ©George H. H. Huey/CORBIS; (icon) Don Couch/HRW; (tr) Sam Dudgeon/HRW; 89 (bc) ©David Muench/CORBIS; (br) Courtesy of Houston Chamber of Commerce; (tc) Corbis Images; (tr) ©D. Donne Bryant Photography; 90 (bl) ©Carmen Lomas Garza, Collection of Paula Maciel-Benecke and Norbert Benecke Aptos, California, photo credit: M. Lee Fatherree; (tl) Courtesy of the San Antonio Public Library; Photographer: Clem Spalding; 91 (bl) ©Jimmy Dorantes/Latin Focus; (br) ©Scott Teven/photohouston; (c) Victoria Smith/HRW; (tl) ©Dave G. Houser/CORBIS; 94 (all except icon) Dennis Fagan/HRW; (icon) HRW; 95 (básquetbol, béisbol, fútbol, fútbol americano, volibol) Peter Van Steen/HRW; (juegos) Victoria Smith/HRW; (tenis) ©Getty Images/Stone; 96 (1, 3) Victoria Smith/HRW; (2) ©Digital Vision; (5) ©Corbis Images/PictureQuest; (6, 8) Dennis Fagan/HRW; (tr) Peter Van Steen/HRW; 99 (c) Sam Dudgeon/HRW; 101 (cl) Digital Image ©2006 PhotoDisc; (cr) ©Peter M. Fisher/CORBIS; (l) CORBIS Images; (r) Dennis Fagan/HRW; 103 (1-ball, 4) Digital Image ©2006 PhotoDisc; (1-raquet) Digital Image ©2006 Artville; (2) Sam Dudgeon/HRW; (3, 5, tr) Victoria Smith/HRW 104 (tl) Marty Granger/Edge Video Productions/HRW; 105 (A, B) Corbis Images; (C) Victoria Smith/HRW; (D) Painet Inc.; (E) ©Nik Wheeler/CORBIS; 106 (tl) Scott Vallance/VIP Photo/HRW; 107 (b) © Andrew Itkoff/Silver Image; (tl) Don Couch/HRW; 108 (bailar, descansar - boy, estudiar, hablar, practicar, tocar - boy, trabajar) Dennis Fagan/HRW; (descansar - lemonade) Victoria Smith/HRW; (icon) HRW; (tocar - piano) Corbis Images; 109 (bc, tc) ©Jimmy Dorantes/Latin Focus; (br) ©Kevin Barry; (tl) Peter Van Steen/HRW; (tr) ©William Boyce/CORBIS; 111 (c) ©BananaStock Ltd.; (tc) ©Stockbyte; 113 (1) Spencer Grant/Photo Edit; (2) David R. Frazier Photolibrary; (3, 4, 5) Michelle Bridwell/Frontera Fotos; (6) Peter Van Steen/HRW; 114 (bl) Bob Daemmrich/The Image Works; 117 (1) Sam Dudgeon/HRW; (2, 4) Victoria Smith/HRW; (3, 5, Sonia-ball) Digital Image ©2006 PhotoDisc; (Sonia-raquet) Digital Image ©2006 Artville; 118 (tl) © John Moran/Silver Image; 119 (tl) Henry Bargas/AP/Wide World Photos; (tr) Corbis Images; 120 (el arco) ©Latin Focus; (el charango) Sam Dudgeon/HRW; (el güiro) Suzanne Murphy-Larronde; (flauta) ©Paul Rodriguez/Latin Focus; (músicos) David Simson/Stock Boston; 121 (t) Eric Gay/AP/Wide World Photos; (b) Chris O'Meara/AP/Wide World Photos; 128 (A, F) Digital Image ©2006 PhotoDisc; (B, C, D) Dennis Fagan/HRW; (E) Corbis Images; 132 (A, C) Peter Van Steen/HRW; (D) Digital Image ©2006 Artville.

CHAPTER 4 All photos by Don Couch/HRW except: page 134 (c) ©Jimmy Dorantes/Latin Focus; (tr) ©Buddy Mays/CORBIS; 135 (bl, cr) Robin Karpan/D. Donne Bryant Photography; (cl) ©Jimmy Dorantes/Latin Focus; (tr) ©Buddy Mays/CORBIS; 136 (br) ©Dave G. Houser/CORBIS; 137 (bl, br) ©Kevin Schafer; 140 (bolígrafos, carpetas, cuadernos, lápices, papel, regla) Victoria Smith/HRW; (icon) HRW Photo; 142 (tl, tr) Victoria

Smith/HRW; 143 (r) Christine Galida/HRW; 145 (r) Marty Granger/Edge Video Productions/HRW; 147 (c) Sam Dudgeon/HRW; 149 (bailar) © Chuck Savage/CORBIS; (descansar) Peter Van Steen/HRW; (pesas) Victoria Smith/HRW; (tarea) ©Stockbyte; (televisión) ©Digital Vision; (trabajar) ©Royalty-Free/CORBIS; 150 Don Couch Photography; 153 (b) Don Couch Photography; 154 (icon) HRW photo; 156 (1, 3) Digital Image copyright ©2006 EyeWire ; (2, 9) Corbis Images; (4, 5, 7, 8) Digital Image copyright ©2006 PhotoDisc; (6) Peter Van Steen/HRW ; (10) Rubberball Productions; 158 Don Couch/HRW Photo; 159 (A) ©Stockbyte; (B) ©Royalty-Free/CORBIS; (C) ©Comstock; (D, r) Sam Dudgeon/HRW; (tr) ©Danny Lehman/CORBIS; 161 (1) Digital Image copyright ©2006 PhotoDisc; (2, 3, 4, t) Peter Van Steen/HRW; 164 © Jeff Greenberg/Alamy Photos; 174 (A) ©Chuck Savage/CORBIS; (B) Corbis Images; (C) Reuters/CORBIS; (D) Victoria Smith/HRW.

CHAPTER 5 All photos by Don Couch/HRW except: page 180 (cl) ©Fernando Paste/Latin Focus; (tr) ©Daniel Rivadamar/Odyssey/Chicago; 181 (bl) ©Wolfgang Kaehler/CORBIS; (br) D. Donne Bryant/D. Donne Bryant Photography; (c) ©Graham Neden/Ecoscene/CORBIS; (tr) David Ryan/D. Donne Bryant Photography; 182 (bl) David Phillips/Words & Images; (tl) D. Donne Bryant Photography; 183 (bc) ©Bettmann/CORBIS; (bl) ©Conde Nast Archive/CORBIS; (br) Fundación de Santiago by Pedro Lira; (c) ©Reuters NewMedia Inc./CORBIS; (tl) Roberto Candia/AP/Wide World Photos; 186 (gato) John Langford/HRW; 187 (azules) ©Royalty-Free/CORBIS; (café) Digital Image ©2006 PhotoDisc; (canoso) ©Image Source Ltd./Alamy Photos; (castaño, negros) ©Rubberball Productions; (corto) Sam Dudgeon/HRW; (largo) Peter Van Steen/HRW; (negro) ©Stockbyte; (verdes) ©CORBIS; 188 (1) ©John Foxx/Alamy Photos; (2) Mark Richards/PhotoEdit; (3) ©Comstock; (4) ©plainpicture/Alamy Photos; 191 (1) Michelle Bridwell/Frontera Fotos; (2) Martha Granger/Edge Video Productions/HRW; (3) David Young-Wolff/PhotoEdit; (4) ©Comstock; 193 (tl) Victoria Smith/HRW; (tr) Peter Van Steen/HRW; 195 (bl) ©COMSTOCK, Inc.; (br) Peter Van Steen/HRW; (cr) ©Digital Vision; (tr) Digital Image ©2006 PhotoDisc; 197 (6:30) Sam Dudgeon/HRW; (all others) Dennis Fagan/HRW; 199 (b) The Granger Collection, New York; 203 (l, r) Digital Image ©2006 PhotoDisc; 206 (bl) Chris Sharp/D. Donne Bryant Photography; 208 (bc, bl, br) Victoria Smith/HRW; 209 (tr) David Phillips/HRW; 210 (br) Peter Van Steen/HRW; (cl) Dennis Fagan/HRW; (cr) Digital Image ©2006 EyeWire; (l) ©Comstock, Inc.; 211 Don Couch Photography; 212 (br) The Museum of Modern Art; (tr) ©Archivo Iconográfico, S.A./CORBIS; 220 (1) Victoria Smith/HRW; (2) Digital Image ©2006 PhotoDisc; (3) Dennis Fagan/HRW; (4) ©Corel; 224 (all) Dennis Fagan/HRW.

LITERATURA Y VARIEDADES: page 228 (c, l) ©Museo Nacional Del Prado; (cr) Don Couch/HRW; 229 (bl, tr) Museo del Prado, Madrid, Spain; Erich Lessing/Art Resource, NY; (tl) Noortman, Maastricht, Netherlands/Bridgeman Art Library; 230-231 (bkgd) Digital Image copyright 2006 PhotoDisc; 230 (bl) Wolfgang Kaehler/CORBIS; (cl) Kevin Schafer/CORBIS; 231 (cr) Doug Wechsler; (t) Michael and Patricia Fogden/CORBIS; 232 (br) Carmen Lomas Garza, Collection of Paula Maciel-Benecke and Norbert Benecke Aptos, California, photo credit: M. Lee Fatherree; 233 (t) 1995 Carmen Lomas Garza, photo credit: Adam Reich, Collection of Aaron & Marion Borenstein, Coral Gables, Florida; 234 (br, c) Jorge Albán/HRW photo; 235 (r, inset) Jorge Albán/HRW photo; 236-237 (bkgd) ©Jeremy Woodhouse, digitalvision; 236 (cl) Book cover (Spanish edition) from La casa de los espirítus by Isabel Allende. Reprinted by permission of HarperCollins Publishers, Inc.; (cr) Book cover (Spanish edition) from Paula by Isabel Allende and trans. by Margaret Sayers Peden. 1994 by Isabel Allende. Translation 1995 by HarperCollins Publishers. Reprinted by permission of HarperCollins Publishers Inc.; 237 (tr) Marcia Lieberman Photography.

NOVELA STILL PHOTOS: Spain, Mexico - Don Couch/HRW; Puerto Rico-John Langford/HRW.

ICONS: (CULTURA) Don Couch/HRW; (VOCABULARIO 1) John Langford/HRW; (VOCABULARIO 2) Don Couch/HRW; COMMUNICACIÓN ICON (l, c) Steve Ewert/HRW Photo; (r) PhotoDisc/Getty Images.